Asymmetric Information, Corporate Finance, and Investment

A National Bureau
of Economic Research
Project Report

Asymmetric Information, Corporate Finance, and Investment

Edited by   R. Glenn Hubbard

The University of Chicago Press

Chicago and London

R. GLENN HUBBARD is professor of economics and finance at the
Graduate School of Business, Columbia University.

The University of Chicago Press, Chicago 60637
The University of Chicago Press, Ltd., London

© 1990 by the National Bureau of Economic Research
All rights reserved. Published 1990
Printed in the United States of America
99 98 97 96 95 94 93 92 91 90   5 4 3 2 1

Library of Congress Cataloging-in-Publication Data

Asymmetric information, corporate finance, and investment / edited by
R. Glenn Hubbard.
        p.   cm. —(A National Bureau of Economic Research project
report)
    Papers presented at an NBER conference held in Cambridge, May 5–6,
1989.
    Includes bibliographical references and index.
    ISBN 0-226-35585-3
    1. Corporations—Finance—Congresses.   2. Investments—
Mathematical models—Congresses.   3. Securities—Congresses.
I. Hubbard, R. Glenn.   II. Series.
HG4006.A89   1990
658.15—dc20   90-11043
                                                                    CIP

Relation of the Directors to the
Work and Publications of the
National Bureau of Economic Research

1. The object of the National Bureau of Economic Research is to ascertain and to present to the public important economic facts and their interpretation in a scientific and impartial manner. The Board of Directors is charged with the responsibility of ensuring that the work of the National Bureau is carried on in strict conformity with this object.

2. The President of the National Bureau shall submit to the Board of Directors, or to its Executive Committee, for their formal adoption all specific proposals for research to be instituted.

3. No research report shall be published by the National Bureau until the President has sent each member of the Board a notice that a manuscript is recommended for publication and that in the President's opinion it is suitable for publication in accordance with the principles of the National Bureau. Such notification will include an abstract or summary of the manuscript's content and a response form for use by those Directors who desire a copy of the manuscript for review. Each manuscript shall contain a summary drawing attention to the nature and treatment of the problem studied, the character of the data and their utilization in the report, and the main conclusions reached.

4. For each manuscript so submitted, a special committee of the Directors (including Directors Emeriti) shall be appointed by majority agreement of the President and Vice Presidents (or by the Executive Committee in case of inability to decide on the part of the President and Vice Presidents), consisting of three Directors selected as nearly as may be one from each general division of the Board. The names of the special manuscript committee shall be stated to each Director when notice of the proposed publication is submitted to him. It shall be the duty of each member of the special manuscript committee to read the manuscript. If each member of the manuscript committee signifies his approval within thirty days of the transmittal of the manuscript, the report may be published. If at the end of that period any member of the manuscript committee withholds his approval, the President shall then notify each member of the Board, requesting approval or disapproval of publication, and thirty days additional shall be granted for this purpose. The manuscript shall then not be published unless at least a majority of the entire Board who shall have voted on the proposal within the time fixed for the receipt of votes shall have approved.

5. No manuscript may be published, though approved by each member of the special manuscript committee, until forty-five days have elapsed from the transmittal of the report in manuscript form. The interval is allowed for the receipt of any memorandum of dissent or reservation, together with a brief statement of his reasons, that any member may wish to express; and such memorandum of dissent or reservation shall be published with the manuscript if he so desires. Publication does not, however, imply that each member of the Board has read the manuscript, or that either members of the Board in general or the special committee have passed on its validity in every detail.

6. Publications of the National Bureau issued for informational purposes concerning the work of the Bureau and its staff, or issued to inform the public of activities of Bureau staff, and volumes issued as a result of various conferences involving the National Bureau shall contain a specific disclaimer noting that such publication has not passed through the normal review procedures required in this resolution. The Executive Committee of the Board is charged with review of all such publications from time to time to ensure that they do not take on the character of formal research reports of the National Bureau, requiring formal Board approval.

7. Unless otherwise determined by the Board or exempted by the terms of paragraph 6, a copy of this resolution shall be printed in each National Bureau publication.

(Resolution adopted October 25, 1926, as revised through September 30, 1974)

Contents

Acknowledgments

These papers were presented at the NBER conference, "Asymmetric Information, Corporate Finance, and Investment" held in Cambridge, May 5–6, 1989. The research represents the culmination of efforts in a three-year project at the NBER under the program on financial markets and monetary economics. I am grateful to Martin Feldstein and especially to Benjamin Friedman for advice and support in the design of the program. Financial support was generously provided by the Ford Foundation, the Lilly Endowment, and the Seaver Institute. Kirsten Foss Davis and Ilana Hardesty spent much time in assuring the quality and efficiency of each meeting.

Finally, I would like to thank my coauthors of papers in this research agenda, from whom I have learned much—Charles Calomiris, Steven Fazzari, Mark Gertler, Kenneth Judd, Anil Kashyap, Bruce Petersen, Peter Reiss, and James Stock.

R. Glenn Hubbard

Introduction

R. Glenn Hubbard

Studies of heterogeneity in firms' terms of trade in capital markets have occupied a prominent place in applied research in financial markets. The National Bureau of Economic Research commissioned monographs on the subject in the 1940s and 1950s—in part because of the differential importance of "financial factors" for the performance of various types of firms during the Depression—and again in the early 1980s.[1] Studies of the growth and development of firms have long proceeded in research in industrial organization, but formal analysis of the role of finance in the development of firms has come much more recently.

Beginning with the seminal work of Modigliani and Miller (1958), the idea that financial structure was indeterminate and irrelevant for investment decisions (apart from tax considerations) heavily influenced modern finance. The major developments in investment research in the 1960s—the neoclassical and q models[2]—made use of Modigliani-Miller propositions in employing variables from financial markets. Empirical work has traditionally produced results inconsistent with the notion of "financial irrelevance," including evidence on the role of breakdowns in financial trade in historically important economic contractions;[3] the role of movements in internal finance in predicting investment;[4] persistent differences in the way certain types of firms raise finance;[5] and the regular cyclical movements of financial variables (e.g., balance sheet positions, liquidity ratios, and bank credit).[6]

Reconciliation of theoretical and empirical research on finance and investment has made use of models in which informational asymmetries between "borrowers" and "lenders" introduce incentive problems in financial relationships, complicating the development of financial contracts and making financ-

R. Glenn Hubbard is professor of economics and finance at the Graduate School of Business of Columbia University and a research associate of the National Bureau of Economic Research.

ing and investment decisions interdependent in specific ways.[7] Much of the new research has proceeded in two agendas, modeling (i) the role of asymmetric information in linking movements in inside finance and investment, holding constant underlying opportunities, and (ii) the importance of information problems in accounting for observed differences in financing patterns and mechanisms for corporate control. These agendas center on the common theme of the importance of particular asymmetries of information between "insiders" and "outsiders" in firm financial transactions and the present testable violations of "financial irrelevance" propositions in studying control and investment decisions. Below I review each in turn, grouping papers presented in the conference accordingly.

Asymmetric Information, Internal Finance, and Investment

One feature of many theoretical models of asymmetric information in capital markets is that the level of internal net worth becomes a critical determinant of the terms under which firms can borrow, holding constant true investment opportunities (see, e.g., Leland and Pyle 1977; Bernanke and Gertler 1990; Calomiris and Hubbard 1990; and Gertler and Hubbard 1988). This role for internal finance in the investment decision is potentially important for models of aggregate investment through two channels. First, to the extent that movements in firms' collateralizable net worth are procyclical, an "accelerator" mechanism emerges (see, e.g., Gertler and Hubbard 1988). This effect would not be present under perfect capital markets. Second, distributional considerations will be important for aggregate investment variability because of the impact of the redistribution on firms' internal net worth. This channel is closely related to the "debt deflation" arguments of Fisher (1933), Kindleberger (1978), and Minsky (1975), among others.

A second mechanism through which informational asymmetries can precipitate a difference in the cost of internal and external finance—that is, making internal net worth more valuable, holding constant investment opportunities—is a "lemons market" problem in valuation. The classic argument (due to Akerlof 1970) is that some sellers with inside information about the quality of an asset will be unwilling to accept the terms offered by a less informed buyer. This may cause the market to break down, or at least force the sale of an asset at a price lower than it would command if all buyers and sellers had full information. This idea has been applied to both equity finance and debt finance.

For equity finance, new shareholders demand a premium to purchase the shares of relatively good firms to offset the losses arising from funding lemons (see, e.g., Myers and Majluf 1984; Greenwald, Stiglitz, and Weiss 1984; and Fazzari, Hubbard, and Petersen 1988). This premium raises the cost of new equity finance faced by managers of relatively high-quality firms above the opportunity cost of internal finance faced by existing shareholders.

In debt markets, Keeton (1979) and Stiglitz and Weiss (1981) have demonstrated that equilibrium "credit rationing" can arise in the presence of adverse selection.[8] In the simplest case, lenders cannot price discriminate (i.e., vary interest rates) between good and bad borrowers in loan contracts, because the riskiness of projects is unobservable. Thus, when interest rates increase, relatively good borrowers drop out of the market, increasing the probability of default and possibly decreasing lenders' expected profits. In equilibrium, lenders may set an interest rate that leaves an excess demand for loans. Some borrowers receive loans, while other observationally equivalent borrowers are rationed. Calomiris and Hubbard (1990) extend this approach by allowing for heterogeneity in borrower types and in endowments of inside finance. Depending on per capita levels of internal net worth, the allocation of new funds across classes of borrowers could either follow the symmetric-information credit allocation or ration funds away from some classes of borrowers who would receive credit in the absence of asymmetric information. A "financial collapse" may occur, in which some or all classes of "asymmetric information" borrowers are denied loans.

In summary, these approaches model the differential cost of external finance from securities and banking markets under asymmetric information and the role of internal net worth in influencing the cost of finance. This suggests that certain classes of borrowers may find it prohibitively expensive to obtain financing by directly issuing securities on the open market. Financial intermediaries help overcome this friction by exploiting scale economies in the evaluation and monitoring of borrowers—thus facilitating the flow of funds between savers and certain kinds of investors. Hence, the terms under which intermediary credit is available are key determinants of investment by firms lacking easy access to direct credit (see Bernanke 1983; and Calomiris, Hubbard, and Stock 1986 for applications of these points).

Most of the research on the importance of asymmetric information in financial markets has focused on specific microeconomic models of market failure in debt or equity markets, as in the studies noted above. To the extent that a sufficient number of firms must raise finance in markets lacking perfect information, microeconomic market failures can generate correlations in aggregate data different from those suggested by standard models of investment or the consequences of macroeconomic policies. In particular, some "price" signals in capital markets will be less important; interest rates would be deemphasized as a determinant of borrowing and investment, with movements in internal net worth of corporate borrowers being relatively more important.

Bruce Greenwald and Joseph Stiglitz consider the effects on investment decisions of equity and credit rationing at the firm level. Positive aggregate profitability shocks raise firms' net worth and inside finance, leading to increases in current and future investment, further stimulating an accelerator mechanism in aggregate investment. Similar logic is applied by the authors to other types of investment as well (e.g., in working capital or employment). They extend these ideas in a model of the banking sector, which is also assumed to be effectively constrained in raising new equity capital. The availability of credit to firms now depends on the financial condition (accumulated internal net worth) of both firms and the banking sector, reinforcing the accelerator mechanism in investment. The Greenwald-Stiglitz model has both short-run and long-run implications. In the short run, the effects of monetary policy on investment and output are magnified through relaxation of financing constraints. Long-run dynamics are driven by rates of accumulation in capital and internal equity. The approach taken by Greenwald and Stiglitz underscores the ability of models of information-related capital market frictions to explain accelerator movements in aggregate variables, dynamics difficult to account for in conventional neoclassical models of investment and growth.

A related application exists for rationalizing the importance of contracting models in macroeconomics. The use of contract-based theories in models of aggregate supply has for some time been standard, most notably in "new Keynesian" explanations of Phillips curve correlations in aggregate time-series data. Roger Farmer employs a different set of contracting theories toward the same end, stressing problems in *financial* contracting in the presence of asymmetric information and limited collateral (self-finance). The transmission mechanism is drawn from models of the role of internal net worth in the investment decision. At high levels of profits or collateralizable net worth, incentive problems are mitigated, and the cost of funds is low, expanding economic activity. Farmer focuses on movements in interest rates in bringing about Phillips curve correlations in data. Deflationary shocks raise real interest rates, reducing the value of internal net worth, with negative effects on economic activity.[9] In addition, he stresses the role of the nominal interest rate; the optimal contract for the firm trades off the opportunity cost of holding liquid balances against the benefits of additional liquidity. The benefits arise from the fact that liquidity buffers permit firms to offer more stable wages, facilitating more efficient employment decisions.

Farmer presents some empirical work in support of the asymmetric-information/limited-collateral approach, with an application to simple Phillips-curve-type models. He finds (using data for the United States over the period from 1931 to 1986) that movements in the unemployment rate are negatively correlated with movements in inflation and corporate profits and positively correlated with movements in nominal interest rates. With the inclusion of the profits variable, the model is stable over subsamples of the postwar period. While the results are open to differences in interpretation, they suggest support for the idea that asymmetric-information problems in financial markets figure importantly in accounting for Phillips curve correlations.

To the extent that credit constraints are important for certain classes of firms, equilibrium models of asset pricing will be affected. William Brock and Blake LeBaron consider the impact of finance constraints on market valuation of firms within a particular class of asset-pricing models. Specifically, they develop a production-based, rational-expectations asset-pricing simulation model with and without credit constraints. "Constrained" and "unconstrained" firms are alike except that the former cannot use noncollateralized debt to finance investment. Unconstrained firms maximize their market value by selecting investment projects that optimally trade off expected returns and systematic risk. The investment of constrained firms, on the other hand, is restricted by past shocks (by assumption), since these firms cannot obtain funds beyond their current resources. Their marginal expected returns will be "too high."

Brock and LeBaron use this setup to analyze the phenomenon, noted in many recent empirical studies, of "mean reversion" in security returns. They show that mean reversion is amplified by financing constraints—positive shocks to productivity affect a constrained firm's investment program more than they affect an unconstrained firm's program. Brock and LeBaron emphasize that binding credit constraints are an important feature of mean-reverting returns in security markets. The authors also discuss a number of suggestive implications of their work, including applications to recent results on seasonal patterns in excess returns for small (a priori, financially constrained) firms.

A key feature of many models of capital market frictions based on asymmetric information is that firm heterogeneity is important. Large, mature enterprises with substantial internal finance relative to their investment opportunities are less likely to have their investment subject to financial constraints than are younger, growing firms with lower net worth. Empirical tests of these ideas have grouped firms according to proxies for the "net worth" distinctions (see, e.g., Fazzari, Hubbard, and Petersen 1988; and Hoshi, Kashyap, and Scharfstein 1990). Michael Devereux and Fabio Schiantarelli pursue this route, motivating finance constraints by including a cost of debt increasing in the level of debt, with the increased cost accounted for by the agency ("financial distress") cost of debt. Their model is an expanded version of the q model used by Fazzari, Hubbard, and Petersen and Hoshi, Kashyap, and Scharfstein.

Devereux and Schiantarelli use panel data on 689 U.K. manufacturing firms over the period from 1969 to 1986 and test for differences in the sensitivity of investment to the availability of internal funds for firms of different sizes and ages. They find that lagged measures of firm cash flow have an economically important effect on investment, holding constant investment opportunities (as measured by q); this effect is present for all size classes of firms. To the extent that information problems are important, one would expect that "age" is a reasonable characteristic by which to group firms according to information intensity. Devereux and Schiantarelli find that cash-flow effects are particularly important for younger, smaller firms. They note that the cash-flow effects for large firms could reflect their more diversified ownership structure and greater associated agency costs of finance.

One problem with many information-based models of links between internal net worth and investment is that it is often difficult to find empirical proxies sufficiently close to variables suggested by theory to permit formal tests. In particular, many theoretical models are cast in terms of relatively small enterprises producing a homogeneous good, with a single measure of collateralizable net worth. Case studies, focusing on firm heterogeneity within an industry, provide a useful alternative to studies based on aggregate time-series data or panel data for a large, diverse cross-section of firms. Peter Reiss uses this approach to analyze investment behavior over the past decade for firms in oil and gas extraction. Oil and gas prices have, of course, been quite volatile over this period, indicating significant fluctuations in both investment opportunities and the value of firms' net worth (as measured by the value of oil and gas reserves in place). Fluctuations in capital spending in the industry over this period were much more pronounced than in the economy as a whole.

Reiss examines the importance of information problems for the investment and financial contracting decisions of a set of "independent" oil and gas firms. His principal findings are two. First, movements in internal finance have systematic effects on investment spending—holding constant the value of drilling investment opportunities—particularly during downturns in oil prices. Second, the availability of internal funds affects drilling firms' ownership stakes in wells, as well as the structure of contracts through which external finance is obtained. The patterns are consistent with the simultaneous determination of financial structure and capital structure decisions under asymmetric information. Reiss's careful case study illustrates the usefulness of more narrowly focused analyses in measuring precisely changes in financial contracting and the costliness of capital market frictions under asymmetric information.

Another explanation of observed correlations between movements in internal finance and investment spending stresses that managers have substantial control over the use of corporate cash flows and have incentives to reinvest these funds in perquisites or non-value-maximizing projects (see e.g., the "free cash flow" model articulated in Jensen 1986). John Strong and John Meyer ask two questions in this line of thought. First, do firms with larger "free" cash flows exhibit different investment behavior? Second, do these differences in investment behavior lead to poorer or better financial performance? Their study centers on an adaptation of the "residual funds" model of Meyer and Kuh (1957). This approach posits that the level (and financing) of firms' capital spending depends on the "residual funds" available after a hierarchy of prior claims on corporate cash flow is satisfied. Likewise, investment spending is decomposed into "sustaining" and "discretionary" categories, the former corresponding to replacement investment and the latter to spending not required to sustain a firm's core business. In the presence of monitoring problems, discretionary investment should depend positively on residual cash flow. Residual cash flow should dominate total cash flow as a liquidity influence in that category of investment.

To test the predictions of their approach, Strong and Meyer consider investment decisions in 34 large paper corporations over the period from 1971 to 1986. The paper industry experienced substantial fluctuations in operating performance over the period and has undergone considerable restructuring. Their evidence for investment is consistent with the view that discretionary investment is influenced by movements in residual funds. Moreover, links between discretionary investment and shareholder returns are consistent with an agency-cost interpretation: higher discretionary expenditures, ceteris paribus, depress shareholder returns. The Strong-Meyer study suggests the benefits of considering other case studies of firms in "mature" and "growing" industries, to contrast links between cash flow and investment.

Finally, the possibility that information problems in lending markets raise the cost of finance for some classes of borrowers raises the question of whether direct government intervention in credit markets would increase the efficiency with which investment funds are allocated. Such a question is of more than academic interest. At the end of 1988, outstanding federal direct loans totaled $222 billion, with, in addition, two and one-half times as much outstanding in the form of loan guarantees. Loan and loan-guarantee programs exist in a number of sectors, including education, agriculture, housing, and small businesses, and the cost of the programs is substantial. Some of these sectors have been identified as prototypes for "credit rationing," at least raising the possibility that credit market interventions would be efficiency improving. Assessing the effectiveness of such policies in the context of formal models of credit rationing in loan markets is difficult and requires a careful specification of the information problem and of the form that potential government interventions would assume.

William Gale takes up these issues in his paper for this volume. He considers (in a model in which borrowers have private information about their risk characteristics) the efficiency costs generated by using collateral as a sorting device when it is worth less to lenders than to borrowers. In equilibrium, relatively high-risk borrowers choose a contract with a high interest rate and low collateral requirement; low-risk borrowers signal their type by choosing to put up substantial collateral in exchange for a lower interest rate. As long as all borrowers have projects whose gross returns are greater than their social opportunity cost (which is assumed in Gale's model), the efficiency loss created by the use of collateral creates a scope for government intervention. In the context of his model, subsidies to unrationed borrowers will reduce the extent of rationing in the whole sector, hence increasing efficiency. On the other hand, interventions targeting borrowers who are denied loans in private credit markets can raise the extent of rationing, reducing efficiency. Analyzing this distinction is important, since most government credit programs are aimed at the low-risk borrower. Gale's paper raises some concerns with this approach and suggests the need to analyze the effects of government credit programs on credit allocation using richer models that incorporate more general financial contracts.

Asymmetric Information, Corporate Control, and Differences in Financing Mechanisms

The problem of monitoring and controlling managers with access to private information about firm opportunities and costs has been noted at least since the seminal work of Berle and Means (1932). Modern theoretical work on principal-agent problems has stressed the endogeneity of financial contracts to align the incentives of "insiders" and "outsiders" in business transactions (see notably Jensen and Meckling 1976, and the large literature that followed). Much attention has been focused on capital structure decisions, in which the use of debt relative to equity is related to, inter alia, the specificity of assets and the relative importance of idiosyncratic and aggregate fluctuations in accounting for firm earnings movements. Other researchers have focused on mechanisms used by capital markets to minimize agency-cost problems.[10]

A key feature of the new research on capital market frictions stemming from asymmetric information is its emphasis on the use of particular forms of contracting mechanisms and monitoring arrangements. These mechanisms are chosen to minimize the added cost of finance under asymmetric information. While much of the traditional literature on capital structure decisions has focused on the choice of "debt" versus "equity," the asymmetric information approach stresses the design of contracts between "insiders" and "outsiders," which will, in general, embody a mixture of debt and equity features along with ancillary monitoring arrangements (see the overview in Gertler and Hubbard 1988). Empirical research here analyzes the determinants of firm financing arrangements, the information content of movements in security prices, and the value of particular monitoring arrangement between insiders and outsiders in corporate finance.

Do firms care who provides their financing? Most studies of capital structure (theoretical and empirical) address factors motivating the *choice of security* (e.g., debt vs. equity) rather than the *provider of funds* (e.g., private vs. public sources). If problems of asymmetric information in capital markets are significant, however, examining variation across firms in who provides funds is likely to be important. Finding that firms do indeed distinguish between private and public and internal and external sources of funds can rationalize observed effects of internal finance on investment. In addition, if credit market segmentation is important, fluctuations in conditions in particular credit markets will have real effects. Jeffrey MacKie-Mason pursues these questions, documenting trends and patterns in incremental sources of financial capital (at the industry and aggregate level) and analyzing a large sample of incremental corporate financial decisions. In particular, he distinguishes between theories that generate predictions for the *type of security* and theories that predict differences in the *type of provider.*

The empirical work begins with the distinction of choices of financial contract by type of contingent financial claim (debt or equity) and by the provider of funds (private or publicly marketed sources). MacKie-Mason uses the nested logit approach to estimate two models—according to whether the firm chooses first whether to use public or private sources, and then debt or equity, or vice versa. The data are drawn from SEC registered offerings that are matched with COMPUSTAT data to obtain information firm characteristics. The patterns of preferences suggested by the data indicate that problems of asymmetric information are an important determinant of financing choices. That is, firms are concerned with who provides their financing, and not just with the standard factors thought to influence the mix of debt and equity finance.

An important feature of many models of asymmetric information in financial markets is that institutional considerations for monitoring and financial contracting are significant. Evidence from a cross section of countries is particularly useful, since one can test whether differences in capital market institutions and financial regulation affect the design of financial contracts. Likewise, given the variation in the tax treatment of alternative sources of finance across countries, a finding of similarities in financing patterns would suggest the relevance of common factors in the costs and benefits of particular forms of financial contracts and arrangements. In his overview of financing patterns in the United States, United Kingdom, Japan, Italy, Germany, France, Finland, and Canada, Colin Mayer outlines a set of stylized facts about the strong common trends in corporate finance. Those patterns include the dominance of internal funds in financing investment, the importance of bank finance as a source of external funds, and systematic variations in financing patterns across firms of various sizes.

Mayer interprets the set of common factors in financing patterns for his set of countries as supporting recent theoretical models linking corporate finance to corporate control. The particular link he stresses is the claim that outside investors can make in the event of a default by insiders. In particular, assets specific to their current employment will be difficult to finance externally, and the use of external finance will be negatively related to the cost of organizing external control. The persistent common patterns in corporate finance across countries that Mayer identifies suggest that information-related capital market frictions are universally important. Further support for this view is provided by departures from common patterns, which can be explained by differences in monitoring and corporate control mechanisms. This suggests that case studies of corporate control mechanisms in particular countries will be useful for analyzing problems of asymmetric information.

To the extent that asymmetric information in financing decisions is important, analyses of seasoned equity issues should be of particular interest. Equity is a residual claim on firms, so that asymmetries of information should figure prominently in the decisions of buyers of common stock issues. In addition, a number of empirical studies have suggested that returns during the period surrounding an equity issue are abnormal, suggesting that information is in fact being revealed during the issue. Robert Koracjzyk, Deborah Lucas, and Robert McDonald address these concerns and develop a model of stock price reactions to equity issues under asymmetric information. They begin by reviewing existing empirical evidence on increases in stock prices just prior to an equity issue and the subsequent drop in stock prices at the issue, noting that most explanations of these patterns individually in the literature cannot explain the two price movements together.

Koracjzyk, Lucas, and McDonald assume that managers—who act in the interest of existing shareholders—have private information about the firm's true value. Consider two firms—one undervalued and one overvalued—that plan to issue equity; because of having to forgo investment opportunities while waiting, postponing the issue is costly to both. Undervalued firms will wait for their price to rise (as their type is slowly revealed to the market) so that their price path rises before an issue. Overvalued firms do not wait, so that their price path is flat prior to the issue. Thus, on average, stock price path prior to issue will be upward sloping. The negative price reaction upon issue can be explained within a "lemons" framework—issuing signals that the firm is on average overvalued, so that the stock price drops.

Another possible explanation for the price rise prior to issue is that the market has learned of the arrival of a "good" project that the firm has yet to undertake. Koracjzyk, Lucas, and McDonald cast doubt on that alternative by demonstrating that price increases also occur prior to secondary issues (large block sales by existing equity holders) which reveal information but have nothing to do with additions to the firm's capital. On the other hand, firms issuing equity experience a rise in Tobin's q prior to the issue and a subsequent fall, a pattern consistent with firms' issuing equity to finance growth opportunities. While the evidence offered by Koracjzyk, Lucas, and McDonald is consistent with the importance of asymmetric information in explaining stock price reactions during seasoned equity issues, it is difficult to make inferences about effects on the efficiency of the investment process. If the stock price declines represent appropriate downward revision in the value of the firm, there has only been a shift in the timing of information about market value. On the other hand, if "bad" firms issue equity to pool with "good" firms, the lemons-market efficiency problems raised by Myers and Majluf (1984) become important.

Takeo Hoshi, Anil Kashyap, and David Scharfstein have focused on Japan as a case study of the development and value of monitoring arrangements in financial markets in the presence of asymmetric information. In their previous (1990) work, these authors examined the effect of internal finance on investment spending by Japanese firms, holding constant investment opportunities (as approximated by Tobin's q). Using panel data, they grouped firms according to whether they were members of *keiretsu* industrial groups. They find that membership in a group and the presence of a group "main bank" are important in the provision of information and the avoidance of credit rationing when investment opportunities are promising. While liquidity effects on investment were found to be important for *nongroup* firms, the investment behavior of *member* firms is well described by a q model.

In their paper for this volume, Hoshi, Kashyap, and Scharfstein extend their earlier work by observing differences in the effects of banking relationships on the sensitivity of investment to internal finance during the 1980s (in the aftermath of a major deregulation of Japanese financial markets). The general features of the deregulation included easing restrictions on issuing bonds abroad and permitting the issuance of noncollateralized bonds in domestic securities markets. Reliance of firms on banks for debt finance diminished substantially during this period. Hoshi, Kashyap, and Scharfstein test for shifts in the investment behavior of group firms, contrasting firms that decreased their reliance on main bank finance (seeking finance instead from the domestic and foreign bond market) and firms who retained their bank ties. For the latter group, investment remained insensitive to movements in firm liquidity (holding constant investment opportunities) before and after banking deregulation. For the former, investment spending became more sensitive to fluctuations in firm liquidity. The key question is, then, the following: If bank monitoring overcomes information problems and relaxes credit constraints, why did some firms sever their bank ties? The authors' work points up important issues to consider in assessing the costs and benefits of banking relationships in Japan, as well as in the design of new theories of the choice between bank debt and public debt.

A variety of strategies is available in capital markets to mitigate the cost of capital market frictions in the presence of asymmetric information. These strategies need not involve modifications in capital structure; it is possible, for example, for outside shareholders in a firm to monitor insiders (managers). Of course, with a large number of shareholders with dispersed holdings, free-rider problems arise. However, large shareholders can realize the benefits of their informed action, and can effectively express their concerns about corporate governance through their voting power. There has been little direct evidence on the question of whether a large shareholder can reduce information-related costs in capital markets, deterring managerial self-interest. To the extent that larger shareholders can accomplish this, they provide a delegated monitoring function, in that their actions provide information to smaller shareholders, who individually do not find it in their economic interest to incur the cost of monitoring.

Richard Zeckhauser and John Pound consider this possibility. After outlining the potential impact of large shareholders on insiders' incentives and the flow of information, they use cross-sectional data on firms to test for systematic variation in performance among firms with large shareholders (after controlling for industry differences). As a proxy for the severity of information problem, Zeckhauser and Pound classify industries according to whether capital and investments are highly firm-specific. The basic idea is that when assets are specific to the management, it is more difficult for large shareholders (acting as monitors) to improve performance; that is, features of asset specificity and closed information structure are assumed to be related. Zeckhauser and Pound find that earnings-price ratios (their measure of performance) are significantly lower for firms with large shareholders in industries with open information structures (i.e., where assets are less specific and monitoring is potentially valuable). There is no comparable "large shareholder" effect for firms in industries subject to closed information structure. The evidence presented by Zeckhauser and Pound provides a suggestive first step toward measuring the benefits of the delegated monitoring mechanism provided by large shareholders.

Notes

1. See, e.g., Koch (1943), Merwin (1942), Lutz (1945), Dobrovolsky (1951), and Friedman (1982b, 1985).
2. See, e.g., Hall and Jorgenson (1967) on neoclassical models. On q models, see Brainard and Tobin (1968), Tobin (1969), and subsequent developments in Hayashi (1982), Summers (1981), and Abel and Blanchard (1986).
3. See the discussion in Calomiris and Hubbard (1989) for the period in the United States prior to the founding of the Federal Reserve and the discussion in Bernanke (1983) for the 1930s.
4. This point was made forcefully by Meyer and Kuh (1957) and Eisner (1978). The development of empirical tests of the role of internal finance in the investment decision is discussed in Fazzari, Hubbard, and Petersen (1988) and extended in the context of Euler equation models of financial constraints and investment by Hubbard and Kashyap (1989), Gilchrist (1989), and Whited (1989).
5. Such patterns were highlighted in an early study by Butters and Lintner (1945). Gertler and Hubbard (1988) review differences in financing patterns by firm size for contemporary data.
6. See, e.g., Wojnilower (1980), Eckstein and Sinai (1986), and Friedman (1982a).
7. This literature is summarized in Gertler (1988).
8. Earlier, Jaffee and Russell (1976) demonstrated that the cost of credit would in general be higher under asymmetric information—the market interest rate must increase, and loan size may be limited, when lenders cannot distinguish borrower quality.
9. Calomiris and Hubbard (1989) have stressed this channel in accounting for Phillips curve correlations in aggregate data for the United States in the period prior to the founding of the Federal Reserve system—a period in which deflationary shocks, investment collapse, and recession were coincident.
10. See, e.g., Easterbrook (1984), Jensen (1986), and Gertler and Hubbard (1990).

References

Abel, Andrew B., and Olivier J. Blanchard. 1986. The present value of profits and cyclical movements in investment. *Econometrica* 54 (March): 249–73.

Akerlof, George A. 1970. The market for "lemons": Quality uncertainty and the market mechanism. *Quarterly Journal of Economics* 84 (August): 488–500.

Berle, Adolph, and Gardiner Means. 1932. *The modern corporation and private property.* New York: Macmillan.

Bernanke, Ben. 1983. Non-monetary effects of the financial crisis in the propagation of the great depression. *American Economic Review* 73 (June): 257–76.

Bernanke, Ben, and Mark Gertler. 1990. Financial fragility and economic performance. *Quarterly Journal of Economics* 105 (February): 87–114.

Brainard, William C., and James Tobin. 1968. Pitfalls in financial model building. *American Economic Review* 58 (May): 99–122.

Butters, J. Keith, and John V. Lintner. 1945. *Effect of federal taxes on growing enterprises.* Boston: Harvard University, Graduate School of Business Administration, Division of Research.

Calomiris, Charles W., and R. Glenn Hubbard. 1989. Price flexibility, credit availability, and economic fluctuations: Evidence from the U.S., 1894–1909. *Quarterly Journal of Economics* 104 (August): 429–52.

———. 1990. Firm heterogeneity, internal finance and credit rationing. *Economic Journal* 100 (March): 90–104.

Calomiris, Charles W., R. Glenn Hubbard, and James H. Stock. 1986. The farm debt crisis and public policy. *Brookings Papers on Economic Activity,* no. 2:441–79.

Dobrovolsky, Sergei P. 1951. *Corporate income retention, 1915–43.* New York: National Bureau of Economic Research.

Easterbrook, Frank H. 1984. Two agency-cost explanations of dividends. *American Economic Review* 74 (June): 650–59.

Eckstein, Otto, and Allen Sinai. 1986. The mechanisms of the business cycle in the postwar era. In *The American business cycle: Continuity and change.* ed. Robert J. Gordon. Chicago: University of Chicago Press.

Eisner, Robert. 1978. *Factors in business investment.* Cambridge: Ballinger.

Fazzari, Steven M., R. Glenn Hubbard, and Bruce C. Petersen. 1988. Financing constraints and corporate investment. *Brookings Papers on Economic Activity,* no. 1:141–95.

Fisher, Irving. 1933. The debt-deflation theory of great depressions. *Econometrica* 1 (October): 337–57.

Friedman, Benjamin M., ed. 1982a. *The changing roles of debt and equity in financing U.S. capital formation.* Chicago: University of Chicago Press.

Friedman, Benjamin M. 1982b. Debt and economic activity in the United States. In *The changing roles of debt and equity in financing U.S. capital formation,* ed. Benjamin M. Friedman. Chicago: University of Chicago Press.

———, ed. 1985. *Corporate capital structures in the United States.* Chicago: University of Chicago Press.

Gertler, Mark. 1988. Financial structure and aggregate economic activity. *Journal of Money, Credit, and Banking* 20 (August, pt. 2): 559–88.

Gertler, Mark, and R. Glenn Hubbard. 1988. Financial factors in business fluctuations. In *Financial market volatility.* Kansas City, Mo.: Federal Reserve Bank of Kansas City.

———. 1990. Taxation, corporate capital structure, and financial distress. In *Tax policy and the economy,* vol. 4, ed. L. H. Summers. Cambridge, Mass.: MIT Press.

Gilchrist, Simon. 1989. An empirical analysis of corporate investment and financing hierarchies using firm level panel data. Mimeograph. University of Wisconsin—Madison.

Greenwald, Bruce C., Joseph E. Stiglitz, and Andrew Weiss. 1984. Information imperfections in the capital market and macroeconomic fluctuations. *American Economic Review* 74 (May): 194–99.

Hall, Robert E., and Dale W. Jorgenson. 1967. Tax policy and investment behavior. *American Economic Review* 67 (June): 391–414.

Hayashi, Fumio. 1982. Tobin's marginal q and average q: A neoclassical interpretation. *Econometrica* 50 (January): 213–24.

Hoshi, Takeo, Anil Kashyap, and David Scharfstein. 1990. Corporate structure, liquidity, and investment: Evidence from Japanese industrial groups. *Quarterly Journal of Economics* 105. Forthcoming.

Hubbard, R. Glenn, and Anil Kashyap. 1989. Internal net worth and the investment process: An application to U.S. agriculture. Mimeograph. Columbia University.

Jaffee, Dwight M., and Thomas Russell. 1976. Imperfect information, uncertainty, and credit rationing. *Quarterly Journal of Economics* 90 (November): 651–66.

Jensen, Michael C. 1986. Agency costs of free cash flow, corporate finance, and takeovers. *American Economic Review* 76 (May): 323–29.

Jensen, Michael C., and William H. Meckling. 1976. Theory of the firm: Managerial behavior, agency costs, and capital structure. *Journal of Financial Economics* 3 (October): 305–60.

Keeton, William. 1979. *Equilibrium credit rationing*. New York: Garland.

Koch, A. R. 1943. *The financing of large corporations, 1920–1939*. New York: NBER.

Kindleberger, Charles. 1978. *Manias, panics, and crashes*. New York: Basic.

Leland, Hayne E., and David H. Pyle. 1977. Informational asymmetries, financial structure, and financial intermediation. *Journal of Finance* 82 (May): 371–87.

Lutz, Friedrich A. 1945. *Corporate cash balances*. New York: NBER.

Merwin, Charles L. 1942. *Financing small corporations*. New York: NBER.

Meyer, John R., and Edwin Kuh. 1957. *The investment decision*. Cambridge, Mass.: Harvard University Press.

Minsky, Hyman P. 1975. *John Maynard Keynes*. New York: Columbia University Press.

Modigliani, Franco, and Merton Miller. 1958. The cost of capital, corporation finance, and the theory of investment. *American Economic Review* 48 (June): 261–97.

Myers, Stewart C., and Nicholas S. Majluf. 1984. Corporate financing and investment decisions when firms have information that investors do not have. *Journal of Financial Economics* 13 (June): 187–221.

Stiglitz, Joseph E., and Andrew Weiss. 1981. Credit rationing in markets with imperfect information. *American Economic Review* 71 (June): 393–410.

Summers, Lawrence H. 1981. Taxation and corporate investment: A q-theory approach. *Brookings Papers on Economic Activity*, no. 1:67–127.

Tobin, James. 1969. A general equilibrium approach to monetary theory. *Journal of Money, Credit, and Banking* 1 (February): 15–29.

Whited, Toni M. 1989. Debt, liquidity constraints, and corporate investment: Evidence from panel data. Mimeograph. Princeton University.

Wojnilower, Albert M. 1980. The central role of credit crunches in recent financial history. *Brookings Papers on Economic Activity*, no. 2:277–326.

1 Macroeconomic Models with Equity and Credit Rationing

Bruce C. Greenwald and Joseph E. Stiglitz

The role played by imperfect information in business fluctuations has received increasing attention since Lucas's early work.[1] However, the locus of that attention has shifted from systematic misperceptions of the sources of price shocks in the original Lucas form of imperfect information to the macroeconomic consequences of information-related microeconomic failures.[2] This paper seeks to summarize a major development of this latter literature, to integrate that development into a standard macroeconomic model and to provide a reformulation that casts additional light on the mechanism by which monetary policy affects the economy. The microeconomic failures in question occur most significantly in financial markets. In credit markets, it is by now well established that lenders who are less well-informed than borrowers about the risk characteristics of the borrower's investment projects may well respond by fixing interest rates and (under certain conditions) rationing credit.[3] In equity markets, it is equally well established that, when potential equity issuers are better informed about their future prospects than potential equity purchasers, raising funds by issuing new equity may be a highly costly, if not prohibitively difficult, undertaking.[4] Briefly and crudely stated, the significant macroeconomic consequences of these financial market failures (which are essentially microeconomic in nature) include an increase in the importance of internally generated funds in determining firm behavior—especially investment behavior; a reduction in the importance of interest rates as a determinant of borrowing and investment (and hence as a macroeconomically stabilizing variable); amplification of the output responses of firms to demand and other disturbances, the risk and cash flow consequences of which cannot be shifted

Bruce C. Greenwald is a member of technical staff at Bell Communications Research. Joseph E. Stiglitz is professor of economics at Stanford University and a research associate of the National Bureau of Economic Research.

either by issuing equity or by increased borrowing (leading to accelerator-like behavior); and significant changes in the likely consequences of macroeconomic policy.

However, financial markets are not the sole area of impact of imperfect information on macroeconomic behavior. Efficiency wage models of labor-market behavior and comparable models of product markets have made important contributions both to understanding macroeconomic phenomena like unemployment and to investigating likely paths of adjustment between macroeconomic equilibria.[5] Thus the paper's basic model of financial market failures is extended to incorporate the impacts of these further informational imperfections in labor and product markets.

The paper consists, therefore, of five sections. The first two describe the impact of imperfect information in financial markets on investment and loan-market behavior, respectively. A third section incorporates these behaviors into a traditional IS-LM model of macroeconomic equilibria. The fourth section then briefly discusses an extension of the model to examine likely paths of adjustment between equilibria when labor and product markets also suffer from information imperfections. Finally, a fifth section investigates the long-run growth implications of the model.

1.1   Firm Behavior and Investment

The model of firm behavior that will be used is essentially that of Greenwald and Stiglitz (1987). Firm decision makers maximize the expected end-of-period equity of the firm minus an expected cost of bankruptcy, which is simply the cost of bankruptcy times the probability of bankruptcy.[6] We assume initially that firms use only circulating capital; inputs must be paid before outputs are available for sale and before output prices are known.[7] Formally, therefore, firms

$$\max \bar{a}(q_t) - c(q_t)P_B,$$

where $\bar{a}(q_t)$ is the expected end-of-period equity, $c(q_t)$ is the cost of bankruptcy, which we will assume is linear in q_t (the size of the firm) so that $c(q_t) = cq_t$, P_B is the probability of bankruptcy, and q_t is the firm's capital stock in period t, which is also, in this circulating capital world, the output that the firm has available for sale at the end of period t. Here, end-of-period equity is

$$\bar{a}(q_t) = \bar{p}_t q_t - (1+\bar{r}_t)\bar{b}_t,$$

where $\bar{p}_t$ is price of output at the end of period t, $\bar{b}_t$ is the firm's indebtedness at the beginning of period t, and $\bar{r}_t$ is the return to borrowers, which is a random variable (as is $\bar{p}_t$) since the firm may go bankrupt and default on its loans. Then

$$\bar{a}(q_t) = q_t - (1 + \bar{r}_t)\bar{b}_t,$$

where $\bar{r}_t$ is the expected value of $\tilde{r}_t$ and the expected price level is normalized at one.

Bankruptcy occurs if the end-of-period value of the firm, a_t, is less than zero; if

$$\tilde{p}_t q_t \leq (1 + r_t)\bar{b}_t,$$

where r_t is the contractual level of interest that the firm promised to pay debtholders at the beginning of period t. The debt incurred by the firm at beginning of period t is

$$\bar{b}_t = w_t \ell_t q_t - a_{t-1},$$

where we assume that output is produced with a constant-returns-to-scale technology using only labor as an input,[8] ℓ_t is the amount of labor needed per unit of output, $a_{t-1} = p_{t-1} q_{t-1} - (1 + r_{t-1})\bar{b}_{t-1}$ is the equity level that the firm inherits from period $t - 1$, and we assume for the moment that no dividends are paid out.

The cost of bankruptcy incurred here represents the cost to managers of the firm (i.e., those deciding on output levels). The justification for such bankruptcy costs is twofold. First, in a world of imperfect information, outside observers cannot distinguish between failure due to incompetent management and failure due to bad luck (which is idiosyncratic to the type of firm in question). As a result, failure will unavoidably stigmatize managers whether it is deserved or not. The negative impact of this failure on their future earnings is, therefore, what is represented by the cost $c(q_t)$.[9] Alternatively, the imposition of a punishment—termination of employment—associated with failure may be one way to structure management incentive contracts that are characterized by sharing rules for positive profits but have no means of credibly forcing managers to participate in losses. And, for these purposes, bankruptcy may be one natural point for assessing such penalties since the ability of management to conceal losses is greatly reduced under such circumstances. Having bankruptcy costs increase with firm size then simply reflects the fact that a larger scale of operation requires more managers. The advantages of this kind of interpretation of bankruptcy cost are, first, that it enables bankruptcy costs to play a larger role in firm decisions than estimates of actual reorganization cost, which are relatively small, would imply;[10] second, that relatively high bankruptcy costs of this kind account for the observed fact that bankruptcy is a rare event that managers appear to strive disproportionately actively to avoid.[11] Finally, we will assume that reorganization costs to debtholders are zero.

We will assume that the contractual rate of interest paid by firms is set to yield an expected return to debtholders that equals a required return, $\bar{r}_t$. For the moment we will assume that the equity-constrained firms are not credit rationed.

Thus, each firm's decision makers maximize

(1) $q_t - (1+\bar{r}_t)(w_t\ell_t)q_t + (1+\bar{R}_t)a_{t-1} - cq_tP_B,$

where the probability of bankruptcy,

$$P_B = F[\bar{u}_t],$$

where $\bar{u}_t \equiv$ price below which firms go bankrupt $= (1+\bar{R}_t)w_t\ell_t - (a_{t-1}/q_t)$, F is the distribution function of $\tilde{p}_t$, and the contractual rate of interest, r_t, is determined, simultaneously with $\bar{u}_t$, by the equation[12]

(2) $(1+\bar{r}_t)[w_t\ell_t - (a_{t-1}/q_t)] = \bar{u}_t[1 - F(\bar{u}_t)] + \int_0^{\bar{u}_t} \tilde{p}_t dF(\tilde{p}_t).$

In this last equation, the right-hand side represents the expected return required by borrowers per unit of output (i.e., the required return, $1+\bar{r}_t$, times the amount borrowed per unit of output). The left-hand side represents the actual expected return to borrowers per unit of output as a function of $\bar{u}_t$. The definition of $\bar{u}_t$ implies that the return from selling the output q_t at $\bar{u}_t$ just covers the contractual return to debtholders (i.e., $1+r_t$). At prices below $\bar{u}_t$, the returns to debtholders are just $\tilde{p}_t q_t$ (since they receive the entire proceeds from sales of output) or $\tilde{p}_t$ per unit of output (see appendix for derivation).

The optimal level of output (and hence investment), q_t, which solves this maximization problem, depends positively and linearly on a_{t-1}, since the maximand, on being divided by a_{t-1}, is a function of (q_t/a_{t-1}) and $\bar{u}_t$ depends on q_t only through (q_t/a_{t-1}).[13] The first-order condition determining the optimal level of (q_t/a_{t-1}) takes the form

$$1 = (1+\bar{r}_t)w_t\ell_t + cP_B + c\frac{d\bar{u}}{d(q_t/a_{t-1})}\left[\frac{q_t}{a_{t-1}}\right]\frac{dP_B}{d\bar{u}}.$$

The left-hand side of this equation is the expected end-of-period return to output (investment) and the right-hand side is the expected marginal cost of output, including the marginal increase in bankruptcy costs associated with higher levels of output (the second and third right-hand-side terms). The output (investment) function of a typical firm can, therefore, be written as

(3) $q_t = h(w_t,r_t,\sigma_t)a_{t-1},$

where σ_t represents the spread of the price distribution, F, and

$$h_w < 0, \ h_r < 0, \text{ and } h_\sigma < 0.$$

The levels of firm output and investment depend not just on the expected return to investment, which depends in turn on wages and interest rates as it does in the traditional case, but also on the firm's equity level and the level of uncertainty concerning future prices. Higher equity levels mean that the same level of output (and hence investment) can be attained with a lower level of borrowing and thus with a lower risk of bankruptcy. Moreover, under quite general circumstances (e.g., if bankruptcy is an event that occurs in the lower tail of a single-peaked distribution of prices), then higher equity levels also lower the incremental risk of bankruptcy associated with any given level of output (investment). This means that higher equity levels reduce the incremental cost of higher output and, thus, lead to increased output and investment.[14]

Increased uncertainty about future profitability has an opposite effect. Greater uncertainty increases both the absolute and incremental risk of bankruptcy under quite general conditions at any level of investment (output) and firm equity. Thus, firms respond by lowering investment (and output) since they cannot absorb the increased risks by issuing more equity.

Complete specification of the output and investment model then requires an equation describing the evolution of equity levels. Substitution from the definitions of $\bar{b}_t$ into the definition of a_t yields

$$\tilde{a}_t = \tilde{p}_t q_t - (1 + \tilde{r}_t)(w_t \ell_t - a_{t-1}).$$

Thus, firm equity levels in period t are firm equity levels in period $t-1$ plus profits (including a shadow return on a_{t-1}). The critical assumption here is that a firm does not have recourse to external equity markets.

The formal rationale for such an assumption is developed in the Appendix below. It is, however, straightforward to describe the arguments involved. Suppose that in addition to the level of output, q_t, prices, wages, and interest rates, the profitability of each firm depends on an unobservable productivity variable. If all firms look identical to potential investors, then firms with high levels of unobserved productivity (and hence future profits) will sell stock on the same terms as those with low levels of unobserved productivity. However, the cost of selling any given amount of stock is higher for the high-productivity firm since the shares that it sells represents a portion of a higher level of profits. Thus, only low-productivity firms would sell stock on these terms.[15] However, in doing so, they would identify themselves as low-productivity firms with a resulting negative impact on their current market values. If, therefore, firms (or their managers) are concerned with the current as well as the future market values of their equity, this second effect may deter even low-productivity firms from issuing equity.

Allowing for dividends leads to only a slight modification of the equity equation as long as dividend levels are fixed. Then, the end-of-period equity of the firm becomes

(4) $$\tilde{a}_t = \tilde{p}_t q_t - (1 + \tilde{r}_t)(w_t \ell_t - a_{t-1}) - d_t,$$

where d_t is the level of dividends. The rationale for such an assumption is similar to that for restricting equity issues. Dividends are negative equity issues to which a firm has made a prior commitment. Only low-productivity firms with a high incremental value for such funds as protection against bankruptcy would seek to abandon this commitment and the consequent negative signal involved should discourage such changes.[16]

If a firm is, in addition, constrained in the amount of debt that it can issue and that constraint is binding, then the output function is even simpler. Let b_t denote the maximum level of allowed borrowing, then

$$w_t \ell_t q_t = \text{dollar amount of investment} = (a_{t-1} + b_t),$$

which is inherited equity plus the level of borrowing allowed under the credit constraint. If the output (investment) of these firms is added to that of firms which are merely equity constrained, then the aggregate investment function will now include the allowed borrowing level, b_t, as an explanatory variable. The investment function of equation (3) can thus be rewritten as

$$(5) \qquad q_t = h(w_t, \bar{r}_t, \sigma_t, a_{t-1}, b_t),$$

where b_t represents the level of rationed credit and $h_b > 0$.

Extending the circulating capital model to incorporate investment in long-lived physical capital is principally a matter of redefining the production period. Consider a firm whose sole investment project consists of a plant with a fixed life of T periods. Assume for simplicity that funds borrowed to support the plant are due to be repaid (including accrued interest) at the end of period T, that input costs and output revenues are contemporaneous in each subperiod $t = 1, \ldots T$ (or at least are subject to minimal uncertainty looking forward from the beginning of each subperiod), and that intervening subperiod profits are reinvested at a safe rate of return, r_t^*, the end-of-period-T return to the plant investment is

$$\tilde{\pi}_T \equiv \sum_{t=1}^{T} \tilde{\pi}_t(k)(1 + r_t^*)^{T-t},$$

where $\tilde{\pi}_t(k)$ is the profit in subperiod t looking forward from the time of the initial investment, which is a random variable and a function of that initial investment, k. The end-of-period $-T$ equity of the firm is then

$$\tilde{a}_T = \tilde{\pi}_T(k) - (1 + r_o)^T b_o,$$

where b_o is the level of initial borrowing and r_o is the contractual rate of return on that borrowing. If $\tilde{a}_T$ is less than zero, the firm goes bankrupt and incurs a bankruptcy cost proportional to its scale of operation, k. Finally, initial borrowing by the firm is simply

$$b_o = p_k k - a_o,$$

where p_k is the price of capital goods and a_o is the initial equity of the firm.

If $\tilde{\pi}(k)$ is linear in k (i.e., constant returns to scale), this long-run investment problem is identical in structure to the circulating capital formulation described above. Thus, nothing in the model restricts the definition of investment to circulating capital and the basic implications of financial market imperfections in the circulating capital model (e.g., the dependence of investment on both inherited equity and the uncertainty of the economic environment),[17] can apply equally well with fixed capital investment.

Several points should be made about the nature of aggregate (and individual firm) investment behavior implicit in equations (4) and (5). First, high profitability in any given period, by generating increases in firm equity levels (for non-credit-constrained firms) and increased cash flow (for credit-constrained firms), will lead to increased future investment. Thus, the model suggests the kind of significant relationship between current operating cash flow and investment found by Hubbard, Fazzari, and Petersen (1988), among others. Also, if high profitability in any period is related to increases in demand in that period, the model will exhibit the kind of accelerator behavior that has been so successful in explaining actual investment behavior.[18] The model can be usefully thought of, therefore, as providing a microeconomic rationale for both the cash flow and accelerator aspects of investment behavior that appear to play such a significant role in practice.[19] Second, firms wishing to borrow pay firm-specific rates of interest, not some average rate on all assets. With imperfectly informed lenders, changes in general market rates do not necessarily lead to changes in the rates charged to borrowing firms.[20] Some part of the shift in loan supply is absorbed by increased credit rationing since charging higher interest rates has an adverse effect on the quality and riskiness of the borrower pool (see below). Thus, the rate, r_t (and the associated expected return to lenders $\bar{r}_t$), which enters the investment model above may vary significantly less than widely observed market rates (such as Treasury-bill rates), which would be available for use in any empirically estimated investment equation. Second, the impact of interest rates tends to be small relative to the impact of changes in a firm's financial position,[21] and real interest-rate series have, until the very recent past, been observably quite stable. Thus, the variability in the financial positions of firms and the perceived riskiness of the environment they face over the business cycle can be responsible for a far greater share of the variation in investment over time than market interest rates. For both reasons, the model provides an explanation for the relatively small and elusive role that interest rates play in empirical investment equations and suggests that interest rates themselves do not play a primary role in macroeconomic stabilization.[22]

Finally, as will be noted extensively in later sections of this paper, investment, although defined for explanatory purposes as investment in physical capital of the usual sort, need not and should not be interpreted so narrowly. Part of investment takes the form of working capital and the hiring and training of workers, and a rise in the cost of investment (because, e.g., of a deterioration in a firm's equity position) will be reflected as a reduction in working capital, in employment, and, since the costs of working capital and hiring are part of the costs that determine aggregate supply, in aggregate supply and labor demand. Pricing, too, may have an important investment component. If future demand depends on current sales, then firms will invest in future demand by lowering current prices and expanding current sales.[23] An increase in the cost of investment will consequently appear as an increase in current prices and a reduction in current output as firms respond by reducing investments in future demand. Again, therefore, a reduction in investment will appear as a reduction in current supply. Productivity growth may also have an important investment component through both research and development spending, the learning associated with the implementation of new technologies embodied in fixed capital investment, and the "learning-by-doing" related to higher current output. Thus, the idea of investment should not be narrowly construed as relating solely to fixed investment, and in what follows we will take such a broad view.

1.2   Credit Rationing and Loan Markets

In describing loan markets, this section will focus on the role of bank lending. The justification for doing this is threefold. First, cyclical changes in firm financing are dominated by changes in short-term bank financing. This is especially true at the peak and during the downward phase of the cycle.[24] Second, the role (or lack of role) of monetary policy is central to macroeconomic theory and, in most modern industrial societies, the proximate impact of monetary policy is on the banking system. Therefore, in examining the role of monetary policy, the banking system is a logical point of departure. Finally, a model of loan markets based on bank lending appears relatively easy to extend to incorporate direct lending to firms, whereas the opposite—extending a direct loan model to incorporate a banking system—seems to be less straightforward.[25]

We will assume, following Stiglitz and Weiss (1981), that lenders are unable to distinguish among borrowers, that borrowers accept a common fixed loan size, and that as the contractual rate of interest charged borrowers rises, the quality of the borrower pool falls.[26] This occurs because the pool of borrowers at high contractual interest rates consists to a disproportionate degree of those who, because they have high expected default rates, do not face comparably high expected interest rates. This means that as contractual interest rates rise, the expected returns on loans may first rise, but ultimately fall as the cost of deterioration in the borrower pool outweighs the direct gains from higher contractual rates. The deterioration in the default rate may also be because of adverse incentive effects. At the same time, the variance of loan returns should rise steadily with rising contractual rates of interest as default rates arise. Changes in contractual rates of interest will, therefore, trace out a mean-variance frontier of loan returns as illustrated in figure 1.1. We will assume that the expected return on this frontier peaks at a contractual interest

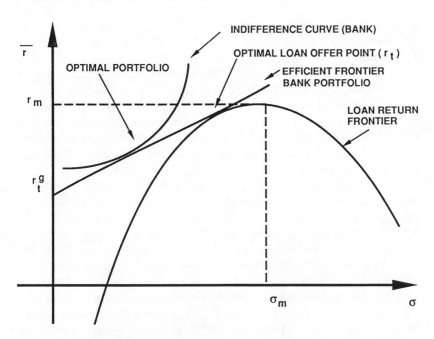

Fig. 1.1   Optimal bank behavior (credit rationing case)

rate, r_m, corresponding to an expected lender return, $\bar{r}_m$, and a return standard deviation, σ_m.[27]

Next we assume that lenders (banks) have a choice of investing in risky loans along this frontier or in safe government bonds that pay a return, r_t^g, in period t. In making this choice we assume that banks are risk averse and characterized by declining absolute risk aversion as their financial positions improve.[28] Like some of the firms to which they lend, banks are assumed to be run by mangers/decision makers who are not fully diversified (i.e., they are disproportionately invested in the banks that they manage).

A useful starting point is to consider a case in which loan demand at any interest rate below r_m exceeds the total lending capacity of banks, and r_t^g is below $\bar{r}_m$. Then banks will always ration credit and the efficient investment frontier for a bank runs along a line from the point r_t^g on the vertical axis to a tangency with the mean-variance loan return frontier traced out by varying contractual rates of interest (see fig. 1.1). (At interest rates on government bonds above $\bar{r}_m$, banks invest entirely in government bonds.) The tangency point on the loan return frontier determines the terms on which bank loans are made. It necessarily occurs at an expected return at or below $\bar{r}_m$ and, thus, entails a contractual loan rate at or below r_m. The fraction of the bank's assets devoted to commercial loans (on the terms determined by the tangency of the efficient frontier and the loan return frontier) is then determined by the tangency of the bank decision maker's mean-variance indifference curve with the efficient frontier. This too is shown in figure 1.1. The position of this tangency point depends on several factors.

As r_t^g falls toward zero, the point of tangency on the loan frontier may move only very slightly, especially if the frontier has a shape like that shown in figure 1.1. As a result, the contractual rate of interest charged borrowers may be highly insensitive to changes in the rate of interest in public securities markets.[29] Nevertheless, as r_t^g falls, the tangency of the efficient frontier with the bank indifference curves may change substantially leading to a significant change in bank lending.

As the financial positions of firms improve, the quality of the overall borrowing pool improves, since firms are less likely to default. This appears as a shift upward in the loan return frontier, since at each contractual rate of interest the expected return on loans rises and the variance of returns falls as default rates decline. The slope of the efficient frontier will then become steeper and the tangency of the frontier with the decision makers' indifference curve will move to the right (i.e., to a steeper point on the indifference curve).[30] Thus, the optimal bank portfolio will consist of a greater fraction of loans and a smaller fraction of government bonds.[31] A reduction in the interest rate on the government bonds will have a similar effect. An improvement in the financial position of a bank can be interpreted as a flattening of the risk-return indifference curves (because of declining absolute risk aversion) and hence a shift to the right in their tangency with the efficient frontier. This implies a greater fraction of commercial lending and less investment in the safe government asset.[32]

The actual level of bank commercial lending is the product of the share of loans in the bank portfolio and the level of bank assets. The latter is, in turn, just the sum of bank capital and deposits. Since we will assume that the money supply consists only of deposits and that reserve requirements are fixed, total loans are

(4)
$$b_t = \left[k\frac{M_t}{P_t} + \gamma_{t-1}^b \right] \beta\ [r_t^g, a_{t-1}, a_{t-1}^b],$$

where $1 \geq \beta \geq 0$ is the fraction of bank assets loaned that depends on r_t^g, the rate of return on government bonds, a_{t-1}, borrowing firm equity positions, and a_{t-1}^b, the equity position of banks as they enter period t with $\beta_1 < 0$, $\beta_2 > 0$, and $\beta_3 > 0$. The variable γ_t^b is bank capital in period t, $k = 1$ minus the required reserve ratio, the nominal money supply is M_t, and P_t is the price level, with all magnitudes except those last two being real variables.

The contractual rate of interest on loans in the rationing equilibrium is

(5)
$$r_t = \alpha(r_t^g, a_{t-1}),\ \alpha_1 \geq 0,$$

and α_2 may be either positive or negative. Higher levels of firm equity lower default rates, and lower default rates should lower r_t, but these higher levels of firm equity also raise demand for funds, which has an opposite effect.

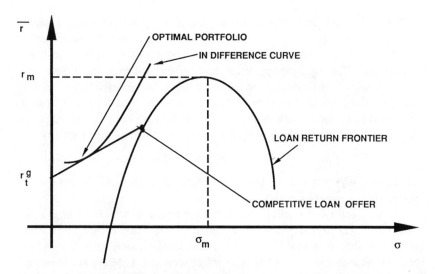

Fig 1.1a   Optimal bank behavior (no rationing case)

The level of bank equity does not affect r_t in the rationing equilibrium because r_t depends only on the tangency of the efficient frontier with the loan return frontier. If, at this contractual interest rate, the demand for loans is less than the amount that bank portfolio decisions make available (i.e., there is no credit rationing), then competition among banks will drive down the contractual rate of interest (given that loan size remains fixed, as in Stiglitz-Weiss 1981). As this occurs bank loan returns move down along the loan return frontier. The available efficient portfolio frontier under these circumstances runs from the point r_t^g on the vertical axis (see fig. 1.1a) to the point of the loan return frontier corresponding to a particular contractual interest rate. Along this new frontier banks select a portfolio mix which is tangent to their risk-return indifference curves. At this tangency, lower contractual returns will lead to less loan investment by banks and hence lower loan supply. At the same time, lower contractual rates of interest increase loan demand. At some point the two just balance and an equilibrium without credit rationing occurs. However, under these conditions, r_t still depends on r_t^g and a_{t-1}, which affects both loan demand and the position of the loan return frontier.[33]

In order to complete the loan sector of the model, we must specify how bank equity and bank capital evolve over time. For simplicity we assume that bank capital may come only from reinvested earning. Bank capital borrowing and new equity, like those of other firms, will be assumed to be impossible.[34] Formally, therefore,

$$\gamma_{t-1}^b = \pi_{t-1}^b + \gamma_{t-2}^b - d_{t-1}^b,$$

where π_{t-1}^b is bank profitability and d_{t-1}^b is the amount in bank dividends in period $t - 1$.

The restrictions on capital borrowing and new equity issues might suggest that bank capital (the net worth that appears in the bank's balance sheet) is also bank equity, the discounted value of the bank's profits. However, that is not the case. The equity of the bank, looking forward from the beginning of period t, include the value of the bank's franchise as perceived by its managers. This will depend, if there are restrictions on entry and deposit interest, on level of the expected future money supply and thus, in turn, on current monetary policy. To keep things as simple as possible we will assume formally that

$$a^b_{t-1} = \gamma^b_{t-1} + \mu_{t-1},$$

where μ_{t-1}, the value of the bank's franchise, depends upon current and expected future monetary policy.

The availability of credit to firms and the terms on which credit is made available, therefore, depends on the financial condition of the firms themselves and that of the banking sector, which reinforces the cash flow and accelerator-like investment behavior noted in section 1.1. Monetary policy affects loan conditions through a number of channels. First, and perhaps least important, monetary policy will affect the interest rate on government bonds. This change in interest rates on government bonds may have a small and even ambiguous effect on interest rates charged borrowers and hence on the demand for funds. Second, changes in monetary policy will lead to changes in the equity of banks due to changes in the perceived value of their franchises.[35] Third, monetary policy increases the assets in the hands of banks that are available for loans to firms. This last effect is an artifact of the assumed restriction of lending in the model to banks. Monetary policy that shifts control over financial investment funds from households to banks naturally increases lending to firms if only banks are able to do this. However, to the extent that banks enjoy special advantages in making loans to firms, a similar impact, but one of lesser magnitude, would occur even if direct lending to firms were allowed. Allowing banks to borrow for capital purposes would also offset this third effect, but again (in the absence of perfect capital markets and perfect deposit competition) only partially. Fourth, changes in monetary policy (reserve requirements and discount rates) directly affect the extent of bank lending and the bank's willingness and ability to lend.

1.3   The Macroeconomic Model

The changes introduced into a standard macroeconomic framework by incorporating the effects of financial market imperfections are extensive. However, much of the familiar structure of the traditional model can be preserved. If the inherited equity levels of firms (a_{t-1}) and the level of environmental uncertainty (σ_t) are treated for the moment as exogenous parameters, then a goods market equilibrium (suppressing these parameters for notational convenience) can be written

(6) $$y_t = i_t(r_t, b_t, w_t) + g_t + c_t (r_t^g, y_t),$$

where y_t is real output, i_t is real investment, g_t is real government spending, and c_t is real consumption, which is assumed to depend on the level of output and the interest rate on government bonds, r_t^g, which in turn is assumed to be the interest rate available to consumers.[36] The principal difference from the traditional IS curve is that financial market conditions are no longer embodied in a single interest-rate variable, but rather in one interest rate facing consumers (r_t^g) and two variables (r_t, b_t) that capture the loan market conditions, involving both price and quantity rationing, facing firms.

The financial market equilibrium (LM curve) interacting with the goods market described above implicitly consists of four financial markets: (1) a money market equating the supply and demand for demand deposits, (2) a government bond market equating the demand for government bonds to the existing supply, (3) the market for loans described in the previous section, and (4) a market for the fixed amount of outstanding common stock of firms.

The last of these markets can be ignored in the analysis which follows. This stock market can be thought of as equilibrating the supply and demand for shares through the determination of a stock price per share. Since equity sales are excluded in the model, this stock price does not influence investment; since in this model consumption does not depend on perceived wealth, it does not affect consumption demand.[37] Nor does its interaction with other asset markets need to be considered. Strictly speaking, stock price should enter the demand curves for both money and government bonds (and loans if banks were allowed to own common stocks), but in this case the stock price could be eliminated by solving for stock prices from the stock supply-and-demand equation and substituting into the money and government bond market equations.

Similarly, the money and government bond demand equations can be solved to yield a reduced-form equation for the government bond interest rate in terms of the real supplies of government bonds and money and the level of output, y_t, which presumably affects money demand. This is roughly equivalent to a traditional LM curve and will be written formally as

(7) $$r_t^g = \ell\left[y_t, \frac{G_t}{P_t}, \frac{M_t}{P_t}\right], \ell_1 > 0, \ell_2 > 0, \ell_3 < 0,$$

where G_t is the outstanding nominal amount of government debt.

The principal innovation that arises from credit rationing is the introduction of equations (4) and (5) describing the loan behavior of banks. These determine r_t and b_t as functions of r_t^g given the equity positions of banks, a_{t-1}^b; the equity positions of borrowing firms, a_{t-1}; the levels of environmental uncertainty (σ_t) and wages (w_t), which affect the demand for bank loans; and the levels of bank capital (γ_{t-1}^b) and the money supply (M_t/P_t), which determine bank resources. For analytical purposes, because two loan-market variables are involved, the simplest approach is to incorporate the loan-market equilibrium into the IS curve by substituting from equations (4) and (5) into the investment function of equation (6). This yields a goods-market equilibrium of the form

$$(8) \qquad y_t = i_t \left\{ r_t \left[r_t^g, \frac{M_t}{P_t}, w_t \right], b_t \left[r_t^g, \frac{M_t}{P_t}, w_t \right] \right\} + g_t + c_t(r_t^g, y_t)$$

where the variables a_{t-1}, a_{t-1}^b, σ_t, and q_{t-1} have been suppressed as parameters. Since r_t is increasing and b_t is decreasing in r_t^g, an increase in r_t^g reduces investment demand and hence aggregate demand. This credit-rationing-modified IS curve is, therefore, downward sloping in the usual way.[38]

The traditional macroeconomic equilibrium is then depicted in figure 1.2 with the intersection of the IS and LM curves determining an equilibrium level of output and the government bond interest rate for any given level of real wages. It also has several familiar properties. An increase in government debt shifts the LM curve upward, leading to an increase in interest rates and a reduction in output.[39] Also, the model is characterized by the standard neutrality result. If the government debt and the money supply are increased proportionately, then prices increase in the same proportion and real magnitudes are unchanged. The same result arises, if the taxes required for debt service are fully discounted by taxpayers and the money supply increases.

However, there are significant differences from a traditional macromodel.

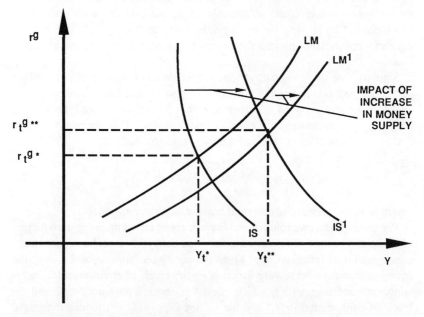

Fig. 1.2   Macroeconomic equilibrium

In particular, an increase in the (real) money supply shifts both the LM curve downward and the modified IS curve to the right, since such a shift directly increases bank lending. As a result it is conceivable, given the relative magnitudes of these shifts, that an increase in the money supply could lead to higher equilibrium output and higher interest rates on government bonds. And, since monetary policy affects the IS curve directly, its effect on total output is likely to be far more significant than that of government debt operations alone, which affect only the LM curve. This seems to be borne out by empirical observations. The added potency of money supply changes arises because it shifts resources into and out of the hands of financial institutions with particular access to borrower information.

Furthermore, unanticipated monetary policy may have stronger impacts still. Assuming that most firms have nominal liabilities (bonds, bank debt, taxes payable, etc.) and real assets, an unexpected monetary expansion may lead to a transfer from lenders (ultimately households) to firms, enhancing the equity positions of firms. This would lead to a further rightward shift in the IS curve, a further increase in output, and more upward pressure on interest rates.

Another exogenous factor that exerts a particular influence in this credit and equity rationing model is an increase in the uncertainties faced or perceived by individual firms. In practice, this could correspond either to an increase in the overall rate of inflation (which has empirically been related to increased relative price fluctuations and to increased variability in the rate of inflation) or to an increase in the unpredictability of monetary policy (as in 1979–82). Such an increase in uncertainty would reduce investment demand both directly and indirectly through its effect on bank lending terms.[40] The IS curve of equation (8) would shift to the left, and equilibrium output and real interest rates would fall (although the change in actual loan rates might be small).

The model is completed by an equilibrium in the labor market that determines the real wage, w_t, as a function of the IS-LM equilibrium. The labor demand curve in this market is just the marginal product of labor at a given level of output net of the incremental risk of bankruptcy borne by managers as output (and employment) increases. This is a downward sloping marginal product curve of the usual sort as shown in figure 1.3. However, this labor demand curve shifts with the financial position of firms. An improvement in a firm's equity position reduces the incremental risk associated with increased output (and employment) at any given output level. Thus, unanticipated shifts in monetary policy that lead to changes in firm equity positions will shift the labor demand curve. Similarly, credit rationing restrictions and the cost of paying workers in advance of production may change the marginal product of labor (net of associated material and interest costs)[41] in response to changes in loan-market conditions.

The labor supply relationship may be embodied in either an upward sloping supply curve of the usual sort or a no-shirking constraint of the kind developed

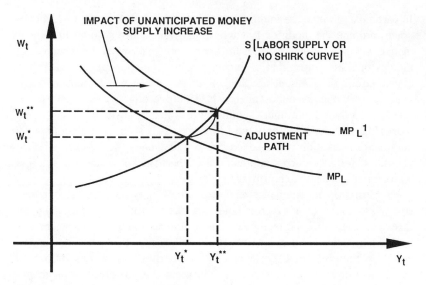

Fig. 1.3   Labor-market equilibrium

in Shapiro and Stiglitz (1984). In both cases, shifts in policy that change the labor demand curve (by inducing shifts in either firm equity positions, loan-market conditions, or the uncertainty of the economic environment) will lead to changes in equilibrium employment, wages, and output (see fig. 1.3). In the case of a labor-supply function there will be no associated unemployment. In the case of a no-shirking constraint (efficiency wage) model, the shift in the labor-market equilibrium will be associated with a change in unemployment. In both cases the change in wages will tend to offset, but only partially, the contemporary change in output at constant wages predicted by the IS-LM interaction. Finally, it should be noted that these changes in output may be relatively short-lived (in contrast to the supply effects of capital accumulation) since firm financial conditions may change relatively quickly (along with loan-market conditions), and they do not depend on any arbitrary nominal price rigidities (in contrast to tradition Keynesian models).

1.4   Short-term Adjustment

The equilibrium shift in output and wages implied by a particular movement in the labor demand curve (see fig. 1.3) should, given the likely slopes of either the labor supply or the nonshirking constraint curve, involve significant changes in both wages and output (employment). However, with imperfect information, the adjustment path to the new equilibrium is likely to involve large initial changes in output (employment) and only small changes in wages. This possibility is based on three simple assumptions in addition to the assumption that firm decision makers are risk averse; namely, (1) that firms are uncertain of the impact of their actions, (2) that this uncertainty increases with the size of movements from the status quo, and (3) that uncertainties associated with price and wage changes are greater than those associated with quantity changes (e.g., in output or unemployment). The first two of these assumptions should be uncontroversial, but the last is central and requires some explanation, which will be provided below.

The reason that rates of adjustment concerning the impacts of different decision variables are related to their relative uncertainties can be seen intuitively as follows. If firms are risk averse, then they will consider both the mean and the variance of the returns yielded by different combinations of changes in decision variables. As firms make adjustments, the expected value and the variance of profits change together. However, if uncertainty concerning the impact of one decision variable A (a price) is greater than uncertainty concerning the impact of another decision variable B (a quantity), then, other things being equal, the optimal portfolio of adjustments will contain less movement in A than B.[42] Following such initial changes, which are greater in B than in A, the expected returns to further changes in A are likely to rise relative to the expected returns to changes in B (since B will now be closer to its new optimal value). Thus, ultimately, A may adjust as extensively as B, but in the short run A will exhibit inertia relative to B.

One important qualification must, however, be made to this simple description. When the consequences of actions are particularly uncertain, and firms are particularly risk averse, it is sometimes suggested that firms will simply maintain the status quo. But what does it mean to continue doing what you were doing before? Does it mean keeping absolute prices fixed, or relative prices? Absolute wages, or relative wages? We provide here an answer: very risk-averse firms will take those actions that minimize the variability of their profits. Thus, in speaking in the previous paragraph of the magnitude of changes in A relative to B, these must be interpreted as changes from the minimum variance point, not as changes from preexisting levels. If the economic environment is one in which the variance of profit is related to relative wages or prices, firms will minimize variance by keeping relative wages or prices fixed. Thus, in the present model, the minimum variance response is one of no change in real magnitudes.[43]

The arguments just given imply that short-term movement in real wages from the no-change point will be relatively small compared to those of output and employment, if firm decision makers face relatively large uncertainties about the effects of wage changes. In efficiency wage models this is likely to be the case. The usual efficiency wage assumption is that average productivities can be observed accurately. Thus, if a large group of workers is laid off or not replaced (where there is substantial normal turnover), the lost labor supply is just the number of workers involved times average productivity. There is little or no uncertainty about this. However, firms are likely to be much less certain of the impact of a wage change on labor supply since this involves estimating the impact of wage changes on turnover (both in quality and quantity) and worker performance. Neither is likely to be known very accurately, nor can these effects be ascertained immediately following any initial wage change (they take time to become manifest). Similarly, if firms who produce to inventory know the impact of output changes on both inventories and costs with little uncertainty, but are highly uncertain of the effects of price changes on both inventories (via sales) and revenues, then these firms will focus predominantly on output rather than price adjustments in the short run. The result will then be a pattern very similar to that which is observed in practice, of adjustment characterized by rapid output and employment changes and small wages and price changes.

1.5   Long-term Dynamics

The long-run dynamics of the model are driven by rates of accumulation in capital and equity and changes in technology, themselves driven by R&D investments. For simplicity, we will assume that bank and firm capital grow in proportion (because of structures of relative profitability in banking and production activities), and that σ_t, the environmental uncertainty, is fixed. The IS-LM labor demand–labor supply equilibrium for given real money and real government debt levels can be solved to yield a level of equity accumulation as a function of a_{t-1} and presumably k_t. In this reduced form function,

$$i_t = g(k_t, a_{t-1}), \ g_1 > 0, \ g_2 > 0.$$

Higher levels of firm equity (and higher levels of physical capital) tend to lead to higher levels of output and investment. In steady state, investment must replace depreciation and equip new workers entering the labor force (if the labor force is growing). Thus, in steady state,

(9) $$i = (\delta + n)k = g(k, a),$$

where n is the rate of growth of the labor force, k and a must now be interpreted as per capita magnitudes, and we assume constant returns to scale (including in the bankruptcy cost function). In a general equilibrium context, g_1 should be less than $\delta + n$ (because increased capital that increases wages and interest rates has a relatively small general-equilibrium effect on new investment demand). Under such a condition, the steady-state levels of a and k in equation (9) are related by an upward sloping curve (see fig. 1.4). This is essentially an equity demand curve. It describes the level of equity per capita in steady state that is required to generate sufficient investment to sustain a particular level of the per capita capital stock. For levels of a below this curve, the per capita capital stock will be declining. For the levels of a above the curve, k will be increasing.

A second steady-state relationship exists between k and a and can be de-

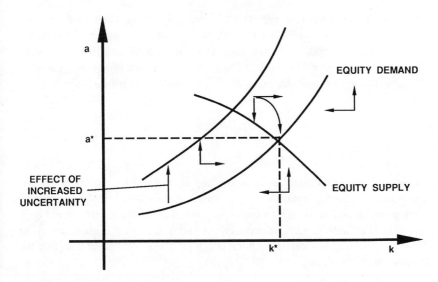

Fig. 1.4   Long-run steady state

scribed as an equity supply curve. Higher levels of both the capital stock and equity tend to increase output, drive up wages, and ultimately reduce profit rates and retained earnings per worker. Since retained earnings are the source of equity growth and since equity per capita must grow in steady-state conditions at a proportional rate n, the steady-state equity demand relationship is

$$(10) \qquad na = h(k, a), \, h_1 < 0, \, h_2 < 0,$$

which is a downward sloping curve (see fig. 4). This second curve intersects the equity demand curve at the long-run steady state of the equity and credit rationing model. A simple phase plane analysis indicates that the equilibrium is stable with dynamic paths that may either return monotonically (most likely) or cyclically to equilibrium. Thus, temporary deviations in firm equity levels, due, for example, to unexpected money supply changes, are ultimately eliminated as the model returns over time to the long-run steady state. Cycles in these models appear, therefore, like most observed business cycles to be self-limiting.

This long-run steady state can also be used to study long-run comparative statics. For example, a sudden increase in uncertainty (σ_I) shifts the equity demand curve upward and yields a new steady state with lower capital and higher equity levels.[44]

1.6   Conclusion

The important point to note about the macroeconomic implications of even the relatively simple model of credit and equity rationing developed here is that this model describes, remarkably accurately, many aspects of observed aggregate behavior, which are difficult to account for in terms of traditional macroeconomic models. At the same time, it embodies realistic microeconomic assumptions about information availability, which produces highly reasonable microeconomic descriptions of firm and lending institution behavior.

Appendix

This Appendix describes the structure of information that underlies the microeconomic description of firm-level behavior in Section 1.1 of this paper. In doing so, it will be useful to begin with the model of the text altered only slightly to include an additive productivity factor, θ_t, which is unobservable to outside investors but known with certainty by a firm's managers, so that the profits of the firm are

$$\pi_t = p_t q_t - (1 + r_t)\bar{b}_t + \theta_t.$$

Substitution from the definition of $\bar{b}_t$, and normalization so that ℓ_t, output per unit of labor, is one, yields

$$\pi_t = [p_t - (1 + r_t)w_t]q_t + (1 + r_t)a_{t-1} + \theta_t,$$

where p_t is the price at which goods are sold at the end of period t, w_t is the wage level, q_t is output (investment) in period t, r_t is the return to lenders, and a_{t-1} denotes the equity funds that the firm inherits from period $t - 1$. At the beginning of each period, each firm receives an independent θ_t draw from a distribution that is the same for all firms.[45] This distribution has $E[\theta_t] = 0$ and a range $[\theta_a, \theta_b]$. At the beginning of a period a firm knows w_t, q_t, a_{t-1}, r_t, and θ_t with certainty. It also knows the distribution of p_t but not the particular realized value of p_t, which materializes only at the end of the period.

At the beginning of period t, neither q_t nor θ_t is observable to outside investors. We will also assume for the moment that lending to firms is done by banks who have access to confidential firm information (i.e., they observe θ_t and q_t), but are constrained not to reveal that information either by revealing borrowing levels, $\bar{b}_t$, or by acting upon it (i.e., by purchasing the stock of a firm in the open market). Thus only a_{t-1} for each firm is observable to outside (i.e., nonbank) investors at the beginning of period t.

We assume that financial contracts are limited to either (1) debt contracts, which provide a fixed return, r_t, if a firm is solvent or, in the event of insolvency, all the assets of the firm, or (2) equity contracts, which provide a fixed fraction of the firm's net worth if the firm is solvent and nothing otherwise. In practice, under equity contracts share owners receive their returns through dividends. We will assume that loans are made by banks, which are owned, in turn, by households, and that equity is held directly by households (i.e., Glass-Steagall-like restraints restrict bank ownership of common stock). We will also assume initially, that all investors are risk neutral and require an expected rate of return, $\bar{r}_t$, on their investments.

Under these circumstances, the equation determining the level of r_t, the contractual rate of return on loans, directly determines the probability that a firm goes bankrupt (i.e., $\pi_t \leq 0$). From the definition of π_t, bankruptcy implies that

$$p_t < (1 + r_t)w_t - \left[\frac{(1 + r_t)a_{t-1} + \theta_t}{q_t}\right] \equiv \bar{u}_t,$$

where, by definition, $\bar{u}_t$ is the price realization below which firms go bankrupt. The expected total return to investors is, therefore,

$$\bar{b}_t E(1 + r_t) = (\bar{u}_t \cdot q_t + \theta_t)[1 - F(\bar{u}_t)] + \int_0^{\bar{u}_t} (q_t p_t + \theta_t)dF(p_t),$$

since, at prices above $\bar{u}_t$, lenders receive $\bar{u}_t$ per unit of output plus θ_t and, at prices below $\bar{u}_t$, lenders as residual claimants receive the entire p_t per unit of output plus θ_t again. The level of r_t, and hence $\bar{u}_t$, is then set so that this expected return is equal to $(1 + \bar{r}_t)\bar{b}_t$. Thus, substitution for $\bar{b}_t$ and rearrangement of terms yield

$$(1 + \bar{r}_t)\left[w_t - \frac{a_{t-1} + \theta_t/(1 + \bar{r}_t)}{q_t}\right] = \bar{u}_t (1 - F(\bar{u}_t)) + \int_0^{\bar{u}_t} p_t dF,$$

which is just the equation of the text modified by the inclusion of the θ_t factor (which is observed by bank lenders).

Expected profits are also a simple extension of those in the text. In particular,

$$E(\pi_t) = [1 - (1 + \bar{r}_t)w_t]q_t + (1 + \bar{r}_t)\left[a_{t-1} + \frac{\theta_t}{1 + \bar{r}_t}\right].$$

Thus, in both instances (expected profits and the definition of $\bar{u}_t$), the effect of the additive productivity factor, θ_t, is to replace a_{t-1} by $a_{t-1} + \theta_t/(1 + \bar{r}_t)$, and the output function of the firm can be written

$$q_t = h(w_t, \bar{r}_t, \sigma_t)\left[a_{t-1} + \frac{\theta_t}{1 + \bar{r}_t}\right],$$

where the function h is exactly that of the text.[46] If therefore, we define

$$z_{t-1} \equiv a_{t-1} + \frac{\theta_t}{1 + \bar{r}_t},$$

then the analysis can proceed directly in terms of z_{t-1} instead of a_{t-1}. Since q_t is linear in z_t and $\bar{u}_t$ is a function of the ratio of q_t and z_t, $\bar{u}_t$ is independent of z_t. Thus, the objective function of firms

$$[1 - (1 + \bar{r}_t)w_t]q_t + (1 + \bar{r}_t)z_t - cq_t F(\bar{u}_t),$$

is linear in z_t, and the end-of-period valuation function for the multiperiod problem is linear in end-of-period equity, as are future expected profits (and their discounted value). The expected end-of-period market value of the firm is therefore,

$$E[V_t] = kE[z_{t+1}] = kE[a_{t+1}] = k'z_t,$$

where k' and k will depend on w_t, $\bar{r}_t$, σ_t and their future expected values, and the second equality follows from the fact that $E[\theta_t] = 0$, ex ante, for each t.

Now consider a decision to raise an amount of equity, e_o. The share of the firm retained by the original shareholders depends on the market value of the firm when it decides to issue equity, V_{ot}, where

$$V_{ot} = \left[\frac{1}{1 + \bar{r}_t}\right] E[V_t] = k'E[z_t]\left[\frac{1}{1 + \bar{r}_t}\right],$$

where the expectations are now taken conditional on the information available to outside equity investors. Thus

$$E[z_t] = a_{t-1} + \frac{E[\theta_t/\text{equity issued}]}{1 + \bar{r}_t}.$$

The share of the firm sold to new shareholders is

$$s = \frac{e_o}{e_o + V_{ot}}.$$

The cost of this equity sale from the perspective of the firm's inside managers is

$$s \cdot k'(z_t + e_o) = sk'\left[a_{t-1} + e_o + \frac{\theta_t}{1 + \bar{r}_t}\right],$$

since they observe θ_t. Since the new equity simply increases a_{t-1}, the value of the equity issue, e_o, is $k' \cdot e_o$. Thus, the condition that firms issue equity is simply

$$e_o k'\left[a_{t-1} + e_o + \frac{\theta_t}{(1 + \bar{r}_t)}\right] \leq (e_o + V_{ot}) \cdot k'e_o,$$

or, after rearranging terms,

(A1) $\theta_t \leq (k' - 1)a_{t-1}(1 + \bar{r}_t) + k'E[\theta/\text{equity issued}].$

With no impediments to issuing equity, k' is equal to one and,[47] the equity issue condition becomes

(A2) $\theta_t \leq E[\theta/\text{equity issued}]$.

This condition implies, in turn, that no equity will be issued. The expectation of θ_t for equity issuers would be derived only from those with θ_t less than that expectation (i.e., those who issue equity according to eq. [A2] above), and this can only occur at θ_a, the lower limit of the θ distribution, where essentially no one issues equity. Thus, no equilibrium without equity issue restrictions is compatible with the information structure assumed here.

However, an equilibrium with such restrictions and consequently $k' > 1$, may exist. In that case, it is still firms for which θ_t is less than or equal to some threshold of those who issue equity (see eq. [A1]) and, in consequence,

$$E[\theta/\text{equity issued}] < E[\theta/\text{no equity issued}].$$

Thus, firms announcing equity issues will face an immediate decline in current market value. If current, as well as end-of-period, market value enters a firm's objective function,[48] this will in turn represent an additional fixed cost of issuing equity and a further deterrent to doing so. In practice, therefore, asymmetric information concerning firm prospects (i.e., θ_t) between managers and outside investors may well restrict equity issues to a small number of firms and an insignificant amount of funds, as appears to be the case in practice.[49] This is the underlying rationale for the equity issue constraint.

In relaxing the informational assumptions described above, the obvious place to begin is with the assumptions of well-informed bank lenders. If banks cannot distinguish among potential borrowers (i.e., they cannot observe q_t or θ_t), then the contractual rate of interest r_t must be set at the same level for all firms. Under these circumstances, the analysis must be adjusted slightly but remains fundamentally unchanged. There is an induced tendency for poor (i.e., low θ_t) firms to borrow more since they have higher default rates and hence lower expected interest costs for any r_t than good (i.e., high θ_t) firms. This does not, however, alter the linearity of the problem in z, so that the basic qualitative results of the fully informed lender case continue to apply (slightly stronger assumptions are needed to ensure that the second-order maximum conditions are satisfied).

A further difficulty is raised if lenders are able to infer θ_t from the level of firm borrowing and reveal this information to investors at large. However, in this case, poor firms would have an incentive to increase borrowing (and invest in nonproduction technologies) to conceal their low θ_t values from the market. At the same time, very poor firms (i.e., those with $z_t < 0$) have an incentive to borrow a great deal (since the probability of bankruptcy declines with output for such firms) so that the need for viable firms to distinguish themselves from very poor firms should set an upper limit on borrowing.

Thus, if lenders attempted to infer firm quality from borrowing levels, there would be a countervailing tendency for all firms to borrow the same amount and equilibria exist in which borrowing levels are constant across firms and uninformative.

Notes

1. See Lucas (1979).
2. See Bernanke and Gertler (1989), Shapiro and Stiglitz (1984), Diamond (1982) and Greenwald, Stiglitz and Weiss (1984) for diverse examples from a large and growing literature.
3. See Stiglitz and Weiss (1981).
4. See Myers and Majluf (1984) and Greenwald, Stiglitz and Weiss (1984). Empirical support for these models is provided by Asquith and Mullins (1986) and in extensive related literature.
5. See Weiss (1980), Shapiro and Stiglitz (1984), Stiglitz (1974, 1976), Akerlof (1984), Bulow and Summers (1985) and Salop and Salop (1976) for examples on efficiency wage models of labor-market behavior; see Stiglitz (1987) on similar models of product markets. For surveys of macroeconomic phenomena see Stiglitz (1982, 1987) and Yellen (1984); on paths of adjustment, see Greenwald and Stiglitz (1989).
6. Similar results obtain if firms maximize an expected utility (or valuation function) of end-of-period equity if the utility function is characterized by decreasing absolute risk aversion.
7. We assume that, for a variety of informational reasons, futures markets are not a significant economic factor (see Greenwald and Stiglitz 1986).
8. The restriction to only labor inputs is made solely for expositional convenience. The effect of relaxing the constant-returns-to-scale assumption is examined in Greenwald and Stiglitz (1986).
9. The importance of bankruptcy itself in this regard is that it represents identifiable failure as opposed to other failures that may be at least partially obscured by accounting flexibility.
10. Although there is some literature stressing that the direct costs of bankruptcy are small, this literature may in fact greatly underestimate the total costs, which include the fact that assets may be tied up during the process of reorganization.
11. In most models in which reorganization costs are small, lenders face imperfect information about the risks of investment projects, and managers serve the interests of shareholders; managers should seek high-risk projects that increase shareholder returns at the expense of lenders. Under these conditions one would expect bankruptcy to be a frequent occurrence.
12. If lenders are risk averse, the required return will be a function of the bankruptcy probability, which in turn depends on $\bar{u}_t$. Formally, eq. (2) holds, with $\bar{r}$ implying a function of $\bar{u}_t$.
13. This result depends on the constant-returns-to-scale production assumption (see Greenwald and Stiglitz 1986 for details), which are quite general.
14. These comparative static propositions depend on imposing restrictions on F, which ensure that the second-order conditions are satisfied.
15. The value of equity in providing protection against bankruptcy is also greater for low- than high-productivity firms, since low-productivity firms are in greater danger of bankruptcy.

16. In practice, since dividend levels typically involve an implied promise of continuity, reducing dividends to obtain equity funds is likely to be less appealing than issuing equity, since the current equity yield is likely to be smaller.

17. However, in practice, there are complications introduced by the existence of long-lived capital. If loans are made on a short-term basis, then a bankruptcy constraint must be defined for each subperiod, t, which, in turn, requires that there be some means of valuing fixed capital at these intervening times. Doing this is not straightforward. Also, firms typically invest in both fixed and working capital. Thus, each individual decision period entails choices of both long-lived investment and current output. The interaction of these two kinds of decisions also significantly complicates the analysis, although it does not change its fundamental implications.

18. See Eisner (1967), Jorgenson (1963) and Lintner (1971) for examples of a large literature.

19. A second accelerator-like effect also arises if there is fixed capital and an increase in demand for a firm's output is persistent. Then past increases in output and profitability are likely to be indicators of future profitability, which would raise the value of a firm's fixed capital stock. In a world without informational imperfections, any such increases in future profitability would be reflected in the market values of firms and would enter a classical investment equation through Tobin's q. In a model with imperfect information, it is the perception of the managers of a firm, based on their private information, which matter, and these perceptions matter in two distinct ways. First, parallel to the classical effect, a rise in future expected return (i.e., an increase in expected prices relative to w_t) will directly elicit higher levels of output. But, in addition, higher future profitability increases the flow of future equity funds and affects output (investment) through that channel as well; this second effect is operative only if the firm cannot raise new capital through new equity issues. In practice, of course, stock market valuations and internal firm assessments may be highly correlated, especially in cross-sectional data, so that the two models will be hard to distinguish. Nevertheless there are important differences between the two. For example, in the past, stock market values have appeared to fluctuate without any clear relationship to future firm profitability and cash flow. Such fluctuations would affect Tobin's q and investment in the classical sense, but would not affect investment in the model presented here.

20. See Stiglitz and Weiss (1981) and the discussion below in sec. 1.2.

21. See Greenwald and Stiglitz (1986).

22. These same factors also explain why properly specified neoclassical investment models like those of Abel (1980) and Abel and Blanchard (1986) perform relatively less well empirically than simple accelerator models.

23. See Phelps and Winter (1970) for a model of this kind.

24. See Zarnowitz (1985).

25. A critical issue to be discussed in subsequent research is the extent to which nonbank lending is a substitute for bank lending. This substitution is of both theoretical and empirical relevance. See Vale (1989).

26. See discussion in the Appendix concerning loan sizes and the information to be derived from observing loan sizes.

27. Since these default risks are, in practice, correlated across borrowers, the law of large numbers does not effectively eliminate the total risk facing even large banks.

28. Note that this represents a departure from the perfectly informed, risk-neutral lenders of sec. 1.1. However, accommodating such behavior does not fundamentally alter the characteristics of the firm-level model.

29. Formally,

$$\lim_{r_t^g \to r^m} \frac{dr_t}{dr_g^t} \to 0, \ \frac{dr_t}{dr_g^t} < 0, \quad \text{for } r_g^t < r^m.$$

30. This is not quite the whole story. The point of tangency with the loan return frontier will also shift—under most circumstances—to the left. Thus the share of loans represented by any point along the horizontal axis will increase, and the total increase in the loan share in the bank's portfolio will consist of the combined effects of the shift in the tangency with the indifference curve and the shift in tangency with the loan return frontier. Also, as the tangency with the loan return frontier changes, the contractual rate of interest charged to firms changes.

31. The substitution effect always leads to more loans. The income effect does too, provided there is decreasing absolute risk aversion.

32. Alternatively, the increase in the bank's financial position could be interpreted as a shift upward in expected terminal wealth, where the mean-variance diagram is taken over values of terminal wealth rather than returns. This would move the whole picture to a region of the indifference map with flatter indifference curves (since absolute risk aversion has declined).

33. If banks can distinguish among categories of potential borrowers, this process of increasing loan demand will entail the making of the loans to successively less attractive groups and rationing the marginal group in equilibrium.

34. The borrowing restriction here has no significant impact on the implications of the model.

35. This is similar in spirit, but likely to be more significant in magnitude than the wealth effect of monetary policy.

36. This consumption function, which is common to traditional macroeconomic models, is used for the sake of simplicity. A full general equilibrium model with intertemporal consumer utility maximization is developed in Greenwald and Stiglitz (1986). A model with a consumption function modified to take account of permanent income in a rational expectations context is developed in Greenwald and Stiglitz (1988). Another general equilibrium alternative is developed by Woodford (1986), who incorporates endogenous borrowing constraints.

37. Relaxing this condition would complicate the analysis without altering its fundamental conclusions.

38. The same results apply, of course, to this noncredit rationed IS curve.

39. This assumes that the increase in the supply of government debt is not completely offset by an increase in demand for government debt in anticipation of higher future taxes. Moreover, since the consequences of the source of the increase in debt (i.e. higher government spending or lower taxes) are not considered, the change should be interpreted in terms of a comparison of a high-debt economy (for historical reasons) to a low-debt economy.

40. These changes in uncertainty also affect the whole curve, shifting the relative demands for different financial assets.

41. Taking into account shadow prices associated with financial constraints and bankruptcy.

42. Uncertainty here is appropriately defined in terms of the covariance matrix of uncertainties concerning the impacts of the several decision variables.

43. These arguments are developed in Greenwald and Stiglitz (1989).

44. If learning by doing is incorporated into the model, different steady states correspond to different growth rates as well as different levels and temporary deviations from steady state have persistent effects on the level of output (see Greenwald and Stiglitz 1989).

45. This restriction is of no practical significance since different θ distributions would correspond to observationally different classes of firms and we need only replicate the analysis for each such class.

46. The use of a more realistic multiplicative productivity factor would merely complicate the analysis without altering its basic implications.

47. In general, k' exceeds one, because without being able to issue unlimited amounts of equity, positive bankruptcy risk ensures that $(1 + \bar{r}_t)w_t < 1$, and firms make positive profits per unit of output. Since equity increases output, it earns these positive profits in addition to the normal return $(1 + \bar{r}_t)$.

48. Such a situation will arise if firms serve existing shareholders and existing shareholders sell a fraction of their current holdings in the beginning of each period (after equity issues have been announced). An overlapping generations model, in which current shareholders are older households consuming wealth at a fixed rate, will give rise to such a situation.

49. With decreasing returns to scale, the value of additional equity is also smaller for high-θ firms than low-θ firms since the extra output made possible by the additional equity is incrementally less valuable at the high-θ firms' higher levels of output. See Taggart (1985).

References

Abel, A. B. 1980. Empirical investment equations: An integrative framework. In *On the state of macroeconomics*, ed. K. Brunner and A. Meltzer, 39–91. Carnegie-Rochester Conference Series on Public Policy, vol. 12.

Abel, A. B., and O. J. Blanchard. 1986. The present value of profits and cyclical movements in investments. *Econometrica* 54:249–74.

Akerlof, G. A. 1984. Gift exchange and efficiency wage theory: Four views. *American Economic Review Papers and Proceedings* 74:79–83.

Allen, F. 1984. Reputation and product quality. *Rand Journal of Economics* 15:311–27.

Asquith, P., and D. Mullins. 1986. Equity issues and stock price dilution. *Journal of Financial Economics* 13:296–320.

Bernanke, B. and M. Gertler. 1989. Agency costs, net worth and business fluctuations. *American Economic Review* 79:14–31.

Bulow, J. I., and L. H. Summers. 1985. A theory of dual labor markets with applications to industrial policy, discrimination and Keynesian unemployment. NBER Working Paper no. 1666 (July).

Diamond, P. A. 1982. Aggregate demand management in a search equilibrium. *Journal of Political Economy* 90:881–94.

Eisner, R. 1967. A permanent income theory for investment: Some empirical explorations. *American Economic Review* 57:363–90.

Fazzari, S., G. Hubbard, and B. Petersen. 1988. Financing constraints and corporate investment. *Brookings Papers and Economic Activity*, 1:141–206.

Greenwald, B., M. Kohn, and J. E. Stiglitz. 1990. Financial market imperfections and productivity growth. *Journal of Economic Behavior and Organization* 13:2–25.

Greenwald, B. and J. E. Stiglitz. 1986. Information, finance constraints and business fluctuations. NBER working paper. Cambridge, Mass. (June).

———. 1987. Imperfect information, credit markets and unemployment. *European Economic Review* 31:223–30.

———. 1988. Money, imperfect information and economic fluctuations. In *Expectations and macroeconomics*, ed. M. Kohn and S. C. Tsiang. Oxford: Oxford University Press.

———. 1989. Toward a theory of rigidities. *American Economic Review* 79 (2):364–69.

Greenwald, B., J. E. Stiglitz, and A. M. Weiss. 1984. Informational imperfections in capital markets and macroeconomic fluctuations. *American Economic Review, Papers and Proceedings* 74:194–99.

Jorgenson, D. W. 1963. Capital theory and investment behavior. *American Economic Review, Papers and Proceedings* 53:247–59.

Lintner, J. 1971. Corporate finance: Risk and investment. In *Determinants of investment behavior*, ed. R. Ferber. New York: NBER.

Lucas, R. E. 1979. An equilibrium model of the business cycle. *Journal of Political Economy* 83:1113–44.

Myers, S. C., and N. S. Majluf. 1984. Corporate financing and investment decisions when firms have information that investors do not have. *Journal of Financial Economics* 13:187–221.

Phelps, E. S. and S. G. Winter. 1970. Optimal price policy under atomistic competition. In *Microeconomic foundations of employment and inflation theory*, ed. E. S. Phelps. New York: W. W. Norton.

Poterba, J., and L. Summers. 1988. Mean reversion in stock prices. *Journal of Financial Economics* 22:27–59.

Salop, J., and S. Salop. 1976. Self-selection and turnover in the labor market. *Quarterly Journal of Economics* 90:619–27.

Shapiro, C., and J. E. Stiglitz. 1984. Equilibrium unemployment as a worker discipline device. *American Economic Review* 74:433–44.

Stiglitz, J. E. 1974. Alternative theories of wage determination and unemployment in LDCs: The labor turnover model. *Quarterly Journal of Economics* 88:194–227.

———. 1976. The efficiency wage hypothesis, surplus labour and the distribution of income in LDCs. *Oxford Economic Papers* 28:185–207.

———. 1982. Alternative theories of wage determination and unemployment: The efficiency wage model. In *Modern developments in public finance: Essays in honor of Arnold Harberger*, ed. M. Boskin. Oxford: Basil Blackwell.

———. 1987. The causes and consequences of the dependence of quality on price. *Journal of Economic Literature* 25:1–48.

Stiglitz, J. E., and A. M. Weiss. 1981. Credit rationing in markets with imperfect information. *American Economic Review* 71:393–440.

Taggart, R. 1985. Secular patterns in the financing of U.S. corporations. In *Corporate capital structures in the United States*, ed. B. Friedman. NBER project report. Chicago: University of Chicago Press.

Vale, B. 1989. Impact of central bank lending under asymmetric information in credit market. Typescript. Stanford University.

Weiss, A. M. 1980. Job queues and lay-offs in labor markets with flexible wages. *Journal of Political Economy* 88:526–38.

Woodford, M. 1986. Expectations, finance and aggregate instability. In *Expectations and macroeconomics*, ed. M. Kohn and S. C. Tsiang. Oxford: Oxford University Press.

Yellen, J. 1984. Efficiency wage models of unemployment. *American Economic Review, Papers and Proceedings* 74:200–205.

Zarnowitz, V. 1985. Recent work on business cycles in historical perspective: A review of theories and evidence. *Journal of Economic Literature* 23:523–80.

2 Collateral, Rationing, and Government Intervention in Credit Markets

William G. Gale

2.1 Introduction

The federal government is the largest single lender in the country. As of the end of 1988, direct loans outstanding exceeded $222 billion, while outstanding loan guarantees were approximately $550 billion (Office of Management and Budget 1989). Federal credit assists borrowers across a wide variety of sectors, including housing, agriculture, small business, and education, in a bewildering array of over 100 programs.[1]

In order to analyze the effects of these policies, this paper focuses on two salient characteristics of virtually all credit programs. First, federal credit is usually intended for those who could not obtain private financing. For example, "a direct loan is best justified when the federal objective could not be met with financing from private sources" (Office of Management and Budget, 1988, F-15). Other programs, such as Small Business Administration loan guarantees, *require* applicants to prove that they could not obtain private financing.

Second, federal credit is provided on easier terms than comparable private credit. These terms can include reduced interest or collateral, longer maturities, grace periods, and so on. These provisions are estimated to reduce the discounted value of borrower payments by amounts that vary widely across programs, but typically range between 10% and 25% (Office of Management and Budget 1989).

William G. Gale is assistant professor of economics at the University of California, Los Angeles.

The author thanks David Butz, Glenn Hubbard, Michael Waldman, and especially Andrew Weiss for helpful comments on recent drafts; Doug Bernheim, Michael Boskin, and John Shoven for comments on a much earlier draft; Lorraine Grams for expert word processing; and the John M. Olin Foundation for financial support.

This paper analyzes the effects of policies with these characteristics in a model where rationing arises endogenously.[2] The underlying model is described in Section 2.2 and is closely related to Rothschild and Stiglitz (1976) and Besanko and Thakor (1987). Investors are divided into two groups, high risk and low risk, and have a choice between investing in a safe project or borrowing to invest in a risky project. For each group, lenders specify a probability of issuing a loan, an interest rate, and a collateral requirement.

Any given amount of collateral is assumed to be worth less to lenders than to borrowers. This feature implies that the use of collateral will generate an efficiency loss. In addition, all projects have expected gross returns greater than their social opportunity cost. Therefore, any amount of rationing represents an additional efficiency loss. The full information equilibrium arises when borrower type is known ex ante, implies no rationing and no collateral, and is thus efficient.

Section 2.3 analyzes situations where each borrower's type is private information. Now, lenders must collectively offer sets of contracts that induce borrowers to self-select into the appropriate contract. In equilibrium, high risks choose a contract with a relatively high interest rate and a zero collateral requirement. Low risks signal their type by choosing to pay high collateral in exchange for a lower interest rate. As long as low risks have sufficient wealth to post as collateral, the equilibrium involves no rationing. Nevertheless, because of the efficiency loss created by the use of collateral, there is a potential role for government.

The principal result of this section is to show that credit policies operate through their effects on the incentive-compatibility constraint, which limits the set of admissible contracts such that high-risk borrowers do not apply for the low-risk contract. For example, a guarantee to low-risk borrowers reduces their interest rate. Since the high-risk contract has not changed, the low-risk collateral requirement must *rise* in order to restore incentive compatibility. The increase in collateral means that guarantees to low risks reduce efficiency.

In contrast, a guarantee to high-risk borrowers makes the high-risk loan more attractive, thereby allowing lenders to reduce the collateral requirement on low-risk loans. Consequently, guarantees to high-risks raise efficiency. Equal guarantees to both groups have similar negative effects on the collateral requirement and positive effects on efficiency.

The major results of the paper are presented in Section 2.4, where it is assumed that borrower wealth is too low to support the collateral requirement outlined in Section 2.3. Because the high-risk contract involves no collateral, it does not change. However, since low-risks can only post a small amount of collateral, the low-risk contract must somehow be made less desirable in order to restore incentive compatibility. The only option is to reduce the probability of granting a low-risk loan; that is, to introduce rationing of low-risk borrowers.[3]

With the existence of rationing, it is now possible to analyze credit policies with the two salient features described above. Suppose the government agrees to offer subsidized credit (either direct or guaranteed loans) to some proportion of the (low-risk) borrowers who are turned down by the private market. The key point is that in the absence of any further changes, these subsidies make the low-risk contract more attractive to high-risk borrowers. Therefore, some other aspect of the low-risk contract must become less desirable in order to restore incentive compatibility. Since the collateral requirement cannot rise, the only alternative is for the overall (public and private) probability of obtaining a loan to fall. That is, increased subsidies to the rationed borrowers *raise* the extent of rationing. Private lending is crowded out on a more than one-to-one basis. It should be emphasized that this is an equilibrium response and is due to the existence of the incentive-compatibility constraint.

Although the subsidies increase the extent of rationing, they raise the ex ante expected utility of low-risk borrowers. This occurs because the benefits of the added cheap government loans outweigh the costs of the increased probability of being rationed. Thus, subsidies to low risks make the representative low-risk borrower better off ex ante but actually reduce the utility of some low-risk borrowers ex post. Since they increase the extent of rationing, the subsidies to low-risk borrowers reduce overall efficiency.

In contrast, subsidies to high-risk borrowers loosen the incentive-compatibility constraint. As a consequence, the extent of rationing of low-risk borrowers falls and efficiency rises.

Section 2.5 offers a short conclusion. The Appendix provides derivations of the various equilibria and proofs of the propositions.

2.2   The Basic Model

2.2.1   Description

The model describes a competitive credit market with many investors, but even more lenders. All agents are assumed to be risk neutral, thus eliminating any insurance role for federal credit, and there is no aggregate risk.

Investors can invest their initial endowment in a safe project that yields a gross return of Z.[4] Alternatively, each investor can borrow $1 and invest that and the initial endowment in a risky project. Investors fall into two categories, which differ according to the probability of having a risky project succeed, π_i, and the gross return to that project, if it is successful, R_i. I assume $\pi_1 > \pi_2$, so that type 1's are low-risk borrowers. Projects that do not succeed yield a gross return of zero. The expected gross return to all projects are equal: $p_i R_i = k$, $i = 1, 2$, where k is a constant. Investors have a certain end-of-period endowment, W. I assume the existence of a sufficient enforcement technology such that W is acceptable to lenders as collateral. The proportion of borrowers that are low risk is given by φ.

Lenders have an alternative safe investment that earns ρ. They offer loans characterized by an interest rate (r), a collateral requirement (c), and a probability of issuing the loan to any particular applicant (p). Following several authors,[5] I assume there is a cost to collateralization. Specifically, the lenders' valuation of \$1 in collateral is given by β, $0 \leq \beta < 1$. Therefore, $1 - \beta > 0$ represents the social cost of transferring the collateral or realizing its value. Competition among lenders generates the following zero-profit condition on loans to each group:[6]

$$(1) \qquad \rho = \pi_i r_i + (1 - \pi_i)\beta c_i, \quad i = 1, 2.$$

Investors are assumed to be able to apply for only one loan. The expected utility of an investor in group i applying for a loan contract meant for group j is

$$(2) \qquad U_{ij} = p_j[\pi_i(R_i - r_j) - (1 - \pi_i)c_j - Z], \quad i, j = 1, 2.$$

Lenders always know the value of φ. In the full information equilibrium described below, lenders also know each borrower's type. In the asymmetric information equilibria, information on borrower type is unavailable to banks on an ex ante basis.

The Nash equilibrium concept is used throughout this paper. A set of contracts is a Nash equilibrium if, holding the current set of contracts fixed, no contract in the set earns negative profits and there is no additional contract which, if offered, would make positive profits (Rothschild and Stiglitz 1976).

2.2.2   Full Information Equilibrium

Although subsequent analysis will focus on markets with asymmetric information, the full information equilibrium is presented first as a benchmark. Because the types are identifiable ex ante, lenders face two distinct loan markets. In each submarket, optimal contracts maximize expected borrower utility U_{ii}, given in (2) subject to (1).

EQUILIBRIUM I.   The full information equilibrium is characterized by

$$(3a) \qquad p_i^1 = 1, \quad i = 1, 2, \quad \text{(no rationing)}$$

$$(3b) \qquad c_i^1 = 0, \quad i = 1, 2, \quad \text{(no collateral)}$$

and

$$(3c) \qquad r_i^1 = \frac{\rho}{\pi_i}, \quad i = 1, 2.$$

With full information, all borrowers receive loans. In addition, since borrowers are indifferent between committing to a dollar of expected interest payments and a dollar of expected collateral, while lenders prefer the former, equilibrium involves complete elimination of collateral. Formally, from (1), the slope of isoprofit curves is

$$\frac{dr_i}{dc_i} = \frac{-(1 - \pi_i)\beta}{\pi_i},$$

while the marginal rate of substitution for borrowers of type i is

$$\frac{dr_i}{dc_i} = \frac{-(1 - \pi_i)}{\pi_i}.$$

Indifference curves (U_1^1 and U_2) and zero-profit curves (I_1 and I_2) for each group are shown in figure 2.1 below. For each group, $\beta < 1$ implies that the isoprofit curve is flatter than the indifference curve. Curves for high-risk borrowers are steeper than those for low-risk borrowers. The full information equilibrium is given by contracts α_1^F and α_2, along with $p_i^1 = 1$.

Substituting (3a)–(3c) into (2) yields

(4) $$U_{ii} = \pi_i R_i - \rho - Z, \quad i = 1, 2.$$

Since $\rho + Z$ is the social opportunity cost of investment, (4) shows that investments are made ($U_{ii} > 0$) if and only if the expected total return exceeds the expected social cost. Therefore, equilibrium is efficient.

2.3 Asymmetric Information and Unconstrained Collateral

2.3.1 Private Equilibrium

When individual investors' types are private information, lenders must design sets of loan contracts that generate self-selection of each borrower type into the appropriate contract. Thus, lenders operate subject to (1) and a pair of incentive-compatibility constraints:

(5a) $$U_{11} \geq U_{12},$$

and

(5b) $$U_{22} \geq U_{21},$$

where U_{ij} is defined in (2). It can be directly verified that the full information equilibrium is not incentive compatible because both types would prefer the low-risk contract.

Instead, with asymmetric information, collateral is used as a sorting device.[7] High-risk borrowers have a stronger preference not to post collateral because they have a larger probability of having to pay it.

Whether collateral can induce complete separation depends crucially on W, the level of borrower wealth. This section examines equilibria and government policy when borrower wealth is sufficiently large to allow complete separation. Section 2.4 examines markets characterized by insufficient wealth.

EQUILIBRIUM II.   When borrower type is private information, and borrower wealth is sufficiently large, equilibrium is characterized by:[8]

(6a) $p_1^{II} = 1,$ $p_2^{II} = 1,$

(6b) $c_1^{II} = \dfrac{(\pi_1 - \pi_2)\rho}{\pi_1(1 - \pi_2) - \pi_2(1 - \pi_1)\beta},$ $c_2^{II} = 0,$

(6c) $r_1^{II} = \dfrac{\rho}{\pi_1} - \dfrac{1 - \pi_1}{\pi_1}\beta c_1,$ $r_2^{II} = \dfrac{\rho}{\pi_2}.$

With imperfect information, high-risk borrowers obtain the same loan contract, and therefore the same utility, as in the full information equilibrium. Low-risk borrowers are not rationed, but their loan terms have changed. Specifically, low-risk borrowers indicate their type by posting collateral. In return, they pay a lower interest rate than in the full information equilibrium.

Substituting (6a)–(6c) into (2) for type 1's yields

(7) $U_{11}^{II} = \pi_1 R_1 - \rho - Z - (1 - \pi_1)(1 - \beta)c_1^{II}.$

Comparing (4) and (7), low-risk borrowers are worse off relative to the full information equilibrium by $(1 - \pi_1)(1 - \beta)c_1^{II}$. The magnitude of the welfare loss increases with c_1.

The equilibrium with asymmetric information and unconstrained collateral is shown in figure 2.1 as (α_1, α_2). High risks obtain α_2, as before. However, any contract offered to low risks must be incentive compatible with α_2. Of all such contracts, α_1 is the most desirable contract for type 1's that also earns nonnegative profits when extended to type 1's. The reduction in low-risk borrowers' utility to U_1^{II} from U_1^{I} is shown by the shift from α_1^F to α_1. Note that (5b) is binding in this equilibrium.

2.3.2   Government Credit

Although there is no rationing in the above model, there is still a role for government policy due to the efficiency losses created by the use of collateral. Because all investors receive loans in the private equilibrium, it seems natural to focus on loan guarantees (rather than direct loans) in this context.[9]

Loan guarantees ensure the lender of receiving an amount γ_i, where $0 \le \gamma_i \le \rho$. The government can set $\gamma_1 = \gamma_2 \equiv \gamma$, or choose the γ_i separately. In return for the guarantee, the lender passes on any collateral collected to the government. The net cost to the government of a defaulted loan is $\gamma_i - \beta c_i^{III}$, where c_i^{III} is the collateral requirement in the presence of the guarantee and is discussed further below. The government is subject to the same information constraints that private lenders face.

With the guarantees in place, expected borrower utility is still given by (2), but the zero-profit condition for lenders is now given by

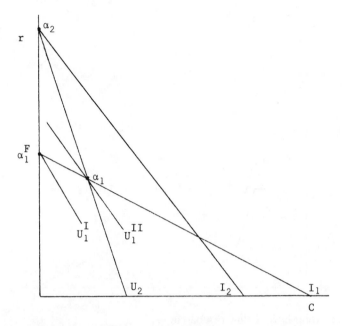

Fig. 2.1   Equilibrium with unconstrained collateral

(8) $$\rho = \pi_i r_i + (1 - \pi_i)\gamma_i, \quad i = 1, 2.$$

EQUILIBRIUM III.   When borrower type is private information and $W > C_1^{II}$, equilibrium with loan guarantees is characterized by

(9a) $\quad p_1^{III} = 1,$ $\hspace{6cm}$ $p_2^{III} = 1,$

(9b) $\quad c_1^{III} = \dfrac{(\pi_1 - \pi_2)\rho}{\pi_1(1 - \pi_2)} - \gamma_2 + \dfrac{\pi_2(1 - \pi_1)}{\pi_1(1 - \pi_2)}\gamma_1, c_2^{III} = 0,$

(9c) $\quad r_1^{III} = \dfrac{\rho}{\pi_1} - \dfrac{1 - \pi_1}{\pi_1}\gamma_1,$ $\hspace{3.5cm}$ $r_2^{III} = \dfrac{\rho}{\pi_2} - \dfrac{1 - \pi_2}{\pi_2}\gamma_2.$

In the preceding private Equilibrium II, banks received βc_1^{II} and 0 in collateral on loans to type 1 and 2 borrowers, respectively. It is easy to verify that if $\gamma_1 = \beta c_1^{II}$ and $\gamma_2 = 0$, (9a)–(9c) reduce to the private equilibrium (6a)–(6c). Only higher guarantee rates have real effects.

Using (9b), increases in γ_1 cause c_1^{III} to rise in equilibrium. This result is contrary to standard intuition, which would suggest that as γ_1 rises, the necessary collateral should fall. However, as γ_1 rises, r_1 falls and the low-risk contract becomes more desirable to high-risk borrowers. Since (5b) binds, c_1 must rise to eliminate the possibility of having high risks masquerade as low risks.

This situation is depicted in figure 2.2. Increases in γ_1 shift the zero-profit line for low-risk lending from I_1 to I_1'. Equilibrium contracts, which are con-

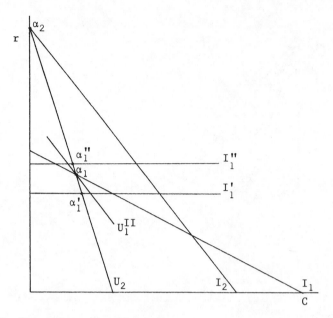

Fig. 2.2   Guarantees to low-risk borrowers

strained by (5a) and (5b), shift from (α_1, α_2) to (α_1', α_2). The collateral required at α_1' is greater than that required at α_1. Therefore, the existence of imperfect information reverses the usual intuition concerning the effect of γ_1 on c_1.

Any guarantee to low risks that reduced the collateral requirement would make them worse off and thus would be rejected in favor of α_1. This is illustrated by a guarantee that shifts the zero-profit curve to I_1'' from I_1' and the low-risk contract to α_1''. It is easy to show that all such guarantees correspond to $\gamma_1 < \beta c_1^{\text{II}}$.

Similar arguments show that c_1^{III} falls with increases in γ_2. As shown in figure 2.3, a rise in γ_2 shifts the zero-profit line for lending to high-risk borrowers from I_2 to I'_2, which raises low-risk utility to U'_2 from U_2. The equilibrium thus shifts from (α_1, α_2) to (α_1^G, α_2^G). At the latter points, *both* groups are better off and the collateral requirement has fallen.

Since the use of collateral creates efficiency losses, these results will have important welfare implications. substituting (9a)–(9c) into (2) yields expected utilities:

$$(10) \qquad U_{11}^{\text{III}} = \pi_1 R_1 - \rho - Z - \frac{(1 - \pi_1)(\pi_1 - \pi_2)}{\pi_1(1 - \pi_2)}(\rho - \gamma_1)$$
$$+ (1 - \pi_1)\gamma_2,$$

and

$$(11) \qquad U_{22}^{\text{III}} = \pi_2 R_2 - \rho - Z + (1 - \pi_2)\gamma_2.$$

Increases in γ_1 raise U_{11}, even though they also raise c_1. For any $\gamma_1 > \beta c_1^{II}$, low-risk borrowers are better off than in private equilibrium. Increases in γ_2 raise both U_{11} and U_{22}. Thus, both types of borrowers are better off with guarantees.

Welfare calculations are based on total expected borrowers' utility minus expected government costs of funding the guarantees. Define overall welfare as

$$(12) \qquad V = \varphi U_{11} + (1 - \varphi)U_{22} - \varphi(1 - \pi_1)(\gamma_1 - \beta c_1)$$
$$- (1 - \varphi)(1 - \pi_2)(\gamma_2 - \beta c_2).$$

The first two terms represent utility of each borrower type, weighted by their population proportion; the last two terms represent net expected government costs of providing guarantees to low risks and high risks, respectively.[10]

PROPOSITION 1.   When borrower type is private information, and $W > c_1^{II}$, the welfare effects of loan guarantees are as follows:

$$(13) \qquad \left.\frac{\partial V}{\partial \gamma_1}\right|_{\hat{\gamma}_2} \quad \begin{array}{l} = 0 \quad \text{if } \gamma_1 < \beta c_I^{II}, \\ < 0 \quad \text{if } \gamma_1 \geq \beta c_I^{II}, \end{array}$$

$$(14) \qquad \left.\frac{\partial V}{\partial \gamma_2}\right|_{\hat{\gamma}_1} \quad > 0,$$

$$(15) \qquad \left.\frac{\partial V}{\partial \gamma}\right|_{\gamma = \gamma_1 = \gamma_2} \quad > 0.$$

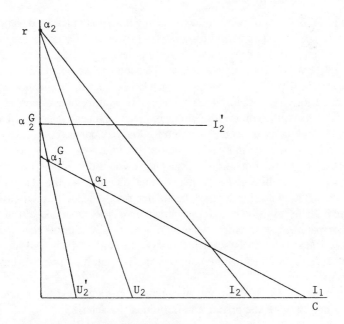

Fig. 2.3   Guarantees to high-risk borrowers

The main result from proposition 1 is that the effects of government intervention depend on how the incentive-compatibility constraint, and in particular the collateral requirement, is affected.

Equation (13) states that increases in γ_1, holding γ_2 constant, reduce welfare. From (10), the guarantee raises U_{11} by $[(1 - \pi_1)(\pi_1 - \pi_2)]/[\pi_1(1 - \pi_2)]$. However, from (12), the marginal cost, per low-risk borrower, of raising γ_1 is $(1 - \pi_1)$. It is easy to show that the marginal costs exceed the marginal benefits. This occurs because the rise in γ_1 raises c_1, which creates an efficiency loss.

The second result states that subsidizing the high-risk group is welfare improving. Using (11) and (12), the government's costs equal the benefits to high-risk borrowers. Since low-risk borrowers are also made better off, there is a welfare gain. The rise in γ_2 increases the attractiveness of the high-risk contract, so that low-risk borrowers can be offered more attractive terms. The fall in c_1 allows for an efficiency gain.

Equation (15) states that raising the guarantee rate on all loans is welfare improving. From (9b), setting $\gamma_1 = \gamma_2 = \gamma$ yields $c_1^{\mathrm{III}}/\partial\gamma < 0$, so that collateral falls as the overall guarantee rate rises. Therefore, the net effect of universal guarantees is to weaken the incentive-compatibility constraint and raise welfare.

2.4   Asymmetric Information and Constrained Collateral

2.4.1   Private Equilibrium

The effectiveness of collateral as a sorting device is crucially dependent on the existence of sufficient end-of-period borrower wealth. For example, if $W = 0$, collateral cannot be used as a sorting device. More generally, suppose $W < c_1^{\mathrm{II}}$, given in (6b); then the low-risk contract offered in Equilibrium II cannot be fulfilled by borrowers. Lenders, knowing this, will not offer the contract. Moreover, because (5b) is binding in equilibrium, if lenders simply reduced c_1 to W, the contracts offered would not be incentive compatible; both groups would prefer the contract meant for low-risk borrowers.

Lenders can resolve this problem by making the low-risk contract less attractive to high-risk borrowers.[11] Raising r_1 would discourage low-risk borrowers more than high-risk borrowers, since the latter have a smaller probability of actually having to pay the higher rate. The only alternative is to reduce p_1. This adjustment will discourage high-risks more and restore incentive compatibility. Therefore, when borrower wealth is insufficient to permit collateral alone to act as a sorting device, rationing of low-risk borrowers ($p_1 < 1$) is required to restore equilibrium. The intuition presented above is summarized in

EQUILIBRIUM IV.   When borrower type is characterized by private information and $W < c_1^{\mathrm{II}}$, the private equilibrium is characterized by[12]

(16) $\quad p_1^{IV} = \dfrac{U_{22}^{IV}}{\pi_2(R_2 - r_1) - (1 - \pi_2)W - Z} < 1, \quad p^{IV} = 1,$

(16b) $\quad c_1^{IV} = W, \qquad\qquad\qquad\qquad\qquad\qquad c_2^{IV} = 0,$

(16c) $\quad r_1^{IV} = \dfrac{\rho}{\pi_1} - \dfrac{1 - \pi_1}{\pi_1}\beta W, \qquad\qquad\qquad r_2^{IV} = \dfrac{\rho}{\pi_2}.$

High-risk borrowers receive the same contract and utility as in Equilibrium II, when $W > c_1^{II}$. In contrast, because they cannot post c_1^{II} in collateral, low-risk borrowers are rationed. Their expected utility is given by

(17) $\qquad U_{11}^{IV} = p_1^{IV}[\pi_1 R_1 - \rho - Z - (1 - \pi_1)(1 - \beta)W].$

2.4.2 Government Credit

In the presence of rationing, the natural government policy to analyze is characterized by p_G, the probability of obtaining a government-guaranteed loan given (1) the borrower cannot obtain private credit and (2) γ_1, defined as before. Although the analysis will focus on subsidized loan guarantees, analogous results can be shown to hold for subsidized direct loans as well.

The interest rate charged on guaranteed loans gives lenders zero profits and is given by

(18) $\qquad\qquad\qquad\qquad r_G = \dfrac{\rho}{\pi_1} - \dfrac{1 - \pi_1}{\pi_1}\gamma_1.$

It is assumed that government charges W as collateral.[13]

With this policy, low-risk utility is given by[14]

(19) $\qquad\qquad\qquad U_{11} = p_1 X_{11} + (1 - p_1)p_G X_{1G}.$

The first term on the right-hand side of (19) represents the probability of obtaining a private loan, p_G, multiplied by X_{11}, the expected payoff to low-risk borrowers of obtaining a private loan meant for low-risk borrowers. The second term represents the probability of obtaining a government-guaranteed loan, $(1 - p_1)p_G$, multiplied by X_{1G}, the expected payoff to low-risk borrowers from that loan. If $\gamma_1 = \beta w$, then $X_{11} = X_{1G}$ and there is no gain to obtaining a government rather than a private loan. If $\gamma_1 > \beta W, X_{11} > X_{1G}$.

The incentive compatibility constraint (5b) is now given by

(20) $\qquad\qquad\qquad U_{22} \geq p_1 X_{21} + (1 - p_1)p_G X_{2G},$

where X_{21} is the expected payoff to high risks of taking a private loan meant for low risks, and X_{2G} is the expected payoff to high risks of taking a government loan meant for low-risks. (These are given in more detail in the proofs of Propositions 2 and 3 in the Appendix.)

EQUILIBRIUM V.   When borrower type is private information, and $W < c_1^{II}$, the equilibrium with loan guarantees is characterized by

$$(21a) \qquad p_1^V = \frac{U_{22} - p_G X_{2G}}{X_{21} - p_G X_{2G}} < 1, \quad p_2^V = 1,$$

$$(21b) \qquad c_1^V = W, \qquad\qquad\qquad c_2^V = 0,$$

$$(21c) \qquad r_1^V = \frac{\rho}{\pi_1} - \frac{1 - \pi_1}{\pi_1} \beta W, \quad r_2^V = \frac{\rho}{\pi_2}.$$

These private loans are, of course, supplemented by government-guaranteed loans to some low-risk borrowers described by (p_G, r_G, W). High-risk borrowers obtain the same contract and utility as in Equilibria II and IV. Low-risk utility is given by (19) with appropriate substitutions for X_{11} and X_{1G}.

Define the probability of low risks obtaining any loan as

$$(22) \qquad p^* = p_1 + (1 - p_1)p_G.$$

Then a proportion $1 - p^*$ of low risks will be rationed.

PROPOSITION 2.   When the initial allocation is given by Equilibrium V, increases in p_G or γ_1 increase the extent of rationing (reduce p^*).

Proposition 2 establishes that government subsidies to borrowers who cannot obtain private financing *increases* the number of borrowers who cannot obtain any financing, public or private. That is, private credit is crowded out on a more than one-to-one basis. Although this result may appear surprising, it is based on the equilibrium response of lenders to the shift in the incentive-compatibility constraint.

For example, in the equilibrium with $W > c_1^{II}$, an increase in γ_1 raised c_1 in order to restore incentive compatibility. Now, however, collateral is constrained to equal W, which is assumed to be less than c_1^{II}. As a consequence, increases in γ_1 (which reduce r_1) require that p_1 fall. From (22), a reduction in p_1, holding p_G constant, reduces p^*. Therefore, raising the guarantee rate to low-risk borrowers increases the extent of rationing.

Similarly, consider a small increase in p_G, holding γ_1 constant. If p_1 were held constant, all borrowers would have an increased chance of obtaining a cheap government loan, which would induce high risks to masquerade as low risks. If p_1 fell such that p^* were unchanged from its previous level, high risks would still prefer masquerading as low risks to taking the high-risk contract. To show this, rewrite (20) as

$$(23) \qquad U_{22} \geq p^* X_{21} + (1 - p_1)p_G(X_{2G} - X_{21}).$$

Recall that this constraint is binding in Equilibrium V. If p_G rises and p^* is held constant, (23) is violated. Therefore, in equilibrium, incentive compatibility requires p_1 to fall enough to make p^* fall in response to the rise in p_G. That is, increases in p_G raise the extent of rationing.

Although they increase the likelihood of any given low-risk borrower being rationed, guarantees raise the ex post utility of those who do obtain government credit; this is caused by the reduced interest rate r_G on guaranteed loans.

The effects of these guarantees on the ex ante expected utility of low-risk borrowers and on welfare is given in

PROPOSITION 3.   When the initial allocation is given by Equilibrium V, the welfare effects of government intervention are

(24a) $$\frac{\partial U_{11}^V}{\partial \gamma_1} > 0,$$

(24b) $$\frac{\partial U_{11}^V}{\partial p_G} > 0,$$

(25a) $$\frac{\partial V}{\partial \gamma_1} < 0,$$

(25b) $$\frac{\partial V}{\partial p_G} < 0.$$

Equations (24a) and (24b) show that guaranteed loans raise the ex ante expected utility of the targeted group. This occurs even though the overall probability of obtaining a loan falls. Therefore, the targeted group prefers to have the policy, even though fewer lower-risk borrowers obtain credit when the subsidy is in place.

Equations (25a) and (25b) show that, as in Proposition 1, guarantees to low-risk borrowers reduce overall welfare. This occurs because the increase in rationing represents an overall efficiency loss. Following the approach taken in Section 2.3 it is straightforward to show that guarantees to the high-risk group reduce the extent of rationing. Intuitively, these guarantees make the high-risk contract (U_{22}) more attractive and, through (21a), raise γ_1. Because of the reduction in rationing, these guarantees raise efficiency.

2.5   Conclusion

This paper analyzes the effects of credit subsidies in markets characterized by adverse selection. The principal result is that the effects of credit subsidies depend on how eligibility is determined. Programs that subsidize the unrationed contract will reduce the extent of rationing and raise overall efficiency. In contrast, programs that target borrowers who cannot obtain private financing raise the extent of rationing and reduce efficiency. The distinction is important precisely because most government credit is designed to provide funds to those who do not receive private loans. In the model presented here, such policies raise the extent of rationing and create inherent tradeoffs among members of the same target group: fewer of them obtain any type of credit, but those that receive government loans are better off.

Two concluding comments should be made. First, the effects described above represent equilibrium responses. In particular, they take into account the need to deter high risks from pretending to be low risks. As a consequence of this incentive-compatibility constraint, whenever the government eases some of the terms on low-risk contracts, the others must be adversely affected in equilibrium.

Second, the paper has focused on a fairly standard adverse selection model, based on Rothschild and Stiglitz (1976). Numerous extensions of that and other models have shown that the nature of equilibrium can be affected by incentive effects (Stiglitz and Weiss 1986), project characteristics, the set of available financial instruments (de Meza and Webb 1987), alternative projects (Chan and Thakor 1987), information sharing (Yotsuzuka 1987), the shape of the production function (Milde and Riley 1988), and other characteristics. The effects of credit policies in such alternative models deserve further exploration.

Appendix

EQUILIBRIUM I.   In each submarket, equilibrium contracts maximize expected borrower utility, U_{ii}, given in (2) subject to (1). Substitution of (1) into (2) for each U_{ii} yields

$$\max_{p_i c_i} L^1 = p_i[\pi_i R_i - \rho - Z - (1 - \pi_i)(1 - \beta_i)c_i].$$

Taking derivatives yields:

$$\frac{\partial L^1}{\partial c_i} = -p_i(1 - \pi_i)(1 - \beta_i) < 0,$$

so that $c_i^1 = 0$, which implies through (1) that $r_i^1 = \rho/\pi_i$. In addition,

$$\left.\frac{\partial L^1}{\partial p_i}\right|_{c_i^1 = 0} = \pi_i R_i - \rho - Z,$$

which is positive if type i investors are applying for loans, implying that $p_i^1 = 1$.

EQUILIBRIUM II.   The remaining equilibria follow a common pattern. Therefore, Equilibrium II is derived in some detail, while the derivations of Equilibria III–V are shorter.

With asymmetric information, equilibrium is obtained by maximizing the population-weighted average of borrowers' expected utility, given by

(A1) $\varphi U_{11} + (1 - \varphi)U_{22}$,

subject to (1), (5a), and (5b). Following Besanko and Thakor (1987), the strategy employed is initially to ignore (5a) and assume $p_i = 1$. Later it will be shown that the optimal solution does satisfy (5a) and $p_i = 1$. Substituting (1) into (A1) and maximizing (A1) subject to (5b) yields the problem:

$$\max_{c_1,c_2} L^{\mathrm{II}} = \varphi p_1[\pi_1 R_1 - \rho - Z - (1 - \pi_1)(1 - \beta)c_1]$$

(A2)
$$+ (1 - \varphi)p_2(\pi_2 R_2 - \rho - Z - (1 - \pi_2)(1 - \beta)c_2$$
$$+ \lambda\{p_2[\pi_2 R_2 - \rho - Z - (1 - \pi_2)(1 - \beta)c_2]$$
$$- p_1[\pi_2 R_2 - \frac{\pi_2}{\pi_1}\rho - \frac{\pi_1(1 - \pi_2) - \pi_2(1 - \pi_1)\beta}{\pi_1}c_1 - Z]\},$$

where λ is the LaGrange multiplier associated with (5b). Setting $p_i = 1$ and setting $\partial L^{\mathrm{II}}/\partial c_1 = 0$ implies

(A3)
$$\lambda = \frac{\varphi(1 - \pi_1)(1 - \beta)\pi_1}{\pi_1(1 - \pi_2) - \pi_2(1 - \pi_1)\beta} > 0,$$

which implies that (5b) is binding. Using (A3), it is easy to show that $\partial L^{\mathrm{II}}/\partial c_2 < 0$, which implies $c_2^{\mathrm{II}} = 0$. Substituting for c_2^{II} in (5b) and solving (5b) for c_1^{II} yields the expression in (6b). Given c_i^{II}, r_i^{II} can be found using (1).

It remains to be shown that (5a) is satisfied at the solution presented above and that $p_i = 1$ is optimal. To show that (5a) is satisfied, note that $U_{11} \geq U_{12}$ if

(A4)
$$\pi_1(R_1 - r_1^{\mathrm{II}}) - (1 - \pi_1)c_1^{\mathrm{II}} \geq \pi_1(R_1 - r_2^{\mathrm{II}}); \quad \text{or}$$
$$\pi_1(r_2^{\mathrm{II}} - r_1^{\mathrm{II}}) \geq (1 - \pi_1)c_1^{\mathrm{II}}.$$

Using (1) and (6b) and some algebra, it can be shown that (A4) holds for the values given in proposition 2 above. By examining figure 2.1, $U_{11} > U_{12}$ can also be seen.

It is also straightforward to show that $\partial L^{\mathrm{II}}/\partial p_2 > 0$, which implies $p_2^{\mathrm{II}} = 1$. Finally,

(A5)
$$\frac{\partial L^{\mathrm{II}}}{\partial p_1} = \varphi[\pi_1 R_1 - \rho - Z - (1 - \pi_1)(1 - \beta)c_1^{\mathrm{II}}]$$
$$- \lambda\left\{\pi_2 R_2 - \frac{\pi_2}{\pi_1}\rho - \frac{\pi_1(1 - \pi_2) - \pi_2(1 - \pi_1)\beta}{\pi_1}c_1^{\mathrm{II}} - Z\right\}.$$

This can be shown to be positive provided that $k - r_1 - Z > 0$. This condition captures the idea that high risks have a higher aversion to posting collateral because they have a larger probability of having to pay it. That is, the same condition implies, from (2), that dc/dp rises with π.

EQUILIBRIUM III.   Guarantees shift the zero-profit condition to (8) from (1). Otherwise, the maximization follows as in Equilibrium II. That is, substitute (8) into (2) for (A1) and maximize subject to (5a), ignoring (5b) and setting $p_i = 1$ for now. The problem is to

$$\max_{c_1,c_2} L^{\text{III}} = \varphi p_1[\pi_1 R_1 - \rho - Z + (1 - \pi_1)(\gamma_1 - c_1)]$$

$$+ (1 - \varphi)p_2[\pi_2 R_2 - \rho - Z + (1 - \pi_2)(\gamma_2 - c_2)]$$

$$+ \lambda\{p_2[\pi_2 R_2 - \rho - Z + (1 - \pi_2)(\gamma_2 - c_2)]$$

$$- p_1\left(\pi_2 R_2 - \frac{\pi_2\rho}{\pi_1} + \frac{\pi_2(1 - \pi_1)}{\pi_1}\gamma_1 - (1 - \pi_2)c_1 - Z\right)\}.$$

Setting $\partial L^{\text{III}}/\partial c_1 = 0$ implies that $\lambda > 0$, which implies that (5b) binds. Given $\lambda > 0$, it is easy to show that $c_1^{\text{III}} = 0$. Solving (5b) for c_1^{III} yields the expression in (9b). Showing that (5a) is satisfied and that $p_i^{\text{III}} = 1$ follow in the same way as Equilibrium II.

PROPOSITION 1.   Expected borrower utilities are given in (10) and (11). The government cost of providing guarantee γ_i is $(1 - \pi_i)(\gamma_i - \beta c_i^{\text{III}})$ for each borrower in group i. The effects of raising γ_1 only or γ_2 only are described in the text. The effects of raising γ are as follows.

If $\gamma < \beta c_1^{\text{II}}$, the only effect of raising γ occurs through raising γ_2, so the increase in γ is welfare improving. When $\gamma \geq \beta c_1^{\text{II}}$, further increases introduce opposing welfare effects. However, the net effect is always welfare improving. Note that, for each high-risk borrower, the benefits of raising γ equal $(1 - \pi_2)\delta\gamma_2$, which equals the cost of providing guarantees for high-risk borrowers. The welfare effects thus depend on comparing $\partial U_{11}^{\text{III}}/\partial\gamma$ and the cost of providing guarantees to low risks, $(1 - \pi_1)$. From (10),

$$\partial U_{11}^{\text{III}}/\partial\gamma = \frac{(1 - \pi_1)(\pi_1 - \pi_2)}{\pi_1(1 - \pi_2)} + (1 - \pi_1) > (1 - \pi_1).$$

Therefore, increases in γ are welfare-improving.

EQUILIBRIUM IV.   The problem is now to maximize (A2) subject to (1), (5b), and a wealth constraint, $W < c_1^{\text{II}}$. As before, taking derivatives with respect to c_2 and p_2 yields $p_2^{\text{IV}} = 1$ and $c_2^{\text{IV}} = 0$, and the latter result implies $r_2^{\text{IV}} = \rho/\pi_2$. The wealth constraint implies that $c_1^{\text{IV}} = W$. The zero-profits condition determines r_1^{IV}. Only p_1 remains to be determined. Optimizing with respect to p_1 implies that $\lambda > 0$ so that (5b) is binding. Solving (5b) for p_1 yields the expression in (16a).

EQUILIBRIUM V.   The problem is now to maximize (A2) subject to (1), (5a), $W < c_1^{\text{II}}$, and (20), and where U_{11} is given by (19). Values for $c_2^{\text{V}}, p_2^{\text{V}}, r_2^{\text{V}}, c_1^{\text{V}}$, and r_1^{V} as derived as in Equilibrium IV. The equilibrium p_1 is determined by solving (20) for p_1.

PROPOSITION 2.   Note that $X_{21} = \pi_2 R_2 - \pi_2\rho/\pi_1 - \{\pi_1(1 - \pi_2) - \pi_2(1 - \pi_1)\beta/\pi_1\}W - Z$, and $X_{2G} = X_{21} + \{\pi_2(1 - \pi_1)/\pi_1\}(\gamma_1 - \beta W)$, where these terms are derived by substituting for r using (1) and (18). Thus X_{11} and X_{1G} are derived analogously. From (22)

$$\frac{\partial p^*}{\partial\gamma} = \frac{\partial p_1}{\partial\gamma}(1 - p_G) = \frac{p_G\pi_2(1 - \pi_1)(U_{22} - X_{21})}{\pi_1(X_{21} - p_G x_{2G})^2}(1 - p_G) < 0,$$

because from (21a), $U_{22} < X_{21}$. Similarly

$$\frac{\partial p^*}{\partial p_G} = \frac{\partial p_1}{\partial p_G}(1 - p_G) + (1 - p_1) = \frac{(U_{22} - X_{21})(X_{2G} - X_{21})}{(X_{21} - p_G x_{2G})^2} < 0,$$

using (21a) and some algebra.

PROPOSITION 3.   Taking derivatives of (19) yields

(A6)
$$\frac{\partial U_{11}^V}{\partial \gamma_1} = \frac{\partial p_1}{\partial \gamma_1}(X_{11} - p_G X_{1G}) + (1 - p_1)p_G \frac{\partial X_{1G}}{\partial \gamma_1}$$

$$= p_G(1 - \pi_1)(1 - p_1)\left\{1 - \frac{\pi_2(x_{11} - p_G X_{2G})}{\pi_1(X_{21} - p_G x_{2G})}\right\},$$

using (21a). The expression in brackets can be shown to be positive, so that (A6) is positive. In addition,

$$\frac{\partial U_{11}^V}{\partial p_G} = \frac{\partial p_1}{\partial p_G}(X_{11} - p_G x_{1G}) + (1 + p_1)X_{1G}$$

$$= \frac{(X_{21} - U_{22})\{X_{21}X_{1G} - X_{2G}X_{11}\}}{(X_{21} - p_G X_{2G})^2} > 0,$$

because the term in brackets can be shown to be positive.

To show the welfare effects of changing γ_1, note that the expresion in (A6) is less than $(1 - \pi_1)$, the marginal costs of raising γ_1 per low-risk borrower. Thus, increases in γ_1 reduce efficiency. Similar results hold for p_G.

Notes

1. For discussions of the features and overall effects of federal credit, see Bosworth, Carron, and Rhyne (1987), Gale (1988a), or Office of Management and Budget (1989).

2. Previous research on federal credit in markets with imperfect information includes Mankiw (1986) and Gale (1988b), who study models with a continuum of borrower types, and Gale (1987) and Smith and Stutzer (1989) who examine models with two types of borrowers. The current paper is based on Gale (1987, app. C). Some of the results are closely related to independent work by Smith and Stutzer (1989).

3. As described in Section 2.4 below, raising the interest rate on the low-risk loan cannot restore incentive compatibility, because low risks are more averse to accepting a higher interest rate than high risks are.

4. The initial endowment could also represent a unit of labor supply, in which case Z would be interpretable as the value of leisure forgone by investing.

5. See Barro (1976), Besanko and Thakor (1987), Bester (1985), and Williamson (1987).

6. In order to focus on the role of collateral and rationing as sorting devices, the paper focuses on separating equilibria. See nn. 8 and 13 below for a discussion of potential pooling equilibria.

7. Besanko and Thakor (1987), Bester (1985), Chan and Thakor (1987), Stiglitz and Weiss (1981, 1986) and Wette (1983) analyze the selection effects induced by collateral.

8. The existence of a separating equilibrium can be ensured by assuming that there is a sufficiently large proportion of high-risk borrowers or that the difference between $\pi_1 - \pi_2$ is large enough. See Rothschild and Stiglitz (1976) or Besanko and Thakor (1987). There are no pooling equilibria under the assumptions in this section.

9. Gale (1987) also examines government policies in which low-risk loans are taxed and high-risk loans are subsidized. These policies operate through the same channels as guarantees and will be ignored here.

10. Therefore, the welfare criterion is total surplus, rather than a Pareto measure. In addition, (12) assumes that taxes are raised in a lump-sum manner.

11. It is impossible to make the high-risk contract more attractive to high-risk borrowers without losing money on high-risk contracts. Because of the Nash assumption, cross-subsidization of contracts will not occur in this model, although it could in other contexts. See Stiglitz and Weiss (1989).

12. Besanko and Thakor (1987) show that, under these circumstances, (5a) requires that $W \geq Z\rho\,(\pi_1 - \pi_2)/\{\pi_1(\pi_2 R - \rho) - Z\pi_2[(1 - \pi_1) + \beta\pi_1]\}$. Loosely speaking, this requires that Z is small relative to W. In order to rule out a pooling equilibrium at $P_i = 1$, $c_i = W$, it if necessary to assume that $\beta < [\pi^*(1 - \pi_1)]/[\pi_1(1 - \pi^*)]$, where $\pi^* = \varphi\pi_1 + (1 - \varphi)\pi_2$. It may be thought that the allocation in Equilibrium V could be broken by an offer that raises p_1 and r_1, holding c_1 at W. Such an offer would earn positive profits if it attracted only low risks. However, from (2), $dr/dp = (k - c - Z)/p\pi - (r - c)/p$. Since this expression is decreasing in π, any offer that raised p_1 and r_1 relative to Equilibrium V would attract both types and thus would not be offered.

13. Reducing the collateral requirement on government loans has the same qualitative effects as raising p_G or γ_1.

14. In order to avoid the prospect of borrowers turning down private loans to accept public ones, I assume $X_{11} > P_G X_{1G}$.

References

Barro, Robert J., 1976. The loan market, collateral, and rates of interest. *Journal of Money, Credit, and Banking* 8 (November): 439–56.

Besanko, David, and Anjan V. Thakor. 1987. Collateral and rationing: Sorting equilibria in monopolistic and competitive credit markets. *International Economic Review* 28, no. 3 (October): 671–89.

Bester, Helmut. 1985. Screening vs. rationing in credit markets with imperfect information. *American Economic Review* 75, no. 4 (September): 850–55.

Bosworth, Barry P., Andrew S. Carron, and Elisabeth H. Rhyne. 1987. *The economics of federal credit programs.* Washington, DC: Brookings Institution.

Chan, Yuk-Shee, and Anjan V. Thakor. 1987. Collateral and competitive equilibria with moral hazard and private information. *Journal of Finance* 42, no. 2 (June): 345–63.

de Meza, David, and David C. Webb. 1987. Too much investment: A problem of asymmetric information. *Quarterly Journal of Economics* 102, no. 2 (May): 281–92.

Gale, William G. 1987. Allocational and welfare effects of federal credit programs. Ph.D. diss., Stanford University.

————. 1988a. Economic effects of federal credit programs. UCLA Working Paper no. 483. Rev. August. Forthcoming, *American Economic Review.*

————. 1988b. Federal lending and the market for credit. UCLA Working Paper no. 504. September. Forthcoming, *Journal of Public Economics.*

Mankiw, N. Gregory. 1986. The allocation of credit and financial collapse. *Quarterly Journal of Economics* 101, no. 3 (August): 455–70.

Milde, Hellmuth, and John G. Riley. 1988. Signaling in credit markets. *Quarterly Journal of Economics* 103, no. 1 (February): 101–30.

Office of Management and Budget. 1988. Special analysis F. *Special analyses: Budget of the United States Government.* Washington, D.C.: Government Printing Office.

————. 1989. Special Analysis F. *Special analyses: Budget of the United States government.* January. Washington, D.C.: Government Printing Office.

Rothschild, Michael, and Joseph E. Stiglitz. 1976. Equilibrium in competitive insurance markets: An essay on the economics of imperfect information. *Quarterly Journal of Economics* 90 (November): 629–49.

Smith, Bruce, and Michael J. Stutzer. 1989. Credit rationing and government loan programs: A welfare analysis. *AREUEA Journal* 17(2): 177–93.

Stiglitz, Joseph E., and Andrew Weiss. 1981. Credit rationing in markets with imperfect information. *American Economic Review* 71 (June): 393–411.

————. 1986. Credit rationing and collateral. In *Recent development in corporate finance,* ed. Jeremy Edwards, Julian Franks, Colin Mayer, and Stephen Schaefer, 101–35. New York: Cambridge University Press.

————. 1989. Sorting out the difference between screening and signalling models. In *Papers in commemoration of the economic theory seminar at Oxford University.* Oxford: Oxford University Press.

Wette, Hildegard. 1983. Collateral in credit rationing in markets with imperfect information: Note. *American Economic Review* 73 (June): 442–45.

Williamson, Stephen D. 1987. Costly monitoring, loan contracts, and equilibrium credit rationing. *Quarterly Journal of Economics* 102, no. 1 (February): 135–46.

Yotsuzuka, Toshiki. 1987. Ricardian equivalence in the presence of capital market imperfections. *Journal of Monetary Economics* 20 (September): 411–36.

3   Do Firms Care Who Provides Their Financing?

Jeffrey K. MacKie-Mason

Most capital structure studies have focused on the type of financial liabilities that firms use to finance their investment.[1] As noted by Robert Taggart, Jr., "primary attention is devoted to corporations' relative use of debt and equity financing. This has been the focal point of most previous attempts to trace patterns in corporate financing and of capital structure theory as well" (1985, 15). The purpose of this paper is to investigate whether firms care from *whom* they get their funds, in addition to caring about the *type* of funds. Finding that firms do distinguish between private and public, internal and external sources of funds, would help to explain the widely documented effect of cash flow on investment. More generally, if firms care about who provides a given type of funds, then credit market conditions are likely to have wide-ranging effects on many types of economic activity.

To address these questions I document aggregate and industry trends and patterns in the incremental sources of financial capital, and then I econometrically analyze a large sample of incremental corporate financial decisions. I find that there are large and persistent differences in the patterns of internal and external financing, both in the aggregate and across industries. The study of financing choices by individual firms shows that firms prefer particular providers of funds under various circumstances. Asymmetric information problems appear to be important determinants of financing choices. Since dif-

Jeffrey MacKie-Mason is an assistant professor of economics and an assistant research scientist of public policy at the University of Michigan, and a faculty research fellow with the National Bureau of Economic Research.

The author would like to thank participants at the NBER Conference on Information, Capital Markets, and Investment for many helpful comments, and members of the 1988 NBER Summer Institute Workshop on Credit Markets and Economic Activity for helpful comments on a preliminary presentation of some results from this paper. The author has particularly benefited from the comments of Glenn Hubbard and David Scharfstein. Superb research assistance was provided by Donna Lawson and Kenneth Kim, through financial support from the Rackham Graduate School and the NBER.

ferent funds providers have different access to information about the firm and different ability to monitor firm behavior, the importance of asymmetric information gives a reason for firms to care about who provides the funds.

Attention to the costs of asymmetric information led Stewart Myers (1984) to propose a "modified pecking order theory" of financing decisions. In this view, firms tend to have hierarchical preferences over sources of funds, first using retained earnings, then private and public debt if necessary, and finally new shares only as a last resort. However, Myers believed that firms would also consider other costs and benefits of debt and equity finance (such as tax advantages). Sometimes a firm will find that other benefits outweigh asymmetric information costs and will choose a funds source lower on the hierarchy than necessary. The results in this paper are consistent with this eclectic view. Firms are seen to care about *who* is providing the money, apparently because asymmetric information problems are important. But there is also evidence that at least some of the time firms calculate the trade-offs between debt and equity *types* of funding as if they were seeking an optimal debt ratio.

In the first section I briefly review some of the major theories of capital structure decisions, emphasizing the distinction between theories that have predictions for the type of security (debt or equity) a firm chooses and those that predict preferences for different types of providers (publicly-marketed or private). In Section 3.2 I present aggregate data on patterns in sources of financial capital, and in Section 3.3 I disaggregate the financing trends into broad industry groupings. There emerges the striking fact that there are persistent trends in the aggregate and differences in financing patterns across industries that cannot be explained if firms care only about the type of financing and not who provides it. This evidence supports the hypothesis that there are important distinctions between types of providers in addition to the distinction between types of funds.

The macro evidence motivates the econometric analysis of individual firm decisions in the second part of the paper. In Section 3.4 I develop a choice model for incremental decisions by individual firms and describe the selection of explanatory variables. The econometric results are presented in Section 3.5.

3.1   Theories of Financing

In this section I distinguish between two major themes in the literature on corporate financing and emphasize the different predictions that emerge from them.[2] The traditional view is that firms consider the costs and benefits of debt and equity then choose an optimal leverage ratio. The more recent view emphasizes costs associated with different providers of funds, rather than with the type of funds provided. It is the latter type of model that provides the central focus of this paper.

The two schools of thought are not mutually exclusive, although almost no theoretical work has appeared that integrates them.[3] I describe them separately not to challenge one with the other, but to highlight the common and distinguishing predictions they make. The data and econometric analysis presented below establish a number of empirical regularities that cannot be explained by the traditional optimal leverage theories. However, the other view—that who provides the funds matters—predicts several of the regularities that I find.

3.1.1   Different Security Types

Most of the financing literature has been concerned with the use of different types of security contracts for funding. Sources of funds can be thought of as contingent claims on the firm's cash flows, with different contingencies distinguishing between types of financing. The best-known examples are simple debt and common equity: debtholders have a senior claim on the firm's cash flows up to a fixed amount, and the equity owners receive the residual. If the firm is unable to meet the fixed interest commitment, the remaining assets are turned over and the equity claims become worthless.

If managers try to maximize shareholder wealth, then new investment should be financed with debt or equity depending on which contributes most to the firm's present value. Three aspects of the different debt and equity contingencies are usually emphasized as benefits and costs for debt and equity: (1) more debt increases the likelihood of bankruptcy, which may impose real wealth costs on shareholders; (2) more debt may distort incremental investment incentives, reducing firm value by the inefficiency cost; and, (3) the government takes different shares of cash flows to debt and equity. These effects are specific to the type of security—that is, the specific contingencies that define the security—and thus have no particular implications for who should provide the funds.

Financial distress and bankruptcy are usually presumed to cause real reductions in shareholder wealth (Miller and Modigliani 1966). Since greater fixed interest obligations increase the probability of financial distress, a firm should use less debt the higher are the expected bankruptcy costs.

A related cost of debt financing is that the fixed interest commitment may distort the managers' incentives for future investment decisions, thus reducing the value of the firm's wealth-increasing opportunities. Firms with large debt burdens may take on projects that are too risky because the shareholders gain if the projects succeed but the debt holders lose if the projects fail (Jensen and Meckling 1976). Myers (1977) and MacKie-Mason (1987) present models in which debt leads to underinvestment in future opportunities because prior interest commitments have first claim on the cash flows from the new project, thus reducing the likelihood that the project will yield a return on its incremental investment cost.

Tax claims also impose benefits and costs on security types. The most important rule is that interest paid is tax deductible for corporations while dividends paid are not. Thus debt financing would appear to be substantially favored, with a horizontal supply curve at the interest rate that equates the after-tax cost of financing with debt and equity. However, Miller (1977) pointed out that the corporate tax advantage to debt could be offset by personal tax disadvantages. He argued that a clientele would form for each firm's securities of investors whose tax rates made them indifferent to the firm's mix of debt and equity payouts, by equating rates of return after corporate and personal taxes. In Miller's model taxes have no effect on the choice of security type.

DeAngelo and Masulis (1980) studied a flaw in the Miller (1977) argument: additional interest commitments reduce the probability that the firm will be paying taxes, and in a zero-tax status the firm loses the benefits of other, non-debt tax shields. Thus, the firm is likely to have an upward-sloping debt supply curve and should have an optimal leverage ratio determined by the intersection of the supply curve and the investor-clientele demand curve.

3.1.2 Different Providers of Funds

A manager's valuation of a claim on a firm's future cash flows depends on what she expects about the firm's future performance. Managers seeking to maximize the wealth of current shareholders will only sell securities if investors are willing to pay as much or more than the managers—given their expectations—believe the securities are worth. Investors determine willingness to pay based on *their* expectations for the future. Investors who believe a firm's prospects are good will offer more than pessimists. The firm will care about who provides the funds because different providers will have different information and expectations, and thus be willing to pay different amounts for the securities.

Suppose managers have better information, and thus more accurate expectations, about the firm than do outside investors. I shall refer to this as the problem of hidden information. Hidden-information problems have quite different predictions for sources of financing than do the optimal leverage discussed above. Hidden-information problems have been proposed as a reason for firms to have hierarchical preferences over various sources of finance by Myers (1984). I place the emphasis somewhat differently: hidden-information problems predict firm preferences over providers of funds but not security types, while the optimal leverage factors affect choice of security types but not of provider funds. This dividing line is oversimplified, but it provides a useful organizing point for the investigation in this paper.

The basic prediction of the hidden-information theory is that investors who believe they have poorer information than managers will pay less for new securities than will better-informed investors. The intuition is simple: since managers sell securities only if buyers are willing to pay as much or more than the managers believe the securities are worth, poorly informed investors will assume that they are being exploited.

This story is a version of the well-known "lemons" model and has been formalized for new share issues by Myers and Majluf (1984). A similar phenomenon can lead to certain investors rationing the amount of financial capital they are willing to provide. Stiglitz and Weiss (1981) present a model in which banks ration credit to various firms because the banks cannot completely distinguish between good and bad firms. At some point no more funds will be offered regardless of the interest rate the firm is willing to promise because of the risk that the firm is a lemon.

Thus firms will prefer to obtain funds from investors who are better informed and do not require as large a premium. For example, firms will prefer to use retained earnings over new share issues: retained earnings are reinvested equity by current shareholders, so there is no possibility for information exploitation to transfer wealth from new investors to existing owners.[4] Likewise firms might prefer borrowing from their regular commercial bankers rather than from publicly marketed bonds if the banker has better access to relevant information (or can verify it more cheaply) than do bond purchasers.

We thus expect that firms care about who provides their financing. In general such asymmetries of information are not related to the *type* of security, and as such do not predict financing preferences over debt and equity *per se*.

3.1.3 Summary

The general predictions of the two views are summarized in table 3.1. Debt/equity choices should depend on tax shields because of crowding out by new interest deductions. The composition of a firm's assets between fixed capital in place and future investment opportunities affects the cost of debt because of the possibility of inefficient future investment decisions. And, firms with a high likelihood of bankruptcy may avoid new debt rather than increase the expected realization of financial distress costs. For the most part these factors are not important for the choice between different providers of funds.

The main predictions of the hidden information view are that firms will seek better-informed investors when the perceived likelihood of a hidden-information advantage is high or when the potential difference in valuations due to hidden-information is high. For example, the probability of financial

Table 3.1   Predicted Effects of Financing Choice Determinants

	Predicted to Have an Effect On	
Potential Determinants	Type of Security	Type of Provider
Tax shields	yes	no
Asset composition	yes	no
Bankruptcy likelihood	yes	maybe
Paying dividends	no	yes
Forecast variance	maybe	yes
Public regulation	no	yes

distress *per se* is not a hidden-information problem if that probability is common knowledge, but the costliness of small information differences is likely to be magnified for a firm near bankruptcy, leading to an indirect effect of potential financial distress on preferences over providers of funds. Thus I have put a "maybe" in the table in that cell.

The other characteristics in table 3.1 are predicted to influence choice of provider, but not type of security. We need to look for publicly observable factors that are likely to indicate significant divergences in information or its value, without actually knowing what hidden information the managers have. For example, if firms pay dividends as a costly and informative signal to reveal hidden information, then hidden information may be a bigger problem for firms that do not pay dividends. When the forecast variance of a firm's earnings is high, a small amount of asymmetric information may be reflected in a big difference between earnings predictions by managers and investors. On the other hand, firms with government rate regulation have much relevant information revealed and validated for investors by the regulatory body. Rate regulation also might intentionally dampen the effects of good or bad surprises.

Specific variables to measure these effects shall be discussed in Section 3.4 below. First, in the next two sections I investigate the trends and patterns in sources of funds in the aggregate and across industries. If firms care only about debt and equity choices, then we should see more or less random variation in the degree of reliance on various providers of funds. Of course this prediction is too strong, and a microeconomic analysis of individual firm financing is necessary if we are to draw strong conclusions. However, from a look at the macro data we shall see important trends and cross-industry variation in reliance on different providers of funds as distinct from different types of securities. These results motivate and reinforce the later analysis of firm decisions.

3.2   Aggregate Sources of Funds since World War II

In this section I present data on sources of funds for the nonfinancial corporate sector since 1945 and discuss the apparent patterns at the aggregate level.[5] These data introduce some of the empirical regularities that will be examined in the econometric analysis of financial choices. Sources of funds are presented as a percentage of total sources in table 3.2. The data are averaged over business cycles (measured from trough to trough, using the nearest quarter) to control for cyclical effects.[6]

Before studying the different patterns in various incremental sources of funds, two broad facts illustrated in figure 3.1 deserve notice. First, the profit flow out of the nonfinancial corporate sector has been very close to zero. That is, predistribution earnings have averaged 97% of total sources of funds, and have rarely strayed far from 100% (table 3.2). Since earnings represent net

Table 3.2   Sources of Funds, by Business Cycle (% of Total Sources)

	Business Cycle									
	45Q4–49Q4	49Q4–54Q2	54Q2–58Q2	58Q2–61Q1	61Q1–70Q4	70Q4–75Q1	75Q1–80Q3	80Q3–82Q4	82Q4–87Q4	Total
Net dividends	28.9	26.8	27.6	27.5	24.3	19.1	19.9	21.1	19.8	23.7
Retained earnings	68.4	68.7	78.4	79.9	73.7	62.0	74.8	72.7	77.6	73.1
Predistribution earnings	97.3	95.4	105.9	107.4	98.0	81.1	94.7	93.8	97.3	96.8
Bank loans	6.9	6.2	5.5	3.7	8.2	11.1	4.1	10.5	5.5	6.8
Mortgages	6.2	3.5	4.6	6.7	3.9	4.0	.3	-4.1	.4	3.1
Trade debt	3.4	-3.9	-2.6	-4.3	-1.8	-2.2	-4.1	3.8	-1.8	-1.8
Other debt	-.3	.8	.6	1.8	2.1	4.0	7.2	8.9	8.3	3.5
Corporate bonds	12.4	11.1	10.9	9.9	11.1	11.2	10.8	6.2	16.0	11.4
Total debt	28.6	17.7	19.1	17.9	23.4	28.1	18.3	25.3	28.3	22.9
New shares	5.3	6.3	5.4	4.2	2.0	6.5	2.4	-.6	-12.8	1.8
Miscellaneous sources	-2.4	7.4	-2.8	-2.0	.9	3.4	4.4	2.6	6.9	2.2
External sources	31.6	31.3	21.6	20.1	26.3	38.0	25.2	27.3	22.4	26.9
Total sources	100.0	100.0	100.0	100.0	100.0	100.0	100.0	100.0	100.0	100.0

Source: Federal Reserve, Flow of Funds Accounts, various issues, 1945–87.
Note: Business cycle troughs are indicated by quarter (Q), but the data are averages of calendar years, split at the closest point to the trough.

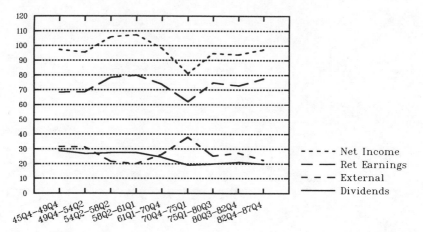

Fig. 3.1   Internal versus external funds (% of total sources)

income after interest payments on debt, the net total flow of financial payments out of the corporate sector has been consistently close to nominal interest payments on debt. Why does the corporate sector maintain a debt level such that investment is almost identical to after-interest earnings?

The second intriguing fact concerns the well-known dividend puzzle. Dividends are a tax-disadvantaged means for transferring funds from the corporate to the household sector. One obvious alternative is to repurchase shares. In fact, firms recently have begun to repurchase huge amounts of equity, but dividends have not declined correspondingly. Although the long-run trend is slightly negative, dividends have been almost a constant share of total sources since 1970, even as new shares have plummeted from 6.5% of total sources over the fourth quarter of 1970 through the first quarter of 1975 (70Q4–75Q1) to − 12.8% in the most recent cycle. It seems that corporations have discovered share repurchases but have not been using them to reduce dividends, at least in aggregate.[7]

Details on the major sources of funds are presented in table 3.3. I distinguish between four major sources: retained earnings, nonpublicly marketed debt, corporate bonds, and new equity share issues. This paper focuses on two dimensions of financing: private versus publicly marketed financing, and debt versus equity financing. Some data on internal versus external sources of funds are also presented. Retained earnings are the only internal source; retained earnings plus private debt constitute private sources.

3.2.1   Internal versus External Sources

Internal and external funds are shown in figure 3.1. Over the entire period nearly three-quarters of funds were provided internally (table 3.2). The reliance on internal funds fluctuates somewhat but the variance is low. If the stag-

Table 3.3   **Internal and External Financing, 1946–1987 (% of Total Sources)**

Year	Retained Earnings	Private Debt	Corporate Bonds	New Shares	Payout Ratio
1946	50.2	50.2	6.1	6.4	39.4
1947	57.7	13.1	12.9	5.0	31.7
1948	72.0	4.1	16.6	3.9	25.6
1949	93.9	−2.6	14.1	5.9	25.0
45Q4–49Q4	68.4	16.2	12.4	5.3	30.4
1950	56.1	10.8	5.1	4.1	30.7
1951	60.5	8.3	10.1	6.5	28.2
1952	82.1	3.7	17.2	8.5	26.7
1953	75.9	3.5	12.0	6.0	27.3
49Q4–54Q2	68.7	6.6	11.1	6.3	28.2
1954	92.4	.2	13.4	6.0	26.5
1955	68.4	11.0	6.9	3.9	25.0
1956	76.4	13.5	8.8	5.7	26.5
1957	76.3	8.2	14.4	5.8	25.8
54Q2–58Q2	78.4	8.2	10.9	5.4	26.0
1958	85.6	.1	15.8	5.5	26.4
1959	71.3	13.3	6.0	4.1	24.4
1960	82.8	10.5	7.9	3.2	25.7
58Q2–61Q1	79.9	8.0	9.9	4.2	25.5
1961	77.0	5.8	9.2	4.4	25.9
1962	77.0	12.8	7.2	.7	24.4
1963	75.5	16.1	6.1	−.5	24.4
1964	79.7	11.2	6.1	1.7	24.3
1965	74.4	16.3	6.1	−.0	24.2
1966	73.1	13.0	11.8	1.5	23.6
1967	74.2	10.8	16.9	2.8	24.2
1968	68.9	14.0	13.5	−.2	25.4
1969	70.0	15.7	12.8	3.7	25.9
1970	67.3	7.8	21.2	6.1	26.2
61Q1–70Q4	73.7	12.3	11.1	2.0	24.9
1971	65.9	4.4	16.6	10.1	23.5
1972	68.0	12.0	9.6	8.6	22.3
1973	53.3	33.2	5.2	4.5	22.6
1974	60.9	17.8	13.4	2.8	25.7
70Q4–75Q1	62.0	16.8	11.2	6.5	23.5
1975	82.1	−7.4	17.9	6.5	19.9
1976	72.5	3.8	11.7	5.4	20.3
1977	74.1	13.0	10.3	1.2	20.3
1978	70.7	16.0	8.2	−.0	20.7
1979	77.2	12.4	6.8	−3.1	21.5
1980	72.3	7.2	10.0	4.7	23.4
75Q1–80Q3	74.8	7.5	10.8	2.4	21.0
1981	68.2	23.7	6.5	−3.3	22.0
1982	77.3	14.4	6.0	2.0	22.9
80Q3–82Q4	72.7	19.1	6.2	−.6	22.5

(continued)

Table 3.3   (continued)

Year	Retained Earnings	Private Debt	Corporate Bonds	New Shares	Payout Ratio
1983	74.6	10.0	4.2	6.1	21.5
1984	75.6	24.5	10.4	−16.8	19.4
1985	81.5	15.3	17.1	−18.8	19.3
1986	73.1	10.7	24.8	−16.5	20.1
1987	83.0	1.2	23.5	−18.0	21.3
82Q4–87Q4	77.6	12.3	16.0	−12.8	20.3
All years	73.1	11.5	11.4	1.8	24.5

Source: Federal Reserve, *Flow of Funds Accounts.*

flation- and OPEC-dominated cycle from the fourth quarter of 1970 to the first quarter of 1975 (70Q4–75Q1) is dropped, the internal/external ratio is extremely stable.

There is no evidence of any long-run trend in internal financing. This finding contradicts Taggart's conclusion that "internally generated funds have also declined relative to total sources during the postwar period" (1985, 28). Taggart examined data through 1979; his conclusion might have been due in part to the abnormally low use of internal financing during 1971–75.[8] Since 1975, retained earnings have hovered around the postwar average of 73%. During the last six years the internal fraction has ranged from 73% to 83%, but those years comprise only the expansion part of the strongest economic boom since 1945.

The dominance of internal equity funding is one of the stylized facts that prompted Myers (1984) to contemplate a hierarchy theory of corporate financing, with retained earnings the most preferred source. Hierarchical preferences follow from some asymmetric information problems. However, firms might prefer internal funds over new shares because of transactions costs and the tax penalty on dividends. Thus observing a high share of internal equity funding need not indicate whether a firm has hierarchical preferences for internal funds over debt. We need to examine the data more carefully before drawing conclusions about the existence of financing hierarchies.

3.2.2 Private versus Public Sources

Another distinction between sources of funds is whether the funds are raised in a public, competitive market. The alternative, which I call "private" sources, is to use retained earnings or debt sold through private placements or negotiated directly with a bank. The shares of private and public sources of funds are shown in figure 3.2. Publicly marketed sources are defined as net new share issues and corporate bonds. Private sources include retained earnings, bank loans, finance company loans, mortgages, and a variety of miscellaneous (but generally small) sources such as taxes payable and net trade debt.

One point appears obvious from the figure: the corporate sector is turning steadily away from public sources of funds. However, we must look separately at the trend components, shown in figure 3.3. Although net public financing has dropped from nearly 20% of total sources during the 1970–75 cycle to almost 0% during the most recent years, the result is entirely due to the strong downward trend in new equity shares. In fact, during seven of the last 10 years net new share issues have been negative (*i.e.*, there have been net repurchases). During 1982–87 new shares have averaged − 12.8% of total sources.

Although net public financing has fallen almost to zero, firms are still turn-

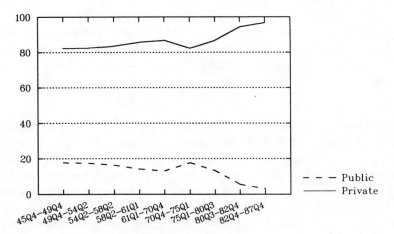

Fig. 3.2 Private versus public sources (% of total)

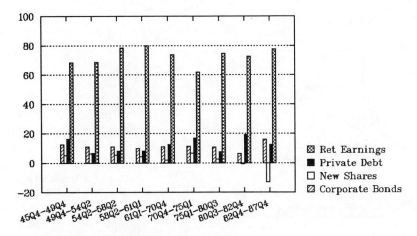

Fig. 3.3 Major sources of funds (% of total)

ing to the public bond market for substantial funds. As seen in figure 3.3, corporate bond financing has been steadily around 10% since 1946. There was a substantial drop during the short 1981–82 cycle, but public bond financing has been significantly above average during the last few years. Thus there is not a consistent trend away from *public* sources of funds; rather there is a trend away from new shares. This observation might be consistent with a financing hierarchy that has new shares as the least-preferred form of finance. On the other hand, if firms have a strong aversion to issuing new shares, we might expect them to invest available cash in liquid financial assets rather than in repurchasing their own shares, building up reserves to reduce the likelihood of needing to issue new shares in the future.

The rising trend in private sources shown in figure 3.2 is also somewhat deceptive. Much of the increase is due to an increase in the funds provided by "miscellaneous sources," consisting primarily of taxes payable and foreign direct investment in the United States. These sources are not easily controlled by individual firms and thus the trend in nonpublic sources may not reflect conscious decisions by managers.

3.2.3   Debt versus Equity

Incremental debt and equity financing are shown in figure 3.4. The first obvious point is that there is little evidence of abnormally high reliance on debt financing during the past decade. Total debt has provided a higher-than-average fraction of total funds during the 1980s; however, the debt contributions have been no greater than they were during the long expansion and following cycle from 1961 to 1975. The debt percentage was also equally high during the first postwar cycle (although this average is due almost entirely to the 54% reliance on debt in 1946). The average debt percentages for the 1980s

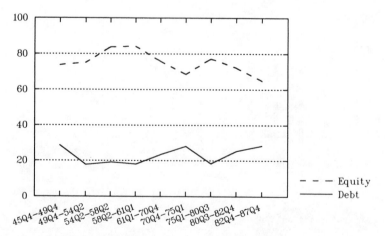

Fig. 3.4.   Equity versus debt sources (% of total)

are well within one standard deviation (1 SD = 8.3 percentage points) of mean postwar debt reliance, although several of the individual years in the 1980s are more than one SD above the mean. Thus in the aggregate recent debt usage does not appear to be alarming. Nonetheless, there may be room for concern about debt usage in some industries or about the riskiness of recent debt issues.

A somewhat more pronounced trend occurs in the equity series. Equity financing has declined fairly steadily since 1958. The share of retained earnings has never again been as high as it was in 1958 (85%), although it came close in 1987 (83%; see fig. 3.3 and table 3.3). New shares have fallen precipitously since 1971. But the difference between total sources and equity sources has been made up largely from miscellaneous sources rather than standard debt sources.

A few interesting facts emerge from this review of aggregate patterns in sources of funds. First, the share of internal financing is dominant and exhibits no long-term trend: since 1975 the share has fluctuated closely around the four-decade average. Second, any strong hierarchical preference for internal funds is offset by an equally strong preference for dividends: in aggregate firms have paid out about 20% of earnings as dividends and simultaneously raised about 20% of their funds from external sources. Third, although there has been substantial movement away from net new share issues, firms still raise a substantial fraction of funds in public debt markets. The persistence in the preference for retained earnings over new shares, and the stability of the share of corporate bonds suggest that firms do care about who provides the funds, rather than selecting randomly from different sources of debt and equity.

3.3.   Industry Variation in Sources of Funds

The main finding in this section is that there are significant and persistent differences in the reliance on internal funds both across industries and over time. These persistent variations support the idea that capital structure decisions involve more than the choice of a debt/equity ratio.

3.3.1   Data

The Federal Reserve does not detail its flow-of-funds accounts by industry. I constructed the data in this section from the 1988 COMPUSTAT database. It is not possible to construct a series strictly comparable to the aggregate Federal Reserve data because COMPUSTAT contains an unweighted sample of only about 6,500 firms.

I constructed industry aggregates directly from the individual firm data. The firm data were selected for use in the econometric analysis below and represent a distinct subpopulation of firms. A firm is included for a given year if long-term capitalization increased that year, that is, if retained cash plus net sales of debt and equity is greater than zero. The restriction to firms with increased capitalization will be justified in Section 3.4 below. For now, notice that the composition of each industry aggregate may change from year to year, either because of an addition to or deletion from COMPUSTAT coverage or because some firms increase their capitalization in some years but not in others.[9] The data were collected for 1977–86.[10] The aggregates are constructed from approximately 1,400 individual firm observations each year. The data are again presented as averages over business cycles; however, both the first and last cycle are incomplete. The industry codes correspond to aggregates of 2-digit SIC codes as detailed in table 3A.1.

3.3.2   Internal Financing by Industry

The shares for internal funds over 1971–87 are presented by industry in table 3.4. The numbers display marked variation in reliance on internal funds across industries and, in many cases, over time within a given industry.

Selected industries are graphed in figures 3.5a and 3.5b. Firms are grouped by similar patterns in the use of internal funds. Figure 3.5a presents the largest

Table 3.4   **Use of Internal Funds by Industry (% of Total Sources over Business Cycles)**

Industry by SIC Code	Business Cycle 1977–80	1981–82	1983–86	Total
100	65.7	104.8	88.0	82.5
1000	66.8	54.8	96.5	76.3
1300	70.8	64.6	80.0	73.2
1500	76.9	68.0	82.7	77.4
2000	78.4	69.2	89.4	81.0
2200	85.0	80.9	77.7	81.3
2800	86.6	73.3	102.7	90.4
2900	95.1	84.6	104.2	96.6
3000	79.5	58.6	78.6	75.0
3400	69.7	86.5	61.8	69.9
3500	82.5	69.8	82.3	79.9
3600	86.8	88.8	80.1	84.5
3700	84.2	80.0	83.4	83.0
3800	87.2	85.1	89.6	87.8
4000	85.2	81.7	79.3	82.2
4500	79.9	52.4	69.6	70.3
4800	70.6	67.9	73.6	71.2
5000	82.1	77.0	71.1	76.7
5200	76.4	78.3	73.6	75.7
7000	64.1	57.3	68.6	64.5
Total	78.7	74.2	81.6	79.0

Note: See table 3A.1 for industry definitions. All results are from author's calculations using COMPUSTAT data.

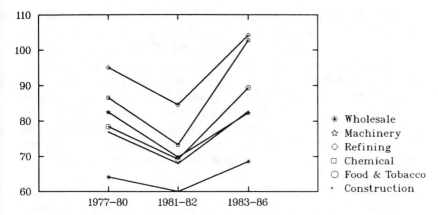

Fig. 3.5a   Use of internal funds, Group I

* Wholesale
☆ Machinery
◇ Refining
□ Chemical
○ Food & Tobacco
• Construction

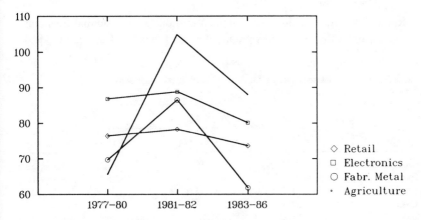

Fig. 3.5b   Use of internal funds, Group III

◇ Retail
□ Electronics
○ Fabr. Metal
• Agriculture

group, for which reliance on internal funds dipped dramatically during 1981–82 cycle, but then rose in the most recent period (usually to even higher levels). Some other industries with this pattern were not graphed for visual clarity. The firms in Group I account for about 74% of the net assets in the sample. The four Group III industries in figure 3.5b (15% of net assets) relied more heavily on internal funds during 1981–82, but (except for Agriculture) ended the period at a lower level than they began. The intermediate group of industries are not graphed (Wholesale Trade, 5000; Textile Mills, Lumber, Furniture, Paper and Printing, 2200; and Ground, Water and Miscellaneous Transport, 4000) due to space limitations. These displayed a slight downward trend in internal funds and almost no change in either debt or equity shares (examined below).

Industries differ in the long run as well as from period to period. At the extremes, the Hotel, Entertainment, and Service aggregate (7000) obtained only 65% of its financing from retentions on average, while Petroleum Refining (2900) provided 96.6% of its funds internally. These two industry groups exhibited the same time-series pattern of internal financing (fig. 3.5a), but are very different in the extent to which they turn to outsiders for new funds.

The variations suggest that the use of internal funds cannot be entirely explained by business cycle effects, secular trends in the economy, or widespread changes in financial practices. Of course the distribution of financing patterns might be due to pure chance rather than to different firm preferences and opportunities. I shall look for systematic determinants of financing decisions in Section 3.5.

Variations in the share of internal financing are offset by changes in external shares. I shall now examine how the shifts in external sources were distributed across debt and equity for different industries.

3.3.3   Debt Financing by Industry

Reliance on debt exhibits substantial variation, as did internal financing. However, firms that followed similar patterns in the use of internal funds do

Table 3.5   Use of Debt by Industry (% of Total Sources over Business Cycles)

Industry by SIC Code	Business Cycle			
	1977–80	1981–82	1983–86	Total
100	31.2	− 15.6	57.1	32.2
1000	23.1	37.4	5.4	18.9
1300	21.3	34.0	20.7	23.6
1500	22.3	12.1	13.3	16.6
2000	16.3	24.8	22.4	20.5
2200	13.0	14.5	22.6	17.1
2800	10.4	11.4	7.7	9.6
2900	4.3	14.7	30.1	16.7
3000	16.4	35.6	16.9	20.5
3400	21.6	8.9	30.6	22.7
3500	11.8	24.0	5.1	11.6
3600	5.5	2.5	14.3	8.4
3700	10.3	16.0	14.6	13.1
3800	8.1	9.4	12.0	9.9
4000	12.9	17.0	16.7	15.3
4500	12.0	38.2	18.9	20.0
4800	18.4	16.2	16.7	17.3
5000	15.8	18.6	17.6	17.1
5200	21.5	14.1	20.1	19.5
7000	29.5	23.5	28.8	28.0
Total	16.3	17.9	19.6	17.9

Note: See note to table 3.4.

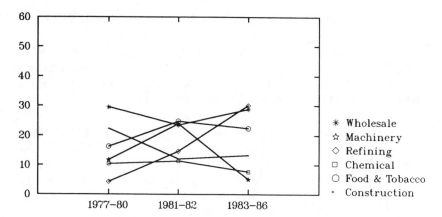

* Wholesale
☆ Machinery
◇ Refining
□ Chemical
○ Food & Tobacco
∘ Construction

Fig. 3.6a   Use of debt, Group I

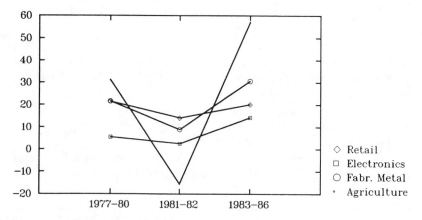

◇ Retail
□ Electronics
○ Fabr. Metal
∘ Agriculture

Fig. 3.6b   Use of debt, Group III

not look similar in their use of debt. The business cycle averages as a percentage of total sources are given in table 3.5. Figures 3.6a and 3.6b graph the industries using the same groupings as before.

I noted in Section 3.2 above that debt usage has increased during the last 10 years, but not dramatically. For this sample, incremental reliance on debt rose from 16% during the first period to 20% during the last period (table 3.5). But while some industries increased their debt use substantially, quite a few decreased.

Figure 3.6a displays a jumbled pattern for the Group I firms. Petroleum. Refining (2900) added huge amounts of new debt, going from an average 4% debt share in 1977–80 to a 30% share during 1983–86. Machinery firms (3500) went from 12% to 24% to 5% debt usage. Metal Mining (1000) dropped from 23% to 5% (see table 3.5). In addition to the time-series variation, the cross-sectional spread in debt usage is large: from about 5% to 30% debt shares both at the beginning and end of the period.

Two other industries greatly increased debt usage: Textile, Lumber, Furniture, Paper and Printing (2200) went from 13% to 23%; and Agriculture (100) went from 31% to 57%, (but with net debt *retirements* of 16% in the middle period). Other industries maintained relatively steady or slightly increased rates of debt usage.

The data reported here contradict Lintner's contention that "there are clear and remarkably persistent patterns in the relative use of debt financing by firms in different industries" (1985, p. 79). At least over the past decade, the use of debt within industries has fluctuated significantly. It may be that the relatively high level of aggregation is masking persistent patterns for more disaggregated industries, and that the changing relative importance of more narrowly defined industries leads to the variation in my aggregate figures. So much variation in the composition of industries over 10 years seems unlikely, however.

3.3.4   New Share Issues

Net new share issues have sharply decreased in recent years and, in fact, have become substantially negative due to repurchases. Shoven (1986) has estimated that cash payments to equity holders through repurchases and cash-financed mergers and acquisitions have been much larger than divided payments during recent years. We shall see that the intensity of equity absorption has been far from uniform across industries.

Table 3.6 presents net share issues by industry. The industries are graphed by group in figures 3.7a and 3.7b. Recall that firms in Group I industries reduced their reliance on internal funds during the middle period, but then moved to higher levels of internal financing during the most recent years (fig. 3.5a). There was no consistent pattern in their debt policies (fig. 3.6a). We can see from figure 3.7a that this group was for the most part alternating between internal and external equity. During the initial stock market rise in 1981–82, many firms brought out new issues; Group I shows constant or increased rates of net new shares during this period.[11] For most of these industries net share issues fell dramatically after 1982 and were negative for several years. From figure 3.7a we can see that most of these industries also were decreasing their use of external debt during the last few years.

The Group III industries are those that increased the share of internal funds in 1981–82, then decreased more recently. Two (Fabricated Metal and Electronics) offset shifts in internal financing with changes in the share of external debt rather than equity; Agriculture (100) decreased and Retail Trade (5200) substantially increased their reliance on new equity (fig. 3.7b). The large negative share for Agriculture is due to major repurchases in 1984 and 1985 by U.S. Sugar, DeKalb, and Castle & Cooke.

Table 3.6   **Use of New Shares by Industry (% of Total Sources over Business Cycles)**

Industry by SIC Code	Business Cycle			Total
	1977–80	1981–82	1983–86	
100	3.1	10.7	−45.1	−14.7
1000	10.1	7.8	−1.8	4.9
1300	7.9	1.4	−0.8	3.1
1500	0.8	20.0	4.0	5.9
2000	5.3	6.0	−11.8	−1.4
2200	2.0	4.6	−0.3	1.6
2800	3.0	15.2	−10.4	0.1
2900	0.7	0.7	−34.3	−13.3
3000	4.1	5.8	4.4	4.6
3400	8.7	4.6	7.6	7.4
3500	5.7	6.3	12.6	8.6
3600	7.7	8.7	5.6	7.1
3700	5.5	4.1	2.1	3.9
3800	4.7	5.6	−1.7	2.3
4000	1.9	1.3	4.0	2.6
4500	8.1	9.5	11.5	9.7
4800	11.1	15.9	9.7	11.5
5000	2.1	4.3	11.4	6.3
5200	2.1	7.6	6.3	4.9
7000	6.4	19.2	2.6	7.4
Total	5.1	8.0	−1.2	3.1

Note: See note to table 3.4.

There is quite substantial cross-sectional variation in the degree of reliance on new shares in the total sample, even with the high level of aggregation. Many industries cluster around 5% net new shares, but several industries use external equity for as much as 15% to 20% of their funds during the 1981–82 period. The range during the last cycle is from −45% to 13%.

It is also important to note that, although in aggregate corporations were absorbing large amounts of equity during the last several years, quite a few industries were using increasing and positive amounts of net new equity: Machinery (3500), Airlines (4500), Fabricated Metal (3400), Ground and Water Transport (4000), and Wholesale Trade (5000). The movement toward nondividend cash distributions was far from universal.

3.3.5 Conclusion

In Section 3.2 I demonstrated that the fraction of nonfinancial corporate funds provided by internal cash has fluctuated somewhat, but the average over business cycles remains fairly stable, around 70%. This contrasts with earlier observations by Friedman (1980) and Taggart (1985), who saw a postwar trend away from internal funds toward debt. By extending the time series past

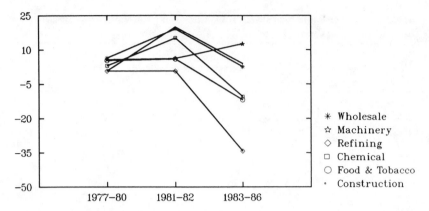

Fig. 3.7a   Use of new shares, Group I

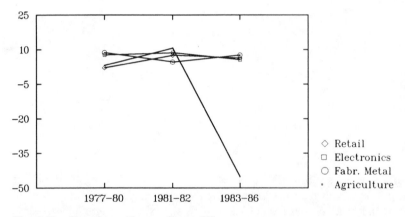

Fig. 3.7b   Use of new shares, Group III

1979 there appears to be no trend away from internal funds, and the movement toward debt (away from external equity) is not outside the normal long-run variation.

The stability of aggregate reliance on internal funds does not carry over to industry patterns of financing. Even at high levels of industry aggregation there is quite substantial variation in both the time-series and cross-sectional patterns of internal financing. The variation is even greater if examined year-to-year rather than as a series of business cycle averages. Many industries shifted significant shares of financing from internal cash to external equity during 1981–82; then they again increased the share of internal funds in more recent years while dramatically decreasing net new share issues, as well as decreasing reliance on debt in some cases. However, several industries exhibited precisely the opposite pattern, and a number of others can not be categorized in either way.[12]

There are large and persistent differences in the degree to which different industries rely on internal funds. There are also significant variations in the pattern of internal financing over time. When the reliance on internal funds changes, the compensating sources of external finance—debt or equity—also vary over time and across industries. We clearly cannot explain the use of internal funds simply with aggregate trends in the economy or in financial institutions and practices. Different firms rely to varying degrees on internal funds. In the next two sections I present an econometric analysis of individual firm financing decisions.

3.4 Determinants of Financial Choices

The data presented in the first two sections showed substantial variations in the use of internal funds that are not explained by business cycle fluctuations. The data also reveal large differences in the use of internal funds across industries. It thus appears that there are nontrivial distinctions between the providers of funds, as well as differences between types (debt and equity).

Are these variations purely random, or are they due to the effects of economic forces on firm financing decisions? As a first step in answering this question, I estimate a simple econometric model of individual firm decisions. Unlike many prior researchers, I distinguish between who provides the funds as well as the type of funds. I find several factors that help to explain firm reliance on various sources.

Some important prior research has indicated that it matters who provides financing. For example, Chris James (1987) examined stock price reactions to announcements of different types of debt financing and found that the market reaction varies with the identity of the provider (*e.g.*, bank, private placement, public bond). In a more direct study of financing preferences, McDonald and Soderstrom (1988) estimate multinomial choice models for dividend and share repurchase decisions. Their approach is quite similar to the analysis in this paper. Their evidence suggests that a financing hierarchy exists and that the marginal source of funds for a firm changes over time.

Although there has been only a little empirical research on this financing question, several studies of investment have allowed for possible effects from distinctions between providers of funds. If there are significant asymmetric information costs for different sources, then the Modigliani and Miller (1958) irrelevance result fails to hold and financing should affect investment. Fazzari, Hubbard, and Petersen (1988) find that investment by those firms most likely to face external credit constraints is significantly determined by cash flow. Blundell et al. (1988) and Devereux and Schiantarelli (ch. 11, in this volume) obtain similar results in two studies of investment by U.K. firms. Whited

(1988) finds that implicit constraints on debt issuance affect investment in a panel of firms. Hoshi, Kashyap, and Scharfstein (1988; ch. 4, in this volume) study investment by Japanese firms and conclude that access to bank finance within a "trading group" increases investment relative to firms unaligned with a bank.

The approach I take to financing distinctions is to study incremental decisions. In the remainder of this section I describe the choice model, the data, and the hypothesized determinants of choice among sources of funds. The results are presented in Section 3.5.

3.4.1 Choice among Financing Alternatives

Consider a firm that wishes to raise new financial capital. I presume that the managers seek to maximize firm value. Funds can be obtained from several sources, each potentially having different effects on firm value. Choices are distinguished by the type of contingent financial claim (debt or equity) and by the provider of funds (private or publicly marketed sources). Thus, I model the alternatives as a multidimensional choice set, with one dimension as $M = \{public,private\}$ and the other choice dimension as $S = \{debt,equity\}$. A financing choice is given by $c_{ms} \in M \times S$, a combination from the two choice dimensions. For example, corporate bonds are denoted by $c_{public,debt}$.

Each source of funds can affect firm value. Let the increment (positive or negative) to the firm's objective function from a particular source be decomposed as

$$V_{ms} = U_m + U_s + U_{ms} + \tilde{\varepsilon}_m + \tilde{\varepsilon}_s + \tilde{\varepsilon}_{ms}.$$

The U terms represent the deterministic effects on firm value peculiar to each financing dimension separately (market, security type), and the effects peculiar to the particular combination (U_{ms}). The $\tilde{\varepsilon}$ terms decompose the random effects on value in the same way. That is, the effect specific to a security being publicly marketed (regardless of whether it is debt or equity) is given by $U_{public} + \tilde{\varepsilon}_{public}$, and likewise for the security dimension. Any interactive effects peculiar to a particular source raised in a particular market setting are captured in $U_{ms} + \tilde{\varepsilon}_{ms}$. This decomposition allows for similarities between sources that share a dimension, but still permits for effects specific to each source.

If we assume that either $\text{var}(\tilde{\varepsilon}_s) = 0$ or $\text{var}(\tilde{\varepsilon}_m) = 0$, and make appropriate assumptions about the distribution of the remaining stochastic terms, then the choice model is known as a nested logit model (McFadden 1981).[13] The restriction that one of the choice dimensions not have its own stochastic component (i.e., the zero-variance condition) limits the description of the possible effects of financing sources on firm value.[14] I estimated both choice models, with the two different variance restrictions. The two models are illustrated in figure 3.8, as choice tree 1 and choice tree 2. The first model, tree 1, has the interpretation that firms choose whether to use public or private sources, and then from one of those branches choose either debt or equity. The second

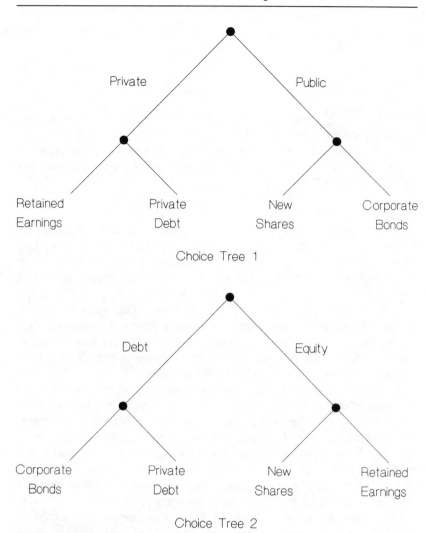

Choice Tree 1

Choice Tree 2

Fig. 3.8.   Financial decision trees

model has the firm choosing debt or equity first, then deciding from what provider to obtain the funds.

To estimate the determinants of choice, I specify U_m, U_s, and U_{ms} as linear functions of hypothesized explanatory variables, X; for example, $U_s = X\beta_s$. The probability that a firm chooses a particular source from the multidimensional choice set can be written as

$$pr(m,s) = pr(s|m)\ pr(m),$$

and with the nested logit stochastic specifications we have

$$\text{pr}(s|m) = \frac{e^{(U_{ms} + U_s)}}{\sum_{s' \in S} e^{(U_{ms'} + U_{s'})}},$$

$$\text{pr}(m) = \frac{e^{(U_m + \bar{I}_m)\alpha}}{\sum_{m' \in M} e^{(U_{m'} + \bar{I}_{m'})\alpha}},$$

where $\bar{I}_m = \ln[\sum_{s' \in S} \exp(U_{ms'} + U_{s'})]$, the log of the denominator of $\text{pr}(s|m)$, and α, a parameter to be estimated. Here $\bar{I}_m$ is known as the inclusive value. Given the probabilities of observing particular choices, the model can be estimated using either maximum likelihood or a nonlinear sequential estimator (McFadden 1981).[15]

3.4.2   The Observed Choices

Two data problems complicate estimating the determinants of financing decisions using a discrete-choice model. First, although firms may be making decisions incrementally and discretely, the sampling frame of the data is more coarsely grained. In MacKie-Mason (1990) only public issues were studied. Since public securities must be registered, SEC data tapes precisely identify each incremental issuing decision. To study financing decisions that include private debt and retained earnings, we must rely on annual accounting statements. Thus the financing decisions must be treated as if the firm chooses its sources of funds once per year. In most cases this means that a single observation actually represents several financing decisions.

Another problem is that firms may raise funds from more than one source at a time. In only a tiny fraction of instances do firms register more than one public security at a time, and in only a few more cases do firms separately register different types of securities within a short time frame. However, in data that combine private and public sources and that are aggregated over a year, the problem will be much more common. In fact, most firms in the COMPUSTAT universe use at least retained earnings and private debt and often one or two of the public sources of funds in a given year.

I have taken the following approach to defining financing choices. My *a priori* logic was suggested by the possibility of a financing hierarchy of the sort proposed by Myers (1984): firms prefer to use internal funds, then private debt, then, only if necessary, publicly marketed securities. This is consistent with the frequencies of public issues in the sample: of the 14,398 observations on firms that increased their capitalization in a given year over 1977–86, only 1,463 were public security issues. Thus, I chose to code the choice variable as "new shares" if the firm issued stock, regardless of other sources of funds; "bonds" if the firm sold corporate bonds; "private debt" if the net increase in debt sources exceeded the net increase in equity sources (but the firm did not issue bonds); and "retained earnings" in all other cases. If the firm did not publicly issue, it is classified as private debt or equity depending on which source contributed the most funds that year. If the firm did publicly issue, it is coded as public debt or equity regardless of issue size.

The sample is drawn from the COMPUSTAT universe. A nonfinancial corporation was included for a particular year if its long-term capitalization (net changes in equity plus net changes in debt) increased that year, according to the Statement of Changes in Financial Position. Most of the tax, moral-hazard, and hidden-information theories that predict financing choices imply that the Modigliani-Miller irrelevance proposition does not hold. That means that the financing choice may depend on the intended use of funds. There is no practical way to measure the nature of the incremental investment decisions made by the firms each year. In order to control for the some of the simultaneity between investment and financing I restrict analysis to firms that increased their total capitalization, thus holding constant the direction of change in the firm's capital stock.

Firms were retained only if complete data were available for the dependent and explanatory variables.[16] Firms that issued publicly were identified by matching the COMPUSTAT sample to the Security and Exchange Commission's Registered Offering Statistics tape, which has records for every registered public offering since 1977.[17] The sample runs from 1977–86. The full sample has 14,398 observations, of which 832 are public stock issues, 631 are public debt issues, 1,720 are coded as private debt, and the remaining 11,215 are coded as private equity (retained earnings).

3.4.3 Explanatory Variables

The explanatory variables were selected from COMPUSTAT as those measures *a priori* expected to best capture the hypotheses discussed in Section 3.1. Most of these variables have found support as financing determinants in other empirical papers. I did not want to contaminate the statistical inference process by pretesting and selecting among possible factors, so all variables were retained in the analysis even if they have insignificant or puzzling coefficients.

To avoid simultaneity, all explanatory variables are measured for the year prior to the financing decision. The variables are described below. Detailed definitions can be found in the appendix to MacKie-Mason (1990). All of the accounting variables that measure levels have been divided by net sales to control for scale effects.

Flotation Costs

We saw in Section 3.2 that retained earnings are the dominant source of funds, followed by private and public debt, with public share issues the smallest source. It is possible that this pattern of financing is due to transactions costs. Issue costs are lowest for retained earnings, low for private debt, higher for public debt, and highest for new shares, with substantial underwriting and registration fees and costs for public issues of both debt and equity.

Borun and Malley (1986) found that underwriting and registration expenses averaged 4.1% of the issue value for new public utility stock. A much older study by the Securities and Exchange Commission (1957) considered costs for different issue sizes; the smallest issues had average flotation costs over 20%, falling to 5.4% for large issues. Flotation costs for debt are generally much lower than for new shares. Blackwell and Kidwell (1988) report average costs of 0.8% for private debt placements and 1.2% for public placements. The SEC study also found that debt issue costs decrease with issue size.

There is no reason, however, to think that flotation costs explain the variation in sources of funds across time, industries, and firms. The analysis below is intended to identify determinants that distinguish between the financing choices made by particular firms. The question asked is whether, *ceteris paribus* (including flotation costs), there are any economic conditions that influence firms' choices over sources of funds.[18]

Hidden-Information Indicators

The hidden-information theories predict that firms will prefer certain types of providers, regardless of the type of security. Since I must rely on publicly available data I cannot hope to measure the extent or nature of any informational advantages possessed by firms at particular times. This may not be a serious problem, however: the investors who decide how large a lemons premium to require do not also possess the firm's private information. What investors can do is use public information to forecast the magnitude and severity of informational asymmetries. I selected several variables as possible indicators of the likely severity of hidden information.

The models of Bhattacharya (1979), John and Williams (1985), and Miller and Rock (1985) suggest that dividend payments function as a signal when managers have private information. If dividends are an effective signal of firm prospects, then investors in non-dividend-paying firms are likely to have less information about what the managers know, all else equal. We should expect non-dividend-paying firms to avoid public market financing. On the other hand, the double taxation of dividends gives firms an incentive to reduce dividends and use retained earnings as a source of equity finance, rather than issue new shares (Auerbach 1983, 1985). Thus we might expect a dividend-paying firm to reduce dividends and finance using internal funds (or to use debt rather than new shares). However, it is well known that firms are very reluctant to cut dividends, suggesting that the signaling value of dividends outweighs the tax savings from financing out of dividends.[19]

A second indicator of potential hidden-information costs is the forecast variance of firm earnings. It has been well established in the accounting literature that earnings follow a random walk (Healy and Palepu 1986; Watts and Zimmerman 1986, chap. 6). Thus, the standard deviation of the first-difference in accounting earnings is proportional to the forecast variance of earnings. If this variance, which I call VEARNA, is large, then investors have relatively little ability to forecast future earnings based on public information. In such a case

I expect that there is a high likelihood that managers have advantageous hidden information and that the correspondingly large lemons premium required by public investors will discourage publicly marketed financing.

Another indicator is a change in the firm's stock price. A number of studies have found that firms tend to issue more new shares when their stock price is high (Taggart 1977; Marsh 1982; MacKie-Mason 1990). If firms were aiming for target debt/equity ratios, then a rise in stock prices should instead lead to more debt usage to restore the ratio. One plausible explanation for market timing has been suggested by Bagnoli and Khanna (1987). They incorporate both real costs of leverage and the Myers and Majluf (1984) hidden-information problem in a financing model. A rising market indicates that investors have become convinced of a favorable improvement in the firm's prospects, and thus are more likely to believe that the firm seeks financing for good projects rather than bad. That is, the market seems to have recently decided that this firm's investments are *not* lemons. To measure a market-timing effect I include the change in the firm's stock price over the previous year.

As another explanatory factor I include a dummy variable for industries that were subjected to economic rate regulation during much of the sample period: namely, trucking, trains, airlines, and telephones. Regulators are hypothesized to play the role of an information collector and validator for public investors, thus ensuring that any substantially bad news is made public. Further, regulation might serve to dampen the effects of good and bad surprises by attempting to stabilize economic returns.[20]

Tax-loss carryforwards may indicate the possibility that any hidden information could be very costly to investors. To see this it is necessary to know something about loss carryforwards. First, a firm is allowed to carry any tax losses back against three previous years of income to obtain an immediate refund. If the loss is carried forward, it is credited against future income without any accumulation of interest. Thus firms almost always carry losses back in order to obtain an immediate tax savings rather than the discounted value of future savings. If a firm has carryforwards it has usually been a poor performer for several years. Further, Auerbach and Poterba (1986) have shown that firms with tax losses tend to persist in that state, further indicating a poor performer. Once a firm is identified by investors as a poor performer, any hidden information that managers might have is likely to have a relatively large impact on the value of new security issues, and thus the required lemons premium will be higher.

A final factor that I expect to influence the firm's preferences over types of providers is the firm's R&D intensity. When a firm is doing a lot of R&D we might expect many instances of managers having important private information about changes in the firm's prospects. Thus, high R&D firms should avoid external financing. The predicted effects of these explanatory variables are summarized in table 3.7.

Table 3.7   Predicted Effects of Explanatory Variables

Potential Determinants	Effect on Private	Effect on Debt
Paying dividends	−	0
Forecast variance (VEARNA)	+	0
Tax-loss carryforwards	+	−
Stock price change	−	0
Regulated	−	0
R&D	+	−
Advertising	0	−
Fraction plant	0	+
Net assets	0	+
Earnings volatility (VEARNB)	0	−
Investment tax credits (ITC)	0	+
ITC/ZPROB	0	−
1/ZPROB	0	−
Debt/assets − average	0	−
Debt/assets	0	+
Cash deficit	0	−

Note: Signs indicate predicted effect on probability of choosing private relative to public sources (col. 1) or debt relative to equity. Zeros indicate no predicted effect.

Optimal Leverage Determinants

As discussed in Section 3.1, the predicted determinants of a firm's optimal leverage ratio are the benefits and costs associated with different contingent claims on cash flow. Three effects have received the most attention: (1) the tax costs from interest deductions crowding out other tax shields; (2) the real wealth costs of bankruptcy (made more likely by higher debt levels); and (3) the costs of inefficient investment decisions resulting from the senior fixed claims of outstanding debt on incremental investment returns. I shall describe several variables used to capture these effects, in reverse order.

Outstanding debt claims create a wedge between the returns to new investment and the firm's shareholders. The more that a firm's value depends on future investment opportunities, rather than on already committed investments, the more costly a debt issue is likely to be. Thus, firms with relatively low implicit collateral in the form of tangible assets are expected to use less debt.

I use several measures of debt capacity. The fraction of plant and equipment in total assets is intended to measure the availability of tangible collateral. Since I am looking at incremental financing (rather than the firm's choice of total debt level), I also expect the firm's size as measured by net assets to matter, since a single new debt issue might be more easily absorbed by a large firm. Bradley, Jarrell and Kim (1984) and Long and Malitz (1985) have suggested that a firm's advertising expenditures and research and development are indicators of intangible assets and thus predict less reliance on debt.[21]

The second type of optimal leverage determinants are the real costs of financial distress. If periods of financial distress or bankruptcy impose costs on shareholder wealth, then new debt—by increasing the likelihood of distress—bears an expected distress cost relative to equity financing. I expect that the increase in bankruptcy likelihood from a new debt issue is larger for a firm already facing a substantial probability of distress than for a healthy firm.[22]

I introduce two variables that measure the likelihood of a firm becoming financially distressed. The first is $1/ZPROB$, which is Altman's (1968) predictor for classifying firms likely to enter bankruptcy.[23] This $ZPROB$ is a weighted average of several balance sheet ratios. The greater is $1/ZPROB$, the greater is the expectation that the firm will enter a state of financial distress. In addition, I have constructed a second variance measure of the firm's operating risk: $VEARNB$. This measure is the standard deviation of percentage changes in earnings. Recall that $VEARNA$ was described above as an indicator of high forecast variance, and thus of potential hidden-information costs. In $VEARNB$ changes are weighted more heavily in years following low earnings (the denominator in the percentage change is close to zero), which should make it a better indicator of bankruptcy likelihood than $VEARNA$. However, both measures are imperfect and we should be cautious in interpreting them as measuring different effects.

The third leverage cost is tax shield crowding out. The higher are a firm's nondebt tax shields, the higher is the expected after-tax interest rate it must pay since there is a greater chance that the firm will be in a zero-tax status. Thus the firm's supply curve of bonds will slope upward.[24] Thus a firm with high nondebt tax shields will prefer to use less debt and more internal funds (retained earnings) or new share issues. However, a firm likely to be tax exhausted is not likely to have high retained earnings for investment. Thus a tax shield effect should primarily distinguish between debt and new shares. Two tax shields I measure are the firm's tax-loss carryforwards (which can offset future tax liabilities) and investment tax credits.[25] Advertising and R&D play the role of tax shields, since they can be thought of as investments that are immediately expensed for tax purposes.

Most studies of debt ratios have failed to find tax shield effects, or have obtained the wrong sign.[26] MacKie-Mason (1990) hypothesized that the investment tax credit (ITC) tax shield might be confounded with ITC acting as a proxy for new physical assets. The moral-hazard theories discussed above predict that firms with physical assets have implicit collateral and are more likely to issue debt. These contradictory effects were successfully distinguished by entering ITC alone, and also interacted with a measure of financial distress. The tax shield effect is more important for firms closer to financial distress since the firm is more likely to be tax exhausted.[27]

Other Variables

I have also included cash flow and past leverage ratio variables in the analysis. A firm with low cash flow is more likely to need external sources of funds. I am using lagged variables to avoid simultaneity, so cash flow will be a good determinant of constraints only if it is a good predictor of the next year's flows. Following Auerbach (1985), I construct a cash deficit variable that is the difference between cash flow and "committed" expenditures (long-run average dividends and the cash necessary to pay for capital expenditures while maintaining the firm's long-run debt-to-assets ratio).

A conflicting prediction on the effect of cash flows is provided by Jensen (1986). If it is costly to monitor managers to ensure that they do not waste uncommitted cash on perquisites and self-interested investments and expenditures, then value might be increased if firms with large free cash flows issue debt in order to increase future cash commitments. Thus, it is not clear if we should see firms with cash surpluses financing internally or externally. When we look at the choice between debt and new shares, however, Jensen's theory predicts a preference for debt to absorb cash flows.

One important reason to study the firm's incremental sources of funds is to avoid the assumption present in most capital structure research that firms have optimal debt ratio targets.[28] Of course, if firms *do* have debt ratio targets, then the effects of the other explanatory variables are conditional on whether the firm is above or below its target debt ratio. I include the lagged debt-to-assets ratio, and the difference between the lagged debt ratio and the long-run (10-year) average debt ratio. If the firm has a stable target ratio, then the latter measure should indicate, on average, which side of the hill needs to be climbed. However, a firm that prefers a high debt ratio will have a high lagged ratio, *ceteris paribus,* and will be more likely to rely heavily on debt for new funding.

Summary

The expected effects of the explanatory variables on debt/equity and private/public choices are summarized in table 3.7. At least to the first order most of the variables are expected to be relevant for one choice dimension but not the other. There are exceptions, such as R&D and *VEARNA*. But there are enough distinctions that it should be possible to obtain clear evidence on whether firms care about the provider of funds separately from the type of financing.

3.5   Econometric Results

The estimation results are presented in tables 3.8 and 3.9 below. The focus of this paper is on the distinction between types of providers (private *vs.* public) so I have presented the top branch (private/public choice) shown in choice tree 1 (see fig. 3.8) in table 3.8, and the two lower branch private/public choices from choice tree 2 in table 3.9. I also include the public debt/equity branch from choice tree 1 in table 3.8 to indicate the ability of the hypothesized debt/equity determinants to explain some debt/equity choices. The other branches of the two models are not directly relevant to the topic of the paper and thus are omitted for clarity of presentation.[29] For private/public choices a positive coefficient indicates a greater probability of private financing; for the public debt/equity branch a positive coefficient indicates a greater probability of debt.

3.5.1   Private or Public Sources?

I first consider the results from dividing the entire sample into private or public, shown in the second pair of columns in table 3.8. Most of the indica-

Table 3.8   Nested Logit Analysis of Financing Choices (Choice Tree 1)

Variable	Public Debt/Equity (Debt = 1, Equity = 0)		Private vs. Public (Private = 1, Public = 0)	
	Coefficient	t-statistic	Coefficient	t-statistic
Constant	− .961	− 1.39	5.58	19.5
Paying dividends	.472	1.75	− .672	− 7.13
VEARNA	− 5.74	− 2.51	1.45	1.89
Tax-loss carryforward	− 3.04	− 1.71	.760	3.41
Price change	− 1.13	− 6.40	− .358	− 7.74
Regulated	− 1.04	− 1.69	− .639	− 2.39
R&D	− 4.41	− .988	− 8.62	− 6.68
Advertising	6.54	2.27	− 3.36	− 2.96
Fraction plant	.0625	.153	− .508	− 2.99
Net assets	.0124	.905	− .101	− 5.36
VEARNB	− .0974	− 2.03	− .00174	− .887
ITC	54.2	1.85	− 5.54	− 1.02
ITC/ZPROB	− 69.7	− 1.92	− 1.70	− .410
1/ZPROB	1.45	2.74	.0810	1.47
Debt/assets − average	− 1.10	− 1.36	2.19	6.47
Debt/assets	− .964	− 1.32	− 4.44	− 16.7
Cash deficit	− 2.49	− 1.66	.0696	.227
Inclusive	. . .	. . .	.0626	1.53
Observations	1463		14398	
Mean of dependent variable	.431		.898	
Log likelihood	− 720.9		− 4165.0	
Lerman's R^2	.289		.583	
Lerman's $\bar{R}^2$	.249		.578	
McFadden's R^2	.279		.120	

Note: The lower branch choice between private debt and equity is not reported for clarity. These results are available from the author. Each branch was estimated with 10-year dummies and 15 industry dummies. The t-statistics are asymptotic.

tors of hidden-information problems have the predicted sign. Firms that were not paying dividends, have volatile earnings (high *VEARNA*) or tax-loss carryforwards, experienced a stock price decline, or were not publicly regulated were more likely to use private sources of funds.

Firms are reluctant to cut dividends, thus paying dividends is a signal that the firm expects to have reliable cash flows. Firms that are unable to signal or choose not to signal expected cash flows through dividends will be subject to a higher "lemons" premium on their public securities and thus prefer to avoid public issues. The same effect is indicated by the positive sign on *VEARNA*: if a firm has volatile earnings, outsiders are more uncertain about future prospects and are less willing to buy public security issues, so such firms prefer to finance privately. On the other hand, hidden-information problems are likely to be less severe for publicly regulated firms (trucks, trains, planes, and telephones) because of public disclosure and some degree of control over rates of return.[30]

Tax-loss carryforwards suggest poor performance by the firm. Loss carryforwards do not appear to be a tax shield effect here, since neither ITC variable is significant. What a loss carryforward does indicate is persistent performance problems since the firm has the opportunity to carry losses back against three previous years of income to get an immediate refund. Further, tax loss firms on average tend to continue as poor performers (Auerbach and Poterba 1986). Such firms are reluctant to seek public financing because they will be subject to high lemons premia.

Firms are much more likely to raise money in public markets if their stock price has risen. A price rise indicates that investors have become convinced that the firm's projects are good ones. Thus the market is more likely to view a new issue as financing needed for good investments rather than bad. Since the firm has been sorted into a "good" category, it will have to pay a smaller lemons premium.

The negative coefficient on R&D is surprising since substantial research was expected to indicate potential hidden information problems. However, the effect of advertising may be consistent with the hidden information story: firms that do lots of advertising tend to be in mature, less innovative industries such as food products or retail. If such firms provide fewer opportunities for unfavorable surprises to investors, then they may be able to obtain public funds without substantial hidden information premiums. Likewise, the net assets and fraction plant coefficients may be indicators of mature, more transparent firms. Large firms are followed much more closely by investment researchers and analysts, so hidden-information costs should be lower.

Most of the variables predicted to affect the choice of *security type* rather than provider type have statistically insignificant coefficients in the private/public choice branch. The likelihood of financial distress as measured by *VEARNB* AND 1/*ZPROB* has small and insignificant effects. The cash flow variable predicted by Jensen's free cash flow hypothesis is near zero and insignificant. The ITC tax shield has no effect. The exceptions are the debt/asset ratios for which I have no explanation. Thus, the predicted distinctions between preferences over type of funds and type of provider appear to be strongly supported.

One possible problem with the model underlying choice tree 1 is that the private funds category combines two very different types of funds—private debt and retained earnings—that are also obtained from rather different types of providers. Although neither source is publicly marketed, which distinguishes them from the other two sources, retained earnings are obtained internally by management decision, while private debt needs the cooperation of external lenders. Choice tree 2 provides a different view (fig. 3.8 and table 3.9). On the lower branches I control for funding type (debt or equity), and examine the private/public choice just between funds of the same type. That is, given equity, when does the firm prefer private (retained earnings) to a new issue, and similarly for debt?

The results presented in table 3.9 corroborate the discussion above, indicating the robustness of the hypotheses. Of all the variables predicted to be the primary determinants of the private/public choice, only *VEARNA* in the equity branch reverses sign, and it is statistically insignificant. For equity, paying dividends, not having tax losses, a stock price rise, and being regulated continue to predict a greater probability of publicly marketed financing. For debt, paying dividends and low earnings forecast variance are still significant; the other effects have the predicted sign but are statistically insignificant (notice, however, that the sample size is much smaller for the debt branch). Also significant for debt are net assets, advertising, and fraction plant, all of which have plausible hidden-information interpretations given above, although the predictions were not as clear *ex ante*.

Tables 3.8 and 3.9 show that a large number of variables help to explain public/private choices in the direction predicted by hidden-information theory. Many of these variables are not plausibly related to preferences between debt and equity, adding support to the hypothesis that firms care independently about who provides the funds. This proposition receives strong support from table 3.9, which reports the analysis of private/public choices conditional on type of funding.

One further piece of statistical evidence is available concerning whether firms care who provides their funds. The inclusive value in choice tree 1 (table 3.8) concerns dissimilarities between alternative providers. Letting α be that coefficient, it can be shown that $1 - \alpha^2 = \text{corr}(V_{m,\text{debt}}, V_{m,\text{equity}})$, that is, the correlation between the values of funds sources that is peculiar to who provides the funds, rather than the type of funds. Thus, if $\alpha = 1$, there is no characteristic of the firm's unobservable preferences that distinguishes public from private sources of funds. The estimated α in this model is more than 25

Table 3.9   Nested Logit Analysis of Financing Choices (Choice Tree 2)

	Private/Public Debt (Private = 1, Public = 0)		Private/Public Equity (Private = 1, Public = 0)	
Variable	Coefficient	t-statistic	Coefficient	t-statistic
Constant	5.13	8.24	5.81	15.6
Paying dividends	−1.09	−4.80	−.441	−4.02
VEARNA	6.37	3.10	−1.32	−1.60
Tax loss CF	.630	1.13	.871	2.20
Price change	−.0462	−.627	−.495	−8.69
Regulated	−.0301	−.0498	−1.14	−3.35
R&D	−12.2	−3.39	−8.62	−5.84
Advertising	−7.34	−2.96	−1.65	−1.05
Fraction plant	−1.55	−4.19	−.0242	−.108
Net assets	−1.10	−9.69	−.0438	−3.51
VEARNB	.0449	1.02	−.00119	−.595
ITC	5.49	.247	−5.20	−.669
ITC/ZPROB	−20.2	−.917	1.40	.235
1/ZPROB	.127	.595	.0276	.442
Debt/asset—average	.782	1.02	1.70	4.10
Debt/assets	−1.48	−2.49	−4.89	−14.8
Cash deficit	4.61	3.82	−.220	−.683
Observations	2356		12042	
Mean of dependent variable	.732		.931	
Log likelihood	−913.0		−2624.2	
Lerman's R^2	.441		.686	
Lerman's $\bar{R}^2$	.416		.681	
McFadden's R^2	.333		.133	

Note: The top branch choice between debt and equity is not reported for clarity. Those results are available from the author. Each branch was estimated with 10-year dummies and 15 industry dummies. The t-statistics are asymptotic.

standard deviations away from one, so we reject the hypothesis of no difference between types of providers with a high level of confidence. The conclusion is that firms do not view private and public sources as interchangeable.

3.5.2   Public Bonds or New Shares?

The first pair of columns in table 3.8 report the estimated effects of the
explanatory variables on firm choices between issuing bonds or new shares,
conditional on going public. This choice is the subject of MacKie-Mason
(1990) and a similar set of results are discussed in detail in that paper. I will
summarize only the main results here.

The evidence supports the importance of tax shield crowding out. Several
variables indicate the likelihood of a firm being tax exhausted: tax-loss carryforwards, *ITC/ZPROB,* and *VEARNB.* Each of these has a significant coefficient indicating that firms likely to be tax exhausted are less likely to issue

debt. *VEARNA*, which was intended to primarily measure hidden-information problems, is also significant, with a sign consistent with its alternative interpretation as another indicator of the likelihood of tax exhaustion.

Firms with cash deficits are more likely to issue equity, again consistent with the firm's desire to avoid committed interest payments that might necessitate reducing the dividend. Viewed another way, firms with surplus cash are more likely to issue debt, which Jensen (1986) predicted as the appropriate way to control the moral-hazard problems from letting the managers have discretionary control over uncommitted cash flows.

Entered by itself, ITC is consistent with the theory that fixed physical assets can secure debt issues, but the plant and equipment fraction of assets and total assets both have no effect on the firm's preference for debt, so the evidence in favor of this moral hazard hypothesis is weak.

3.5.3 Summary

Many estimated effects have been discussed in this section. To summarize, it is useful to again refer to the predictions shown in table 3.7. Most of the predictions have been supported by the data, some quite strongly and robustly. Several variables expected to affect choice of provider but with no obvious importance for type of security indeed had the predicted signs and were significant. The results were obtained both for the private/public distinction in the entire sample (table 3.8) and for the private/public choice conditional on debt or equity financing (table 3.9).

The models fit the data reasonably well, considering the underdeveloped state of structural theory in this area. Lerman's R^2 statistic (which has the usual "explained variation" descriptive content as the R^2 in a linear regression) ranges from 0.44 to 0.69 in the private/public choice models. McFadden's R^2 measures the incremental contribution by the explanatory variables beyond a naive model that simply predicts the mean. This statistic is low but still substantial for a discrete-choice model. So much of the variation in the data is explained by the dominant use of retained earnings (93% of all equity choices) that there is not much left to explain after the naive model. Naturally much of the residual will not be explained by the descriptive proxy variables selected for the analysis. It is notable, however, that in the debt-only branch of choice tree 2 (table 3.9), in which the split between private and public is more balanced (73% private), the McFadden R^2 is 0.33, which is quite large for a discrete-choice model.

Thus, there still remains much to be learned about firm preferences for different sources of funds. But the evidence thus far is clear and strong that firms do care about who provides the funds, as distinct from the type of security.

3.6   Conclusion

This paper has presented data on the incremental financing behavior of U.S. nonfinancial corporations since 1945. The main conclusion is simple and is reinforced with evidence throughout the paper: firms are concerned with who provides their financing, not just with the debt/equity distinction. Debt is more than just debt; equity is more than just equity.

Most optimal leverage theories in the literature have concerned solely the debt/equity distinction. Stated simply, firms are believed to balance the tax advantages, real bankruptcy cost disadvantages, and investment incentive inefficiencies of debt. More recently, the possibility that information asymmetries might affect financing decisions has received substantial attention. Hidden-information models explicitly direct our attention to distinctions other than the debt/equity choice. In particular, it becomes crucial to know who the parties providing the funds are and what information is available to them.

This paper has provided substantial evidence that hidden-information problems are important. In the aggregate there are large and persistent differences in the patterns of internal and external financing. Different industries—with different information characteristics—exhibit substantial variations in reliance on internal funds both over time and across industries. When the incremental financing decisions of individual firms were analyzed, we saw significant and coherent distinctions between the providers of funds.

Internal financing is different from external. Private financing is different from public. These facts should encourage more research into the nature of financial choices by firms and into the implications of hierarchical financing preferences and credit market constraints on investment and other firm activities.

Appendix

Table 3A.1   Industry Definitions

Code	SIC Coverage	Description
100	100–200	Agriculture
1000	1000–1200, 1400	Metal Mining, Coal, Miscellaneous Mining
1300	1300	Oil & Gas Mining
1500	1500–1700	Construction
2000	2000–2100	Food & Tobacco
2200	2200–2700	Textile Mills, Lumber, Furniture, Paper, Printing
2800	2800	Chemical & Allied
2900	2900	Petroleum Refining
3000	3000–3300	Rubber, Plastic, Leather, Stone, Clay, Glass, Primary Metal
3400	3400	Fabricated Metal
3500	3500	Machinery excluding Electrical
3600	3600	Electronics, Electrical Machinery
3700	3700	Transport Equipment
		Measuring Instruments, Photo, Watches,

(continued)

Table 3A.1   (continued)

Code	SIC Coverage	Description
3800	3800–3900	Miscellaneous Manufacturing
4000	4000–4400, 4600–4700	Ground, Water, & Miscellaneous Transport
4500	4500	Airlines
4800	4800	Communications
5000	5000–5100	Wholesale Trade
5200	5200–5900	Retail Trade
7000	7000–8999	Hotels, Entertainment, & Services

Notes

1. See, *e.g.*, Auerbach (1985), Bartholdy, Fisher and Mintz (1989), Bradley, Jarrell and Kim (1984), Long and Malitz (1985), Ang and Peterson (1986), and Williamson (1981).

2. In recent years a number of good overviews of capital structure theory have appeared. See, *e.g.*, Myers (1984), Auerbach (1985), Taggart (1985). I shall not provide a redundant development of the standard models.

3. Myers (1984) described his view as an eclectic, "modified pecking order theory," but did not integrate the elements into a careful model.

4. The literature on managerial capitalism (*e.g.*, Berle and Means 1932, Lieben-stein 1966) suggests that managers act at least in part in their own interest, rather than in the interests of current shareholders. One effect of managerial opportunism on financing is examined in my discussion on the role of cash flow, in Sec. 3.4.

5. The discussion of aggregate sources of funds updates some of Raymond Goldsmith's flow-of-funds studies done for the National Bureau of Economic Research (Goldsmith 1956; Goldsmith, Lipsey, and Mendelson 1963).

6. The last cycle is shown to end in 1987 because more recent data were not available; the economy was still expanding at least into the middle of 1990.

7. See Shoven (1986) for a detailed look at repurchasing behavior.

8. Further, the averages he reports appear to be in error, although the discrepancy might be the result of revisions of the series by the Federal Reserve.

9. The temporary disappearance of a firm from an industry aggregate may have a substantial impact on levels of the variables, but will only affect the relative shares that are reported here inasmuch as that firm deviates substantially from the industry mean.

10. Earlier data were not collected because the other information needed for the econometric analysis is unavailable before 1977.

11. This sample misses the huge boom in initial public offerings during those years, because newly public firms are usually too small to be immediately covered by COMPUSTAT.

12. We must be careful about drawing inferences from relative financing shares. There is an important distinction between extent to which a firm relies on a particular source and the exposure of that firm to particular markets. Even a firm relying predominantly on internal sources may face the external market quite often. For example, firms in this industry on average provided 96.6% of their funds internally (table 3.4). However, these companies also obtained large amounts of debt financing: debt sources were equivalent to 30% of total sources during 1983–86 (table 3.5). The large influx of debt was offset by equally large share repurchases, with net new shares at −34%

during the period. Thus the industry provided 104% of total funds through internally generated cash, but the firms were heavily involved in external securities transactions as well. We cannot necessarily take high reliance on internal funds as measured above to be support for Donaldson's hypothesis that internal financing "avoids the glare of publicity and shareholder attention which accompanies the decisions and actions of management if externally financed" (1961, 54). In fact the financial decisions of petroleum firms were among the most publicized and scrutinized during recent years.

13. This structure avoids the problem of independence of irrelevant alternatives (IIA) that characterizes a better-known model, the multinomial logit. If IIA *were* imposed it would mean, for example, that the probability of choosing public equity over public debt would be unaffected by whether or not it was possible to use retained earnings. That is, internal equity would substitute identically for either public equity or public debt. The model I use avoids this implausibly extreme independence.

14. A more general model is the multinomial probit, which allows for any pattern of correlations among the choices. I attempted to estimate a multinomial probit model, but found it computationally infeasible for this sample. Each evaluation of the likelihood function requires the calculation of a triple integral. With about 14,000 observations and 30 iterations this procedure involved over 500,000 triple integrations for each estimation run. A further complication is that some of the covariances appeared to be poorly identified, possibly because about 80% of the choices were of one source (retained earnings).

15. For computational feasibility I used the sequential estimator, and calculated standard errors corrected for the two-stage method.

16. Because of the small size of the subsample that issued publicly, I made an effort to fill in as much missing COMPUSTAT data as possible for these observations by a hand search through Moody's Manuals and the firms' 10-K reports to the SEC. Public utilities were dropped because flow-of-funds data are not available for them on COMPUSTAT.

17. The SEC tape contains records for registrations beginning with 1974. However, the tape layout was changed in 1977 at which time the SEC tried to recode the old observations according to the new format. I discovered that the recoding was done incorrectly, and after discussions with programmers at the SEC I determined that it was not possible to recover any correct registration data for 1974–76.

18. One factor that might measure variation in flotation costs across firms and time is the size of the financing, since unit issue costs are known to vary with issue size. However, issue size is clearly endogenous, both because a firm may be able to make its public issues less frequently to reduce flotation costs and because the investment and the financing decisions will not be independent if asymmetric information is important. To avoid simultaneity bias I do not include issue size in my list of reduced form explanatory variables.

19. McDonald and Soderstrom (1988) study this question.

20. Electric utilities are another obvious industry in which to look for regulation effects because of the close regulatory oversight and the heavy and regular new financing undertaken. Unfortunately, Standard and Poor's does not provide the flow-of-funds data that I need for electric utilities in the COMPUSTAT data base.

21. Note that R&D is expected to indicate both future discretionary opportunities and the potential for hidden-information problems. As we shall see below, advertising and R&D can also be viewed as tax shields.

22. This would be the case in a simple model in which earnings changes are distributed normally and for firms with less than a 50% chance of bankruptcy. The critical point in the distribution, below which the firm is distressed, will be closer to the mean for weaker firms (higher probability) and thus a given shift in that critical point from an increased debt burden will add a greater portion of the distribution than for a firm

with only a small-tail probability of bankruptcy. Above a 50% chance of bankruptcy the effect becomes ambiguous in this simple model, but such instances are unlikely to be quantitatively important in my sample.

23. This measure has been effectively used in MacKie-Mason (1990), Bartholdy, Fisher and Mintz (1989), and Whited (1988).

24. The same effect would follow from a higher corporate tax rate, but there is no variation in the corporate tax rates during the sample period to identify a rate effect.

25. Auerbach and Poterba (1986) have noted that book tax-loss carryforwards may substantially mismeasure the actual loss carryforwards available to the firm for tax purposes. This problem with the data was discussed in MacKie-Mason (1990). Also in that paper, a short corrected time series constructed by Auerbach and Poterba was tested with no discernible effect on the results of estimating the choice between public debt and equity issues.

26. For example, Titman and Wessels (1988), Ang and Peterson (1986), Long and Malitz (1985), Bradley, Jarrell and Kim (1984), Marsh (1982), and Williamson (1981).

27. See the example above in n. 22 and the related text discussion.

28. This point is discussed in MacKie-Mason (1990).

29. Coefficients were also estimated for each year and 15 industry dummies to control for time and fixed industry effects; these results and the omitted branch results are available from the author.

30. There was substantial deregulation for most of these firms during the sample period, but none of these industries have been completely deregulated.

References

Altman, E. I. 1968. Financial ratios, discriminant analysis, and the prediction of corporate bankruptcy, *Journal of Finance* 23:589–609.

Ang, J. S., and D. R. Peterson. 1986. Optimal debt versus debt capacity: A disequilibrium model of corporate debt behavior. In *Research in finance*, vol. 6, ed. A. W. Chen. Greenwich, Conn.: JAI.

Auerbach, A. J. 1983. Stockholder tax rates and firm attributes. *Journal of Public Economics* 21:107–27.

———. 1985. Real determinants of corporate leverage. In *Corporate capital structures in the United States,* ed. B. M. Friedman. Chicago: University of Chicago Press.

Auerbach, A. J., and J. M. Poterba. 1986. "Tax loss carryforwards and corporate tax incentives. Working paper. Massachusetts Institute of Technology, Cambridge, Mass. Department of Economics.

Bagnoli, M., and N. Khanna. 1987. Equilibrium with debt and equity financing of new projects: Why more equity financing occurs when stock prices are high. Working paper. University of Michigan, Department of Economics.

Bartholdy, J., G. Fisher, and J. Mintz. 1989. Some theory of taxation and financial policy with application to Canadian corporate data. Working paper. Queen's University.

Berle, A., and G. Means. 1932. *The modern corporation and private property.* New York: Macmillan.

Bhattacharya, S. 1979. Imperfect information, dividend policy, and the "bird in the hand" fallacy. *Bell Journal of Economics* 10:225–35.

Blackwell, D., and D. Kidwell. 1988. An investigation of cost differences between public sales and private placements of debt. *Journal of Financial Economics* 22:253–78.

Blundell, R., S. Bond, M. Devereux, F. Schiantarelli. 1988. Does Q matter for investment? Institute for Fiscal Studies Discussion Paper no. 87/12a. London.

Borun, V., and S. Malley. 1986. Total flotation costs for electric company equity issues. *Public Utilities Fortnightly* (February), pp. 33–39.

Bradley, M., G. A. Jarrell, and E. H. Kim. 1984. On the existence of an optimal capital structure: Theory and evidence. *Journal of Finance* 39:857–78.

DeAngelo, H., and R. W. Masulis. 1980. Optimal capital structure under corporate and personal taxation. *Journal of Financial Economics* 8:3–29.

Donaldson, G. 1961. *Corporate debt capacity: A study of corporate debt policy and the determination of corporate debt capacity.* Boston: Division of Research, Harvard Business School.

Fazzari, S., R. Hubbard, and B. Petersen. 1988. Financing constraints and corporate investment. *Brooking Papers on Economic Activity,* no. 1, pp. 141–95.

Friedman, B. 1980. Postwar changes in the american financial markets. In *The American economy in transition,* ed. M. Feldstein. Chicago: University of Chicago Press.

Goldsmith, R. 1956. *A study of saving in the United States.* Princeton, N.J.: Princeton University Press.

Goldsmith, R., R. Lipsey, and M. Mendelson. 1963. *Studies in the national balance sheet of the United States.* Princeton, N.J.: Princeton University Press.

Healy, P. M., and K. Palepu. 1986. Corporate financial decisions and future earnings performance: The case of initiating dividends. Typescript. Massachusetts Institute of Technology, Sloan School of Management.

Hoshi, T., A. Kashyap, and D. Scharfstein. 1988. Corporate structure, liquidity, and investment: Evidence from Japanese panel data. Sloan Working Paper no. 2071. Massachusetts Institute of Technology.

James, C. 1987. Some evidence on the uniqueness of bank loans. *Journal of Financial Economics* 19:217–35.

Jensen, M. C. 1986. Agency costs of free cash flow, corporate finance, and takeovers. *American Economic Review* 76: 323–29.

Jensen, M. C., and W. H. Meckling. 1976. Theory of the firm: Managerial behavior, agency costs and ownership structure. *Journal of Financial Economics* 3:305–60.

John, K., and J. Williams. 1985. Dividends, dilution, and taxes: Signalling equilibrium. *Journal of Finance* 40:1053–70.

Liebenstein, H. 1966. Allocative efficiency vs. X-efficiency. *American Economic Review* 56 (June): 392–412.

Long, M. S., and I. B. Malitz. 1985. Investment patterns and financial leverage. In *Corporate capital structures in the United States,* ed. B. M. Friedman. Chicago: University of Chicago Press.

McDonald, R., and N. Soderstrom. 1988. Dividend and share changes: Is there a financing hierarchy? Working paper. Northwestern University, Kellogg School of Management.

McFadden, D. 1981. Econometric models of probabilistic choice. In *Structural analysis of discrete data with econometric applications,* ed. C. F. Manski and D. McFadden. Cambridge, Mass.: MIT Press.

MacKie-Mason, J. 1987. Long-term contracts and sequential economic decisions. University of Michigan working paper. Ann Arbor, Mich.

———. 1990. Do taxes affect corporate financing decisions? *Journal of Finance,* forthcoming.

Marsh, P. R. 1982. The choice between equity and debt: An empirical study. *Journal of Finance* 37:121–44.

Miller, M., and K. Rock. 1985. Dividend policy under asymmetric information. *Journal of Finance* 40:1031–51.

Miller, M. H. 1977. Debt and taxes. *Journal of Finance* 32:261–75.

Miller, M. H., and F. Modigliani. 1966. Some estimates of the cost of capital to the electric utility industry, 1954–1957. *American Economic Review* 56:333–91.

Modigliani, F., and M. H. Miller. 1958. The cost of capital, corporation finance, and the theory of investment. *American Economic Review* 48:261–97.

Myers, S. C. 1977. Determinants of corporate borrowing. *Journal of Financial Economics* 5:147–76.

———. 1984. The capital structure puzzle. *Journal of Finance* 39:572–92.

Myers, S. C., and N. S. Majluf. 1984. Corporate financing and investment decisions when firms have information that investors do not have. *Journal of Financial Economics* 13:187–221.

Securities and Exchange Commission. 1957. *Costs of flotation and directly placed corporate securities, 1951–1955*. Washington, D.C.: Government Printing Office.

Shoven, J. 1986. New developments in corporate finance and tax avoidance: Some evidence. NBER Working Paper no. 2091.

Stiglitz, J., and A. Weiss. 1981. Credit rationing in markets with imperfect information. *American Economic Review* 71:393–410.

Taggart, R. 1977. A model of corporate financing decisions. *Journal of Finance* 32:1467–84.

Taggart, R., Jr. 1985. Secular patterns in the financing of U.S. corporations. In *Corporate capital structures in the United States*, ed. B. Friedman. Chicago: University of Chicago Press.

Titman, S., and R. Wessels. 1988. The determinants of capital structure choice. *Journal of Finance* 43:1–18.

Watts, R. L., and J. L. Zimmerman. 1986. *Positive accounting theory.* Englewood Cliffs, NJ: Prentice-Hall.

Whited, Toni. 1988. Debt, liquidity constraints, and corporate investment: Evidence from panel data. Working paper. Princeton University.

Williamson, S. 1981. The moral hazard theory of corporate financial structure: An empirical test. Ph.D. diss., Massachusetts Institute of Technology, Sloan School of Management.

4 Bank Monitoring and Investment: Evidence from the Changing Structure of Japanese Corporate Banking Relationships

Takeo Hoshi, Anil Kashyap, and David Scharfstein

4.1 Introduction

Economists typically view banks as intermediaries that serve to channel funds from individual investors to firms with productive investment opportunities. This commonly held view, however, is difficult to reconcile with the assumption of frictionless capital markets: in frictionless markets, firms would raise capital directly from individual investors and avoid the costs of intermediation.[1]

This paper offers empirical evidence on the benefits of intermediation. Our explanation for the existence of financial intermediaries derives from the view that there may be important capital-market frictions created by information problems between firms and investors. We view banks and other financial intermediaries as institutions designed in part to circumvent these capital-market imperfections. Specifically, banks serve as corporate monitors who pay the costs of becoming informed about their client firms and who try to ensure that the managers of these firms take efficient actions.

This view of the role of banks is not new. Schumpeter (1939) argued informally along these lines, and Diamond (1984) has constructed a formal model

Takeo Hoshi is assistant professor of economics at the Graduate School of International Relations and Pacific Studies, University of California, San Diego. Anil Kashyap is an economist in the Division of Research and Statistics at the Board of Governors of the Federal Reserve System. David Scharfstein is associate professor of finance at the Massachusetts Institute of Technology, Sloan School of Management.

The authors thank Glenn Hubbard for useful conversations on numerous occasions. They are also grateful to Yasushi Hamao, Takatoshi Ito, Jim Kahn, John McMillan, Jim Poterba, and conference participants for helpful comments and to Masako Niwa, William Kan, and Andrew Wiedlin for valuable research assistance. The data were generously provided by the Nikkei Data Bank Bureau. The views expressed in this paper are those of the authors and do not necessarily reflect the opinions of the Board of Governors of the Federal Reserve or its staff.

that captures these and related ideas. Diamond shows that delegating the task of monitoring to a financial intermediary minimizes monitoring costs. The alternative—issuing securities like public debt and equity—may be inefficient either because monitoring costs are needlessly duplicated among individual security holders or because monitoring is a public good that no one has an incentive to provide. Of course, this raises a potentially troubling question: Who ensures that banks monitor the firms in which they invest? Diamond shows that bank diversification plays a key role in ensuring that banks indeed monitor their client firms. His is the first model that takes full account of monitoring costs and shows that financial intermediation can be the most efficient monitoring mechanism. Ramakrishnan and Thakor (1984) and Williamson (1986) make similar points.

Our goal in this paper is to analyze empirically the role of banks in monitoring firms when there are information problems in the capital market. The focus of our study is the Japanese economy where historically banks have played a much more important role in financing investment than in the United States.[2] However, in the past decade the importance of bank financing in Japan has declined dramatically. While bank borrowing comprised 84% of all external financing between 1971 and 1975, it was only 57% in the 1981–85 period. In large part, this resulted from considerable deregulation of Japanese capital markets—enabling firms to raise capital directly from financial markets in the form of bonds and other debt-linked instruments. The result has been a substantial disintermediation of the Japanese financial system.

These regulatory changes offer us an excellent opportunity to study the role of financial intermediation. Our research strategy is to examine the investment behavior of a panel of firms before and after deregulation. In the period before deregulation all of the firms in our sample had close ties to a bank or set of banks. After deregulation, some of these firms loosened their ties to banks and relied more heavily on direct capital-market financing. Another set maintained their close banking ties. Our goal is to see whether the investment behavior of firms that have maintained their bank relationships exhibit the features of a bank-monitored firm. Moreover, we wish to detect changes in the investment behavior of firms that have loosened their bank ties: Do they exhibit behavior that reflects the fact that they were monitored before but not after deregulation?

Of course the crucial step in this analysis is identifying investment behavior that distinguishes between firms that are monitored and those that are not. In this regard we build on our earlier work in Hoshi, Kashyap, and Scharfstein (1990), which also examined the relationship between liquidity and investment for firms with different degrees of bank affiliation. We argued in that paper that essentially all models that posit some sort of information problem in the capital market predict that liquidity should be positively related to investment. This prediction arises, for example, in Myers and Majluf (1984). In their model, managers are privately informed about the value of investment.

This means that equity will sometimes be underpriced. Managers will therefore be reluctant to issue equity to finance investment: indeed, they may turn down positive net present value investments that they would otherwise accept if they had the internal funds to finance the investment. This model generates the prediction that, all else equal, more liquid firms should invest more. One can derive similar predictions from models that assume different information asymmetries and moral-hazard problems.

Bank monitoring is one way of overcoming these information problems. If banks lend a large fraction of a firm's debt as well as own a portion of its equity (as they do in Japan), then they have strong incentives to become informed about the firm and its investment opportunities. It is also in their interest to ensure that managers make efficient business decisions. In this case, the theory would predict that there should be little relationship between investment and liquidity for bank-monitored firms. If firms need funds to finance investment they can go directly to their informed bank to raise the money. Provided the project is valuable, the bank should be willing to provide the capital.

To explore these ideas, we start with a sample of firms all of which had close bank ties before deregulation. Investment by these firms is not sensitive to their liquidity during the 1977–82 period. We identify 1983 as the first year in which the effects of deregulation were fully felt. By that time, there is a set of firms that have significantly reduced their bank borrowing and increased their direct capital-market financing. These firms exhibit a strong sensitivity of investment to cash flow in the later period. By contrast, the firms that maintained bank ties show no sensitivity of investment to cash flow in both periods—before and after deregulation.

These results complement our earlier work (Hoshi, Kashyap, and Scharfstein 1990), which compared the investment behavior of this sample of firms to the investment behavior of firms without close banking ties during the period 1977–82. In that paper we found that the investment of the latter set of firms was quite sensitive to liquidity whereas it was not so for firms with close bank ties. The most interesting aspect of this paper is that we explore the investment behavior of the *same set* of firms over different periods. In some respects, it is more compelling to establish that, *for the same firm,* liquidity is more important as it weakens its banking ties.

These results raise the natural question of why a firm would choose to weaken its bank ties and incur this cost. Obviously, the answer must be that there are compensating benefits from raising funds directly from the capital market or costs of maintaining bank ties. These costs and benefits, while potentially important, are poorly understood and difficult to quantify. The conclusion, Section 4.4 below, includes some conjectures about what these costs and benefits may be. The more limited goal of this paper is to establish the facts about what happened to investment behavior as a result of deregulation.

The remainder of the paper is organized as follows. The next section reviews the regulatory changes in Japan that have enabled firms to issue directly placed securities. We trace the changes in aggregate financing patterns between 1971 and 1985. We then present financing statistics for the firms in our panel. These results are consistent with the aggregate changes. Section 4.3 presents our main empirical evidence. In that section we also entertain other explanations for our findings. Finally, Section 4.4 contains concluding remarks. It also includes some speculative comments about the factors that might explain why some firms have shifted to direct financing and others have not.

4.2   Deregulation and Changes in Japanese Corporate Finance

Until recently bank debt was the predominant form of financing for Japanese firms. In large part this was due to regulations that made it difficult or even impossible to raise funds directly from securities markets. During the early 1980s a series of regulatory reforms were implemented that increased significantly the financing options of Japanese corporations. The result has been a dramatic transformation in the structure of Japanese corporate finance. This section reviews those regulatory reforms and presents aggregate-level and micro-level evidence on their impact on financing patterns.

The Japanese government's security-market regulations reduced both the supply and demand for corporate debt. First, on the supply side, the government required all domestically issued bonds to be fully secured against a firm's assets. It is widely believed that Japanese managers were reluctant to issue secured debt. The Nihon Keizai Shimbun-sha (1987) cites the administrative cost of establishing collateral as one of the most important reasons for the stagnant growth of domestic straight bond issues. There were no prohibitions against unsecured bank debt. According to Yoshihara (1987, p. 130), as of March 1981, less than 40% of all lending done by banks required collateral. These regulations therefore encourage bank financing.

A second supply-side regulation required firms to receive government permission to issue bonds in foreign markets. Unlike domestic bonds, these bonds could be unsecured. Nevertheless, foreign bonds were infrequently used because the government—for a complicated set of reasons—appears to have been reluctant to grant permission to issue these bonds.

Finally—and perhaps most important—there were interest-rate ceilings that reduced the demand for bonds. Holders of corporate bonds thus earned below-market yields. For example, Shimura (1978) reports that the difference between the subscribers' yield and the market yield of corporate bonds was as high as one percentage point in the late 1960s. While there were also interest-rate ceilings on bank debt, it is widely believed that banks were able to get around these restrictions by requiring firms to hold low-interest-bearing accounts at the bank (see, e.g., Aoki 1984, pp. 20–21).

The result, as one would expect, is that bank borrowing was the primary source of external funds for most firms. Nasu (1987) reports that from 1976 to 1980, 80% of manufacturing firms' external funds came through borrowing from financial institutions.

The move toward deregulation was initiated in the government bond market. Until 1977, there was essentially no secondary market for government bonds. Instead, the Ministry of Finance put pressure on the banks to hold these low-yielding bonds. During a time in which government debt was quite low, this was acceptable to the banks. High growth helped sustain such practices because the Bank of Japan could (and actually did) monetize the bonds without fear of inflationary consequences. But as the government deficit grew and growth slowed after the first oil shock, this policy became more costly to the banks. They began to put pressure on the government to loosen its interest-rate restrictions. The government finally agreed to do so, and by June 1978 the Ministry of Finance began selling bonds through public auctions. Relaxation of interest-rate ceilings in the corporate bond market soon followed as it became apparent that the demand for corporate bonds would have been destroyed by the liberalization of the government bond market. As evidence of this change, the mean difference between the subscribers' yield and the market yield in the 1980–88 period was -54 basis points, whereas it was 32 basis points between 1973 and 1979. Interest-rate ceilings still exist, but they are adjusted frequently in line with market conditions.[3] In addition, the interest rates on convertible bonds are not regulated (Shinkai 1988, p. 288).

The government's second major reform was the loosening of its restrictions on foreign bond issues. Following the passage of the Foreign Exchange Law Reform of 1980, firms were no longer required to have government permission before issuing bonds on overseas markets; instead they were only required to notify the government that they intended to make such an issue.[4] According to the Ministry of Finance, by 1983 Japanese firms raised almost half their capital in overseas securities markets.

A third important reform was the government's legalization of warrant bonds in June 1981. These bonds come with an option to buy shares at a specified price during a certain period. This option was initially nondetachable, but it became detachable after December 1985. The Ministry of Finance reports that by 1986 over 20% of all new funds were raised using warrant bonds.

Finally, in January 1983 the government phased in new regulations allowing firms to issue unsecured bonds. Before then, only Toyota Motors and Matsushita Electric were permitted to issue unsecured bonds in domestic securities markets. In January 1983, an additional nine firms were permitted to issue unsecured straight debt and 23 more firms were allowed unsecured convertible bonds. In several stages over the subsequent four years, these privileges were gradually expanded; by February 1987, 180 firms could issue unsecured straight bonds, and 330 firms could issue unsecured domestic convertible bonds.

Together these reforms facilitated a pronounced shift in the aggregate financing patterns away from (indirect) bank borrowing and toward (direct) bond financing. Table 4.1 reproduces Nasu's (1987) statistics on financing patterns since 1971. As the table shows, between 1981 and 1985, the aggregate percentage of external funds raised by bank borrowing was 57%, which was down from 80% in the preceding five-year period. In contrast, the percentage due to bond financing rose from 2% between 1976 and 1980 to 22% between 1981 and 1985. The percentage of external funds raised through equity issues also increased slightly from 12% between 1976 and 1980 to 16% between 1981 and 1985.

The remainder of this section examines whether these general patterns also hold for a particular set of manufacturing firms. The firms in question represent a subset of the Japanese manufacturing firms that have been continuously listed on the Tokyo Stock Exchange since 1965. Since the data are described at length in Hoshi, Kashyap and Scharfstein (1990), we omit an extended description of the data.[5] This particular subset comprises 121 nonfinancial firms that we previously classified as having a close affiliation to a single bank in the 1972–82 period. The question we ask is: Have these firms that already had well-established banking relationships followed the general movement away from bank borrowing? In the next section, we examine whether any such moves have affected the firms' investment behavior.

To address this first question, we supplemented the balance sheet data that we have previously used with detailed data on borrowing patterns. These data are available from the publication *Keiretsu no Kenkyu,* which is also one of the original sources underlying the identification of these firms as having a strong bank relationship from 1972 to 1982.[6] Our strategy in collecting the data was to pick two years that would permit a comparison of the borrowing patterns before and after the reforms discussed above. We chose 1977 as the early year for two reasons: it is well before any of the important regulatory changes and it is the first year for which we had the stock price data needed to

Table 4.1   Composition of External Funds Raised by Manufacturing Firms (%)

	1971–75	1976–80	1981–85
Securities:	11.6	14.3	38.2
Stocks	7.0	12.1	15.5
Bonds	4.6	2.2	22.7
Borrowings from financial institutions:	84.0	80.3	56.6
Notes discounted	13.7	27.5	− .6
Short-term borrowings	31.8	47.0	49.6
Long-term borrowings	38.5	5.8	7.6
Other borrowings	4.4	5.4	5.2

Note: The data are taken from table 3-10 in Nasu (1987, p. 85).

compute Tobin's q (which we need later in analyzing investment). We compare the corporate financing patterns in 1977 to those in 1986, the most recent year for which data are available.[7] While post-1986 data would be helpful, it is not necessary; by then many of the key regulatory changes that have enabled firms to reduce their dependence on bank financing were already in place.

In collecting the data we found that 12 of the 121 firms either did not have complete data in *Keiretsu no Kenkyu* or had switched largest lenders by 1986. These firms no longer satisfy our definition of a firm with a close bank relationship. For the remaining 109 firms, table 4.2 compares data on some key variables in 1977 and 1986.

The first observation is that for these firms the 10 years between 1977 and 1986 have been ones of steady growth. The real capital stock increased by 50% over this period. Judging from the recent data, the growth of the capital stock appears to be continuing: in 1977, the median value of Tobin's q was 1.32, while the median rate of investment (relative to the capital stock) was .07; in 1986, these numbers were 1.68 and .19, respectively.[8] Thus, the period we are analyzing is one in which there was considerable investment, and financing needs were likely to have been important.

The change in the debt-equity ratio during this period is perhaps the most striking piece of evidence from table 4.2; in 1977, the ratio was 1.26; by 1986 it had fallen to .37. These numbers primarily reflect the steep rise in the Japanese stock market. During this 10-year period the aggregate equity value of these firms rose by more than fourfold, an annual growth rate of over 15%. While equity values have soared, there has been a much smaller increase in debt financing; the median nominal market value of debt rose only 3%, amounting to a real decline of about 11%.

The aggregate shift away from bank borrowing toward bond financing that was mentioned earlier is also evident for these firms. Table 4.2 shows that the book value of bank borrowing has fallen in real terms, with the median value falling by 24% and the mean falling by 11%. In addition, long-term bank borrowing was a much smaller fraction of all long-term liabilities, falling from 66% in 1977 to 31% in 1986.

One historically important source of bank financing are banks affiliated with a firm's *keiretsu* or industrial group. These groups are loose affiliations of firms (many of which have trading relationships with each other) centered around a core group of banks and other financial intermediaries. The 109 firms in our sample can all be considered members of one of the six largest industrial groups during the 1972–82 period. It is widely believed that for these firms group financing was the most important source of capital.[9]

There are a number of important differences between borrowing from a group bank and borrowing from other banks. First, group banks are likely to hold more debt in these firms than other banks and hence have stronger incentives to monitor them. In 1977, in our sample, group banks held, on average,

Table 4.2   Group Firms Characteristics in 1977 and 1986:
                   Summary Statistics for Selected Variables

	Medians Only	
	1977	1986
Real capital stock—Depreciable assets (in millions		
of 1981 yen)	11,239	16,867
Tobin's q (for all assets)	1.32	1.68
(Investment)/(Capital)	.07	.19
(Market value of debt)/(Market value of equity)	1.26	.37
(Borrowing from group)/(Total bank borrowing)	.31	.29
(Total bank borrowing)/(Total debt)	.93	.88
(Borrowing from group)/(Total debt)	.28	.22
(Total bank borrowing)/(Capital)	1.75	1.01
(Borrowing from group)/(Capital)	.51	.30

	Medians (Means)	
	1977	1986
Nominal market value of total debt	18,819	19,404
	(64,988)	(77,399)
Nominal book value of bonds	950	3,580
	(6,947)	(16,703)
Nominal book value of bank borrowing	16,763	15,187
	(57,434)	(59,189)
Nominal book value of group borrowing	5,097	4,265
	(13,759)	(14,557)
	.66	.31
(All long-term borrowing)/(All long-term liabilities)	(.59)	(.38)
(Bonds)/(All long-term liabilities)	.09	.18
	(.11)	(.26)

Note. Capital and investment refer to real depreciable assets.

24% of all bank debt. In addition, group banks also tend to hold more equity in their client firms; this too gives them more powerful incentives to monitor. Moreover, group banks have in the past been active at helping member firms in financial distress; other banks often defer to the group banks, expecting them to take the lead in organizing any financial workouts for distressed firms (Sheard 1985). Finally, former bank executives are often placed in top managerial positions at these firms. This may facilitate the flow of information between the bank and its client firms.

Table 4.2 reveals that firms have become much less dependent on group financial institutions for their financing. The book value of borrowing from group financial institutions has dropped substantially, with the median falling 33% in real terms and the mean 4%. Interestingly, this change has mirrored changes in the amount of total bank borrowing. As the table shows, while the overall level of group borrowing has fallen as a fraction of total bank borrowing, this form of borrowing has remained roughly constant.

So far we have focused on the changes in the level of bank and group borrowing. Of course, these changes could in principle reflect a decline in the financing needs of Japanese corporations. To give us a more meaningful measure of the change in the composition of financing, we control for the change in firms' financing needs by normalizing the borrowing numbers by the market value of the firms' debt and by the market value of their depreciable assets.[10]

These ratios reinforce the view that both bank and group borrowing have become less important funding sources. Relative to total debt, both types of borrowing show modest declines—by 5% in terms of all bank borrowing and by 21% in terms of group borrowing. However, these declines come on top of the previously mentioned downward trend in debt financing, so that they understate the movement away from bank financing. For this reason, the ratios that compare the borrowing numbers to the capital stock are better measures of these level effects; relative to the capital stock, both borrowing measures fell by over 40% from 1977 to 1986.

Table 4.2 also indicates that along with the shift away from bank financing there has been a move toward bond financing. The median book value of bond financing rose by over three-and-a-half times in real terms. As a fraction of long-term liabilities, bonds have risen twofold. A more detailed look at the bond patterns reveals that most of the increase in bond financing has come from the issue of convertible bonds. In 1977 the average amount of outstanding convertible bonds accounted for 30% of all bond financing. This percentage and the amount of outstanding convertible bonds were both roughly constant until the 1983 regulatory changes. Since then, convertible bonds have gained in use, so that by 1986 their face value was nearly five times the level in 1977. Even with the rise in straight bond financing, convertible bonds accounted for 60% of all bond financing in 1986.

A simple pattern emerges from table 4.2. The period of steady growth from 1977 to 1986 accompanied a marked decline in debt-equity ratios. In particular, the bank-borrowing component of debt, the traditional source of financing, became much less important. This is reflected in declines in borrowing from both group banks and other banks. The recent data suggest that when firms need outside financing, they are increasingly turning to the stock market and the newly developed bond market.

While this message is consistent with the aggregate evidence presented earlier, it is somewhat misleading; table 4.2 masks some interesting heterogeneity in the data. Not all of the firms have been so aggressive in cutting back on debt financing, nor have all the firms had such steady growth. In fact, the performance and general financing patterns of firms that have reduced their dependence on bank financing are quite different than firms that have maintained their banking relationships.

Table 4.3   Characteristics Sorted by Movements in Group Borrowing to
                   Total Debt Ratio

	Medians Only			
	69 Firms Where GB/D Fell		40 Firms Where GB/D Rose	
	1977	1986	1977	1986
Real capital stock—Depreciable assets (in millions of 1981 yen)	10,877	20,674	15,123	16,115
Tobin's q (for all assets)	1.34	1.74	1.24	1.46
(Investment)/(Capital)	.07	.19	.04	.15
(Borrowing from group)/(Total debt)	.28	.17	.25	.31
(Borrowing from group)/(Capital)	.53	.17	.50	.53
	Medians (Means)			
Nominal market value of total debt	16,531	17,118	24,871	20,243
	(63,378)	(81,061)	(67,766)	(71,080)
Nominal book value of bonds	1,166	7,162	286	0
	(7,730)	(21,470)	(5,596)	(8,481)
Nominal book value of group borrowing	4,934	2,967	5,438	7,736
	(14,265)	(13,527)	(12,890)	(16,308)

Note: Capital and investment refer to real depreciable assets. GB/D stands for the ratio of group borrowing to total debt.

Table 4.3 demonstrates this point by separately showing the relevant statistics from table 4.2 for two sets of firms: those for whom the ratio of group borrowing to total debt has decreased and those for whom it has increased. The same basic pattern would emerge if we classified these firms according to changes in the ratio of total bank borrowing to debt.

This table brings out two important points. First, the firms that have reduced their dependence on group financing (and bank financing, more generally) have had much higher growth than the firms that have increased their dependence on group financing. In 1986, the real capital stock of the median firm in the former set of firms is over twice its size in 1977—a real growth rate of over 6% a year. In contrast, the real capital stock of the median firm that has increased its group borrowing has risen by less than 1% per year.[11]

The second important difference between the two sets of firms is their changes in q. Despite the large increase of the capital stock for the firms that have become less dependent on group financing, their q's have risen appreciably. The increase in q for these firms is roughly twice as large as for the other firms.

These data suggest that decisions regarding the mix of debt financing are not arbitrary; Diamond (1989) presents a theory of this choice. This raises an important issue for our paper when we come to compare the investment behavior of the two sets of firms: Are the factors that determine firms' financing choices correlated in some way with their investment behavior? If so, our results will be biased. After discussing what we think determines firms' financing choices, we present evidence and argue that this issue probably does not explain our results.

4.3   Financing Patterns and Investment

4.3.1   Approach

The objective of this section is to investigate whether the documented changes in Japanese financing patterns have had an impact on corporate investment behavior. As discussed in Section 4.1, essentially all models that posit information problems in the capital market predict that more liquid firms undertake more investment. We have argued that close bank relationships are a means of mitigating information problems; banks with large debt and equity stakes in firms have strong incentives to monitor them. In contrast, firms without investors who have large financial stakes at risk are more likely to face information problems when it comes to raising capital.

In Hoshi, Kashyap, and Scharfstein (1990) we showed that during the period when these firms all had close banking relationships, 1977–82, liquidity was not a significant determinant of investment. The question we ask here is whether, for the set of firms that have loosened their ties to banks, liquidity is a more important determinant of investment. Moreover, does liquidity continue to be unimportant for firms that maintain close bank ties?

The main empirical obstacle in determining the importance of liquidity is the possibility that liquidity is correlated with other variables that affect investment. In particular, if the fundamental determinants of investment are unobservable, then the liquidity coefficient in an investment regression will be biased to extent that liquidity is correlated with the fundamentals. The standard claim is the such correlation exists: strong current performance as evidenced by high liquidity signals that future performance is likely to be good and hence that investment is worthwhile. Thus, a regression of investment on some measure of liquidity may simply be picking up the relationship between current and future performance, inducing an omitted variable bias.

Fazzari, Hubbard, and Petersen (1988) take two steps toward addressing this problem. First, they estimate an equation that contains both liquidity and an explicit proxy for the value of investment opportunities. They argue that since q is a forward-looking measure of profitability, it is useful in this regard. We believe that q is an imperfect measure of investment opportunities,[12] so that some component of liquidity still reflects these opportunities. Nevertheless, to the extent that q does reflect investment opportunities it will reduce the omitted variable bias of the liquidity coefficient.

The more innovative approach to this problem is to compare the effects of liquidity across two sets of firms. Fazzari, Hubbard, and Petersen (1988) identify a set of firm that they believe on a priori grounds are likely to face information problems in the capital market and identify another set that are not likely to face such problems.[13] They then estimate the investment equations for these two sets of firms, comparing the estimated effects of liquidity. Under the null hypothesis of perfect capital markets there should be no difference in the estimated liquidity coefficients provided the omitted variable bias is the same for the two sets of firms. Thus, if one is to explain the finding that liquidity is more important for one set of firms under the null hypothesis, one has to argue that the omitted variable bias is greater for that set of firms: either that q is a particularly bad proxy for investment or that liquidity is particularly good proxy. Below, we discuss two arguments along these lines, but do not find compelling evidence for them. Absent such a compelling argument, the findings are consistent with the existence of liquidity constraints.

4.3.2 Regression Equations

The evidence we will present is obtained by regressing investment in depreciable assets (normalized by the stock of depreciable assets) on a set of yearly dummies, a tax-corrected version of q for depreciable assets, cash flow, lagged production, and the beginning of period stock of marketable securities. The last three variables were all normalized by the stock of depreciable assets and all the data were first differenced.

This regression equation is the same as the one estimated in our previous paper. Essentially all of the nonliquidity variables are included to reduce the possibility that the liquidity variables might be proxying for unobservable determinants of investment. We briefly discuss why these variables should reduce this possibility. The yearly dummies are included to filter out any common macroeconomic shocks.[14] Other firm or industry-specific shocks are eliminated by first differencing (at the cost of losing one year of data). Since this transformation induces a moving-average term into the residual, all the standard errors reported below are computed using a robust method that allows for first-order moving-average errors (see White 1984).

For the reasons given above we include q in the regressions. In fact, we actually use both beginning- and end-of-period q in all of our regressions. We include both measures because it is possible that cash received during the period contains information about investment opportunities not contained in the beginning-of-period q. Including the end-of-period q addresses this problem at the cost of obscuring the interpretation of the coefficients on q.[15] Since these regressions are not designed to test the q theory of investment, this trade-off is one we are willing to make. The results are not affected by the inclusion of end-of-period q.

We also include production over the previous year in our regressions. There are several reasons to include production. The most important is that the empirical investment literature has repeatedly shown the existence of an accelerator effect in the data. Our previous paper confirms the importance of the effect for these firms. Blundell et al. (1987), Fazzari, Hubbard, and Peterson (1988) and Whited (1990) establish that the accelerator effect is important even in models with q for firms in Britain and the United States. If we were to drop production, it is possible that the liquidity variable would be proxying for accelerator effects since production and liquidity are typically correlated. The inclusion of both variables eliminates this problem. In addition, theoretical arguments based on the presence of monopolistic competition in the product market can also be used to justify the inclusion of a production term in the investment equation (see Schiantarelli and Georgoutsus 1987). We emphasize, however, that these results do not depend on the inclusion of production.

Finally, since the focus of the investigation is the sensitivity of investment to liquidity, we include two measures of liquidity. The first variable is current cash flow, which is defined as income after tax plus depreciation less dividend payments.[16] We also include the firms' holding of marketable securities as a proxy for the stock of a firm's liquid assets. These securities are identified by the firms as assets that can readily be converted into cash. In most years, the median firm's holdings of these cash equivalents is as large as the median amount of investment.

4.3.3 Findings

As a starting point for our discussion, we estimate the basic regression for the 109 firms over the 1978–82 period—specifically, from April 1978 to March 1983. The results are shown in the first column of table 4.4. As would be expected from our previous work, neither cash flow nor the stock of liquidity is a significant determinant of investment over this preregulation period.

Table 4.4   Investment and Internal Funds before and after Deregulation

	All 109 Firms	All 109 Firms
Fiscal years	1978–82	1983–85
Average q (beginning of	$-.002$	.010
period)	(.005)	(.005)
Average q (end of period)	.002	$-.009$
	(.005)	(.006)
$\left(\dfrac{\text{Cash flow}}{K}\right)_t$	$-.008$	.161
	(.036)	(.149)
$\left(\dfrac{\text{Marketable securities}}{K}\right)_{t-1}$	.041	.037
	(.031)	(.040)
$\left(\dfrac{\text{Production}}{K}\right)_{t-1}$	.019	$-.009$
	(.002)	(.011)

Note: Dependent variable is I/K. All regressions include a set of yearly dummies and are done using first-differenced data. The standard errors are reported in parentheses below the coefficient estimates and they have been corrected for the moving average introduced by the first differencing.

The coefficients of both variables are precisely estimated and small, which suggests the interpretation that these variables are not important determinants of investment.

As the second column of table 4.4 shows, the results are less clear-cut over the 1983–86 period. The point estimate of the cash flow coefficient is much larger, but it is imprecisely estimated so that at conventional levels of significance it is indistinguishable from zero. The seemingly large standard errors suggest that there is substantial heterogeneity in the data. Below, we establish that this is the case.

It is worth pointing out that, as so much previous work has shown, q does not appear to be the key variable that determines investment. Also, production is no longer significant in the later period. Given the reduced-form nature of the regression, this change is hard to interpret.

We now consider the natural question raised by the results in table 4.4. Is the increased sensitivity of investment to cash flow in the later period related to the changes in financing patterns that occurred at the same time? To address this question, we separated the sample into two sets of firms, those that increased and those that decreased their reliance on bank financing. As a measure of the strength of a bank relationship we used the ratio of group borrowing to debt. We focus on group borrowing rather than total bank borrowing because, as discussed above, group borrowing is probably associated with more intensive monitoring. However, it is worth indicating that other measures of the dependence on bank financing yield similar results.

We ran the above regressions for the two sets of firms. The first two columns of table 4.5 show that for the pre-deregulation period, the sensitivity of investment to internal funds does not seem to depend on whether or not firms subsequently changed their group borrowing to total debt ratio. Put differently, splitting the sample in the 1978–82 period does not reveal a tendency for either class of firms to invest more when their liquidity is higher.

Since the two samples are independent, hypothesis tests comparing individual coefficients between the two sets of firms can be conducted without being concerned about covariances. As the table shows, the sampling variation is large enough so that none of the individual coefficients are statistically different for the two groups. In most cases, the coefficients are also precisely estimated so that such comparisons are meaningful. The only exception is for the marketable securities variable, where the coefficient is very difficult to pin down for the firms that have maintained strong ties to the groups. Overall, these findings support our previous work: during this period when all of these firms had close banking ties, liquidity does not drive investment.

The third column of table 4.5 demonstrates the first of the two main findings of the paper: firms that have loosened their ties to group banks exhibited a marked increase in the effect of liquidity on investment. The coefficient on cash flow for these firms increased by a factor of five from .082 to .479 between the pre- and postderegulation periods; the t-statistic on cash flow in-

Table 4.5   **Investment and Internal Funds before and after Deregulation (Controlling for Movements in Group Borrowing to Total Debt Ratio)**

	GB/D Down, 69 Firms	GB/D Up, 40 Firms	GB/D Down, 69 Firms	GB/D Up, 40 Firms
Fiscal years	1978–82	1978–82	1983–85	1983–85
Average q (beginning of	−.003	−.003	.005	.016
period)	(.006)	(.008)	(.008)	(.004)
Average q (end of period)	−.003	.016	−.007	−.008
	(.006)	(.008)	(.009)	(.005)
$\left(\dfrac{\text{Cash flow}}{K}\right)_t$	.082	−.064	.479	−.049
	(.100)	(.035)	(.140)	(.098)
$\left(\dfrac{\text{Marketable securities}}{K}\right)_{t-1}$	.044	.139	.049	−.187
	(.029)	(.130)	(.027)	(.102)
$\left(\dfrac{\text{Production}}{K}\right)_{t-1}$	.013	.020	−.020	.012
	(.007)	(.002)	(.013)	(.015)

Note: GB/D stands for the ratio of group borrowing to total debt. Dependent variable is I/K. All regressions include a set of yearly dummies and are done using first-differenced data. The standard errors are reported below the coefficient estimates and they have been corrected for the moving average introduced by the first differencing.

creased from .8 to 3.4. Using a one-sided test, the postderegulation coefficient is significantly larger than the prederegulation coefficient at the 5% level. The other coefficients for these firms are mostly unaffected; none are statistically different across the two periods.

The paper's second major result, shown in the last column of the table, is that for firms that have maintained their ties to group banks, liquidity continues to be unimportant even after deregulation. For these firms, both before and after the regulatory changes, cash flow is statistically insignificant with a coefficient that is tightly estimated and close to zero. The effect of holdings on marketable securities is hard to pin down in either period, but neither coefficient is significant. Individual comparisons of the other variables in the equation also suggest that there are no statistically significant differences across the two periods, although the standard errors on coefficients for beginning-of-period q are rather large.

The analysis suggests that bank relationships relax liquidity constraints. Before accepting this interpretation of the evidence, however, we explore an alternative explanation of our results. As we discussed above, the characteristics of firms that have loosened their bank ties differ substantially from those that do not. In particular, firms that reduced their dependence on banks had higher growth and higher q's. This suggests that there are some underlying economic forces that determine corporate borrowing patterns. Diamond (1989) analyzes models along this line. It is possible that the factors that determine this choice are correlated with firms' investment behavior.

One explanation for the result that liquidity is unimportant for firms that maintain their bank ties is based on the observation that these firms generally have low q. These firms would not be expected to invest heavily and their investment opportunities are probably poor. It might be argued that for these firms neither liquidity nor any other variable should forecast investment. In contrast, successful firms with high q tend to use the public capital markets. These firms have better investment opportunities and one might expect that other variables like liquidity would predict investment. Hence, in this view, the omitted variable bias is more severe for the firms that have loosened their bank ties, and it is not surprising that the estimated effects of liquidity are larger for these firms. By this reasoning, any selection mechanism that simultaneously partitions firms on the basis of q implicitly uncovers an investment-liquidity linkage that is driven by these consideration rather than the selection rule.

To address this alternative explanation, one must show that a selection rule that explicitly conditions on performance does not explain the observed differences in the relationship between investment and liquidity. Table 4.6 reports the estimated regression equations after sorting firms into low and high q groups. The partition is made on the basis of average q for all assets in 1977.[17] To save space, we only report results for the partition that separates the top one-third and bottom two-thirds of the firms: this amounts to separating firms with q above and below 1.5. Similar results would apply for a partition based on the median firm. It also does not matter whether we partition based on q in 1977 or in 1986.

Table 4.6 suggests that our main findings are not explained by the possibil-

Table 4.6   **Investment and Internal Funds before and after Deregulation (Separating High- and Low-q Firms)**

	34 Firms $q \geq 1.5$ in 1977	75 Firms $q < 1.5$ in 1977	34 Firms $q \geq 1.5$ in 1977	75 Firms $q < 1.5$ in 1977
Fiscal years	1978–82	1978–82	1983–85	1983–85
Average q (beginning of period)	−.001 (.008)	−.007 (.008)	.016 (.007)	.005 (.008)
Average q (end of period)	−.002 (.008)	.008 (.006)	−.004 (.007)	−.012 (.009)
$\left(\dfrac{\text{Cash flow}}{K}\right)_t$	−.048 (.047)	.069 (.061)	.097 (.158)	.350 (.205)
$\left(\dfrac{\text{Marketable securities}}{K}\right)_{t-1}$	.038 (.058)	.059 (.038)	−.033 (.066)	.064 (.038)
$\left(\dfrac{\text{Production}}{K}\right)_{t-1}$	.016 (.010)	.018 (.002)	−.003 (.019)	−.007 (.013)

Note: Dependent variable is I/K. All regressions include a set of yearly dummies and are done using first-differenced data. The standard errors are reported below the coefficient estimates and they have been corrected for the moving average introduced by the first differencing.

ity that cash flow contains differential information for high and low q firms. The first two columns show that, for both sets of firms, liquidity was unimportant in the prederegulation period; both the flow and stock measures of liquidity are tightly estimated and insignificant. The last two columns show that similar—although somewhat ambiguous—results hold for the postderegulation period. Over this period, cash flow is harder to estimate precisely with relatively high standard errors. None of the coefficients is significant. The coefficients for the low and high q firms are not significantly different from each other, although the point estimate for the low q firms is higher. We also sorted simultaneously by both q and the ratio of group borrowing to debt. Both low and high q firms that reduced their group borrowing showed a strong sensitivity of investment to cash flow, whereas both types of firms that continued to rely on group banks showed much lower sensitivity of investment to cash flow.

To assess further the importance of this problem, we sorted the sample on the basis of whether investment in the postderegulation period was above or below average. In general, this selection rule will be problematic since it implicitly sorts on the basis of the residuals in investment equation. But in this case, it is perhaps the cleanest way to test whether performance or strength of affiliation is more important in determining the investment/cash flow linkages. We found that the high-investment firms that maintained their group ties showed no significant relation between investment and cash flow, while the high-investment firms that moved away showed a very strong and significant relation. The low-investment firms showed a similar pattern although here the strongly attached group firms actually had a significantly negative cash flow coefficient, while the firms that loosened their ties had a positive and significant coefficient. Hence, group attachment and not stock market indicators such as q or even realized investment rates seem to be the key determinant of whether cash flow helps to predict investment.

Of course, q and observed investment rates are imperfect measures of a firm's prospects. It is conceivable that a firm's financing patterns are in fact better indicators. For example, it may be that only firms with excellent investment opportunities reduce their bank ties so that for them liquidity is particularly informative about investment opportunities. Unfortunately, it is impossible to determine whether the financing behavior itself is a better measure of future performance. Thus, to accept our interpretation of the facts one must believe that q and investment rates themselves are reasonable measures of future performance.

4.4 Conclusion

This paper presents evidence on the role of banks in monitoring firms. We argued that bank monitoring mitigates information problems in the capital market. This is manifested in the investment behavior of firms with close bank relationships; these firms do not appear to be liquidity constrained. We started with a sample of firms with close bank ties and showed that their investment was not sensitive to their liquidity. Regulatory reforms created new possibilities to raise money directly from the capital market. We found that the investment of firms that chose this new financing option and weakened their bank ties was much more sensitive to liquidity than firms that continued to borrow heavily from banks.

This analysis raises an obvious question: If indeed bank monitoring overcomes information problems and relaxes liquidity constraints, why did some firms weaken their bank ties? This question points to the need for a theory of the choice between bank debt and public debt. Except for Diamond's (1989) recent theoretical contribution, we know very little about this trade-off. Diamond argues that young firms, or older ones that have done poorly, will borrow mainly from banks and that older, more successful firms will use public debt. The idea is that successful firms have more "reputation capital" at stake and hence have more to lose by taking inefficient actions. These firms do not need to incur the monitoring costs associated with bank borrowing. By contrast, younger firms have not yet developed a reputation and older, less successful firms do not have a good reputation to lose. It is therefore efficient for these firms to incur the costs of bank monitoring.

The results presented here suggest that monitoring and other costs associated with bank financing must be large. Otherwise, firms would not have chosen to weaken their bank relationships until they had enough collateral (both tangible and intangible) to be able to get around liquidity constraints. Unfortunately, we can only conjecture what these costs might be. Beyond direct monitoring costs, three others come to mind. The first obvious cost stems from regulations requiring banks to hold a fraction of their assets in non-interest-bearing accounts. This reserve requirement means that the costs of funds to banks exceed those of individual investors; as a result, they will require a higher gross rate of return on their investments.[18] In addition, bank loans are generally less liquid than publicly traded debt. The difficulty that banks face in adjusting their loan portfolio may also mean that they will require a higher gross return.

Finally, a more subtle cost of bank financing may arise from the different objectives of banks, corporate managers, and shareholders. Since banks mainly hold debt claims, they receive little of the up side from unusually good firm performance (of course, to the extent that they own equity they will participate in some of the gains). Shareholders, in contrast, care only about maximizing the up side. This conflict may result in excessively conservative investment policies if banks control corporate investment decisions. It may therefore be efficient to reduce bank ties to avoid this problem at the expense of becoming more liquidity constrained. As firms generate more cash from ongoing operations, they may be more willing to make this transition. In addition, managers may prefer to have more control over operating decisions than a bank is willing to allow. Managers may choose to weaken the firms' bank ties and incur greater financing costs because it gives them more control despite the fact that it is inefficient to do so. Again, as firms become more liquid, managers may be more willing to incur these costs.

We conclude by emphasizing that this empirical analysis (and that of MacKie-Mason, in this volume) as well as the theoretical work of Diamond (1989) suggests that there is more to financing decisions than the choice of a debt-equity ratio. A crucial decision that firms face is the actual source of financing regardless of whether it is in the form of debt or equity. The recent changes in Japanese financing arrangements were particularly useful in addressing this issue.

Obviously, Japan is not the only country in which this issue is important: firms operating in the context of other financial systems face the very same set of questions. And, Japan's is not the only financial system in the midst of rapid change. Along with the increase in leverage in the United States there have been dramatic changes in who holds corporate debt and equity. Firms are increasingly relying on private equity markets for their financing; for many firms much of the equity is held by management and large institutional investors. This movement away from passive shareholders with small equity stakes to larger, more active shareholders may have important consequences for the link between the financial and real sides of the firm. In addition, there have been striking changes in the structure of debt markets: junk bonds and the increased reliance on private placement are two recent phenomena. While firms in Japan have moved towards direct capital-market financing, in some ways the move in the United States has been in the opposite direction. Understanding the forces underlying these changes is one of the important challenges facing students of corporate finance.

Notes

1. The costs include administrative expenses in excess of underwriting fees, reserve requirements that raise the cost of funds to banks, and the illiquidity of bank loans.
2. See, e.g., Hamada and Horiuchi (1987), Royama (1982), Suzuki (1974).
3. According to Shinkai (1988) these rates are said to " 'respect' the market rates."
4. The government can still intervene to block an issue, but such interventions are very unusual.
5. To simplify the calculations, we restricted the sample to firms with accounting years ending in March. After imposing this restriction and removing outliers, we are left with 337 firms. Most of the data on them comes from the Nikkei Financial Data Tapes.
6. In fact, we used Nakatani's (1984) refinement of *Keiretsu no Kenkyu,* which eliminates firms that switched their lender or merged.
7. The dates here refer to the end of a fiscal year, so that when we say 1977 it refers to March 1977.

8. Our measure of Tobin's q is the ratio of the market value of debt and equity (correcting for taxes) to the replacement cost (measured at market values) of all assets. The construction of q is discussed at length in Hoshi and Kashyap (1990). Throughout this section, we compare the median value for the firms at two points in time. Even though the median firm is generally different at each point, for ease of exposition we discuss the comparison as if the same firm is being studied.

9. See, e.g., Hodder and Tschoegl (1985).

10. In both these ratios, the denominators are nominal market-value numbers while the numerator is a nominal book-value number. Given that most bank borrowing is short term, the book-value numbers for borrowing should not be very different from the market-value numbers for borrowing. Hence these ratios should be straightforward to interpret.

11. Note that we use the debt normalization rather than the asset normalization. We do this because the asset-based measure is low for high-asset firms so that one would expect to observe these patterns by the very nature of the construction.

12. In calculating Tobin's q one must make numerous assumptions that no doubt introduce measurement error. For example, one must convert book-value measure of asset values into market-value measures, a very imprecise task.

13. They argue that firms with low divident payouts are more likely to face information problems since they seem to prefer retaining their earnings.

14. Since the length of the panel is so short, it is difficult to make any further corrections for possible serial correlation.

15. End-of-period q is endogenous since it includes the end-of-period replacement cost in its denominator, which in turn includes the replacement cost for investment made during the year. Accordingly, the coefficient associated with end-of-period q will be biased toward zero.

16. It is not clear if dividends are discretionary and whether they belong in a measure of liquidity; however, when we estimate our model including dividends in our liquidity measure, our results do not change.

17. The q's that appear in the regressions pertain only to depreciable assets, that it is they are constructed by subtracting the replacement cost of nondepreciable assets from the market value of the firm and dividing this difference by the replacement cost of depreciable assets. This measure of q and Tobin's q, which is based on all assets, are very highly correlated (see Hoshi and Kashyap 1990).

18. Fama (1985) and James (1987) document an interesting fact along these lines. They show that yields on bank certificates of deposite and bankers' acceptances are no different than the yield on comparable maturity government bonds and commercial paper. Thus, given reserve requirements and their greater costs of funds they must be losing money on these securities and earning profits on their other activities, perhaps corporate-lending activities. To be earning profits in this activity they must offer a differentiated product: borrowing from a bank must be different from borrowing directly from the capital market. Of course, this fact does not tell us in what way the two sources of funds are different.

References

Aoki, Masahiko. 1984. Aspects of the Japanese firm. In *The Economic Analysis of the Japanese Firm*, ed. M. Aoki, 3–43. North-Holland Elsevier.

Blundell, Richard, S. Bond, M. Devereux, and F. Schiantarelli. 1987. Does Q matter for investment? Some evidence from a panel of U.K. companies. Working Paper no. 87/12. Institute for Fiscal Studies.

Diamond, Douglas. 1984. Financial intermediation and delegated monitoring. *Review of Economic Studies* 51:393–414.

———. 1989. Monitoring and reputation: The choice between bank loans and directly placed debt. Typescript. University of Chicago.

Fama, E. 1985. What's different about banks. *Journal of Monetary Economics* 15: 29–36.

Fazzari, Steven, R. G. Hubbard, and B. Petersen, 1988. Investment and finance reconsidered. *Brookings Papers on Economic Activity,* no. 1, pp. 141–195.

Hamada, Koichi, and Akiyoshi Horiuchi. 1987. The political economy of the financial market. In *The political economy of Japan,* vol. 1, *The domestic transformation,* ed. Kozo Yamamura and Yasukichi Yasuba, 223–60. Stanford, Calif.: Stanford University Press.

Hodder, James, and A. Tschoegl. 1985. Some aspects of Japanese corporate finance. *Journal of Financial and Quantitative Analysis* 20:173–90.

Hoshi, Takeo, and A. Kashyap. 1990. Evidence on q and investment for Japanese firms. *Journal of the Japanese and International Economies.* In press.

Hoshi, Takeo, A. Kashyap, and D. Scharfstein. 1990. Corporate structure, liquidity, and investment: Evidence from Japanese industrial groups. *Quarterly Journal of Economics.* In press.

James, Christopher. 1987. Some evidence on the uniqueness of bank loans. *Journal of Financial Economics* 19:217–36.

Keiretsu no Kenkyu (Research on industrial groups). (annual publication). Tokyo: Keizai Chosa Kyokai.

Ministry of Finance. Japan. *Security Bureau Annual Report* (annual publication).

Myers, Stewart, and N. Majluf. 1984. Corporate financing and investment decisions when firms have information that investors do not have. *Journal of Financial Economics* 13:187–221.

Nakatani, Iwao. 1984. The economic role of financial corporate grouping. In *The Economic Analysis of the Japanese Firm,* ed. M. Aoki, 227–58. North-Holland Elsevier.

Nasu, Masahiko. 1987. *Gendai Nihon No Kin-yu Kozo* (Financial structure in contemporary Japan). Tokyo: Toyo Keizai Shinpo-sha.

Nihon Keizai Shimbun-sha. 1987. *Ko-Shasai Hakko Shijo* (The bond issuing market) Tokyo: Nihon Keizai Shimbun-sha.

Ramakrishnan, Ram, and A. Thakor. 1984. Information reliability and a theory of financial intermediation. *Review of Economic Studies* 5:415–32.

Royama, Shoichi. 1982. *Nihon no Kin'yu System* (Japanese financial system). Tokyo: Toyo Keizai Shimpo-sha.

Schiantarelli, Fabio, and D. Georgoutsos. 1987. Monopolistic competition and the Q theory of investment. Working Paper no. 87/11, Institute for Fiscal Studies.

Schumpeter, Joseph. 1939. *Business cycles.* New York: McGraw Hill.

Sheard, Paul. 1985. Main banks and structural adjustment. Research Paper no. 129. Australia Research Center.

Shimura, Kaichi. 1978. *Gendai Nihon Ko-Sha-sai Ron* (Government and corporate bonds in contemporary Japan). Tokyo: Tokyo Daigaku Shuppan Kai.

Shinkai, Yoichi. 1988. The internationalization of finance in Japan. In *The political economy of Japan,* vol. 2, *The changing international context,* ed. T. Inoguchi and D.I. Okimoto, 249–71. Stanford, Calif.: Stanford University Press.

Suzuki, Yoshio. 1974. *Gendai Nihon Kin'yu Ron* (Money and banking in contemporary Japan). Tokyo: Toyo Keizai Shimpo-sha.

White, Halbert. 1984. *Asymptotic theory for econometricians*. Orlando, Fla.: Academic Press.

Whited, Toni. 1989. Debt, liquidity constraints, and corporate investment: Evidence from panel data. FEDS Working Paper no. 113. Federal Reserve Board.

Williamson, Stephen. 1986. Costly monitoring, financial intermediation, and equilibrium credit rationing. *Journal of Monetary Economics* 18: 159–79.

Yoshihara, Shozo. 1987. *Ginko Torihiki no Chishiki* (Knowledge of bank transactions). Tokyo: Nihon Keizai Shinbum-sha.

5   Sustaining Investment, Discretionary Investment, and Valuation: A Residual Funds Study of the Paper Industry

John S. Strong and John R. Meyer

The agency theory of corporate takeovers and restructurings argues that neoclassical approaches to investment decision making fail to capture the incentive and monitoring problems related to cash flow. In particular, Jensen (1986) and Griffin (1988) have argued that managers have substantial control over the allocation of corporate cash flows and incentives to reinvest these flows in unnecessary or wasteful projects. These uneconomic investments, it is argued, lead to poor performance and lower valuation. To a crude (ceteris paribus) first approximation therefore, a negative relationship should be observable between the relative extent of "free" cash flow for a firm and the rate of change in its market valuations.

Unfortunately, empirical testing of this hypothesis is complicated by the possibility (increasingly recognized in economic theory and long recognized empirically) that for some firms there may exist a hierarchical ordering to the costs of different sources of financing (as induced say, by information, tax or other asymmetries).[1] Typically, internal cash flow would be among the cheapest sources that is at the base of this hierarchy. In such circumstances, a firm's investment may be limited by the availability of internal cash flow. This, in turn, could limit the growth and general performance of the firm. In short, internal cash flow can be a source for not only financing permissive managerial extravagances but, in a world of information and tax asymmetries and other financial market imperfections, can also be a means for a firm achieving higher growth rates and equity valuations than might otherwise be possible.

John S. Strong is an assistant professor of finance at the School of Business Administration, College of William and Mary, and a research fellow of the Center for Business and Government, Harvard University. John R. Meyer is the Harpel Professor of Capital Formation and Economic Growth, Center for Business and Government, Harvard University.

The authors would like to thank Steven Fazzari, R. Glenn Hubbard, Larry Pulley, and Kim Smith for helpful comments and Susan Swartz for research assistance.

Accordingly, while the agency theory of corporate restructurings is appealing, empirical verification has proceeded slowly. In particular, empirical testing has focused only on small parts of the model. What is required is an examination of the relation between cash flows and investment, and then between those investments and longer-term financial performance. First, do firms with larger "free" cash flows exhibit different investment behavior? Second, do these differences in investment behavior lead to poorer or better financial performance and, more precisely, under what circumstances?

5.1. A Review of the Agency Model

Agency theory emphasizes the conflicts that arise between management and stockholders.[2] This approach holds that increased cash flows reduce shareholder incentives for monitoring performance while increasing managerial discretion. Managers are believed to take advantage of this discretion by directing cash flows to projects over which they retain supervision. Since this control cannot be achieved by dividend or share repurchase policies, managers choose to emphasize capital expenditures. These capital projects are believed to be uneconomic at the margin in many cases, thereby producing the consequences of the agency problem.

This argument depends on a number of critical assumptions. For example, as already noted, if a firm faces a pronounced hierarchy in its financing possibilities, preference for capital investment may increase value if the set of investment opportunities is attractive (Fazzari, Hubbard, and Petersen 1988). However, previous research (Griffin 1988; Jensen 1986) on the agency theory of restructurings has studied situations in which economic rents on older assets were present and investment opportunities were unattractive. In contrast to this research, McConnell and Muscarella (1985) found that corporate capital expenditure announcements are associated with significant positive increases in share values, consistent with a view that managers seek to maximize the value of the firm when making investment decisions.[3]

Similarly, corporate debt that reduces the agency problem by reducing cash flows available to managers may concomitantly reduce financial capacity, thereby limiting the firm's ability to undertake positive net present value (NPV) projects if they present themselves. The agency model implicitly assumes that the costs of managerial discretion in allocating cash flows outweigh the benefits of reserve financial capacity.[4] Donaldson (1984) points out the difficulty in sorting out this trade-off. He finds that managers of large firms were not oriented toward maximization of the value of the firm, but rather by "the aggregate purchasing power available to management for strategic purposes during any given planning period."[5] The difficulty, emphasized in agency theory, is whether this strategic resource flexibility is used to increase the value of the firm over the longer term.[6]

Furthermore, the market for corporate control may fail to serve as a foil for reducing managerial cash-flow discretion. Rather than that market acting as a discipline for cash-rich firms, managers may choose acquisitions as an alternative to capital investment projects. For example, if conditions of information asymmetry lead managers to know of their excess cash flows before potential acquirers, these cash flows might lead to dubious acquisitions that enhance or create agency problems, rather than being the solution to them.[7] This relation was found by Bruner (1988) in a study of mergers in which firms with excess cash and debt capacity were more likely to be bidders for companies with less liquidity and debt capacity.

5.2 An Alternative Model: The Residual Funds Approach

The agency model is not very precise in its definitions of cash flows and capital investment, nor does it spell out the decision-making and funds-allocation processes within the firm. As an alternative, we believe that a residual funds model better captures the behavioral dimensions of corporate capital budgeting and related resource allocations. The residual funds approach first was presented by Meyer and Kuh (1957) and extended by Kuh (1963), Meyer and Glauber (1964), and Dhrymes and Kurz (1967). More recently, the notion of a hierarchy of financing choices has been extended to capital structure analysis by Myers (1984) and to the interaction of investment and financing decisions by Myers and Majluf (1984), Petersen (1988), Fazzari, Hubbard and Petersen (1988), Bernstein and Nadiri (1986), and McDonald and Soderstrom (1986).

The residual funds approach argues that the amount and financing of capital investment by firms is in part a function of the "residual funds" available after proceeding down a hierarchy of prior claims on corporate cash flow. The starting point is the total cash flow generated by the firm, which provides the base amount for distribution to various claimants and investment opportunities. The first priority is for servicing established levels of debt, incorporating both interest payments and associated principal obligations (either at maturity or via sinking funds requirements). The established level of debt will presumably reflect a firm's evaluation of what constitutes its best mix of debt and equity financing, trading off tax aspects and other features, and (where applicable) expected allowance for growth in core lines of business.

The funds available after debt service are then used to pay preferred dividends. The next claimants on the funds, following Dobrovolsky (1951) and Lintner (1956), and as amplified by more recent signaling concepts (Ross 1977; Bhattacharya 1979; Hakansson 1982; Bernheim 1988; Crockett and Friend 1988), are the common shareholders, who receive dividends at a previously established "regular" *pattern* of payments per share.[8] This pattern includes established or expected growth in dividends and, for some firms, where nonrecurring dividends have become a characteristic feature of cyclical upturns, these "extra" payments as well. Following common dividends, the residual funds are then available for capital investment of several types. First, mandated investments, such as safety needs or pollution control equipment are put in place. Second, investment aimed at replacing or improving the efficiency of established productive capacity is implemented. Third, new investments for capacity expansion of established product lines are undertaken, followed by capital needed for expansion into closely related products. Finally, capital investment outside the existing lines of business will be considered, but generally only if some internal funds remain after meeting prior claims in the hierarchy.

To see that the residual funds approach can produce outcomes consistent with those of the agency model of free cash flow, it is useful to consider both the determinants of capital investment and the dual position of common stockholders in the funds-distribution process. To start, capital investment is only partially a search for positive net present value projects, in which prior investments are continually reevaluated and potential new investments analyzed in a neoclassical profitability framework.[9] Rather, when the level of capital investment is conditioned by the amount of residual cash flows, an important distinction arises concerning *types* of capital investment. If we assume that the baseline financial commitments of debt and dividends were founded on an extrapolation of current product mix, scale and market trends, and so on, then capital investment may be classified into two types. First comes *sustaining investment,* that amount which is necessary to provide a level of funds commensurate with existing financial and core business requirements. In general, this should approximate replacement investment, although short-term fluctuations in economic rents and longer-term changes in productivity relationships may make this correspondence less than one-to-one. Next comes *discretionary investment,* defined as that which is *not* required to sustain the firm's core business at its current level and trend of operations.

Preference for "cheap" internal finance will cause a firm to use residual funds to pay for sustaining investment whenever possible. By contrast, discretionary investments are more likely to be undertaken when a pool of residual funds remains available after sustaining investments have been made. In the event the available funds are absorbed by prior claims, discretionary investments are less probable, a result consistent with both agency and residual funds hypotheses. Thus, sustaining investment will tend to be more related to existing capital stocks and neoclassical profitability approaches, while discretionary capital expenditures will depend on the existence of residual funds. Resort to external financing also could be described as residually derived, since it depends on the relationship between internal cash flows, prior financial claims, and sustaining investment requirements. The cyclical asymmetry observed by Meyer and Kuh (1957) between accelerator and cash-flow effects on investment could be similarly explained; the dominance they observed of the accelerator during cyclical upswings might be expected to correspond with periods when sustaining investment exceeded the available pool of residual funds. In short, discretionary investment serves as a buffer, tending toward zero when no residual funds are available and competing with nonroutine shareholder distributions when a surfeit of internal funds exists.

Indeed, if at all possible, all necessary projects will be financed internally. If, as in many cases, this is not possible, the residual funds will be used as the basis for establishing the amount of required external financing. Because of tax considerations (at least in the United States) debt will usually be the lowest-cost source of external finance and will be used, especially if it can be accommodated within accepted capital structure targets.[10] These targets will incorporate information on ability to pay debt service from cash flow without jeopardizing other established claimants, especially prior debt servicing requirements, preferred dividends, and the preexisting pattern of common dividends. New equity becomes attractive only under highly specialized conditions; for example, at very high antidilutive price/earnings ratios or where additional debt bears a high-risk premium. If, on the other hand, any internal funds remain after "established" financial and investment claims have been met, then these funds can be distributed to shareholders, used to replenish liquidity positions on the balance sheet, or to finance "discretionary" investment. It is at this point that the agency problem comes to the fore. There are obviously many "slippages" and possible alternatives, further complicated by the fact that hierarchical considerations enter on *both* the financial and real side. Nevertheless, the residual funds approach will often provide a good approximation to the real world of corporate capital budgeting. The approach also helps explain why cash-flow variables consistently do well in empirical models of investment even though not specified by theories assuming perfect financial markets.

An interesting issue arises at this point concerning major acquisitions, a special case of discretionary investment. Here, widespread use of debt finance and the frequency of postmerger leveraged recapitalizations might seem at odds with the residual funds model. However, such acquisitions are likely to change the scale, mix, and trend of the firm's "core business," thus modifying sustaining investment requirements. At the same time, associated changes in asset ownership and operations will induce a rethinking of the financial structure of the combined entity. In particular, major acquisitions are likely to reorient firms away from internal growth of core businesses.[11] If this occurs, a reordering of cash flows toward financial claimants is probable. Of course, restructurings generally include assumption of the prior debt obligations of the acquired firm, but these claims, along with dividend policies, may be substantially changed following a restructuring. Thus, the preference for internal finance in the residual funds model is conditioned by mergers and acquisitions, which introduce changes in the hierarchies of both investment and financing and require adjustment to a new residual funds regime.

The second principal feature of the residual funds approach is that common shareholders occupy two places in the hierarchy of funds distribution. The two positions correspond to the two sources of return—dividends and capital appreciation through retention. The dual position of the common stockholder enhances his monitoring ability, for example, by separating the signals produced by the regular pattern of dividends from those created by increases in the dividends, or by the use of external finance. To illustrate, the behavior of ongoing dividends provides information as to the value of the existing businesses, while incremental distributions through repurchases or extraordinary dividends may convey negative information about investment opportunities.[12] Under the residual funds approach, *changes* in the pattern of dividends, and what such changes signal, are most important; as a corollary, financing constraints are perhaps as well identified by changes in dividend policy as by payout levels.[13]

Compared with the agency model, the residual funds approach posits a relationship not between total cash flow and investment, but between a quite restrictive notion of residual cash flow and discretionary investment. Again, the relevant residual cash flow involves cash available *after* established debt service, dividends, and sustaining investments have been made. Empirically, this means that "free" cash flow in a residual funds model might well be periodically negative even for otherwise very successful enterprises. Indeed, for the very successful firm participating in a strong growth sector, free cash flow might be persistently negative. Financial policies that serve to make such cash flows even more persistently negative by additional debt or dividends, as recommended by some applications of agency theory, could therefore be questioned in some circumstances.

5.3 Data

Time-series data from 1971–86 for the paper and allied products industry are used to test the residual funds approach. The paper industry was selected for study for several reasons. To start, it experienced two important factor price shocks, in 1973–74 and in 1979, due to energy prices. Also, the production technology of the industry is well defined and relatively homogeneous. The industry is about average in cyclical sensitivity but has experienced substantial fluctuations in operating performance over the period studied.[14] Over that study period, the returns to paper industry shareholders have neither consistently outperformed nor lagged behind the stock market as a whole, as shown in figure 5.1. The range of company total returns encompasses overall market returns, suggesting that the paper industry provides a better test of the relationship between cash flows, investment, and performance than industries in which most firms have performed persistently above (or below) the economy as a whole.

Compared to the petroleum industry studied by Griffin (1988), the paper industry has experienced sizable sustaining investment requirements due to factor price changes, though in recent years it has not required much addi-

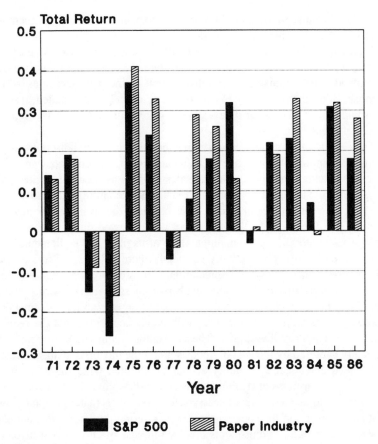

Fig. 5.1   Total return to shareholders: paper industry and S&P 500

tional capacity investment. Thus, the investment opportunity set may have shifted from the sustaining class in the 1970s to being more discretionary in nature in the 1980s. In addition, the cash flows generated by the firms in the paper industry have not been driven by huge swings in product prices, so that capital investment in response to nonrecurring economic rents are not so dramatic as in petroleum. Finally, the industry has undergone considerable restructuring, principally taking the form of industry consolidation of assets, rather than diversifying mergers or acquisitions. This activity provides an opportunity to examine the degree to which those firms with larger residual cash flows sought to acquire those companies whose cash flows impaired their ability to make sustaining investments.

Thirty-four firms constitute the data set. Annual balance sheet, income statement, and funds flow data were obtained from COMPUSTAT tapes, while monthly financial series were constructed from the COMPUSTAT PDE files. While most of the variables are self-explanatory, the investment and cash-flow series require additional discussion.

Total capital investment was compiled from the funds flow statements for each firm for each year. The variable was defined as the sum of reported capital expenditures, acquisitions, and investments (principally securities held for purposes other than liquidity). Share repurchases were not included. Acquisitions and longer-term security investments were defined directly as discretionary investment.[15]

The separation of capital expenditures into sustaining and discretionary investment components was done by using accounting data on replacement depreciation, with adjustments for real sales growth, as described below. With the advent of Statement 33 from the Financial Accounting Standards Board (FASB), current replacement cost data began to be available in the early 1970s. Each firm's quarterly 10-Q report was reviewed for information as to the age, estimated life and remaining value of its plant and equipment. When this information was not explicitly provided, Internal Revenue Service guidelines on asset class lines and depreciation were used to supplement the company's quarterly disclosures. The result is a constructed series of "replacement" capital investment for each firm, based on accounting information.[16] These amounts were then combined with adjustments to reflect the required amount of inventory investment. These inventory requirements are not automatically captured by the cost of goods sold on the income statement. Cost of goods sold and related inventory accounts exhibited wide variations in the degree of last-in-first-out (LIFO) versus first-in-first-out (FIFO) accounting.[17] In addition, adjustments were necessary for those firms that dipped into lower cost LIFO layers on their income statements during the late 1970s and early 1980s. The inventory adjustments involved the use of current-cost inventory data when possible and information from the most recent quarterly financial report on LIFO cost of goods sold and changes in the LIFO reserve. The effect of these calculations is to reflect more accurately the sustaining expenditures on physical assets required for ongoing operation at prior or established levels of activity.

However, such a series does not incorporate those capital investments required to maintain established growth patterns or trends. To do this, further adjustments were necessary to distinguish the growth-related component of sustaining investment from discretionary expenditures. To incorporate this effect, each firm's real sales growth was calculated, and this growth factor applied to the required replacement investment calculated above.[18] When added together, the result is an estimate of sustaining investment for each year.[19] The difference between total capital expenditures and sustaining investment provides our estimate of discretionary investment.[20]

Residual cash flow was estimated by indirect construction. Reported net income (before extraordinary items) was combined with noncash expenses (principally depreciation, amortization, and the change in deferred taxes) to generate a total cash-flow measure. Construction of the residual cash-flow measure began with net operating income before interest and taxes. Consistent with the hierarchical model, interest payments on existing debt and taxes were then subtracted.[21] The subsequent set of cash distributions involve provisions of returns to financial claimants *at previously established levels,* for example, net debt issuance, sinking fund requirements, preferred dividends, and common dividends at the same level as the previous year.[22] Following these distributions, sustaining investment (as described above) was subtracted. The amount of funds available after this entire series of distributions was defined as the residual cash flow.

5.4   Empirical Tests of Cash Flow–Investment Relationships

Summary statistical information for the paper industry is presented in table 5.1 for the entire 1971–86 period, and the 1971–80 and 1981–86 subperiods. The 1971–80 subperiod reflects the years of large energy and capital shocks, while the 1981–86 period covers years of stable or falling energy costs and a different investment environment. In particular, while capital expenditures as a percentage of total assets has remained stable, there was more acquisition

Table 5.1   **Summary of Cash Flow and Investment Data, Paper Industry**

Variable	1971–86	1971–80	1981–86
Return on assets	4.316	4.79	3.804
	(1.839)	(1.91)	(2.057)
Residual cash flow as % total cash flow	.499	.644	.311
	(.512)	(.737)	(.533)
Residual cash flow as % of common equity (book value)	.120	.131	.092
	(.068)	(.084)	(.078)
Capital expenditures as % of total assets (annual average)	.102	.119	.097
	(.023)	(.039)	(.038)
Dividend payout ratio (average)	.202	.165	.201
	(.201)	(.227)	(.246)
Debt/asset ratio	.449	.425	.477
	(.069)	(.146)	(.135)
Total share repurchases as % beginning equity	.151	.055	.106
	(.173)	(.069)	(.127)
Discretionary investment as % of total capital investment	.287	.320	.252
	(.354)	(.382)	(.114)
Residual cash flow as % of capital expenditures (% internal financing)	.682	.763	.576
	(.365)	(.400)	(.452)
Acquisitions and investments as % of beginning common equity	.503	.271	.469
	(.633)	(.179)	(.491)
Average total return to shareholders	.155	.168	.175
	(.095)	(.077)	(.187)

Note: Mean is given for each category with SD in parentheses below.

activity and less nontakeover discretionary investment in the 1980s. Consistent with the free cash-flow hypothesis and our residual funds model, this decline in nontakeover discretionary investment occurred at the same time as increases in leverage and dividend payout. Within the possible discretionary uses of residual funds, the main change has been the importance of share repurchases, which doubled (on average) between the two periods.

Traditional investment analysis assigns a large role to profitability (net present value) as a determinant of investment behavior. A difficulty arises in distinguishing between the profitability of investment opportunities at the margin as distinct from the overall profitability of the firm (returns from the flow of new projects relative to returns from the stock of prior investments). As proxies, our model employs a set of return on assets (ROA) variables and a measure of Tobin's q, the ratio of the market value of the firm to the replacement cost of assets.[23] The first of our ROA variables is the firm's ROA for the previous year, to reflect the "best" historical information that managers might have on recent performance. The second variable is the ROA that actually occurred for the current and succeeding year, which is intended to serve as a proxy for reasonably perfect foresight about investment returns. The third measure is the overall industry average ROA for the prior year, current year, and following year. This measure also incorporates foresight, intending to measure the general industry outlook at the time the investment was made. While the effect of including both past and future (perfect foresight) ROA measures might be expected to overstate the strength of the profitability-investment link, it does provide a more stringent test of incremental influences of cash flow on sustaining and discretionary investment.

Three alternative cash-flow measures are employed: total cash flows, residual cash flows, and residual cash flows net of ROA effects. The last of these measures was constructed by regressing residual cash flows as a percentage of common equity on the firm's ROA, and defining the regression errors as residual cash flows net of ROA effects. This measure embodies a rigorous test of the independent effect of cash flow on investment, since arguably it could be claimed that ROA or other profit measures incorporate cash-flow financial considerations.

In pooling the cross section time-series data set, we used both standard ordinary least squares (OLS) estimation with a single intercept and a fixed-effects model utilizing separate dummy intercepts for each firm. The former model depends on inter- as well as intrafirm variation, whereas the fixed-effects model depends solely on interfirm variation. Generally, the fixed-effect model is preferred because of the asymptotic efficiency of its estimators. The fixed-effects model has the further advantage of controlling for omitted firm-specific effects. Consequently, the cash-flow parameter estimates in the fixed-effects model are more likely to reflect their hypothesized influences rather than merely serve as a proxy for omitted neoclassical profit-related variables.

Table 5.2 presents results for the determinants of sustaining investment,

Table 5.2   **Dependent Variable: ln(Sustaining Investment)**

Equation	Constant	ln(ROA) − 1	ln(IND ROA) (−1, 0, +1)	ln(q)	ln(EXP ROA) ln(ROA 0, +1)	ln(TCF)	ln(RCF)	ln(RCF Net of ROA Effect)	R^2	F	Durbin-Watson Statistic
(1)	.832	.292	.147	.026	.258	.255			.623	288.3	1.72
	(2.63)	(3.47)	(2.78)	(1.37)	(2.05)	(3.64)					
(2)	.684	.238	.124	.025	.192		.248		.656	240.3	1.67
	(2.23)	(2.64)	(1.75)	(1.38)	(1.96)		(3.41)				
(3)	.955	.215	.209	.014	.265			.285	.651	235.3	1.62
	(3.48)	(2.88)	(1.68)	(1.18)	(2.33)			(3.03)			
(4)		.192	.304	.303	.284	.390			.739	271.2	1.93
		(2.82)	(2.94)	(2.34)	(2.71)	(2.36)					
(5)		.196	.196	.256	.273		.434		.712	287.1	1.61
		(3.54)	(2.33)	(1.85)	(3.03)		(2.72)				
(6)		.387	.121	.298	.392			.417	.741	212.4	1.74
		(4.21)	(2.26)	(2.19)	(2.44)			(2.03)			

Note: t-statistics are in parentheses. ROA = returns on assets; IND ROA = industry returns on assets; EXP ROA = expected returns on assets; ln = natural log; TCF = total cash flow; RCF = residual cash flow.

expressed in log transformations. Equations (1), (2), and (3) are OLS estimates for each of the different cash flow measures, while equations (4), (5), and (6) are the corresponding fixed-effects estimates. Of the profitability measures, the firm's recent ROA and its expected ROA (in a perfect foresight framework) are relatively consistent and significant. In addition, industry average ROA exerts a positive, albeit smaller, effect on sustaining investment. The q variable is small and insignificant in the OLS equations, but larger and more significant in the fixed-effects models. The magnitude of the q coefficients is consistent with the estimates of Salinger (1984), Summers (1981), Hayashi (1982), and Schaller (1988). The added significance of q in the fixed-effects regressions suggests that q models should carefully control for firm-specific effects. This may help to better control for interfirm differences in market power or other product market imperfections.

The cash-flow variables in table 5.2 are significant and roughly the same magnitude as the individual profitability variables. However, the profitability effects taken together are still larger than the cash-flow influences. Also, the significance of the residual cash-flow variable drops when it is measured net of ROA collinearity.

The residual funds hypothesis asserts that residual cash flows, while having some effect on total capital expenditures, should be of greater importance in determining discretionary investment. In table 5.3, fixed-effects estimates of discretionary investment equations are shown. The first three regressions in table 5.3 introduce the three alternate cash-flow measures and are estimated using the entire pooled sample, including those observaitons where residual cash flows are negative. However, a "strong form" of the residual funds model would argue that, since discretionary investment cannot fall below zero, the residual cash flow–discretionary investment relationship might differ in those situations where residual cash flows are negative. To evaluate this, equation (4) of table 5.3 estimates the fixed-effects model without those observations in which residual cash flows were below zero. Negative residual cash flows occurred in at least one year for 19 of the 34 firms, but accounted for only 16% of the total observations. As equation (4) shows, the coefficient estimates are relatively uninfluenced by this change, suggesting that the logarithmic structure of the model is reasonable.[24]

The lagged ROA effect is always negative, with marginal significance. Expected ROA does have the hypothesized positive effect and is somewhat significant. Both industry ROA and q effects are insignificant and negatively associated with discretionary investment. By contrast, the cash-flow estimates are positive and significant in all equations. Furthermore, residual cash flows are both larger and more significant than total cash flows as determinants of discretionary investment. The residual cash-flow measures apparently incorporate few profitability effects, as there are only slight differences in the estimated coefficients (and significance) for the "raw" residual cash-flow measure and for the same variable purged of ROA effects.

Table 5.3   Dependent Variable: ln(Discretionary Investment)

Equation	ln(ROA) (−1)	ln(q)	ln(IND ROA) (−1, 0, +1)	ln(EXP ROA) ln(ROA 0, +1)	ln(TCF)	ln(RCF)	ln(RCF Net of ROA Effect)	R^2	F	Durbin-Watson Statistic
(1)	−.311 (1.94)	.002 (.38)	−.216 (1.54)	.306 (1.48)	.471 (2.92)			.582	291	1.84
(2)	−.227 (2.09)	−.002 (.20)	−.163 (1.35)	.226 (2.10)		.570 (3.43)		.511	259	1.89
(3)	−.217 (1.84)	.001 (.23)	−.126 (.82)	.183 (1.66)			.524 (2.14)	.493	254	2.15
(4)	−.189 (1.99)	.003 (.47)	−.171 (1.49)	.199 (2.03)		.539 (2.86)		.498	237	1.96

Note: *t*-statistics are in parentheses. ROA = returns on assets; IND ROA = industry returns on assets; EXP ROA = expected returns on assets; ln = natural log; TCF = total cash flow; RCF = residual cash flow. Discretionary investment measured as actual capital expenditure minus replacement cost depreciation of physical assets adjusted for real sales growth.

Comparing tables 5.2 and 5.3, the profitability variables' coefficients are larger for sustaining investment than for discretionary expenditures, while the cash-flow measures are substantially more important for discretionary investment. In most of the equations, ROA is negatively related to discretionary investment, yet positively associated with sustaining expenditures. Since the ROA variables reflect returns on existing assets, they would be expected to exert a more direct and pronounced influence on sustaining than on discretionary investment. Lower profitability also may signal an orientation toward discretionary expenditures outside of the firm's current operations.

Table 5.4 presents fixed effects estimates of the determinants of merger and acquisition activity (within the industry).[25] Resources used for within-industry acquisitions or similar investments can be thought of as a particular class of discretionary investment. In this case the profitability variables are negatively related to acquisition activity, although with only marginal significance. The major negative relation is with expected ROA, which suggests that poorer prospects may induce consolidations and outside acquisition activity. In all three equations, cash-flow measures are significant and positive. Moreover, the residual cash-flow coefficients dominate those for the total cash flows in magnitude and are roughly equal or better in significance, again supporting the link between residual cash flow and discretionary investment.

5.5 Residual Cash Flows, Discretionary Investment, and Financial Performance

The agency model of the market for corporate control contends that free cash flows create incentives for wasteful capital expenditures, which then hurt financial performance and reduce the value of firms. The previous sections found considerable evidence of a link between residual cash flows and the level of discretionary investment. It remains to be determined whether these discretionary investments harm financial performance. To analyze this, shareholder returns must be examined. Since most investments are multiyear in nature, a long-term review is needed; we chose to measure shareholder returns as the price relative of common stock for the 1971–80 and the 1981–86 periods. The price-relative measure cumulates the price and dividend components of shareholder returns. It is superior to the average total return because it takes into account wealth positions reinvested on an ongoing basis, rather than only short-term trading returns.

The results for the 1971–80 and 1981–86 subperiods are presented in table 5.5. Most of the estimated coefficients are similar for both periods; however, the sustaining investment and dividend payout ratio variables have statistically significant coefficient changes. Capital expenditure on sustaining investment was associated with higher returns in the 1970s than in the 1980s. This may reflect a high marginal return on replacement of existing assets in the wake of two major energy price shocks during the earlier period. Conversely, sustain-

Table 5.4   Dependent Variable: ln(Acquisitions and Investments)

Equation	ln(ROA) (−1)	ln(q)	ln(IND ROA) (−1, 0, +1)	ln(EXP ROA) ln(ROA 0, +1)	ln(TCF)	ln(RCF)	ln(RCF Net of ROA Effect)	R^2	F	Durbin-Watson Statistic
(1)	−.163	.531	−1.440	−.103	.463			.477	5.46	1.64
	(1.88)	(2.08)	(1.54)	(2.69)	(2.82)					
(2)	−.199	.302	−.644	−.118		.658		.503	8.38	1.72
	(1.44)	(1.84)	(1.25)	(2.47)		(3.31)				
(3)	−.167	.325	−.694	−.141			.577	.485	5.97	1.62
	(1.58)	(2.24)	(1.32)	(2.99)			(2.58)			

Note: t-statistics are in parentheses. ROA = returns on assets; IND ROA = industry returns on assets; EXP ROA = expected returns on assets; ln = natural log; TCF = total cash flow; RCF = residual cash flow.

Table 5.5   Dependent Variable: Price Relative of Common Stock (Total Return to Shareholders over Entire Period)

Variable	1971–80	1981–86
Constant	1.831	.827
	(.72)	(.94)
Sustaining investment as % of total assets	2.381	.944
	(2.63)	(1.90)
Discretionary capital investment as % of total assets	− 1.417	− 1.612
	(− 3.12)	(− 3.20)
Cumulative ROA	.834	.938
	(2.66)	(3.14)
Orthogonalized residual cash flow as % of total assets	.886	.964
	(− 2.19)	(2.52)
Dividend payout ratio	.402	.652
	(− 1.56)	(1.76)
Share repurchases as % of equity	− 1.441	1.718
	(− 1.46)	(3.15)
Acquisitions and investments as % of common equity	2.781	2.182
	(2.41)	(3.18)
(Sales + inventory change as % of total assets) ×	.545	.304
(sustaining investment as % of total assets)	(2.84)	(2.46)
$\bar{R}^2$	.568	.558
F-statistic	3.39*	2.74*

Note: t-statistics are in parentheses.
*p = .01.

ing investment in the 1980s was done in an environment largely characterized by excess industry capacity, so that maintenance of the existing asset base may have resulted in lower returns.

In considering the possible influence of sustaining investment on returns, the interaction of capacity utilization and investment requirements must be considered. Specifically, the closer a firm is to full capacity, the more likely growth in sustaining investment will be required. Since firm-specific capacity utilization measures are not available, a proxy was constructed as (sales + change in inventories) divided by total assets.[26] This variable then was multiplied by (sustaining investment/total assets) to create an interactive variable. The coefficient of this measure is positive and significant in both periods, although much larger in the 1970s. One reason for this change may be that capacity utilization in the earlier period was much higher; in the 1980s, many plants did not achieve 80% utilization until late 1985. This result also suggests that sustaining investment may be quite stable during periods of excess capacity, but that nonlinearities are introduced once capacity utilization passes some threshold.[27]

In both periods, a larger share of discretionary capital expenditure was significantly negatively associated with stock price relatives, lending strong credence to at least the major tenets of the Jensen agency hypothesis. However, acquisition activity (a component of discretionary investment) was positively and significantly associated with higher shareholder gains. At least for the paper industry, distinguishing between sustaining and discretionary investment may not go far enough; the positive effects of acquisition activity suggests that discretionary investment classification should be further disaggregated.[28]

The availability of residual cash-flow financing is positively related to shareholder wealth in both periods, even after orthogonalizing for profitability effects. One possible explanation is the value of such residual cash flows as reserve financial capacity, akin to Donaldson's (1984) and Myers and Majluf's (1984) concept of financial slack. Thus, residual cash flows may provide financial flexibility to undertake positive net present value projects if they appear; however, the negative relation between discretionary investment and shareholder returns suggests that the key component in the agency model of corporate control lies not in residual cash flows as much as in the uses to which those funds are committed.

5.6 Summary

This paper develops two distinctions in evaluating the linkages between cash flows, investment, and financial performance. The first is the difference between sustaining and discretionary investment. Sustaining investment is aimed at maintaining the productive capacity of the firm's existing assets. Discretionary investment reflects capital expenditures that are not required for core business purposes, yet are undertaken in lieu of dividend increases, share repurchases, or other stockholder distributions. A major contention of this paper is that the determinants of these two types of corporate investment are quite different. In fact, the logic of the residual funds approach is that it is inherently a misspecification to use total capital expenditures as a dependent variable in analysis of investment, since total capital expenditure comprises at least two different components.

At the same time, a distinction was made between total cash flow and residual cash flow. The total cash-flow measure is more closely tied to profitability, while residual cash flows takes into account a hypothesized hierarchy of claims, only some of which embody legally established priority obligations. Residual cash flows were defined as funds that remain after debt service, taxes, sustaining investment, and "established" dividends were paid. This set of payments to financial claimants, in conjunction with sustaining investment, is a vital means of signaling information as to the value of the firm's existing assets. Once this is done, residual cash flows, discretionary investment, and changes in dividend policies provide information concerning a firm's prospects and investment opportunities.

The disaggregation of investment and cash-flow data is important in empirical analysis of both agency and asymmetric information models. The observed relationship between residual cash flows, discretionary investment, and financial performance is consistent with agency hypotheses. Discretionary expenditures are negatively related to shareholder returns, but acquisitions (mostly related to core business activities) are positively associated with shareholder wealth. This strongly suggests that further disaggregation and specification of the different constituent parts of both corporate cash flow and capital budgets would be worthwhile. Some important nonlinear relationships also may be present and need to be explored.[29] Finally, this paper examined only one industry; any substantial generalization awaits a broader investigation into other industries, locales, and time periods.

Of particular interest would be investigations of other industries at different stages of product maturity and with different cash-flow characteristics. For example, the behavior of reputedly "mature" industries such as railroads, steel, and tires might be contrasted with those industries based on relatively new technologies, such as electronics and some pharmaceuticals. Natural resource-based industries subject to product price volatility also would provide a different body of experience for investigation.

In each of these cases, of course, difficult data and definitional problems are present. However, such problems also are endemic when attempting to adapt accounting information to measure other economic concepts (as, say, when attempting to measure q). Furthermore, if the paper industry results are not too atypical, then efforts to define and measure discretionary investment and residual funds are valuable, at least by the empirical standard of better identifying underlying behavioral regularities in investment and financial decisions.

Notes

1. The theoretical base in this area has been developed over a 20-year period in a series of papers by Joseph Stiglitz (1969, 1973, 1974, 1982, 1988). See also B. Greenwald, J. Stiglitz, and A. Weiss (1984), J. Stiglitz and A. Weiss (1981), Stephen Ross (1977), and Hayne Leland and David Pyle (1977). An excellent review of these issues is found in Auerbach (1983).

2. For a review of these issues, see Amir Barnea, Robert A. Haugen, and Lemma W. Senbet (1986); also, Michael C. Jensen and Clifford W. Smith, Jr. (1985).

3. However, the study only analyzes stock price effects of the announcement of capital spending plans, so that the longer-term valuation effects of actual capital expenditures are not considered.

4. Early discussions of debt capacity include John R. Meyer and Edwin Kuh (1957) and Gordon Donaldson (1961). Recently, Stewart Myers's (1984) notion of "financial slack" is quite similar.

5. Gordon Donaldson (1984, 3).

6. Much of the empirical work in support of agency perspectives on corporate control and the problem of managerial discretion relies heavily on stock price event stud-

ies, which typically cover only a short period, most commmonly 60 days surrounding the event.

7. Information asymmetry arguments must be carefully drawn in the context of acquisitions outside of core businesses. In those cases, the acquiring firm's managers may have no information advantage or, possibly, an information disadvantage. This may explain (in part) the lack of gains to shareholders of acquiring firms during merger activity.

8. A review of signaling aspects of alternative financing is presented in P. Asquith and D. Mullins (1986). See also J. Crockett and I. Friend (1988).

9. K. Smith (1989) finds little evidence of a relation between the sophistication of investment review and control systems and financial performance.

10. See Alan J. Auerbach (1984).

11. This has been true in the natural resource industries and in financial institutions, where growth has occurred through acquisition rather than internal expansion. This reorientation may also account for critiques of such restructurings, which raise concerns about diversion from long-term to short-term goals.

12. In a recent paper, Bernheim shows that dividends and repurchases can serve different signaling functions analogous to the distinction between sustaining and discretionary activities. See B. Douglas Bernheim (1988). See also Kose John and Joseph Williams (1985).

13. This contrasts with Fazzari, Hubbard, and Petersen (1988), who separate firms on the basis of payout levels in their analysis of investment decisions.

14. The average equity beta for the sample of paper companies is 1.17; the asset-weighted average beta is 1.04.

15. The discretionary nature of such activities depends in part on the degree to which acquisitions involve operations related to core business, as distinct from unrelated diversification. The COMPUSTAT and DISCLOSURE data only provide aggregate dollar amounts of each firm's acquisitions and investments. A search of *the Wall Street Journal Index* and *the New York Times Index* identified corporate acquisitions and a few acquisitions of plants or divisions, but for these asset purchases terms typically were not disclosed.

16. Use of replacement depreciation as a proxy for sustaining investment may overstate actual sustaining investment, to the extent that such replacement is unwarranted. This might be true, e.g., in declining industries, or where technological change has increased the flow of capital services from a given stock of capital assets.

17. This information was gathered from the footnotes of each firm's financial statements for each year.

18. These adjustments were made using the Consumer Price Index.

19. An alternative measure of sustaining and discretionary investment was constructed using a distributed lag model for each company. The model was used to construct a baseline "expected" level of capital expenditures for each firm for each year. While the two measures of sustaining investment had a correlation of .74, the estimate of sustaining investment from the distributed lag model is consistently higher than that employing adjusted accounting data. This result might be expected, since any "average" level of capital expenditures is likely to include some discretionary component.

20. Although we do present a model of total gross capital expenditures below, our focus is on the relation between cash flow and discretionary investment, which should be largely unrelated to capital stock per se. Since our construction is based on replacement depreciation from financial statements, capital stock effects thereby are incorporated. In the total investment model, Goldfeld-Quandt tests for heteroscedasticity were rejected. Given reasonably homoscedastic residuals, Kuh and Meyer (1955) argue that deflating by assets may introduce spurious correlation in the ratios.

21. This subtraction introduces a degree of measurement error becasuse taxes payable for financial reporting purposes may differ from the actual amount of taxes paid.

22. Net debt issuance is included here as a means by which companies can maintain target capital structures.

23. In our regressions, our measure of q is unadjusted for taxes and reflects the market and asset values at the beginning of each year. While a more detailed construction of q could change our reported results, Fazzari, Hubbard, and Petersen (1988) find little difference in their results using adjusted or unadjusted measures of q. Schaller (1988), however, finds the estimates of the effects of q on investment to be quite sensitive to measurement issues.

24. The model's fit is enhanced slightly, due to the nonlinearity of discretionary investment-residual funds relationship around zero.

25. The partitioning of total expenditures into sustaining and discretionary components is always open to criticism. However, the clear discretionary nature of acquisitions and investments provides a good test of the residual funds approach.

26. Since the valuation equations are cross-sectional, industry capacity utilization for each subperiod does not capture intrafirm differences very well. While the (sales + inventory change)/total assets measure does suffer from flow-stock incongruity, it does measure asset-use intensity. To check the relation with capacity utilization, the constructed (sales + inventory change)/total assets variables were combined into an asset-weighted average for each year. The correlation of this measure within the time series of paper industry capacity utilization was .71.

27. Further analysis of this point introduces measurement problems as well, since a reliance on historically based accounting or investment relations may be unreliable as a guide to future sustaining investment needs.

28. Given that most of the paper industry merger and acquisition activity involved consolidation rather than diversification, the positive valuation effects of acquisitions support well-established business policy views on the value of "sticking to one's knitting" in seeking mergers and acquisitions within the core business or in closely related activities. See M. E. Porter (1987).

29. Dhrymes and Kurz (1967) contend that study of investment and financial policies generally requires use of simultaneous-equations methodology, given the prevailing endogeneity; they gave particular emphasis to the problem of dividend payout and retention. This approach, while worthy of exploration, may not apply as directly to the residual funds model, in that the strict accounting and financial identities are not present in our hierarchical model of financial and investment allocation.

References

Asquith, P., and D. Mullins. 1986. Signalling with dividends, stock repurchases, and equity issues. *Financial Management* 15:27–44.
Auerbach, A. 1983. Taxation, corporate finance, and the cost of capital. *Journal of Economic Literature* 21:905–40.
———. 1984. Taxes, firm financial policy and the cost of capital: An empirical analysis. *Journal of Public Economics* 23:27–57.
Barnea, A., R. Haugen, and L. Senbet. 1986. *Agency problems and financial contracting.* Englewood Cliffs: Prentice-Hall.
Bernheim, B. D. 1988. Dividends versus share repurchases as signals of profitability. Unpublished manuscript. Northwestern University, Kellogg School of Management.

Bernstein, J., and M. I. Nadiri. 1986. Published in Peston, M. and Quandt, R., editors, *Prices, competition, and equilibrium*. London: Philip Allan/Barnes and Noble.

Bhattacharya, S. 1979. Imperfect information, dividend policy, and the "bird in the hand" fallacy. *Bell Journal of Economics* 10:259–70.

Bruner, R. 1988. The use of excess cash and debt capacity as a motive for merger. *Journal of Financial and Quantitative Analysis* 23:199–217.

Crockett, J., and I. Friend. 1988. Dividend policy in perspective: Can theory explain behavior? *The Review of Economics and Statistics* 70:603–13.

Dhrymes, P., and M. Kurz. 1967. Investment, dividend, and external finance behavior of firms. In *Determinants of investment behavior*, ed. R. Ferber. New York: Columbia University Press.

Dobrovolsky, S. 1951. *Corporate income retention*. New York: NBER.

Donaldson, G. 1961. *Corporate debt capacity: A study of corporate debt policy and the determination of corporate debt capacity*. Boston: Harvard University, Graduate School of Business Administration, Division of Research.

———. G. 1984. *Managing corporate wealth*. New York: Praeger.

Fazzari, S., R. G. Hubbard, and B. Petersen. 1988. Financing constraints and corporate investment. *Brookings Papers on Economic Activity*, no. 1, pp. 141–95.

Greenwald, B., J. Stiglitz, and A. Weiss. 1984. Information imperfections in the capital market and macroeconomic fluctuations. *American Economic Review* 74:194–99.

Griffin, J. 1988. A test of the free cash flow hypothesis: Results from the petroleum industry. *Review of Economics and Statistics* 70:76–82.

Hakansson, N. 1982. To pay or not to pay dividends. *Journal of Finance* 37:415–28.

Hayashi, F. 1982. Tobin's marginal q and average q: A neoclassical interpretation. *Econometrica* 50: 213–24.

Jensen, M. 1986. Agency costs of free cash flow, corporate finance, and takeovers. *American Economic Review* 76:323–29.

Jensen, M., and C. Smith. 1985. Stockholder, manager, and creditor interests: Applications of agency theory. In *Recent advances in corporate finance*, ed. E. Altman and M. Subrahmanyam, pp. 93–136. Homewood, Ill.: Irwin.

John, K., and J. Williams. 1985. Dividends, dilution, and taxes. *Journal of Finance* 40:1053–70.

Kuh, E. 1963. *Capital stock growth: A microeconometric approach*. Amsterdam: Elsevier.

Kuh, E., and J. R. Meyer. 1955. Correlation and regression estimates when the data are ratios. *Econometrica* 23:400–416.

Leland, H., and D. Pyle. 1977. Information asymmetries, financial structure, and financial intermediation. *Journal of Finance* 32:371–87.

Lintner, J. 1956. Distribution of incomes of corporations among dividends, retained earnings, and taxes. *American Economic Review* 46 (May): 97–113.

McConnell, J., and C. Muscarella. 1985. Corporate capital expenditure decisions and the market value of the firm. *Journal of Financial Economics* 14:399–422.

McDonald, R., and N. Soderstrom. 1986. Dividend and share changes: Is there a financing hierarchy? NBER Working Paper no. 2029.

Meyer, J. R., and R. Glauber. 1964. *Investment decisions, economic forecasting, and public policy*. Boston: Harvard University, Graduate School of Business Administration, Division of Research.

Meyer, J. R., and E. Kuh. 1957. *The investment decision*. Cambridge, Mass.: Harvard University Press.

Myers, S. 1984. The capital structure puzzle. *Journal of Finance* 39:575–92.

Myers, S., and N. Majluf. 1984. Corporate financing decisions when firms have investment information that investors do not have. *Journal of Financial Economics* 13:187–221.

Petersen, B. 1988. Capital markets imperfections and investment fluctuations. *Economic Perspectives,* 12:3–12. Chicago: Federal Reserve Bank.

Porter, M. 1987. From competitive advantage to corporate strategy. *Harvard Business Review* 65:43–60.

Salinger, M. 1984. Tobin's q, unionization, and the concentration-profits relationship. *Rand Journal of Economics* 15:159–70.

Ross, S. A. 1977. The determination of financial structure: the incentive-signalling approach. *Bell Journal of Economics* 8:23–40.

Schaller, H. 1988. Why doesn't Q investment theory work? Evidence from U.S. firm data. Typescript, Department of Economics, MIT.

Smith, K. 1989. Effects of investment control systems. Ph.D. diss., University of Maryland.

Stiglitz, J. 1969. A re-examination of the Miller-Modigliani Theorem. *American Economic Review* 59:784–93.

———. 1973. Corporate financial policy and the cost of capital. *Journal of Public Economics* 2:1–34.

———. 1974. On the irrelevance of corporate financial policy. *American Economic Review* 64:851–66.

———. 1982. Information and capital markets. In *Financial economics: Essays in honor of Paul Cootner,* ed. C. Cootner and W. Sharpe, pp. 118–58. Englewood Cliffs, N.J.: Prentice-Hall.

———. 1988. Why financial structure matters. *Journal of Economic Perspectives* 2:121–26.

Stiglitz, J., and A. Weiss. 1981. Credit rationing in markets with imperfect information. *American Economic Review* 71:393–410.

Summers, L. 1981. Taxation and corporate investment: a q-theory approach. *Brookings Papers on Economic Activity,* no. 1, pp. 67–127.

6   Are Large Shareholders Effective Monitors? An Investigation of Share Ownership and Corporate Performance

Richard J. Zeckhauser and John Pound

6.1   Introduction

Large shareholders, who hold a sizable fraction of all voting shares in publicly held corporations, may solve a fundamental problem of modern capital markets: the difficulty outside claim holders have in monitoring corporate management. For an individual shareholder, the costs of obtaining information may outweigh its benefits. In addition, the holdings of dispersed individual shareholders are too small to influence corporate outcomes, even if the benefits are great enough to provide adequate incentives to become informed.[1] Large shareholders potentially solve both of these problems. They can reap large benefits for themselves and other shareholders by becoming informed and possibly by influencing corporate outcomes because they hold a block of voting power.

In recent years, empirical studies have confirmed that the arrival of new large shareholders causes significant stock price increases in target corporations (Mikkelson and Ruback 1985; Holderness and Sheehan 1985). This pattern implies that the accumulation of a new, large position conveys significant benefits to other shareholders of the corporation. However, the most dramatic of these gains come when the large shareholder is perceived to be trying to gain control of the target firm. In this case, large shareholders convey benefits not because they engage in long-term monitoring and thereby insure against

Richard J. Zeckhauser is the Frank P. Ramsey Professor of Political Economy at the John F. Kennedy School of Government, Harvard University, and a research associate at the National Bureau of Economic Research. John Pound is an assistant professor of public policy at the John F. Kennedy School of Government, Harvard University.

This research was conducted under the auspices of the Corporate Voting Research Project at the John F. Kennedy School of Government. The authors acknowledge their debt to Francois Degeorge for research assistance. Comments by participants at the NBER conference and the Sanwa Bank Conference on International Financial Markets, July 1989, Tokyo, are greatly appreciated.

poor performance, but rather because their arrival indicates takeover pressure directed against the firm. They represent a one-time catalyst for sudden change in corporate structure or strategy.

An unanswered question—and perhaps one more fundamental to the broad process of corporate governance—is whether the ongoing presence of a large shareholder has significant effects on corporate performance, assuming no explicitly activist or control-oriented short-term plan. If large shareholders monitor corporate activity, they could deter managers from securing benefits at the expense of shareholders. (Managerial self-dealing arises because the shareholders are either unable to determine what is happening or powerless to stop the process.)

Our principal interest in this analysis is not self-dealing but another undesirable practice that arises from asymmetries in information between shareholder and manager, namely performance tilting. Let us assume that some aspects of firm performance (A) can readily be monitored by shareholders, whereas others (B) cannot. A manager intent on demonstrating that he is performing ably will tilt performance by fostering A at the expense of B. For example, A might be sales levels, which are attested to by accountants; B might be the training of young employees, an effort that affects the balance sheet or income statement only after many years. In this vein, managers are often criticized for paying too much attention to a short-term, bottom-line view.

Note that performance tilting involves neither diminution of managerial effort nor excess pay. If both A and B could be monitored, the manager would produce a more balanced portfolio of outputs. The shareholders would be better off, and, presumably, the manager would reap extra benefits as well.

As monitors—of self-dealing, performance tilting, or both—large shareholders would constitute a part of the incentive structure of the firm. They would interact with management and affect the formulation of corporate strategy. They would lessen the need for takeovers and other control-transferring activities by imposing discipline on corporate operations. To accomplish this, they need not issue any threats. As we will show, large shareholders may raise the value of the company merely by indicating that it is safe to take results at their face value, without worrying about managerial duplicity or distortion.

In this paper, we examine how large shareholders might affect long-term corporate performance, and whether they in fact do so. We first discuss the potential impact of large shareholders on corporate incentives and information flow. Our particular focus is on the much-discussed trade-off between short- and long-term performance. Our central argument is that current results are easier to observe than future prospects; hence they are overemphasized by managements that may no longer be in office when prospects become reality. A good example of this phenomenon relates to the choice of accounting methods for inventories. Assuming rising prices, first-in-first-out (FIFO) accounting results in higher stated earnings than last-in-first-out (LIFO) accounting. Higher stated earnings in turn means higher taxes and less money to reinvest or pay dividends to the shareholders. (If a firm uses LIFO for tax purposes, it must also use LIFO for reporting purposes.) Even though the choice of accounting methods is easily observed, a management worried about maintaining announced share earnings, the most monitorable output quantity, might elect FIFO, reducing the short- and long-term cash flow of the corporation.

The choice of accounting methods bears a parallel to paying dividends, a costly measure, to signal the financial condition of the firm. Dividend signaling (if the practice exists) also sacrifices shareholder interests to convey favorable information to the market. In both cases a scrupulously honest, impartial monitor would avoid this waste and therefore benefit both shareholders and management.

Our empirical work employs cross-sectional data to infer the presence or absence of performance tilting. Our principal focus is on the possibility of excessive present orientation due to difficulties in monitoring the future. Thus, we test for systematic differences in expected future performance among firms with large shareholders, compared with firms in the same industries that do not have such shareholders. We also examine whether the presence of large shareholders affects corporate financial policies that are determined, in part, by the size of agency problems within the firm and, in part, by the need to signal future performance to the market.

We examine two financial policy choices that are frequently described as signaling instruments: dividend payouts and capital structure. High dividend payments, relative to industry norms, may be an attempt to signal higher future profits to the market (Bhattacharya 1979). Alternatively, by requiring the firm to go to the capital market more frequently, such payments could provide for monitoring (Rozeff 1982; Easterbrook 1984). If either of these forces is significant, large shareholders may reduce the need for dividend payments. At the opposite end of the scale, it has been alleged that in firms with unappealing prospects, self-aggrandizing managements may reinvest profits at below-market rates. (Supposedly, large oil companies invested in uneconomic exploration in the era before takeover threats curbed such action.) Large shareholders may force larger dividend payouts from such firms. Similarly, large shareholdings and leverage may be systematically related. The agency costs of debt (Jensen and Meckling 1976) may be affected by large shareholders. Alternatively, as with dividends, large shareholders may reduce the need for other financial signals of future performance (Ross 1977). Our tests thus provide indirect evidence on the hypothesis that dividends and leverage are used as signals.

In our tests, we distinguish firms operating in two types of industries: those in which capital and investments are highly firm specific and those in which they are not. When assets are unique to the firm and its management—when, for example, there is a high level of R&D activity—monitoring by shareholders will be difficult. When firms have assets that are specific to management, large shareholders cannot as easily improve performance even if they find that management's current performance is lacking. It is therefore harder, for example, to restructure the asset base of a computer company than that of a steel or oil company. In addition, we conjecture that firms with a high degree of asset specificity are also likely to have a closed information structure—that is, the investment decisions of management are likely to be difficult to analyze. In these industries, we hypothesize, large shareholders are not likely to have a significant monitoring effect.[2] Our main results are as follows.

6.1.1   Earnings/Price Ratios

In industries with relatively low asset specificity and a relatively open information structure, including, for example, machinery, metal fabricating, and paper products, the presence of a large shareholder leads to significantly higher expected future performance. Across eleven such industries, we find that earnings/price (E/P) ratios for large-shareholder firms are lower by an average of approximately 10%. This indicates a higher average expected earnings growth rate in large-shareholder firms. In industries with high asset specificity and, implicitly, a closed information structure, including computers and pharmaceuticals, large shareholders are not associated with lower E/P ratios. This may suggest that when the nature of the firm's investment and production decisions make outside monitoring difficult, large shareholders cannot solve this problem.

6.1.2   Dividend Payout Rates

Within an industry, there is no significant difference in dividend payout rates between firms with and without large shareholders. This finding indicates that dividend payments and large shareholdings are not substitute forms of monitoring.

It also suggests that the predominant monitoring function of large shareholders is not to force increases in payout ratios. That might have been the case if the overriding agency problem solved by large shareholders were insufficient payouts from free cash flows. (Of course, it is conceivable that large shareholders force payouts up to industry norms from a level that would otherwise have been suboptimally low.)

6.1.3   Leverage Ratios

In industries with both open and closed information structures, the leverage ratio is not connected with the presence of a large shareholder. This implies that large shareholders do not guard against the agency costs of debt by deterring investments that compromise the interests of preexisting debtholders. Large shareholders are typically not also debtholders and thus probably lack the incentives to protect debtholder interests. Given the absence of such incentives, indeed, we might actually expect large shareholders to compete with bondholders over the use of corporate resources, with the shareholders pushing on average for more risky activities.

6.2   Large Shareholders and Corporate Oversight

Our central argument is that large outside shareholders can play an important role by monitoring management actions and influencing management decisions to favor shareholders, thereby improving the performance of a corporation and raising the price of its stock. We shall refer to this process as monitoring, but it should be understood to involve as well a decision-altering ingredient that may deter or compel management actions. Our monitor may well be a disciplinarian.

If monitoring can play this valuable role in reducing agency losses in the management-shareholder relationship, why do we not see large shareholders everywhere? What elements of performance will large shareholders affect? How is the market equilibrium established with large shareholders? What returns and costs do large shareholders reap and incur? Do large insider shareholders—presumably even more capable of monitoring—not play an equivalent role?

The model outlined below provides a framework in which to address these questions. Our principal interest is in the intuitive concepts. Thus, we shall rely on partial equilibrium analyses, focusing on one or two factors at a time. Our analysis is developed under four headings: upward-sloping supply curve, large shareholders, the nature of market equilibrium, and monitoring earnings flow and the E/P ratio effect.

6.2.1   The Upward-sloping Supply Curve

The cornerstone of our assumed market for the stock of a company is an upward-sloping supply curve: as one buys more stock the price of an additional share increases. We shall assume that buyers can be perfect monopsonists, purchasing their way up the supply curve.[3]

A number of factors may contribute to the upward slope. We shall mention four, by way of illustration. First, there is heterogeneity among sellers (e.g., different tax positions, different strategies of investing, and different perceptions about the appropriate price for the stock). Thus, their reservation prices differ. Second, inferences about private information can be based on purchases and sales. (The stock price incorporates available information, and a large purchase, e.g., implies the appropriate equilibrium price is higher than the one that previously prevailed.) Third, there may be limited supply of a stock that contributes useful market diversification. Fourth, changes may result from a large buyer's behavior (e.g., he may be considering a takeover or putting the stock in play; alternatively, people may just believe his monitoring will be beneficial to future performance).[4] Any one of these reasons would be sufficient to produce an upward-sloping supply curve. Let us leave aside for the moment the specifics of the supply curve and examine the benefits and costs that return to a large shareholder who monitors.

6.2.2 Large Shareholders

The protagonist in our model is a large shareholder, denoted LS, who assumes a substantial position and then monitors the performance of the company. Given his influential position, he improves that performance on behalf of all shareholders.

To simplify, we will assume that the large shareholder's only productive role is as a monitor. The increment that he offers in performance of the company, and hence stock price, is positively related to the size of his position. There is likely to be a range of increasing returns. Below some threshold he may not be given information or a board seat. Moreover, his own incentive to monitor increases proportionately with holdings. A hypothetical relationship between monitoring gain and size of position is shown as the dashed "large shareholder's marginal value curve" in figure 6.1. This curve shows the LS's average per share increment in value above current market price.

When LS sells out his holding, must he sell back down the supply curve? The answer will depend on how he sells out: Does he transfer a large block to a single purchaser (say, as part of a takeover) or merely put his stake on the market? If he has held the stock for a long time and reaped substantial dividends along the way, that element of his return, which is equal per share held, will tend to level the total return per share. (If LS intends to hold for only a short time, and if he must sell his holdings down the supply curve, then the dashed curve will begin to decline beyond some point.)

Conventional wisdom might suggest that the large shareholder should con-

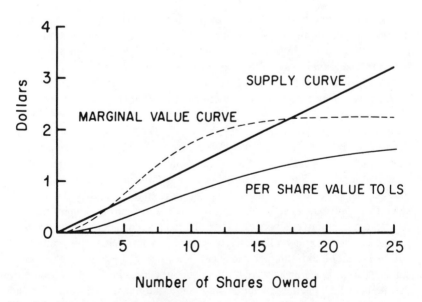

Fig. 6.1 Returns to large shareholder

tinue to purchase shares only so long as the market price is below his value for an additional share of stock, as indicated by the bottom curve in figure 6.1. This rule is not correct, however, for his purchases also influence the performance of the shares he already owns. Thus, he might be willing to pay $41 for a stock that he believes is worth only $40, if this additional purchase increases the value of his previous holdings by more than $1 total.

For decision-making purposes, LS's only concern should be with his marginal valuation curve, which is indicated as the dashed line in the diagram. The third curve shown, which is solid, is the upward-sloping supply curve for the stock. Obviously, if the slope of the supply curve is sufficiently steep there will be no size of position that will enable the large shareholder to break even or make a profit. We illustrate the complementary case, where participation may be worthwhile, where the dashed (marginal benefit) curve crosses the solid (marginal cost) curve.

Let n be the number of shares LS buys, treated as a continuous variable. Consider the case in which each of LS's shares is worth the same, namely $V(n)$, with $P(n)$ being the cost of a marginal share. Thus $V(n)$ would be the dashed curve in the diagram and $P(n)$ the heavy curve. We are assuming that the large shareholder can buy his way up the supply curve. We would expect $P'(n) > 0$, and that $V'(n) > 0$ over the relevant range. Here LS wishes to maximize

$$(1) \qquad nV(n) - \int_0^n P(x)dx,$$

with respect to n. Taking the derivative and setting it equal to zero yields

$$(2) \qquad nV'(n) + V(n) - P(n) = 0,$$

or

$$(3) \qquad nV'(n) = P(n) - V(n).$$

The left-hand side of (3) gives the gain in value to all of LS's existing shares, namely the dashed curve. The right-hand side gives his immediate loss in value due to paying more than the stock is worth.[5]

It may be easier to think of n as the percentage of total available stock rather than as numbers of shares. Our formula implies that an individual who owned 8% of the stock in a company selling at 40 would buy additional stock at 41 if the gain in performance of the company for each percent purchased were $\frac{1}{8}$ of a point.[6]

The LS's analysis would be the same if the increment in value associated with the size of his holding depended on factors other than monitoring. These could include private benefits relating, say, to a takeover, greenmail, or establishing beneficial business relationships. Then the monitoring gains would be mostly a lagniappe. In what follows, we consider large purchases that are primarily designed to improve performance through monitoring.

Does the large shareholder incur costs beyond the money he must expend? Other shareholders will free ride on his shoulders, of course, but that is not a cost to the large shareholder, just a benefit for which he is unable to charge. A loss of diversification will be a significant cost for some large shareholders, say the offspring of the founder of the company, who will find themselves overconcentrated in the stock. This loss will be less severe for large pension funds or mutual funds, which may be able to take large positions in a number of companies and are likely to have holdings in other securities that are significant even in comparison with large positions within single companies.

6.2.3 The Nature of Market Equilibrium

The supply curve we described serves many classes of customers, including speculators, potential large shareholders, individuals who wish to bring information to the market, and sellers with other motivations, such as the need to finance a Porsche purchase.

Other Market Participants

An intriguing group of participants are those who bring information to the market. Some of them may have information of the form, "The price of stock X should be $50." The trouble with this type of information is that individuals with inconsistent beliefs can come into agreement on a market price either by buying or selling amounts so large that risk and/or capital constraints come into play or by curtailing their activities because they realize that the other players have contrary, possibly valid, information.

More often, we believe, information is of the type: "I know some good news about company X, which is unlikely to be fully reflected in the market price. The degree of underreflection is $1." With the latter type of information, the individual would expect to move the price by $1. But given all the noise associated with stock prices, it may be hard to tell when he has had that effect. And is his proper purchase 1,000 shares or 100,000 shares?

Let us take the most favorable situation, in which everyone understands the structure of the supply curve and thus knows how many shares must be purchased or sold in response to particular quantities of information. (Noise in securities markets might otherwise make this hard to determine.) This amount—in effect the local slope of the supply curve—would seem to be somewhat arbitrary. That is, the market could be in equilibrium if it took 1,000 shares to reflect a particular amount of information or if it took 100,000 shares, so long as everybody knew the number. This argument may have a familiar ring from other market situations. For example, only relative prices are determined through market processes, not the overall price level.

Fortunately, several additional mechanisms could help to define the supposedly arbitrary quantity "slope of supply curve." Say the market were highly responsive, so that if someone had a substantial amount of negative information he would sell only a small number of shares, with the market price dropping quickly. We shall now argue that such a situation could not characterize the equilibrium.

Some individuals buy or sell shares for reasons other than bringing information to the market, say, because an estate is being settled, or because they are trading on an uninformed basis, or they are selling all their holdings after listening to John Granville. Under the circumstances described, movements from their purchases (sales) would tend to push the market price of the stock up (down) too much. Arbitragers would recognize that a substantial proportion of price movement in the stock was due to noninformational sales and would correct the market accordingly. Thus, the equilibrium would be altered to become less responsive. (The role of these uninformed traders resembles that of hedgers in providing stability in a conventional hedgers-speculators model.)

A second equilibrating mechanism could be the ability of potential market participants to gather information. If the market were too responsive, then people who acquired information would not be able to reap much profit. Information purchases would diminish. As less information was purchased, a smaller proportion of the activity on the exchange would be due to information. Actions of arbitragers would flatten the supply curve until equilibrium was reached.

Some of the purchases and sales in the market for a stock are true signals. They might be labeled action shares (shares that might do something such as launch a takeover) and knowledge shares (shares that know something). Noise shares are those that are sold by uninformed traders, estates that must be liquidated, and so on. Noise shares are likely to be less affected by the slope of the supply curve than signal shares. Figure 6.2 shows the relationship between the quantities of these different types of shares and the slope of the supply curve.

The Equilibrium Number of Large Shareholders

Let us now turn to the market equilibrium. Arbitragers try to deduce information from market movements. If there is a high signal-to-noise ratio among purchases, then the arbitragers will help to establish a steep slope for the supply curve in the market. This behavior pattern is represented as the arbitrage relationship curve in figure 6.3. The market response curve in that diagram is computed from figure 6.2, where knowledge shares and action shares are amalgamated as the signal component. The intersection of these two curves simultaneously determines the slope of the supply curve and the signal-to-noise ratio in the market.

In the real world, many companies do not have large shareholders. (In two-thirds of the companies we sampled for our empirical work, no shareholder owned over 15% of the shares). One possibility is that there are just not

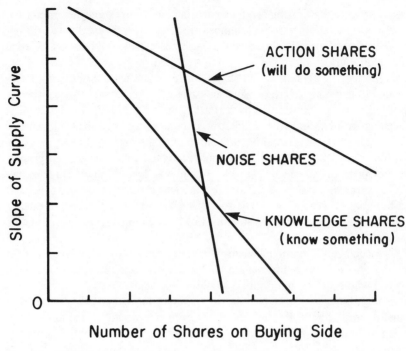

Fig. 6.2   **Different types of shares as a function of slope of supply curve**

enough large players to go around. That explanation is inconsistent with the anecdotal evidence about securities markets. Indeed, there are many large players—such as hundreds of pension and mutual funds—that do not attempt to take monitoring positions in any specific companies.

A more persuasive explanation, we believe, is that some special and scarce skill may be required to produce an upward-sloping curve of the type presented in figure 6.1; that is, the ability to monitor may potentially earn significant rents. Moreover, different holders will be better able to monitor different companies. For some companies no one may be a sufficiently effective monitor to overcome the market-moving costs of securing and disposing of a large position.

Our empirical analysis suggests a third possibility. Some companies do not need (will not yield significant gains to) a large-shareholder monitor. Some companies may already be run effectively on behalf of shareholders and may be expected to be run effectively in the future, perhaps because they have particularly transparent information structures. Alternatively, a company's operations may be so difficult to understand—so "opaque"—that even a large shareholder could not monitor it effectively. Companies with substantial R&D components may often fall into this category. Such companies may still have large shareholders, but not primarily for monitoring reasons (e.g., large downstream firms frequently take large holdings in high tech firms in order to understand, anticipate, and contract for technological innovations). As we discuss below, a fourth reason for the paucity of large shareholders may be that a steep supply curve makes it not worthwhile for large-shareholder monitors to enter.

6.2.4   The Monitoring Process

When large shareholders monitor, how do they increase the value of the company? Their basic role, we believe, is to change the actions of the management. We are concerned with monitoring of (1) self-serving behavior and (2) performance slanting.

Self-serving behavior favors management at the expense of shareholders. In economic models such behavior has been called shirking (in an allusion to the moral-hazard literature), suggesting that, without monitoring, managements do not work as hard as they should. Casual observation of corporate executives, however, suggests that indolence is not a major problem. Shareholders are more likely to be hurt by management's choosing to pay itself more than would be required by competitive conditions. Two factors allow managers to overpay themselves: (1) agenda control (management and its board supporters make the proposals, while shareholders, despite ostensible

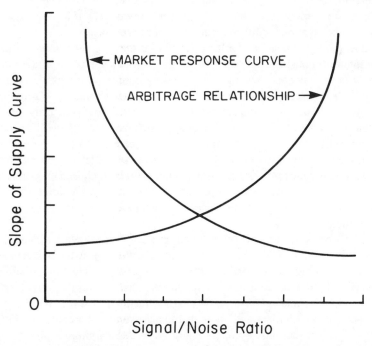

Fig. 6.3   Determination of market equilibrium slope and signal-to-noise ratio

control, have no way to coordinate themselves to oppose); and (2) impenetrability (e.g., compensation arrangements have become so complex that shareholders cannot readily determine what executives are paid).[7]

Performance slanting is the central concern in this analysis. Managements wish to demonstrate that they are performing effectively. If all information flowed freely, and if management could be penalized for poor performance, then trade-offs among corporate accomplishments would be brought more into accord with shareholder preferences. For example, to determine how much the company should spend on maintenance to save future repairs, managers would just use their shareholders' discount rate and undertake any projects with a positive present value. This prescription is fine so long as shareholders can monitor all of the outputs. However, some outputs are more easily observed than others.

Current profits are observable and are defined according to accounting convention. Future profits are always speculative. Managements are usually optimistic but cautious about making specific predictions, particularly given the current litigious environment. It is often alleged that the American economy suffers because stock buyers pay too much attention to the latest quarterly earnings reports. Assuming this to be the case, the manager who can boost current profits by $1 at the expense of $3 in five years might do so, even if the shareholders' trade-off would be $1 for $2. The manager might not be around to reap the benefits of those higher profits, and he does not have a way to demonstrate today that profits will be higher subsequently. If he did, presumably that information would be incorporated into the stock price.[8]

If the manager knew he would be around for the long run, he would have little interest in pushing up today's stock price, p, at the expense of the future price. But he may not know his future. Moreover, his tenure prospects diminish with the stock price. Say his probability of being retained is $q(p)$, where $q' > 0$. Given that most managers have substantial amounts of firm-specific capital, the value of q' need not be great for the manager to be willing to tilt earnings substantially on behalf of today's stock price.[9]

Consider a company with a management that wishes to maximize current stock price. For the purposes of this example, management, like its shareholders, is risk neutral. Management confronts a production possibility frontier relating current earnings, c, and discounted expected future earnings, f. Call this relationship $f = F(c)$.

Let us first consider a situation where this curve is known, say the solid curve in figure 6.4. With the stock price, p, equal to $c + f$, the management chooses to operate at point E, where the slope of the production possibility curve is -1. Stockholders know only about c, but they draw correct inferences about f. If management reports higher than expected first-period earnings, say c', stockholders will know that management is beggaring the future to boost present earnings by operating at D. Future earnings would be predicted as f'. The share price will fall.

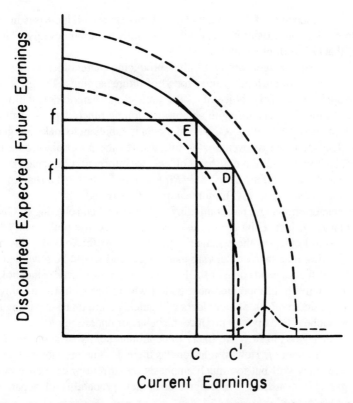

Fig. 6.4   Potential trade-offs between current and discounted future earnings

But this seems a strange story. An announcement of higher than expected current earnings usually boosts rather than diminishes stock price. Present earnings convey a strong message about the overall well-being of the company, the success of its products, its manufacturing prowess, and so on. This signal overwhelms the negative inference that higher earnings send about borrowing from the future. The correct diagram would not have a single production possibility frontier, but rather a distribution of such curves. Such additional production possibility frontiers are shown by the dashed curves in figure 6.4; the dashed bell-shaped curve shows their distribution.

Note the inherent asymmetry of information in this situation. The stockholder does not know management's observation, s, about the state of the world. With the certainty formulation, we had the management select c to maximize p given that $f = F(c)$, where $F(c)$ was assumed to be known to stockholders. Once uncertainty enters the picture, we have a more complex situation. Now $f = G(c,s)$, which collapses to a one-variable formulation $f = F(c)$ in the special cases of no uncertainty or where s is known. We shall assume that G is well behaved, so that the production possibility frontier is convex and the value of c for which $G_1 = k$ increases with increases in s; that is, the production possibility curve does not shift out too unevenly. (This requires that $G_{12} > 0$, given that $G_{11} < 0$.)

Assume that managers are faithfully reproducing shareholder wishes. They will trade off $1 of current earnings for $1 of future earnings. The greater is s, the greater will be their choice of c. The unraveling shareholders will project future earnings, f^*, according to an upward-sloping function of c—call it the revelation curve $f^* = R(c)$. A 2-period model is sufficient to make our general point. The sequence of events is as follows: (1) the uncertainty on s is resolved, and managers, but not shareholders, are informed; (2) managers select c; (3) shareholders infer f from $f^* = R(c)$, where $R' > 0$; (4) a share price is determined as $p = c + f$; (5) future earnings f are revealed.

A manager knowing s has conflicting incentives when selecting c. Given a particular $R(c)$, increasing c will raise share price because both c and f^* will be increased. Let us say the manager is going to be in office only for this single period, knows that shareholders are using $R(c)$, and would be rewarded with some bonus that depends on c or p. He will simply maximize c. Shareholders, of course, will be disappointed next period when f turns out to be below the value suggested by $R(c)$. Shareholders will quickly learn that a departing manager cannot be relied upon to produce the behavior underlying $R(c)$.

Most managers, in fact, are likely to be around next year, and hence have some concern about f. However, as long as there is some probability that they will leave, they will put too much emphasis on current price, hence current earnings. This distortion will be greater if their probability of departure is related to c or p.

Say managers wish to maximize $c + qf$, where q is the probability that they are around in the second period, with the form $q = Q(c)$, with $dq/dc > 0$.[10] Differentiating this expression with respect to c and setting the result equal to 0 gives $f/c = -[1 + (dq/dc)f]/q$.

It would be optimal for the shareholders to set $f/c = -1$, that is, to trade off one future dollar for one current dollar. Here q is less than 1, f and dq/dc are positive, all of which implies $f/c < -1$; more than $1 of future earnings will be traded for $1 of current earnings. Shareholders are not fooled, of course. They will simply employ a more pessimistic revelation function, where a lower f^* is projected for every c. The more likely shareholders think the manager is to leave, the more closely his departure is related to current earnings or share price, the more pessimistic the revelation function will be.

This formulation assumes that shareholders can monitor only c. In fact they may have some direct information about s or f. As long as shareholders are less than perfectly informed, however, c will be an informative signal about s. The forces outlined here will lead managers to select a c that is too great.

Take a simple numerical example. Say that earnings prospects s define the relationship

$$s = c^2 + f^2,$$
$$\text{so that } f = (s - c^2)^{1/2}.$$

If the manager is seeking to maximize $c + f$, he will simply set

$$c = f = (s/2)^{1/2}.$$

Shareholders will untangle this relationship and infer that $f^* = c$, and p will be set in the market to equal $c + f^*$. Expectations will be realized. By contrast, consider the manager seeking to maximize $c + qf$. To simplify, we assume q is constant and independent of c. He will set

$$cq = (s - c^2)^{1/2},$$

or

$$c = [s/(1 + q^2)]^{1/2}.$$

If $q < 1$, say because the manager might leave, then c will be set "too high" for shareholder interests. Assume that shareholders know q; they will disentangle this information, of course. Rather than assessing $f^* = c$, as they would if q were 1, they will set $f^* = q[s/(1 + q^2)]^{1/2}$, or $f^* = qc$.

The information is disentangled, but the distortion persists. Moreover, the stock price, $p = c + f$, will appropriately reflect prospects consistent with the efficient market theory. It might seem that if the shareholders understood the situation, they could correct the management's incentives. However, as long as payment is based on current earnings and stock price, nothing can be done. If shareholders are worried about tilting to the present, they might give a larger bonus for lower current earnings. But this would defeat another purpose of the arrangement from which we have abstracted. Presumably, the manager's compensation (and possible tenure) is based on earnings or share price at least in part to give him an incentive to work harder. If he is rewarded for lower current earnings, he could simply slack off or even destroy earnings. The only arrangement that works is to assure him a bonus that depends on f as well as c, even if he should depart before f is realized.

The essence of the problem is that current earnings are informative about s. Unless shareholders know s for sure, any bonus arrangement based on current earnings or current share price will induce an earnings tilt toward the present, even though all information is fully disentangled and the share price reflects value.

6.2.5 Overcoming Performance Slanting

Is there any way out of this dilemma, in which value is lost although all information is revealed? One way around this problem would be to raise the value of q and reduce its responsiveness to current earnings. (The example of the previous section had q as constant, and thus avoided this problem.) Guaranteeing the manager tenure or making tenure independent of performance would hardly seem desirable, however. Two basic types of approaches might ameliorate the problem: pushing management incentives toward longer-term performance and improving the information flow.

Management incentives can be better aligned with those of shareholders if managers' pay is based not on present earnings and present stock prices, but on future stock price. Stock options are the obvious mechanism, though management should be prohibited from selling the stock for a period of time (perhaps lengthy) after its purchase. (Stock itself gives less incentive for a given size of bonus to the manager.) However, responsibilities and compensation cannot always wait until all of the information is in. If current earnings are increased, an executive's salary (granted options) or expected tenure would be expected to increase as well. Some degree of performance tilting must be expected.

The second approach would be to convey additional information about s.[11] This will be directly costly, say, because additional accounting fees are required, to attest to the maintenance level of the facility or the R&D-related prospects for eventual new products, or to chronicle employee morale. Indirect costs will come from revealing valuable information to competitors. There is another possibility. Shareholders may gain information about s, or assurances that earnings are not being tilted, through the presence of a monitor.

6.2.6   Insider Monitors

Could insiders be trusted to monitor? In some circumstances the answer is yes. If their shareholdings are exceptionally large relative to other elements of their compensation, or if their reputation as effective managers weighs heavily relative to their financial returns, or if they can develop a reputation for future orientation, there may be a chance. No one thinks a Warren Buffett or Lawrence Tisch is indifferent to long-term share price performance. But they are exceptional investors, with secure tenure, massive holdings, and international reputations.

Obviously, insiders cannot be trusted to monitor management perks. But what about the more intriguing problem of earnings tilts? Suppose insiders were given stock options and everyone believed that they would therefore appropriately weight the future. This would boost equilibrium price/earnings (P/E) ratios, which in turn would increase the insiders' incentive to boost present earnings at the expense of the future. Only if we could provide the insiders with secure tenure and require them to hold their options for a long time could we have any assurance that they would provide appropriately for future earnings. A manager's reputation for sufficient future orientation would be valuable, but it is difficult to see how such reputations could develop within many companies.[12]

6.2.7   Outside Monitors

Notice that the performance-tilting management does not benefit from shareholders' inability to monitor perfectly.[13] Managers would be better off if they could demonstrate or warranty their beliefs to the public. More insightful accounting procedures might help, though it is hard to see how accountants could measure employee morale or the expected returns from R&D expenditures. Undoubtedly helpful would be a monitor who was allowed to see, and who had the incentive to review, a great deal of (possibly inside) information about the company.

The monitoring large shareholder thus enters the scene. He can review future plans in detail, looking at data that are difficult to comprehend or would hurt the company if released to the world at large. And he must have the incentive to take action, such as fostering a takeover, blowing the whistle (as H. Ross Perot did with General Motors), or merely selling his stock quietly if management refuses to respond appropriately. With a takeover, management is out of a job. A blown whistle or the information that a large monitoring block has been sold can also punish management by depressing the share price.

In the model we have sketched, the ability to demonstrate to a monitor that future earnings will be higher is an advantage to management. There will be no need to tilt earnings. For any reasonable compensation schedule, managers will be better off financially for having such a monitor, for he provides them with a mechanism to verify reported information and make commitments. Under these circumstances, discounted expected future earnings will be greater for any given level of current earnings. The observable effect should be an increase in the P/E ratio. We test for this prediction below. Our model would also predict that in the presence of a monitoring large shareholder, other costly devices that signal future success might be used less extensively.

6.2.8   Summary

Our central empirical hypothesis is that, other factors equal, firms with large outside shareholders will have a higher price relative to their reported earnings. Our primary empirical test is thus to ask whether the presence of large insider shareholders shifts the relationship between company earnings and stock price. Large shareholders might be able to assess managements' efforts to boost training, promote R&D, or postpone sales so as to yield greater profits subsequently. A monitoring shareholder might also encourage management to defer earnings so that the government could not take an early tax bite. In sum, when a company acquires a monitor, earnings will be pushed more toward the future, and the sum of current plus expected discounted future earnings should increase. Recognition of this effect would tend to raise the price associated with any given level of earnings.

6.3 Sample

To test the relationship between large shareholdings, corporate performance, and corporate financial structure, we drew a sample of 286 firms, dispersed across 22 industries. Of these industries, we classified 11 as likely to
have low asset specificity and an open information structure and 11 as likely
to exhibit high asset specificity and a relatively closed information structure.

Our sample was based on the Value Line Investment Survey, whose industry classifications are generally more reliable than rules based on SIC codes
and other quantifiable measures. In addition, Value Line's data on ownership,
price, and accounting performance are consistent and can be used for comparisons both within and across industries.

We began by sampling randomly from industries in which Value Line followed more than eight firms. We included an industry in the sample if there
was at least one firm in which a single outside shareholder owned more than
15% of total common stock. We continued this industry-by-industry sampling
regimen through 22 industries, a number we believed would be sufficient.

We used a 15% threshold because this level of ownership seemed likely to
imply significant voting power over the company. A number of corporate
charter provisions and state laws give 15% owners an effective veto over major corporate decisions. Examples are corporate supermajority provisions and
the new Delaware state antitakeover code. In addition, 15% appears to verge
on an ownership level that many analysts construe to have serious control
implications. For example, many states have recently passed so-called control
share acquisition provisions, which stipulate that shareholders passing a 20%
ownership threshold are considered to have a clear control intent. Thus, the
structure of corporate charters and state laws both suggest that if any large
shareholders exhibit a significant monitoring or control effect over the corporation, this effect should certainly be observable when the large shareholders
own a stake more than 15% of voting equity.

Neither the structure of corporate law nor the structure of corporate charters
would necessarily suggest that, in equilibrium, a 5% ownership stake would
be sufficient to have a significant impact on management. Indeed the only
reason that 5% ownership has been hypothesized to be important is because
the disclosure laws required potential corporate acquirers to disclose their acquisition program to the market at the 5% ownership threshold. (We investigated the shareholdings-performance relationship for those firms in our
sample with large shareholders who had between 5% and 15% ownership; no
relationship was apparent.)

We next partitioned our sample of 22 industries according to the information and asset structure of the industry. This classification effort is necessarily
judgmental and somewhat qualitative. However, we attempted to make it rigorous by the following methodology. For each industry, we gathered data on
research and development expenditures and sales ratios for 1988, for all firms

listed in the relevant SIC code in the Compustat database. We then used the R&D/sales ratio as a proxy for the information structure of the industry. We assumed that the higher the R&D intensity of firms in the industry, the more closed is the information structure, and the more difficult would be outside monitoring. The idea is similar to the asset-specificity concept described in Titman and Wessels (1988). They hypothesize that with higher R&D/sales ratios, debt is riskier because assets are more management specific and less liquid. Similarly, we hypothesize that the higher are R&D/sales, the more difficult it is for outsiders to make detailed assessments of the corporation's likely future performance.

The industries in our sample are listed in table 6.1. Open and closed information structure industries are listed separately. The dividing line was set at an R&D intensity of 1% of sales. That is, industries with average R&D/sales

Table 6.1   **Sample Industries**

Industry	No. of Firms	No. with Large Shareholders	% with Large Shareholders	Average R&D/Sales Ratios	% Reporting R&D
		A. Transparent Industries (Easy to Monitor)			
Apparel	12	4	33	.14	07
Building materials	13	6	46	1.40	14
Food processing	16	7	44	.50	25
Metal fabricating	12	5	42	.80	48
Paper products	13	4	31	.35	35
Petroleum	11	4	36	.50	47
Publishing	11	4	36	.44	09
Restaurants	13	4	31	.00	00
Retail stores	18	9	50	.00	00
Telecommunications	8	3	38	.45	11
Textiles	8	3	38	.41	26
		B. Opaque Industries (Difficult to Monitor)			
Aerospace	18	6	33	4.0	100
Chemical manufacturing	13	5	38	4.2	100
Computer software	13	3	23	14.0	80
Computers	13	1	8	9.0	67
Drugs	9	1	11	31.0	59
Electronics	17	6	35	3.0	64
Machinery	14	3	21	2.5	54
Medical supplies	15	5	33	56.0	64
Office equipment	14	5	36	1.0	61
Precision instruments	14	4	29	6.0	69
Semiconductors	11	3	27	7.0	68

Source: Value Line Investment Survey.
Note: A large shareholder is defined as a single entity owning 15% or more of the outstanding voting stock of the corporation.

ratios above 1% are characterized as opaque, while industries with averages below 1% we labeled transparent. The same division results when the industries are grouped according to whether at least half of the firms report any R&D expenditure (last column of table 6.1). Firms reporting no R&D expenditures enter our average calculation as zero observations. The table shows, for each industry, the number of firms with a large (over 15%) shareholder and the percentage of the industry sample with such a shareholder.

While our 1% cutoff is obviously somewhat arbitrary, its results are roughly consistent with an intuitive assessment of the information structure of the industries in our sample. Included in the opaque category are industries such as drugs, computers, and chemicals. The transparent industries include food, apparel, and textiles, among others. As we show in the next section, raising the transparency cutoff—to 5% R&D intensity, for example—does not materially affect our results. The use of the R&D/sales measure to stratify industries by information structure thus appears to create relatively little sensitivity or arbitrariness.

Only one industry in our sample, building materials, involves any classification judgment. This industry is relatively small, including only 14 firms under the Compustat classification. One small firm reports an R&D/sales ratio of 20%, while the other firms, many much larger, report no R&D expenditures. Nominally, the weighted average R&D/sales ratio for this industry is 1.4%, and it should thus be included in the opaque category. But it seems clear that the mean is the wrong measure in this case, and we include this industry in the transparent category. (It clearly falls into that category if we consider the percentage of firms reporting R&D expenditures.) Industry descriptions by analysts, such as Value Line, confirm that this industry is not characterized by research or technology-intensive activity.

6.4   Large Shareholders and Expected Performance

To examine the difference in expected performance between firms with and without large shareholders, we concentrate on one widely used measure of corporate performance—E/P ratios. (Because earnings can sometimes be negative, or sufficiently close to zero that price/earnings ratios are meaningless, the earnings/price ratio provides a more meaningful figure.) The E/P ratios indicate expected earnings growth rates. Other cross-sectional measures, such as price/book ratios and Tobin's q (which is usually derived from book value calculations), are generally less reliable because they involve implicit assumptions about asset value. So long as E/P ratios are adjusted to remove extraordinary items, they provide a more consistent picture of the discount placed on current and future profits by the market.

To calculate E/P ratios across the sample, we take the last full fiscal year of earnings—1988 in virtually all cases—and divide it by the market price of the company's stock on the date of issue of the first-quarter 1989 Value Line report for that industry. This yields an E/P ratio for each firm. We then take an unweighted average of E/P ratios for the relevant sample (e.g., metal industry firms with large shareholders).

To test for differences in E/P ratios for firms with and without large shareholders, we aggregate the data in two different ways. First, we calculate for each industry the average E/P ratio for large-shareholder firms and the average for firms without a large shareholder. We then take the difference between these averages for each industry and calculate the average difference across the industries in our sample. This calculation weights each industry average equally in the comparison, rather than weighting each firm in the larger sample.

Next, we standardize E/P ratios for firms within each industry by dividing each firm's E/P ratio by the industry mean E/P. Using these standardized ratios, we pool all firms that have a large shareholder, and those that do not, to form two large samples. We then calculate average standardized E/P ratios for these large samples. This comparison weights each firm, rather than each industry group, equally.

We perform these two tests separately for each of our two broad industry samples—open-information-structure (transparent) firms and closed-information-structure (opaque) firms. Because we expect large shareholders to have different effects in these two types of industries, we do not pool the data from these two industry categories (although the tables allow direct comparison of the results across the two subsamples).

Table 6.2 displays the E/P ratios for firms with and without large shareholders for each of the 22 industries in our sample. We find quite large differences in E/P ratio for the 11 open-information-structure industries, with E/P ratios being substantially lower in the presence of a large shareholder (pt. A). The pattern for the 11 closed-information-structure industries (pt. B) is considerably less strong. The sign of the effect is the same for most of the industries, but the average magnitude is smaller.

Table 6.3 presents our two statistical tests for systematic differences in E/P ratios for firms with and without a large shareholder. For the open-information-structure industries, the test statistics reject the hypothesis of equal average E/P ratios at the 5% level. In contrast, for the closed-information-structure industries, neither test allows rejection of the hypothesis that E/P ratios are equal in the presence and absence of a large shareholder.[14]

In opaque industries, which are much less hospitable to the type of monitoring that we describe, approximately 27% of our sample firms have large shareholders. Presumably these shareholders are there for some other reason, perhaps because of history (e.g., the heirs of the founding family), or the need to foster business relationships, or to spur new business developments. Presumably some large shareholders are present in transparent industries also for nonmonitoring reasons. If so, the differences that we observe understate the actual returns to monitoring. If only half of the large shareholders in our transparent industry sample are monitors, for example, then the differences that we find may represent half of the effects of monitoring. (This of course assumes that nonmonitoring large shareholders do not affect the variables that we are studying).

These data imply that the hypotheses advanced in Section 6.2 have some merit. Corporations in which there is a large shareholder in the ownership

Table 6.2   Earnings/Price Ratio (E/P) for 22 Industries

Industry	E/P with Large Holder	E/P without Large Holder	Difference
	A. Transparent Industries (Easy to Monitor)		
Apparel	9.74	10.21	.27
Building materials	15.02	17.35	2.33
Food processing	7.98	7.94	− .03
Metal fabricating	9.77	10.29	.52
Paper products	13.89	13.50	− .39
Petroleum (integrated)	9.49	9.49	.00
Publishing	5.66	7.40	1.74
Restaurants	11.91	11.68	− .23
Retail stores	11.78	14.27	2.49
Telecommunications equipment	10.15	13.50	3.35
Textiles	5.90	8.89	2.99
Average			1.19
Standard error			.42
t-statistic			2.81
	B. Opaque Industries (Difficult to Monitor)		
Aerospace	15.14	14.46	− .68
Chemical manufacturing	8.32	8.94	.62
Computer software	13.98	14.34	.36
Computers	15.63	15.63	.00
Drugs	9.84	10.78	.94
Electronics	14.44	14.58	.14
Machinery	7.89	8.63	.74
Medical supplies	12.10	12.46	.36
Office equipment	14.11	13.15	.96
Precision instruments	12.79	12.25	.54
Semiconductors	14.08	15.46	1.38
Average	.22		
Standard error	.21		
t-statistic	.99		

Source: Value Line Investment Survey.
Note: A large shareholder is defined as a single entity owning 15% or more of the outstanding voting stock of the corporation.

Table 6.3   Comparison of Standardized E/P Ratios for 286 Firms

Sample	Average E/P (%)	No. of Firms
	A. Transparent Industries (Easy to Monitor)	
With large shareholder	93.81	53
Without large shareholder	104.00	82
	B. Opaque Industries (Difficult to Monitor)	
With large shareholder	99.12	42
Without large shareholder	100.32	109

Note: *t*-statistic for hypothesis that there is no difference between the sample means in part A is 2.87; in part B 0.31. E/P ratios were standardized within each industry by dividing each firm's E/P ratio by the industry average and multiplying by 100.

pool display, on a cross-sectional basis, a higher market premium, indicating a higher level of anticipated future performance relative to present performance. This suggests an ongoing beneficial governance effect arising from the presence of large shareholders. It also suggests that the market recognizes the expected effects of large shareholders on fundamental corporate performance, and incorporates that effect into security prices. In other words, large shareholders are interpreted by the market as signals of higher future performance, relative to the currently observed level of profits.

6.5   Large Shareholders and Dividend Payout Decisions

At least three primary hypotheses may be advanced about how the presence of large shareholders affects dividend payouts. First, dividend payouts may constitute an alternative form of capital market monitoring (Easterbrook 1984; Rozeff 1982). Corporations with high payout rates will be forced to go to the market relatively more often to secure funds for new investment. This subjects the investment decisions to outside scrutiny. Thus, when large shareholders are not present in the ownership pool, the market may demand other forms of monitoring—such as dividend payouts—as substitutes. We might expect to observe an inverse relationship between dividend payouts and the presence of large shareholders.

Second, a primary policing function of large shareholders may be to increase dividend payout rates. Perhaps large shareholders do not monitor management decisions themselves, but rather change corporate payout policies so that management can be monitored by the appropriate parties. If this is the case, then large shareholders would force an increase in dividend payouts so that firms would be forced to go outside to raise investment funds and thereby subject themselves to capital market monitoring. An alternative possibility is that large shareholders counter a tendency to excessive retention of cash flow by management, due to a preference to reinvest and build the size of the corporation, and hence expand the domain under their control (Jensen 1986). Under this hypothesis, higher dividend payout rates are not a monitoring device, but an end in themselves.

Third, and implicit in our arguments of Section 6.2, dividends may be a signal sent by management to inform the market of higher expected future profits.[15] If the primary function of dividends is to signal, then there may be less need for dividends in the presence of a large shareholder, because the large shareholder is a substitute (and more credible) signal of good future performance. This could imply that firms with large shareholders should have lower dividends than similar firms without large shareholders.

To investigate dividend payout behavior, we calculate dividend payout rates as a function of current earnings for each firm. That is, we look at the rate of voluntary dividend payout as a fraction of current after-tax profits, which represent the available pool of corporate resources that management can either pay out or retain for internal use.

To compare dividend payout rates, we use the same statistical tests as we described in the previous section. We first look at the average difference in dividend payout rates within each industry, comparing firms with and without large shareholders, and take the average of this difference over the industries in our sample. This approach weights each industry equally in the test. Next, we standardize dividend payout rates within each industry by the industry mean, and pool observations across industries. This comparison weights each firm equally.

Tables 6.4 and 6.5 present summary data on the dividend payout rates across our sample of industries. Payout data for firms with and without large shareholders are given in table 6.4. Table 6.5 presents summary tests for differences in payout rates. The presence or absence of large shareholders seems to make no significant difference in dividend payout rates across either opaque or transparent industries. (We have not investigated the tax status of large shareholders, which might make them more or less eager than the average shareholder for dividend payouts.)

Along the lines of our earlier discussion, these results are open to several interpretations. They certainly do not imply that large shareholders and dividend payouts are alternative forms of monitoring. The results are consistent with the hypothesis that large shareholders enforce higher dividend payouts, but only if the hypothesis is more specifically that large shareholders bring below-average dividend payout levels up to industry norms. The results do suggest, however, that in the presence of a large shareholder, higher dividends do not have a useful role as a signal of higher expected future profits, assuming they perform this function in the absence of such a shareholder. Firms with large shareholders are expected to have differentially higher future profit rates, and this mitigates the need for other financial policies to convey this information to the market.

Table 6.4   **Average Dividend Payout Ratios for 286 Firms in 22 Industries**

Industry	Payout with Large Holder	Payout without Large Holder	Difference
Apparel	.39	.36	−.03
Building materials	.25	.26	.01
Food processing	.51	.46	−.05
Metal fabricating	.36	.38	.02
Paper products	.31	.25	−.06
Petroleum (integrated)	.37	.43	.06
Publishing	.38	.50	.12
Restaurants	.06	.13	.07
Retail stores	.21	.16	−.05
Telecommunications equipment	.07	.01	−.06
Textiles	.85	.32	−.54
Average			−.05
Standard error			.05
t-statistic			−1.00
	B. Opaque Industries (Difficult to Monitor)		
Aerospace	.26	.22	−.04
Chemical manufacturing	.55	.58	.03
Computer software	.07	.05	−.02
Computers	.20	.02	−.18
Drugs	.44	.25	−.19
Electronics	.13	.12	−.01
Machinery	.26	.34	.08
Medical supplies	.08	.14	.06
Office equipment	.33	.30	−.03
Precision instruments	.03	.14	.11
Semiconductors	.01	.05	.04
Average			−.01
Standard error			.03
t-statistic			−.33

Note: Large holder is defined as a single entity owning more than 15% of outstanding voting stock. Dividend payout ratio is calculated by dividing the last full fiscal year's per share dividend payment by the last full fiscal year's earnings per share.

6.6   Large Shareholders and Capital Structure

How might large shareholders affect corporate capital structure? Conceivably, large outside shareholders may solve the monitoring problem that creates agency costs from debt financing. Specifically, large shareholders' monitoring may ensure that management does not shift the firm's investment policies away from those projects preferred by (and expected by) debtholders. If large shareholders do lower the agency costs of debt in this way, firms with a large shareholder in the ownership pool should have lower costs of debt capital. This, in turn, implies that leverage ratios should be higher for firms with large

Table 6.5   Comparison of Standardized Dividend Payout Ratios for Pooled
                   Sample of 286 Firms

Sample	Average Dividend Payout (%)	No. of Firms
A. Transparent Industries (Easy to Monitor)		
With large shareholder	111.51	53
Without large shareholder	92.56	82
B. Opaque Industries (Difficult to Monitor)		
With large shareholder	98.02	42
Without large shareholder	100.76	109

Note: t-statistic for hypothesis that there is no difference between the sample means in part A is 1.71; in part B 0.21. Payout ratios were standardized within each industry by dividing each firm's dividend payout ratio by the industry average and multiplying by 100. Dividend payout ratios were calculated for each firm by dividing the last full fiscal year's dividend payout per share by the last full fiscal year's earnings per share.

shareholders than for other firms in the same industries without large shareholders.

However, large shareholders will perform this role only if they have the right incentives. In the United States, national laws prevent some major debtholders (e.g., banks) from also being large shareholders. In addition, institutional investors, who are typically large debtholders and large shareholders, typically administer their debt and equity holdings through different channels. For example, most investment companies offer bond mutual funds and stock mutual funds, but there are relatively few combined funds. Thus, because of these structural problems, it seems unlikely that large shareholders in the United States will have the incentives to solve the agency cost problem for debtholders. In fact, large shareholders may compete against debtholders. If they can push the firm to partially expropriate debtholders, inefficient financial policies will result. But efficiency could be enhanced, for example, if the presence of large shareholders creates a balance of power with debtholders, whose ownership tends to be more concentrated.

A second hypothesis is that, as with dividends, the presence of large shareholders mitigates against the corporation's tendency to assume debt as a signal of differentially better expected future performance. A high level of debt has been seen as a particularly credible signal because it puts management's control of the company directly at risk should they fail to meet the performance guarantee (Ross 1977; Gilson 1989). If the presence of a large shareholder is an effective signal, the firm may be able to avoid additional debt commitments, increasing its financial flexibility while still conveying information about superior future performance to the market.[16]

We test these propositions using our samples of large-shareholder and no-large-shareholder firms. Once again, to examine differences in leverage we compute two complementary tests for our large-shareholder and no-large-shareholder samples. First, we calculate the difference in leverage within each industry, and then take an unweighted average across industries. This weights each industry equally in the calculation. Next, we standardize statistics and pool all firms in the sample. This weights each firm equally in the average.

Tables 6.6 and 6.7 display these data. Industry-specific ratios are shown in table 6.6, which breaks out firms with and without large shareholders. Table

Table 6.6   **Average Leverage Ratios for 286 Firms in 22 Industries**

Industry	Leverage with Large Holder	Leverage without Large Holder	Difference
	A. Transparent Industries (Easy to Monitor)		
Apparel	.275	.254	− .023
Building materials	.291	.236	− .055
Food processing	.113	.139	.026
Metal fabricating	.219	.260	.041
Paper products	.287	.253	− .034
Petroleum (integrated)	.265	.334	.069
Publishing	.039	.120	.081
Restaurants	.093	.266	.172
Retail stores	.226	.191	− .036
Telecommunications equipment	.085	.185	.100
Textiles	.342	.310	− .032
Average			.03
Standard error			.02
t-statistic			1.50
	B. Opaque Industries (Difficult to Monitor)		
Aerospace	.224	.272	.046
Chemical manufacturing	.123	.125	.002
Computer software	.202	.151	− .050
Computers	.268	.191	− .076
Drugs	.025	.213	.188
Electronics	.188	.179	− .009
Machinery	.182	.250	.068
Medical supplies	.122	.296	.174
Office equipment	.116	.141	.025
Precision instruments	.161	.134	− .027
Semiconductors	.230	.228	− .002
Average			.03
Standard error			.03
t-statistic			1.00

Note: Large holder is defined as single entity owning more than 15% of outstanding voting stock. Leverage ratio for each firm is calculated by dividing the book value of total debt by the book value of total debt plus the market value of equity.

Table 6.7   Comparison of Standardized Leverage Ratios for Pooled Sample of
                   286 Firms

Sample	Average Leverage Ratio (%)	No. of Firms
A. Transparent Industries (Easy to Monitor)		
With large shareholder	89.80	53
Without large shareholder	106.59	82
B. Opaque Industries (Difficult to Monitor)		
With large shareholder	91.61	42
Without large shareholder	103.26	109

Note: t-statistic for hypothesis that there is no difference between the sample means in part A is 1.71; in part B 1.16. Leverage ratios were standardized within each industry by dividing each firm's leverage ratio by the industry average and multiplying by 100. Leverage ratio for each firm was calculated by dividing the book value of total debt by the book value of total debt plus the market value of equity.

6.7 gives summary and test statistics for the two full-sample tests. These data show no significant difference in average leverage ratio in the presence of large shareholders, in firms with either open or closed information structures. Leverage ratio differences in the presence of large shareholders are small in economic terms.

Large shareholders apparently perform a monitoring function only for equity owners and do not seem to have a positive impact on debtholders, or to reduce the agency costs of debt. This is probably because of the effective separation of equity and debt management in major U.S. financial institutions, which is partially (but not entirely) due to regulatory constraints. Managers of large equity positions are typically not also concerned with the value of large debt holdings, even if the same institution holds a large debt position in the firm in question.

The data also suggest that, consistent with the hypotheses advanced in Section 6.2, the presence of a large shareholder may reduce the need to signal differentially higher future performance through corporate financial policy. Firms in the large-shareholder sample have higher expected earnings growth rates, yet do not signal these rates to the market through leverage ratios.

6.7   Conclusion

This study investigates the effects of large outside shareholders on corporate performance and corporate financial policy. The first portion of the paper presents a theoretical model that reveals the incentives for monitoring by large shareholders and the nature of market equilibrium with monitors. In particular, the presence of large-shareholder monitors is hypothesized to discourage tilting of performance toward present results. Higher price earnings ratios are the natural result.

Our empirical study employs a sample of firms from 22 industries to test whether the presence of large shareholders is associated with systematic differences in expected earnings growth, dividend payout ratios, or leverage ratios. We break our sample of firms into two types of industries: those in which the information structure of firms makes it possible to monitor management's investment decisions; and those in which outside monitoring, even by a large shareholder, may be exceedingly difficult or impossible. We hypothesize that, if large shareholders are to have a significant effect, it will be seen in the former rather than the latter type of firms.

Overall, we find that in 11 industries with a relatively open information structure, large shareholders are associated with significantly higher expected earnings growth rates. Using earnings/price ratios to measure expected earnings growth, we find about a 10% difference associated with the presence of large holders. This difference is not present in 11 industries with relatively closed information structures, suggesting that these firms are more difficult to monitor. Given that in transparent industries there are also likely to be large shareholders whose primary purpose is not monitoring, our assessed difference is likely to understate the effects of monitoring.

Across all industries in our sample, we find no significant differences in dividend payout ratios in the presence and absence of large shareholders. These results are consistent with the hypothesis that higher earnings prospects are signaled by the presence of large shareholders, and hence that these firms do not need to make higher-than-average dividend payments as an additional signal to the market. The results do not imply that dividends and large shareholdings are alternative forms of monitoring, or that the principal role of large shareholders is to force an increase in dividend payout rates. Nor do they indicate that not paying dividends is necessarily self-dealing on the part of management.

Finally, we find no difference in leverage ratio in the presence or absence of large shareholders for any type of industry that we examine. Once again, this result is consistent with the hypothesis that large shareholders are a substitute form of signal of future performance. In transparent industries, the presence of a large shareholder signals differentially better future performance, and hence there is less need to assume higher than average-debt-loads to alert the market to the good performance prospects. The results also suggest that large shareholders do not lower the agency costs associated with debt financing, by monitoring so as to protect debtholders' interests. This is not surprising, because in the U.S. market large equity and debt holdings are typically managed independently.

Our data support the view that large holders help to solve an informational problem in capital markets by monitoring management—and not merely during a takeover process. Large but passive long-term holders seem to have a significant ongoing effect on corporate governance and performance. Large shareholders can be viewed, quite contrary to common public perceptions, as particularly patient investors. By certifying future-oriented information, they allow management to concentrate more on the long term, without demanding that the corporation adopt costly financial strategies involving dividends or debt to signal directly its long-term commitments.

Our empirical results beg a fundamental question, however. If large shareholders significantly improve corporate performance, why do all firms not have a large shareholder? Or, put another way, what motivates large shareholders to take positions in particular firms? Surely if the market were fully efficient, large shareholders would be most likely to take positions in firms that would otherwise exhibit poor performance, thereby bringing their performance closer to industry norms. In this case, with the presence of large shareholders being determined within the process, the systematic performance differences that we have documented might not exist. (If the poor-performance-attracts-large-shareholders phenomenon is significant, our findings understate the contribution of large shareholders.)

Fortunately for our empirical studies, there are widely differing structural incentives for large shareholders to take positions in particular firms. A steeper supply curve, which might come about because substantial new information was regularly supplied to the market, could be a deterrent, as might various aspects of the firm's corporate governance and corporate control profile. For example, large shareholders might be less likely to take positions in forms that bristle with antitakeover devices; if performance deteriorates the large shareholder has little recourse but to sell back down the supply curve. An investigation of what determines the structure of large share ownership constitutes a promising avenue for further exploration of the relationship between share ownership and corporate performance.

Our theoretical discussion suggests that management will have an incentive to tilt earnings toward the present and that outside monitors can ameliorate this distortion. Our empirical analysis does not conclusively prove any particular hypothesis. However, it is consistent with our theory. Firms with large shareholders command lower E/P ratios than those without, which implies a brighter future relative to the present. In the final assessment, large shareholders may free management to pursue beneficial policies. As is often the case, there are strong elements of symbiosis in the relationship between the monitor and the monitored.

Notes

1. Olson (1971) discusses the dilemma that leads voluntary efforts to underprovision when the beneficiaries are small and dispersed.
2. A more refined hypothesis might suggest that some firms would be so transparent

that they can be monitored even by dispersed shareholders, and that large shareholders play their most significant role with relatively, but not fully, transparent firms.

3. In most circumstances, purchases will be made in blocks, pushing up the price of inframarginal shares within each block. If the blocks themselves are small relative to the total purchase, this effect will not be significant.

4. For evidence that this does indeed occur, see Pound and Zeckhauser (1990), Mikkelson and Ruback (1985), and Holderness and Sheehan (1985).

5. The discrete version of (3) is $(n - 1)[V(n) - V(n - 1)] \geq P(n) - V(n)$.

6. We recognize that this result may appear counterintuitive to some potential large shareholders. All of the essential points in our model obtain even if large shareholders do not purchase beyond the point (if any) where value falls below price. In the diagram shown, this restriction would exclude a large shareholder even though his participation would be profitable. Even when value exceeds price at some point, there is likely to be a minimum purchase required to break even because there is an initial range in which purchases lose money.

7. A typical 10K form will list a variety of stock options and pension benefits as well as salary. Salary captures the most attention and is most easily interpreted. Hence we suspect that compensation is increasingly being provided through indirect means.

8. For a recent discussion of the hypothesis that management may focus on the short term, see Stein (1988, 1989).

9. We should make clear that the market is not "fooled" by this tilting; it expects managers to operate with a higher effective discount rate than would shareholders. Moreover, if a manager could demonstrate a future orientation, leaving dividends aside, this would raise the present stock price. The rate of appreciation in the stock price, however, would be no different from that for a company with fiercely present-oriented managers.

10. This formulation is purely for illustration. This would be the objective of a risk-neutral manager who was paid a bonus in proportion to earnings and, if fired, would receive the same salary elsewhere, but would have no bonus prospects.

11. In practice some elements contributing to the prospects of the firm can be monitored more easily than others. Retained earnings or a new building are easy to observe. Improved employee training or better relations with customers are less evident. Our theory would suggest that when providing for the future, managements would focus disproportionately on benefits that can be observed, then on those that can be inferred, and finally on those that are not revealed.

12. For an analysis of inside ownership and market valuation, see Morck, Shleifer, and Vishny (1988).

13. Some of the ideas outlined in this section are treated in greater detail in Zeckhauser and Marks (1989).

14. Our original analysis included a twenty-third industry, Canadian energy, which was subsequently deleted because the Compustat files on which we base our R&D/sales criterion include no separate industry classification for these firms. Assuming that this industry would have an R&D/sales ratio roughly in line with that for U.S. petroleum, it would belong in our transparent sample. Its inclusion would strengthen our results. Canadian energy has an E/P ratio with large shareholders of 8.88, an E/P without large shareholders of 13.52, producing a difference of 4.64, which is by far the largest difference among the industries in our sample.

15. It is true, however, that if the future is bright, then ceteris paribus, both management and shareholders would wish to pay out lower dividends and concentrate on investment. Thus, if dividends are used to signal, this use may conflict with the optimal full-information strategy of the company.

16. In contrast to the situation with dividends, brighter future prospects mean that greater leverage is less costly. Leverage signaling, in effect, cuts in the right direction.

References

Bhattacharya, S. 1979. Imperfect information, dividend policy, and the "bird in the hand" fallacy. *Bell Journal of Economics* 10:259–70.

Easterbrook, F. 1984. Two agency-cost explanations of dividends. *American Economic Review* 74(4):650–59.

Gilson, S. 1989. The rule of boardholders in financing troubled firms. Working paper. University of Texas, Austin, School of Business.

Holderness, C., and D. Sheehan. 1985. Raiders or saviors? The evidence on six controversial investors. *Journal of Financial Economics* 14(3):555–79.

Jensen, M. 1986. Agency costs of free cash flow, corporate finance, and takeovers. *American Economic Review* 76:323–29.

Jensen, M., and W. Meckling. 1976. Theory of the firm: Managerial behavior, agency costs, and ownership structure. *Journal of Financial Economics* 3:305–60.

Mikkelson, W., and R. Ruback. 1985. An empirical investigation of the interfirm equity investment process." *Journal of Financial Economics* 14(3):523–55.

Morck, R., A. Shleifer, and R. Vishny. 1988. Management ownership and market valuation: An empirical analysis. *Journal of Financial Economics,* 20:293–316.

Olson, M. 1971. *The logic of collective action: Public goods and the theory of groups.* Cambridge, Mass.: Harvard University Press.

Pound, J., and R. Zeckhauser. 1990. Clearly heard on the street: The effects of takeover rumors on stock prices. *Journal of Business.* Forthcoming.

Ross, S. 1977. The determinants of financial policy: The incentive signalling approach. *Bell Journal of Economics* 8:23–40.

Rozeff, M. 1982. Growth, beta, and agency costs as determinants of dividend payout ratios. *Journal of Financial Research* 5(3):249–59.

Stein, J. 1988. Takeover threats and managerial myopia. *Journal of Political Economy* 96(1):61–80.

———. 1989. Efficient capital markets, inefficient firms: A model of myopic corporate behavior. Working paper. Harvard Business School.

Titman, S., and R. Wessels. 1988. The determinants of capital structure choice. *Journal of Finance* 43:1–19.

Zeckhauser, R., and D. Marks. 1989. Sign-posting: Selected product information and market function. Working paper. Harvard University, Kennedy School of Government (April).

7   Economic and Financial Determinants of Oil and Gas Exploration Activity

Peter C. Reiss

7.1   Introduction

In 1981, domestic oil companies spent a record $55.7 billion exploring for and developing oil and gas reserves in the United States. In 1986, they spent less than one-half that amount, a six-year low of $26.6 billion. This $29.1 billion drop in capital spending is impressive by any standard. It was more than one-half of domestic corporate R&D spending in 1986 and more than 10% of net corporate additions to new plant and equipment. Many factors contributed to this precipitous decline in exploration and development expenditures. From 1978 to 1981, world events such as the Iran-Iraq war and increased cooperation within OPEC caused the average domestic price of oil to jump from $8 to over $35 per barrel. As world oil prices rose, so did domestic exploration: large onshore and offshore projects were planned and undertaken; previously uneconomic leases became the object of renewed drilling efforts; and many firms began to experiment with expensive new drilling and completion techniques.

During the latter half of 1981 and early 1982, oil prices softened. While some oil companies cut back on their exploration and development efforts, most firms and analysts remained optimistic. Many firms, for example, continued to issue new shares and long-term debt to finance additional increases in their exploration and development activities. By 1986, however, spot prices for West Texas intermediate crude had fallen below $10 per barrel. As revenues fell and debt burdens increased, firms cut back on exploration and devel-

Peter C. Reiss is associate professor of economics at the Stanford Business School and a faculty research fellow at the National Bureau of Economic Research.

The author thanks the Olin, Sloan, and Fletcher Jones Foundations for financial support. He would also like to thank Glenn Hubbard and John Meyer for their useful comments on earlier versions.

opment. These cutbacks had a pronounced effect not only on the oil and gas industry but also on economic and financial activity in a number of oil-producing states. Hardest hit were Texas, Louisiana, Oklahoma, Kansas, Colorado, and Alaska.

Gyrations in natural gas prices also contributed to the dramatic swing in domestic exploration and development activity. From 1978 to 1983, prices for newly found gas rose from less than $1.00 to over $2.70 per mcf (thousand cubic feet). Part of this increase occurred because of natural gas price and pipeline deregulation; part occurred because of end-user substitution from oil to natural gas. A series of mild winters in the northern United States in the mid-1980s stopped the upward trend in gas prices. By December 1986, a severe gas glut had dropped the price of newly found natural gas from $2.70 to under $1.65 per mcf.

These unprecedented oscillations in energy prices provide economists with a unique opportunity to compare alternative models of investment. In particular, because investment costs and returns changed at different rates, one can assess separately the effects of each on investment spending. Further, because the escalation and decline in prices was so rapid, one can examine whether a firm's liquidity position affects its investment spending plans. Although several empirical studies have concluded that financial liquidity plays a role in firms' investment decisions, relatively few of these studies have had data covering periods in which the demand for external investment capital was known to have changed.[1]

The structure of the oil and gas industry also provides economists with a unique opportunity to study the inputs and outputs of investment projects. Accounting standards in this industry require firms to release detailed information on their capital structures and investment spending. These data contain not only different measures of the returns to investment but also detailed information on firms' finances. In addition, the oil and gas industry provides a useful reference industry for evaluating the predictions of theoretical investment models. It has price-taking firms, each producing a relatively homogeneous good. Most of these firms use the same exploration and production technologies. They also use the same input markets. Thus, in contrast to investment studies that have samples of diversified firms with different production technologies, here we can hold constant many technological differences that affect the returns to investment.

The next section provides background information on the oil and gas industry. It describes the exploration and development process. It also provides information on the costs of exploration and development projects. Section 7.3 builds a model of exploration and development. This model resembles conventional investment models, but also includes specific features of the oil and gas exploration process. The latter part of Section 7.3 estimates the parameters of this exploration model using annual data from 1978 to 1986 on the operations of 44 independent oil and gas firms. In addition to finding that firms face constant returns to scale in exploration, we find that liquidity variables explain some of the major changes in investment activity during this period. Section 7.4 considers ways in which firms' financial positions may affect their investment decisions by relating the structure of financial contracts to informational asymmetries between producers and outside equity or bond holders. It appears that when a firm's reserve collateral falls significantly (as was the case with the general deflation in oil and gas prices), financial contracts often limit discretionary investment spending. These contract provisions point to general difficulties that outside investors have in evaluating oil and gas firms' requests for, and uses of, external financial capital. Outside investors recognize that, as a firm's financial position deteriorates, the firm's opportunity cost of internal capital rises relative to that of external capital. In addition, as the probability of bankruptcy increases, the firm has incentives to take greater risks with outside capital. Investors recognize this problem and include clauses in their financial contracts that place restrictions on firms' discretionary investment. These contracts create a link between a firm's liquidity position and its investment decisions, but only during periods of firm or industry distress.

7.2 Background on Oil and Gas Exploration

7.1.1 Exploration versus Development

Oil and gas firms divide their exploration and development capital expenditures into three categories: exploration, development, and property acquisition. Of the $30 billion oil and gas firms spent on capital outlays in 1986, approximately 37% went for exploration and 59% went for development investment. Firms spent most of the remaining portion acquiring undeveloped oil and gas properties.

The division of oil and gas capital spending into exploration and development parallels the distinction drawn in manufacturing between "research" and "development." Exploratory, or "wildcat," drilling takes place on unexplored land or at unexplored depths. In addition to drilling expenses, exploration expenditures include those for basic and applied geologic research (e.g., seismic testing). For a typically exploratory well, firms spend anywhere from several hundred thousand to several million dollars. Table 7.1 summarizes trends in domestic exploratory drilling activity and expenses during the years 1978–86. In 1985, 12,208 exploratory wells were completed in the United States. Most of these wells were drilled in Texas (4,174) and Kansas (1,503). Of the roughly 12,000 exploratory wells drilled, very few uncovered large amounts of oil or gas. Indeed, from 1978 to 1986 only about one in four exploratory wells yielded commercial quantities of oil and gas.

Development takes place on properties proven to contain oil or gas. Development drilling usually involves locating a series of wells that "step out" from

Table 7.1　　　　　**U.S. Oil Industry Statistics, 1978–1986**

A. Prices

| Year | Average U.S. Oil Price | | Average U.S. Gas Price | | U.S. Finding Cost |
	$ per Barrel	1967 $ per Barrel	$ per MCF	1967 $ per MCF	($ per BOE)
1978	8.96	4.28	.91	.43	6.64
1979	12.51	5.31	1.18	.50	11.74
1980	21.59	8.03	1.59	.59	10.66
1981	31.77	10.83	1.98	.68	12.17
1982	28.52	9.53	2.46	.82	11.57
1983	26.18	8.64	2.59	.86	9.24
1984	25.88	8.34	2.66	.86	6.61
1985	24.09	7.80	2.51	.81	8.76
1986	12.66	4.21	1.87	.62	6.96*

B. U.S. Exploration and Development

	Development Expenditures[a]	Exploration Expenditures[a]	Oil Reserve Revisions + Additions[b]	Exploratory Wells Completed	Exploratory Dry Holes	Success Rate (%)
1978	11.0	9.4	2.58	11,030	8,055	.270
1979	17.3	15.6	1.41	10,375	7,479	.303
1980	19.6	20.8	2.97	12,870	9,008	.300
1981	25.0	30.7	2.57	17,430	12,247	.297
1982	25.9	27.9	1.38	15,882	11,229	.293
1983	25.2	21.1	2.90	13,845	10,062	.273
1984	26.6	21.5	3.75	15,138	11,216	.259
1985	27.2	16.4	3.02	12,208	9,201	.246
1986	16.4*	8.5*	N.A.	7,192	5,469	.240

C. U.S. Drilling Statistics

	Total Drilling Costs[a]	Average Drilling Cost per Well[c]	Total U.S. Lease Acreage[d]	Active Drilling Rigs
1978	13.1	280	431	2,255
1979	16.1	331	449	2,176
1980	22.8	368	473	2,910
1981	36.7	454	513	3,970
1982	39.4	514	539	3,105
1983	25.1	372	586	2,229
1984	25.2	326	588	2,428
1985	23.7	417	N.A.	1,969
1986	13.6*	366*	N.A.	964

Sources: Oil and Gas Journal Database, Oil Industry Comparative Appraisals, Basic Petroleum Data Book, and *Oil and Gas Reserve Disclosures.*
Notes: A * denotes author's calculations. N.A. means not available.
[a]In billions of dollars.
[b]In billions of barrels.
[c]In thousands of dollars
[d]In millions of acres.

the initial exploratory play or find. Firms also drill development wells to improve the recovery of oil from nearby wells. Development expenditures include those for drilling and completion; they exclude expenses associated with the actual pumping or transportation of oil and gas. Development wells generally cost less than exploratory wells and have a much higher probability of success. During 1986, roughly 32,000 development wells were completed in the United States, about 4.5 development wells for each exploratory well. Table 7.1 also contains information on U.S. development spending.

7.1.2 Firms

Three types of firms explore for oil and gas: major, diversified, and independent companies. Major companies rank among the top 10–15 firms in the industry (e.g., Exxon, Texaco, and Mobil). These firms participate in all segments of the petroleum market: exploration, production, transportation, refining, and marketing. They usually conduct their exploration activities with large staffs of geologists and drilling experts. They also own their own drilling equipment. Diversified companies are somewhat smaller than the majors. They too participate in most segments of the petroleum industry; they, however, typically have a much smaller fraction of their operations in oil and gas (e.g., Pacific Lighting and Union Pacific). Independent oil and gas firms, or "operators," are smaller firms. They tend to concentrate their operations mainly in oil and gas exploration and production. These firms range in size from several-person "firms" (e.g., Willard Pease Oil Co. and Bronco Oil and Gas) to large producing firms (such as Adobe Oil and Gas and Dyco Petroleum). Independent operators mainly explore and develop onshore properties. They also tend to emphasize natural gas exploration over oil exploration (Arthur Andersen 1986).

7.1.3 The Exploration Process and Well Costs

U.S. oil companies currently explore for oil and gas in 41 states. While most companies have operations in several states, independent operators often concentrate their drilling in specific geologic horizons. Other than the major companies, relatively few domestic firms operate overseas; many diversified companies do, however, operate in Canada.

Exploration for oil and gas typically proceeds in one of two ways. Large firms use their in-house staff and public and private geologic data bases to identify prospects. Smaller firms typically rely on independent geologists and lease brokers. Most companies spend considerable amounts on research, seismic testing, and leases before drilling. Frequently, companies also lease large blocks of land surrounding potential prospects. This latter practice mitigates common pool problems and preempts other operators from free riding on a firm's success. Block leasing can, however, be costly. Roberts Oil and Gas provides a typical, although by no means unusual, example. In 1982, Roberts Oil and Gas earned $640,000 in oil and gas revenues from wells on

1,719 (net) acres of developed leasehold property. At the same time, Roberts held over 17,193 (net) acres of undeveloped leasehold property, much of which was never developed.

Oil and gas leases have quite elaborate and curious contractual provisions. These provisions respond to informational asymmetries and incentive problems between the lessee and the lessor. In general, private mineral leases grant the holder drilling and subterranean development rights for a fixed number of years.[2] In return, the landowner usually receives a per acre fee and a production bonus, termed a *royalty interest*. Operators commonly grant landowners a one-eighth (12.5%) royalty interest in the gross revenue generated by wells on their property. In some states, such as California, royalties may run as high as one-sixth. Some lease contracts also involve third parties who put together the deal, such as geologists or lease brokers. These dealmakers receive, without cost, an *override royalty*. Occasionally, an operator may also reserve an override royalty for its employees or shareholders. Override royalties may amount to between 1/32 and 1/16 of gross revenues.

In a standard lease agreement, the operator incurs all drilling and production costs—the so-called *working* or *operating interest* in the well.[3] In return for assuming all costs, the operator receives the remaining revenue streams from the well—that is, all gross revenues net of the front-end load from royalty payments. Operators term the remaining interest the *net revenue interest*.[4] To finance the working interest, the operator must often line up substantial financial capital in advance. This capital covers the front-end costs associated with drilling and completing a well. The operator's front-end costs differ by well type, location, and initial tests. All wells have substantial variable drilling and test costs; only successful wells incur completion costs. Accountants define drilling costs as all costs incurred to the "casing point"—the stage at which the operator lines the walls of the well with special pipe. Major drilling expenses consist of intangibles such as site preparation (5%–15%), drilling contract work (45%–55%), logging and testing (5%–10%), consultant fees (5%), and contingencies, damages, and survey work. Tangible costs include drilling mud, water, and chemicals (5%–15%), and permits, miscellaneous equipment, piping, and the casing head (1%–15%).[5]

Exploratory wells have greater sunk set-up costs. These sunk costs include those for lease inspection, drilling platforms, geophysical research, and site development. Development wells offer more opportunities for spreading costs, as suggested in their names: "offsets," "work-overs," "secondary extension," and "stepouts." Well costs differ across development wells for a variety of reasons, including depth, location, the availability of inputs (e.g., water and drilling mud), climate, and chance.[6] Table 7.1 summarizes average well costs. In 1984, the average well cost about $326,000 and the average cost per foot was about $75.

To complete a successful well, firms must test, line, perforate, and stimulate the well.[7] Depending on the drilling process used and the well test results, completion costs can double or triple the cost of a well. For example, according to a recent issue of the *Oil and Gas Investor,* Donald Slawson, an independent operator, recently developed several 8,000-foot wildcat wells in the Wyoming Powder River basin. Each well cost about $150,000 to drill. Completion costs on the successful wells were an additional $225,000 per well. In contrast, Foreland Company drilled similar 7,500–8,500-foot wildcat wells in tighter formations in eastern Nevada. Foreland's drilling costs averaged $700,000 per well. Completion costs were an additional $600,000 per well (Daviss 1987, 29–31).

The above examples of the capital required by an operator to drill and complete a successful well do not factor in an important element of cost—the probability of success. Dry holes account for a majority of all well expenditures. According to table 7.1, the average exploratory well is successful one out of four or five tries. If these attempts were independent, then the expected cost of a successful exploratory well would range from between one to $2 million. (This does not include the additional costs of abandoning wells or of complying with environmental regulations.) Thus, operators require substantial financial capital to obtain a successful well.

7.3   An Empirical Model of Exploration and Development Investment

Having described the costs associated with exploration and development, we now model the investment process. This investment model describes how the returns to exploration and development vary with changes in input and output prices. It provides a baseline investment specification against which we can assess the effect of financial variables on investment decisions.

To reduce the complexity of the model, we assume that firms explore for and produce a single, homogeneous product, oil. This assumption parallels an industry convention that quotes volumes of natural gas and condensate in oil "equivalent barrels."[8] Firms explore for oil each period by drilling w_t^e and w_t^d exploratory and development wells. Each well costs a constant amount, p_t^e or p_t^d.[9] Drilling adds to a firm's existing stock of reserves R_t according to the discovery function $A_t = A(w_t, L_t, R_t, X_t)$, where L_t denotes other inputs required to produce reserves, such as undeveloped leaseholdings, and X_t represents a firm's cumulative discoveries as of date t. We include both the reserve stock and cumulative discoveries in $A(\cdot)$ to allow for vintage and learning effects in the discovery process. Although in principle firms could sell newly discovered reserves and not extract them, almost all firms choose to hold reserves. In this model, firms hold reserves for three reasons. First, larger inventories reduce firms' extraction costs. We include this effect by assuming that total production (extraction) costs, $C(q_t, R_t)$, have the property that $C_{R_t} = \partial C(q_t, R_t)/\partial R_t < 0$. Second, larger inventories improve the chances of recovering significant reserves through secondary or tertiary drilling. Third, increases in the level of reserves increase the productivity of exploration and development through learning (here represented by X_t).

Given these technological specifications, we assume firms maximize profits by choosing their drilling and extraction policies over a finite lifetime T. Formally, firms maximize

$$\max_{\{q_t, w_t\}} \sum_{t=0}^{T} [P_t q_t - C(q_t, R_t) - D(w_t)] \rho^t,$$

subject to

$$X_{t+1} - X_t = A(w_t, L_t, R_t, X_t),$$
$$R_{t+1} - R_t = A(w_t, L_t, R_t, X_t) - q_t,$$

with R_0 and X_0 given, and R_t, q_t, w_t, and P_t greater than zero for all T periods. This formulation presumes firms discount profits at a constant rate ρ and it ignores uncertainty. Reiss (1989) has derived conditions on the functions $A(\cdot)$ and $C(\cdot)$ that relate the solutions of this problem to those in a model where discoveries occur randomly.

Solving this problem for the optimal production and exploration policies yields the following first-order necessary conditions for an interior optimum:

(1)
$$P_t - C_{q_t}(q_t, R_t) = \rho \lambda_{t+1},$$

and

(2)
$$-\frac{\partial D(w_t)}{\partial w_t} + \rho \frac{\partial A(w_t, L_t, R_t, X_t)}{\partial w_t} (\lambda_{t+1} + \theta_{t+1}) = 0.$$

In these equations, λ_t represents the shadow value of reserves and θ_t the shadow value of cumulative discoveries.[10] The first equation states that in equilibrium the net price of oil taken out of the ground must equal the shadow price of an additional unit of reserves. To interpret the second equation, we divide through by $A_{w_t} = \partial A(w_t)/\partial w_t$ and substitute for λ_{t+1}, giving

(3)
$$\text{MDC}(A) = \frac{D_{w_t}}{A_{w_t}} = P_t - C_{q_t} + \rho \theta_{t+1}.$$

This equation relates the marginal discovery cost of a barrel of oil to the shadow value of an additional unit of reserves. (Recall that reserves serve both to lower future production costs and to increase the productivity of exploration). To relate exploration and development expenditures per addition to the discovery function input elasticities and the shadow value of reserves, we multiply both sides of this equatioan by $\alpha_w = A_{w_t} w_t / A$, giving

(4)
$$FC_t = \frac{p_{w_t} w_t}{A_t} = \alpha_w [P_t - C_{q_t} + \rho \theta_{t+1}].$$

Industry analysts commonly use the left-hand side of this equation, a firm's finding cost, to evaluate the performance of oil company exploration programs. The right side of equation (4) measures the production value of an additional unit of (capital) reserves. Thus, equation (4) relates the market value of an additional unit of reserves to their current replacement cost. In essence, the variables in this investment equation look much like those in a "q" investment specification: the higher the market value of current additions, the greater the firm's incentive to invest.

When cumulative discoveries and reserves do not affect the productivity of exploration programs, the shadow price of past discoveries, θ_t, does not vary through time. In this particular case, equation (4) states that capital spending increases proportionately to net increases in the price of oil (holding additions and the input elasticity of the discovery function constant). When cumulative discoveries and reserves affect the productivity of exploration, then θ varies with time. Solving for these shadow prices and substituting them back into equation (4) gives an autoregressive equation for finding costs

$$(5) \qquad FC_t = \gamma FC_{t-1} + \bar{\alpha}_w(P_t - C_{q_t}) - \frac{\bar{\alpha}_w}{\rho}(P_{t-1} - C_{q_{t-1}}),$$

where $\bar{\alpha}_w = \alpha_w/(1 - A_{x_t})$ and $\gamma = 1/[\rho(1-A_{x_t})]$. This equation shows that capital spending has an autoregressive component when cumulative discoveries affect the productivity of exploration.

The finding-cost equations (4) and (5) characterize how oil and gas firms' investment policies change as a function of output prices and the technology of exploration (as embodied in the input elasticity α_w). Although the analysis was framed in terms of a single input, w_t, we can aggregate finding-cost equations across inputs to form a single finding-cost equation. Of the theoretical constructs in these equations, we observe or can estimate all but the marginal production cost of oil and the shadow value of cumulative discoveries. The absence of data on firm's *marginal* finding costs makes it impossible to estimate equations (4) or (5) directly. If we assume that average finding costs equal marginal finding costs, then we can estimate either (4) or (5) using accounting measures of firm's average production or "lifting" costs. When firms have constant unit production costs, however, the first-order conditions of the model do not uniquely determine their production rate, q_t. As an alternative to using only accounting cost data, I approximated the marginal costs with a rational function that varies with output and reserves. Specifically, I used

$$C_{q_t}(q_t, R_t) = \phi_0 + \frac{\phi_1}{R_t} + \frac{\phi_2 q_t}{R_t}.$$

In this cost specification, the ϕ_i are unknown, constant parameters. Because the last term in this equation involves firm output, I used instrumental variables for specifications that include this term.

To estimate equations (4) and (5) as linear regressions, I assume that the discovery function has constant input elasticities. Following the discussion of exploration in the previous section, I assume that w contains four inputs: exploratory wells drilled (w_e), development wells drilled (w_d), proved developed leaseholdings (L_p), and undeveloped leaseholdings (L_u). These inputs generate reserves according to the constant elasticity discovery function

$$(6) \qquad A = \alpha_0 w_e^{\alpha_e} w_d^{\alpha_d} L_u^{\alpha_u} L_p^{\alpha_p} \psi.$$

The parameters α_e, α_d, α_p, and α_u represent the factor input elasticities. Constant returns to scale in discovery hold when $\alpha_e + \alpha_d + \alpha_p + \alpha_u = 1$. The variable ψ represents random factors in the discovery process. I assume that these factors follow an independently distributed, lognormal (ln) random process, with $\ln\psi$ having a mean of zero and with a standard deviation σ.

Using the discovery equation (6) and either (4) or (5), we can jointly estimate the parameters of the discovery process and characteristics of firms' costs. This model provides a simple description of how capital investment for oil and gas firms changes with swings in oil and gas prices. It does not, however, consider how a firm finances its exploration and development investments. In practice, independent oil and gas firms invest heavily up front to drill; only much later do the wells produce significant revenues. The lag between the initial expenditure of investment capital and the sale of reserves varies considerably, but many industry sources place the average payback period of a successful well at between 5 to 10 years. Unless the firm has internal capital from previous successes, it frequently must borrow or sell equity to finance additional exploration. In a world with perfect capital markets and perfect monitoring, asymmetries in information among borrowers and lenders should not affect firms' investment decisions. Indeed in the above model, one would model "finance" by simply adding interest payments to exploration costs. In practice, however, lenders do not have perfect information about the riskiness of a firms' projects and the firm itself. In such a world, one would expect that lenders and equity holders would insist on contingent contracts that limited their financial exposure to bad drilling projects. If such contracts were enforceable, they would most likely affect a firms' investment spending when the firm runs into financial trouble. We return to this point below after we have discussed the empirical results of the standard exploration model.

7.3.1 The Sample of Firms and Variable Definitions

To examine the investment process for oil and gas firms, capital spending, reserve, and financial data were assembled for a sample of 44 independent oil and gas firms. The data begin in 1978 because of a revision of oil and gas reporting requirements.[11] They end in 1986 because of reporting lags. The sample of firms was chosen at random from the *Oil and Gas Journal*'s 1983 list of the top 400 oil and gas firms. Major and diversified companies were automatically excluded because of the geographic diversity of their operations. Independent firms were selected as follows. From the initial list of 400 firms, 70 firms were selected at random. Twelve independents were eliminated from consideration because they had substantial foreign operations. Another 14 were subsequently eliminated because of insufficient or unreliable data (e.g., accounting convention changes or their oil and gas operations were not summarized in sufficient detail). It is not surprising that the eliminated firms tended to be very small or very large. The remaining 44 independents have mostly U.S. operations (an average of 95% or more of their production must be in the United States during the sample period).[12]

Information on the operations of these companies was gathered from a variety of public and private sources, including: SEC 10K filings, annual reports, the *Oil and Gas Investor,* the *Oil and Gas Journal, Moody's,* J. S. Herold, Inc., and conversations with several company officials. During the sample period, several firms were acquired or merged with other firms. If a sample firm acquired another large oil and gas firm (e.g., Discovery's acquisition of Texo Oil), the firms' data were pooled for prior years. When the acquired firm was small (e.g., Vanderbilt's 1978 purchase of Bell Western) or the acquired firm's assets were sold off, no adjustments were made to the data. Appendix A lists the firms in the sample, and Appendix B defines variables. Table 7.2 provides descriptive statistics on these firms and their operations by year. The average firm in the sample drilled between 15 and 30 net wells per year and in the process spent $10–$20 million on exploration and development. The average firm also divided their capital spending evenly between exploration and development.

7.3.2   Estimation Issues

Both the finding cost and discovery equations can contain endogenous variables on the right-hand side. Each model also implies a set of cross-equation restrictions among the coefficients and the error variance-covariance matrix. Finally, the discovery function contains nonlinearities. Below I report both ordinary least squares (OLS) and instrumental-variables estimates of the discovery function and finding-cost equations. Systems and least squares estimates of (5) did not produce dramatically different parameter estimates. Of more importance in the estimation was the issue of how to model firm heterogeneities in production and discovery. The theory of this section does not predict whether firms will have different discovery and cost functions. I allowed for productive heterogeneities by including additional regressors in the discovery specifications. In general, it was difficult to find geographic or firm-specific covariates that explained firm-level differences in investment. I therefore report firm and time fixed-effects specifications only when these specifications produced significantly different slope coefficients from the restricted specifications reported here.

Table 7.3 reports OLS and single equation instrumental-variables estimates of the discovery function.[13] The dependent variable is the natural logarithm of

Table 7.2   Annual Averages of Sample Variables

A. Year

	1979	1980	1981	1982	1983	1984	1985	1986
OIL PRICE	16.55	29.65	33.49	31.07	29.08	28.21	25.27	15.92
GAS PRICE	1.44	1.90	2.38	3.08	3.19	3.17	2.89	2.18
EWELLS	8.5	9.3	9.6	5.1	4.0	5.0	3.7	1.2
DWELLS	15.9	21.6	27.6	17.1	11.9	16.5	14.1	5.0
NRI PRD EWELLS	.29	.31	.32	.26	.24	.23	.22	.27
NRI DRY EWELLS	.31	.28	.29	.22	.22	.24	.27	.24
NRI PRD DWELLS	.31	.36	.37	.28	.27	.30	.27	.28
NRI DRY DWELLS	.31	.30	.34	.24	.26	.35	.27	.20
EWELL COST	.75	2.21	1.70	1.63	1.15	2.59	2.43	1.36
DWELL COST	1.47	1.55	.72	1.17	1.03	.87	.85	2.82
MBOE PRODUCTION	375.7	401.9	371.4	320.1	318.6	418.6	432.6	463.0
MBOE ADDITIONS	508.0	561.9	593.2	424.1	501.3	512.2	409.3	238.4
LONG-TERM DEBT	27.9	30.0	46.4	52.2	50.0	54.0	65.8	70.8
O&G REVENUE	21.9	30.9	31.4	29.8	27.8	31.1	21.6	22.0
EXPLORATION	4.06	7.32	11.5	8.27	4.23	4.93	7.28	1.57
DEVELOPMENT	4.71	9.92	13.1	8.58	6.64	7.78	3.13	3.39
Observations	26	27	34	38	35	32	27	23

| | B. Production Size Class | | |
	Less than 250 MBOE	Less than 250 MBOE and Greater than 500 MBOE	Greater than 500 MBOE
EWELLS	3.04	3.04	11.10
DWELLS	6.57	10.80	31.19
EWELL COST	1.64	.84	2.01
DWELL COST	1.55	1.35	.79
MBOE PRODUCTION	82.6	397.6	2673.5
MBOE ADDITIONS	558.4	950.1	3684.1
LONG-TERM DEBT	5.4	13.3	116.9
O&G REVENUE	6.4	9.0	53.0
EXPLORATION EXPENDITURES	1.53	2.13	12.60
DEVELOPMENT EXPENDITURES	1.42	3.74	17.30

Notes: The first part of the table omits the 1978 observations. The oil and gas prices are January to December averages. Because not all firms have fiscal years that end in December, prices and revenue figures were adjusted so as to represent end-of-year averages. O&G stands for oil and gas.

Table 7.3   Discovery Function Estimates
                     $A = G(w) = \alpha_0\, w_e^{\alpha_e}\, w_d^{\alpha_d}\, L_p^{\alpha_p}\, L_u^{\alpha_u}\, \psi$

	OLS (1)	OLS (2)	IV (3)	IV (4)	IV (5)
CONSTANT	4.56	4.60	3.54	4.63	4.35
	(28.04)	(15.25)	(12.52)	(6.84)	(10.15)
ln EWELLS	.11	.12	.54	.75	.69
	(1.64)	(1.62)	(1.48)	(2.17)	(3.59)
ln DWELLS	.44	.44	.42	.38	.26
	(6.64)	(6.62)	(1.32)	(2.80)	(2.81)
ln DEVELOPED LAND	.35	.36	.36	.07	.15
	(5.37)	(5.08)	(1.41)	(.21)	(1.94)
ln UNDEVELOPED LAND	. . .	−.01	. . .	. . .	. . .
		(−.16)			
SIZE1	. . .	. . .	. . .	−2.26	−.52
				(−5.31)	(−1.23)
SIZE2	. . .	. . .	. . .	.28	.10
				(.75)	(.97)
SIZE3	. . .	. . .	. . .	−.12	.34
				(−.30)	(.01)
SEE	1.19	1.18	1.84[a]	1.61[a]	.82[a,b]

Note: [a] indicates unadjusted IV estimate; [b] includes firm effects. Asymptotic *t*-statistics are in parentheses. The label OLS stands for ordinary least squares and IV stands for instrumental variables. The standard errors of estimate (SEE) have been adjusted for possible heteroscedasticity. $N = 215$.

the firm's annual oil equivalent discoveries, denominated in thousands of barrels. ("Oil equivalent" means that gas reserves have been converted into oil reserves.) Table 7.2 defines most of the independent variables and gives their units. The size dummies categorize each firm's average level of production during the sample period. The dummy variable SIZE1 equals one if the firm produces fewer than 100 MBOE per year; SIZE2 equals one for firms that produce more than 100 but fewer than 250 MBOE per year; and SIZE3 equals one for firms who produce more than 250 but less than 500 MBOE per year. The omitted category contains all firms producing more than 500 MBOE per year. These production cutoff levels were chosen to divide the firms into four roughly even size classes.

The OLS estimates in table 7.3 suggest that the discovery function exhibits slight decreasing returns to scale, while the instrumental-variable estimates suggest increasing returns to scale. In both cases, hypothesis tests do not reject the null hypothesis that exploration and development exhibit constant returns to scale. It is somewhat surprising that the two sets of estimates produce dramatically different estimates of the value of exploratory and development drilling. The OLS estimates suggest that a 1% increase in the number of exploratory wells drilled will increase reserves by .12%, while a 1% increase in development drilling will increase reserves by about four times that amount. The two-stage least squares estimates lead to a different conclusion. In particular, they indicate a high return to exploratory wells. I tested whether the differences in these two sets of estimates reflected a bias caused by the endogeneity of the discovery function inputs. Wu-Hausman tests indicate that each of the inputs should be treated as variable factors. Thus, more weight should probably be placed on the instrumental-variable estimates.

The last two columns of table 7.3 examine the issue of whether size plays a role in the productivity of firms. Column 4 provides some evidence of a size effect in discovery; namely, very small firms have lower productivities. The inclusion of nonredundant individual firm effects (col. 5) reduces the statistical significance of this result. Further analysis of the individual firm effects also suggests that only the smallest firms (less than 75 MBOE) have low productivities.

Estimates of the investment or finding-cost equation (4) appear in table 7.4. The first three columns of table 7.4 examine how closely investment follows energy prices (assuming no unit production cost effects). While the parameter estimates are plausible, only the estimates that use firm gas prices have estimated input elasticities comparable to those in table 7.3. Consider, for example, the coefficient on the per barrel equivalent oil price (BOE). It indicates

Table 7.4   **Finding-Cost Function Estimates**

$$\frac{D(w)}{A(w)} = \alpha_A P + \phi(q_t, R_t)$$

	OLS	OLS	OLS	IV	OLS	OLS
CONSTANT				10.31	9.02	12.73
				(3.12)	(5.06)	(3.21)
OIL PRICE	.39					
	(15.89)					
GAS PRICE		.65				
		(14.65)				
BOE PRICE			.26	.12	.30	.37
			(15.20)	(1.97)	(3.37)	(1.71)
$1/R_t$				.18		
				(1.31)		
q_t/R_t				−.11		
				(−1.20)		
CF_{t-1}/R_t					.21	
					(3.12)	
CM_{t-1}/R_t						−.08
						(−2.51)
SEE	9.62	10.06	9.86			

Note: Asymptotic *t*-statistics are in parentheses. The standard errors have been adjusted for possible heteroscedasticity. When an estimate of lifting costs (including windfall profits and severance taxes) is subtracted from prices in the first three columns, the elasticity estimates (*t*-statistics) are, respectively, .44 (16.17), .83 (14.36), and .28 (15.45).

that an increase (decrease) in the price of oil by $1 during this period would increase (decrease) capital spending per barrel of oil found by 26¢. The third column allows unit production costs to vary with (beginning of the period) firm reserves and production. These estimates imply that reserves and output do not affect production costs. In other words, production costs were relatively constant over the range of outputs observed during the sample period. The estimated price effect falls from 26¢ to 12¢, suggesting that the cost terms only marginally affect the estimated productivity effects. Experimentation with firm and time effects failed to change these conclusions.

Several studies of investment have found that financial variables such as cash flow affect investment spending.[14] Following this earlier work, I included each firm's cash flow from the previous year (divided by its reserves) in the finding-cost regression. Under the null hypothesis that the neoclassical model is correctly specified, a firm's liquidity position should not affect investment, nor explain the apparently low price effects. Including cash flow improves the overall fit of the model and increases the estimated effect of price on capital spending. The estimated coefficient implies that a decrease in cash flow last period of $1 will reduce overall capital spending by 21¢, holding price and the relevant bases constant. Various specifications that introduced linear splines in cash flow were also tried. For example, the cash-flow effect was allowed to differ by firm size, year, and net income class. None of these specifications revealed significant nonlinear cash flow effects.

During the deflationary period from 1982 to 1986 the liquidity of oil and gas firms also was affected by increased debt service. (Table 7.2 documents the increase in long-term debt.) As oil prices declined, bank loans and other medium-term debt contracts placed increased demands on firms' internal funds. To explore whether falling oil and gas revenues, combined with increased debt service payments, may have affected investment, current maturities of debt were included in the investment equation. Only lagged current maturities $(CM[-1])$ had a significant effect on capital spending. Estimates of this relationship appear as the last column of table 7.4. The negative coefficient suggests that an increase in current maturities due last period significantly diminished investment spending in the subsequent period.

7.4   Financing Arrangements in Oil and Gas

The previous section showed that after controlling for investment opportunities, financial variables explained additional variation in oil and gas investment spending. Other empirical investment studies have found similar so-called liquidity effects.[15] How one interprets the presence of significant liquidity effects depends upon a variety of economic and econometric issues. Some researchers interpret the significance of these variables as evidence of liquidity constraints. Others interpret them as evidence of serious flaws in conventional investment specifications. Previous studies have had difficulty discriminating between these alternative interpretations of the evidence, largely because they do not test explicit liquidity theories. Recent empirical research on liquidity has sought instead to confirm liquidity hypotheses by choosing statistical designs that isolate firms experiencing liquidity problems. (See, e.g., the Hoshi, Kashyap, and Scharfstein, and Meyer and Strong papers in this volume.) Unfortunately, not much is known about the mechanisms by which these problems arise or how liquidity problems actually affect investment plans. The remainder of this paper discusses how financial contracts in this industry may create a link between a firm's liquidity position and its investment spending plans. It appears that financial contracts in this industry can have real consequences for managements' control over funds during deflations in oil and gas prices. This section starts by describing various ways in which firms finance oil wells. It concludes with some observations on incentive and contracting problems in this, and possibly other, research-intensive industries.

7.4.1 Shared Financing

One of the most curious features of oil and gas exploration is that few small- and medium-size oil companies chose to drill "heads up"; instead, most firms drill wells with the financial backing of outside investors. This has been true in good times and in bad, when companies have had ready internal finance and when they have not. It is surprising that many of the major companies also rarely finance wells on their own. Outside investors range everywhere from other oil and gas firms, banks, financial service companies, pipeline companies, and refiners to individual investors. When the outside investors are other oil and gas firms, these outside firms typically have an active interest in the operator and the operator's wells. For example, oil and gas firms sometimes combine their resources to manage common pool problems. Companies with complementary assets (e.g., drilling equipment, transmission lines, and input supplies) also choose to pool their resources so as to reduce transactions costs. "Farm outs" constitute another common form of joint venture. In a farm out, a leaseholder allows another firm to drill wells on its leases in return for an override or revenue interest. Typically the leaseholder uses this arrangement when it needs extra drilling rig capacity or when it wishes to purchase expertise in drilling a particular geologic horizon.

While technological complementarities and common pool problems provide partial explanations for the joint participation of firms in drilling projects, they do not completely explain why oil and gas firms regularly sell equity interests in their projects. Some industry experts believe that bankruptcy risks provide firms with incentives to form joint ventures. While the pooling of projects can provide insurance, why should firms with asymmetric information pool risks? Firms can self-insure by diversifying their geographical operations. Moreover, they can cheaply diversify by buying equity in other firms (as opposed to specific investment projects). Some industry analysts have argued that tax advantages cause firms to pool their funds. By supplying up-front capital, outside investors purchase immediate tax offsets. They then defer taxable income streams to later (presumably lower) tax years.[16] Oil companies find it profitable to sell their tax benefits whenever they know that they will have little income against which they can deduct drilling expenses.

7.4.2 Financial Terms

Although capacity constraints, common pool problems, bankruptcy risk, and tax incentives may explain why firms seek external funds to finance exploration and development, they do not explain the idiosyncrasies of equity participation contracts. Equity contracts in this industry incorporate many provisions that address asymmetric information and adverse selection problems. These problems occur because the operator has private information about the prospects of joint exploration and development projects. Thus, even though a project may contain substantial tax advantages, these gains may go unrealized because the operator cannot credibly transfer all of them to investors. Although the theoretical contracting literature suggests that the firm and its investors could commit to complete contingent contracts to overcome these incentive problems, firms and investors face two major problems when writing contracts. First, in many instances the operator has private information about *what* contingencies might arise. The operator need not have any incentive to reveal these contingencies at the time the parties contract. Second, lenders face substantial monitoring and verification costs when trying to enforce contracts. For example, while investors in this industry can file due diligence suits against operators, they frequently have a hard time proving that management contributed to a bad outcome. Statements indicating the difficulty of assessing a project's risks regularly appear in public prospectuses. For example, one operator warns investors, "With new investors what I try to do is make them clearly understand that if they can't afford to take their money and flush it down the toilet, they can't afford to be in the oil business, because chances are that is what they are doing" (Treibitz 1985, 47). Given the difficulty outside investors face in writing complete contingent contracts and in verifying investment outcomes ex post, one might expect to see few inexperienced investors in the oil and gas industry. Curiously, this is not the case. Thus, there must be other mechanisms by which outside investors affect an operator's drilling plans.

The terms on which outside equity investors participate in drilling projects differ across deals for a variety of reasons. Most equity deals, however, have the following structure. The outside investor agrees to pay some fraction of the working interest in a series of wells. The investor receives in return a net revenue interest in each well. Occasionally large outside investors receive the same terms as the operator: the investor pays 1% of the costs and receives 1% of the net revenue. The typical outside investor purchases a *carried interest* in a series of oil and gas wells. A common carried interest is stated as "one-third buys one-quarter." Under these terms, the outside investor receives .75 percent of the net revenue for each percentage point of the project's costs he has assumed.[17] The outside investor thus "carries" one-quarter of the operator's costs. In return for carrying the operator, outside investors often require the operator to own a significant interest in the project, typically at least a one-eighth interest. Industry analysts claim that this capital requirement insures that operators will complete wells with due diligence. Although operators do not always require outside investors to commit minimum sums, it appears that operators prefer for investors to purchase at least a one-sixteenth share in a series of wells.

When an outside investor purchases a working interest in a well, the investor assumes some of the liability for the operation of the well. Should the operator go bankrupt, those with the remaining working interest are liable for completing or abandoning the well. Should the well have a blow out, they are also responsible for additional costs (or the insurance deductible). Thus, a working interest in the well carries with it large potential liabilities. These liabilities may not be completely insurable at a reasonable cost (Fraser 1986). During the 1970s, alternative financing arrangements arose to reduce operators' incentives to expose outside investors to large legal liabilities (such as those associated with deep offshore wells). Most of these arrangements reduce agency problems by shifting risks onto the operator. The most common of these arrangements was the oil and gas limited partnership. Under this arrangement, outside investors (the "limited partners") contributed money to a partnership in return for tax benefits. The general partner (typically the well operator) drilled its own prospects with these funds and bore most of the partnership's operating liabilities. While these partnerships limited the legal exposure of participants, they raised their own set of incentive problems. In order to remove the partners from legal liabilities, the partners typically had to engage in "arm's length" transactions with the general partner. While some oil and gas partnerships were dedicated to drilling specific projects or areas, many partners simply funded vague portfolios of drilling projects or even "blind pools." Thus, these partnerships often allowed the general partner wide discretion in drilling and completion decisions. Although some industry experts believe that when general partners repeatedly seek funds they have sufficient incentives to offer good projects to outsiders, some argue that reputations matter little in this business.

In all of the aforementioned financing arrangements, the lender has a very difficult time mitigating agency problems that arise when the operator has better information. Over time, outside investors have designed several new financing arrangements to deal with these informational asymmetries. These new arrangements typically place constraints on the operator's discretionary investment spending, particularly when the operator has bad luck or runs into financial trouble. One common way in which outside investors control operators' incentives is through *"back-in"* or *revisionary interest* contracts. These contracts give the operator an interest (or an additional interest) in a well when the well reaches a certain stage. Typically the operator "backs in" after production begins or after production has covered all of the well's costs. Once the operator has backed in a revenue interest, the operator assumes a fraction of the remaining costs and revenues just as the other investors do. In essence, this arrangement mitigates agency and information problems by only allowing the operator into a deal after the well pays off. This makes the operator less likely to under-complete profitable wells.[18] On the other hand, these contracts may provide the operator with an incentive to over-complete marginal wells.

7.4.3   Empirical Evidence

The previous subsections underscored two important features of the exploration process: the amount of capital required before production can occur and the inability of investors to write complete contingent contracts that resolve investment incentive problems. If capital markets were perfect, and lenders could perfectly evaluate projects and costlessly monitor the performance of operators, then these costs should not affect the real investment activities of oil and gas firms. Moreover, one would expect to see few differences across firms in their capital structures or the terms on which they obtained their investment financing. Risk-neutral firms requiring external finance would simply borrow at risk-adjusted rates of return or offer equity. Bad luck, or a string of dry holes, would not affect the ability of firms to raise capital for future projects, except insofar as it changed general perceptions of risk. Risk-averse firms would also face few constraints in raising capital, since they could easily diversify risk across other firms.

In practice, it appears that there are systematic differences in the ways oil and gas firms finance their exploration activities. Table 7.5 provides some evidence on how firms' net revenue interests in wells vary with their financial position. The table reports regression results for equations that explain a firm's average net revenue interest in their exploratory (EWELL) and development (DWELL) wells. To control for possible size effects, production size dummies were included on the right-hand side. (The intercept term reflects the mean effect for the largest size class.) Also included were lagged cash flow and a second variable that was zero when cash flow was positive, and cash flow when cash flow was negative. These results show that smaller firms in the sample maintain significantly smaller average net revenue interests in the wells they drill. More important, even after controlling for size effects, it appears that the cash flow position of the firm during the previous year significantly affects the firm's net revenue interest in exploratory wells. This same effect appears, but is somewhat weaker, in the final development-well interest equation. Specifications that include firm or time effects do not change these basic conclusions.

7.4.4   Bonds and Other Debt Contracts

Debt contracts in this industry also recognize agency problems and attempt to control them by limiting operator discretion. Just as outside equity holders have problems controlling the quality of an operator's drilling projects, so too

Table 7.5   Net Revenue Interest (NRI) Equations

	EWELL NRI	EWELL NRI	EWELL NRI	DWELL NRI	DWELL NRI	DWELL NRI
CONSTANT	.36	.36	.36	.44	.44	.44
	(16.76)	(16.79)	(16.75)	(15.69)	(15.66)	(15.64)
SIZE1	−.17	−.18	−.18	−.21	−.18	−.21
	(−5.52)	(−5.67)	(−5.59)	(−5.37)	(−5.68)	(−5.08)
SIZE2	−.08	−.08	−.08	−.11	−.08	−.11
	(−2.97)	(−2.98)	(−2.97)	(−3.21)	(−2.98)	(−3.20)
SIZE3	−.06	−.06	−.06	−.12	−.06	−.12
	(−2.26)	(−2.27)	(−2.26)	(−3.25)	(2.27)	(−3.23)
$CF(-1)/R_t$		.05	.04		−.01	−.02
		(1.97)	(1.83)		(−.35)	(−.49)
$CF(-1)/R_t < 0$			.02			.12
			(2.03)			(1.89)
SEE	.17	.16	.16	.14	.14	.13

Note: Asymptotic *t*-statistics are in parentheses. The standard errors have been adjusted for possible heteroscedasticity.

do debt holders. Debt holders also have a difficult time securing their loans with firms' assets. While they can formally attach a firm's primary source of collateral, its reserves, outsiders have a hard time determining the market value of a firm's reserves and, hence, its total net worth.

Banks and insurance companies provide most of oil companies' debt capital. These institutions rarely make loans for specific drilling projects; instead, they issue lump sum amounts of credit or revolving lines of credit. To mitigate incentive problems, they often place covenants and penalties in their debt contracts. These debt covenants require specified repayments and penalize the firm when it gets into financial trouble. (Contracts usually define trouble as the failure to maintain certain financial ratios.) Typically, the debt covenants limit the flexibility of both the lender and the borrower should the firm encounter financial troubles. The debt covenants for Arapaho Petroleum provide a good example of these limitations: "The loan is collateralized by United States proved oil and gas properties, gas gathering systems, and certain partnership interests. Agreements issued in conjunction with this debt specify among other things that Arapaho maintain certain operating and financial ratios, limit payment of cash dividends, prohibit redemption of its common stock, and under certain circumstances incurring additional indebtedness, merging with another entity, and entering into a new business" (Moody's *OTC Industrial Manual* 1986).

These provisions clearly limit what Arapaho could do in response to changes in its financial position. For instance, the contract may force the company to curtail capital spending on good projects in order to meet its financial obligations on others. This contract also prohibits it from borrowing additional funds or from other joint venture arrangements. Banks claim that they must include these provisions to deter firms from taking unacceptable risks. In practice, however, banks cannot credibly commit to enforcing these provisions should the firm run into financial trouble. This insistence on constraining the discretion of firms in bad times appears in even relatively flexible loan arrangements. For example, consider the terms of Hadson Oil's revolving credit agreement: "Long-term debt consists of a secured note payable to a bank under a revolving credit agreement which provides for a total line of credit of $25 million. The amount which the company may borrow is limited to a loan base amount which is based on an analysis of oil and gas reserves. . . . The note is secured by these reserves" (Hadson Oil Annual Report 1986). In this agreement, the bank attaches the firm's oil and gas reserves as collateral to the loan. Notice, however, the loan's provisions do not distinguish between events within Hadson's control and events outside their control. Thus, while the amount of credit available depends on the market value of recoverable assets, the contract does not distinguish between fluctuations in firm value caused by market conditions versus changes due to management's actions. Thus, these contracts potentially limit the ability of capable managers to respond to downturns in energy prices. When energy prices fell in 1985 and 1986, for example, Hadson's access to capital was limited.

Although the use of reserves as collateral may seem like a very practical way of aligning the firm's incentives with the lender's, these contracts introduce their own incentive and moral-hazard problems. Reserve estimates are subjective. Even with outside appraisals, lenders rarely have a complete picture of firms' reserve collateral. Geologists, for instance, define reserves based upon what they estimate a firm can "economically" recover. Sometimes a firm's reserve base may double or fall in half simply because the firm declares certain reserves may no longer be recoverable. This discretion introduces the possibility of moral hazard in firms' operating decisions. Consider the position of Discovery Oil and Gas in 1984. "The Company's continuation as a going concern appears to be dependent on its ability to generate sufficient [internal] cash flow from operations or the sale of assets, or make arrangements for alternative sources of capital [as may be permitted by the debt covenants] . . . in order to reduce its outstanding bank indebtedness and to return to profitable operations" (Discovery Oil Annual Report 1986).

That some firms actually had difficulty in meeting their obligations in these contracts is apparent in Alamco's 1986 Auditor Report: "The Company's liquidity has been impaired due to significant decreases in its revenues and the debt service associated with its long term debt and capital lease obligations. Although the company has continued to meet its obligations as they mature, it is in technical default on a substantial portion of its long term debt and capital lease obligations" (Moody's *OTC Industrial Manual* 1986, 1473–74). During 1986 Alamco stopped doing any significant exploration and development at the insistence of its creditors. Less than five months after the above report appeared, Alamco filed for bankruptcy and the company proceeded to liquidate its assets. While this is perhaps one of the most dramatic cases of outside investors affecting the investment decisions of an independent operator, it does illustrate that outside investors can place real constraints on investment activity.

7.5 Conclusions

This paper considered what effects liquidity and other financial factors may have on the exploration and development activities of oil and gas firms. It started by noting that there were dramatic changes in the oil and gas industry between 1978 and 1986 that affected both firms' investment opportunities and their financial viability. Using an investment model that controlled for firm's investment opportunities, we found that financial factors such as cash flow and current maturities of long-term debt explained some variation in investment spending.

In the latter half of the paper, descriptive evidence on the financial terms used in the financing of wells was considered, and the role of debt contracts in placing constraints on the firm was noted. In particular, the use of oil and gas reserves as collateral was seen to have potentially important implications for how much firms could borrow during deflationary periods. Additional regression evidence suggested that firms' ownership positions in wells are affected by the availability of internal finance. Much remains to be done to convincingly tie this descriptive evidence to more formal theories and tests of liquidity theories of investment. The detail of the oil and gas industry, however, provides a useful starting point for further theoretical and empirical work. In particular, future research might consider how much control firms have over their liquidity positions. Clearly, the availability of finance depends not just on the availability and cost of external finance, but also on the internal conditions that determine how a firm allocates its own resources.

Appendix A
Firms in the Sample

Adams Resources and Energy
   (formerly ADA Resources)
Alamco, Inc.
Alta Energy Corporation
Arapaho Petroleum
Argo Petroleum
Argonaut Energy Corporation
Aztec Resources
Century Oil and Gas
Chaparral Resources

Conquest Exploration
Damson Oil
Diablo Oil Corporation
Discovery Oil
Double Eagle Petroleum and Mining Company
Dyco Petroleum
Galaxy Oil
Hadson Corporation
   (formerly Hadson Ohio Oil)
Mitchell Energy

Roberts Oil and Gas	Unit Drilling
Royal Resources Corporation	Usenco
Sabine Corporation	Valex Petroleum, Inc.
Seneca Oil Company	Vanderbilt Energy
Statex Petroleum	Wainoco Oil
Striker Petroleum	Western Energy Development
Summit Energy	Whiting Petroleum
Target Oil and Gas	Wichita Industries
Templeton Energy	Wiser Oil Company
Texas International	Woodbine Petroleum
Tipperary Corporation	Woods Petroleum
Towner Petroleum	Worldwide Energy

Appendix B
Variable Definitions

OIL PRICE	=	dollars per barrel;
GAS PRICE	=	dollars per mcf (thousand cubic feet);
EWELLS	=	exploratory wells;
DWELLS	=	development wells;
MBOE	=	thousand barrels of oil equivalent;
ADDITIONS	=	discoveries in thousands of barrels (MBOE);
EXPLORATION	=	exploration expenditures ($ million);
DEVELOPMENT	=	development expenditures ($ million);
EWELL COST	=	exploration expenditures per exploratory well ($ million);
DWELL COST	=	development expenditures per exploratory well ($ million);
NRI	=	net revenue interest;
PRD	=	producing wells.

Notes

1. In related work, Bernanke (1983) studied the effects of the Great Depression deflation on bank capital. Much earlier, Meyer and Kuh (1957) emphasized that small firms' investment programs were sensitive to large downturns in demand.

2. A private landowner owns both surface rights and (unassigned) subsurface rights. These rights are transferred whenever the property is sold. The landowner may choose to sell all mineral rights to the property separately at any time. The landowner may also restrict the depth of the mineral rights. Federal leases involve somewhat different allocations of rights. Federal royalty contracts, however, do not typically differ from those in private contracts.

3. The term "operator" usually identifies the firm drilling the well. The term "operator of record" identifies the entity responsible for well logs and drilling liabilities. The operator may or may not own an operating interest in any particular well.

4. Consider the following example. An operator signs a lease promising the landowner a 12.5% royalty. In addition, the operator pays a 2.5% override royalty to a

lease broker. Upon completion, the operator pays 15% of any revenues to these parties. The operator receives in return 85% of the revenues but pays 100% of the costs.

5. These figures come from sample well budgets reported in issues of the *Oil and Gas Investor.*

6. The American Petroleum Institute and the Independent Petroleum Association publish annual survey estimates of drilling costs by date, location, type, and depth of well. Academic studies of these drilling costs include those by Fisher (1964), Epple (1975) and others.

7. To perforate a well, the operator fires metal bullets or pressurized gas into the walls of the well. These "shots" increase the flow of oil and gas into the drill hole. Stimulation includes additional measures to increase the flow of oil and gas, such as injecting water into the ground surrounding the well or pump.

8. Firms convert the two using the BTU equivalence: 6,000 cubic feet of gas equals one barrel of oil. A barrel of oil contains 42 gallons.

9. I assume that the price of a well does not depend on individual firms' drilling decisions. The price can change over time, however, because of movements in the aggregate supply curve of drilling services.

10. For related exploration models see Pindyck (1978), Uhler (1978), and Livernois and Uhler (1987).

11. In December 1977, the Financial Accounting Standards Board (FASB) issued statement 19. This statement established uniform accounting conventions for oil and gas firms. Statement 19 was later amended by Securities and Exchange Commission Accounting Series Releases 253, 257, and 269. These releases added requirements or amendments affecting reserve reporting and the definitions of exploration and development expenditures. See, e.g., Moore and Grier (1982) and Magliolo (1986).

12. The initial subsample was limited to 70 firms because of data collection costs. I focus on independents with limited foreign operations to reduce variation in firms' investment opportunities. Fewer than 2% of the sample firms had significant foreign operations.

13. The instrument list included fixed effects, annual price indexes for the inputs (from the *Basic Petroleum Data Book*), oil and gas prices, beginning of period reserves, and geographic and geologic dummy variables. The dummy variables include variables summarizing the presence of offshore, Alaskan, Gulf Coast, and California operations.

14. In addition to the empirical chapters in this volume, see Fazzari, Hubbard, and Petersen (1988) and the references therein.

15. For a review of aggregate and disaggregate studies on U.S. data see Fazzari, Hubbard and Petersen (1988). Meyer and Strong's paper in this volume provides another industry study. The Hoshi, Kashyap, and Scharfstein paper provides evidence from Japan.

16. Special oil and gas investment offsets also attract individual investors. Until the recent tax reform act, most intangible drilling costs were fully deductible. Under functional allocation programs, the firm sold these deductions to individual investors. Recent revisions in the tax code reduce the incentives for individuals to use these shelters. For example, individuals must now assume part of the working interest in order to take tax deductions. The new tax law also limits the types of income individuals may offset with oil and gas revenue.

17. Under "one-third buys one-quarter," if the outside investor paid 50% of the costs of the well, the investor would receive $50 \times .75 = 37.5\%$ of the net revenue interest in the well. If the well operator pays 15% in front-end royalties, then the investor receives $31.875 = 85 \times .5 \times .75\%$ of the well's gross revenues.

18. Wolfson (1985) notes that because exploratory well results provide information

externalities for other wells, operators may choose not to complete successful wells. Part of the monitoring problem investors face is one of cost—it is extremely expensive to verify that the operator has correctly reported the costs and results of a well. In many cases, there is always residual uncertainty about outcomes. In the words of one operator, "I can think of three wells that I have drilled that I can hardly wait until I get to Heaven [so that I can] see what was really down there, to look down and see where that oil was" (Treibitz 1985, p. 49).

References

American Petroleum Institute (API). *Basic petroleum data book: Petroleum industry statistics*. Annual. API: Washington, D.C.

Arthur Andersen, Inc. 1986. *Oil and gas reserve disclosures*. Houston: Arthur Andersen.

Bernanke, B. 1983. Nonmonetary effects of the financial crisis in the propagation of the Great Depression. *American Economic Review* 73: 257–76.

Daviss, B. 1987. Venturing into the wild. *Oil and Gas Investor* 7(1): 26–31.

Epple, D. 1975. *Petroleum discoveries and government policy: An econometric analysis of supply*. Cambridge: Ballinger.

Fazzari, S., R. Hubbard, and B. Petersen. 1988. Financing constraints and corporate investment. *Brookings Papers on Economic Activity* no. 1, pp. 141–95.

Fisher, F. 1964. *Supply and costs in the U.S. petroleum industry: Two econometric studies*. Baltimore: Johns Hopkins University Press.

Fraser, B. W. 1986. The cost of doing business just went up. *Oil and Gas Investor* 5(6): 38–41.

J. Herold, Inc. *Oil Industry Comparative Appraisals*. Annual. Greenwich, Conn.: J. Herold Investment Service.

Livernois, J. R., and R. Uhler. 1987. Extraction costs and the economics of nonrenewable resources. *Journal of Political Economy* 95:195–203.

Magliolo, J. 1986. Capital market analysis of reserve recognition accounting. *Journal of Accounting Research* 24:69–108.

Meyer, J., and E. Kuh. 1957. *The investment decision*. Cambridge, Mass.: Harvard University Press.

Moore, C., and J. Grier. 1983. *Accounting standards and regulations for oil and gas producers*. Englewood Cliffs, N.J.: Prentice-Hall.

Office of Technology Assessment. *U.S. oil production: The effect of low oil prices*. Annual. Washington, D.C.: Government Printing Office.

Pindyck, R. 1978. The optimal exploration and production of nonrenewable resources. *Journal of Political Economy* 86:841–61.

Reiss, P. 1989. Exploration as research. Stanford Business School Research Paper. Stanford University.

Treibitz, C. H. 1985. Deal terms 1 & 2. *Oil and Gas Investor* 5(5): 46–49.

Uhler, R. 1976. Costs and supply in petroleum exploration: The case of alberta. *Canadian Journal of Economics* 9:72–90.

———. The rate of petroleum exploration and extraction. In *Advances in the economics of energy and resources*, vol 2, ed. R. S. Pindyck.

Wolfson, M. 1985. Empirical evidence of incentive problems and their mitigation in oil and gas tax shelter programs. In *Principals and agents: The structure of business*. Cambridge, Mass.: Harvard University Press.

8 AIL Theory and the Ailing Phillips Curve: A Contract-Based Approach to Aggregate Supply

Roger E. A. Farmer

8.1 Introduction

My focus in this paper is the role of certain recent microeconomic contract-based theories in helping us to understand the theory of aggregate supply. Typically, these theories are viewed as part of a search for the underpinnings of Keynesian explanations of the Phillips curve. Contract theories are supposed to explain why prices are sticky and thereby help us understand why unemployment may temporarily deviate from its "natural rate." I shall argue that this view of the role of contract theories is fallacious. Contract theories do not justify the status quo; instead they provide a powerful alternative to both neo-Keynesian and New-Classical theories of aggregate supply.

The group of theories that I am referring to is a subset of the class of all contract theories that takes, as its starting point, two important premises. The first of these premises is that contracts are written between parties who are asymmetrically informed about the state of the world. The second premise is that agents have limited access to collateral. To differentiate the members of this class of theories from more familiar insurance-based approaches to contract theory I shall refer to them as asymmetric information limited liquidity theories or *AIL theories*.[1]

The most prominent feature that separates AIL theories from both neo-Keynesian and New-Classical theories of aggregate supply is that AIL theories deny the utility of the concept of the natural rate of unemployment. According to standard popular approaches to macroeconomics, cyclical variability of the level of economic activity is due either to intertemporal substi-

Roger Farmer is an associate professor at the University of California, Los Angeles.

This work was supported by NSF grant SAS-8722432. The author thanks Glenn Hubbard for his comments.

tution of leisure or to sticky prices of one kind or another. In either case, short-run fluctuations in employment occur mainly as a result of the failure of agents to perfectly forecast future economic conditions. The long-run upward movements in unemployment rates that have occurred in both the United States and Europe in recent years are perceived to be due to structural adjustment problems or hysteresis effects that have altered the natural rate. The AIL contract-based alternative, on the other hand, explains both cyclical and long-run movements in the unemployment rate as rationally anticipated fluctuations in an equilibrium rate of unemployment that are caused by movements in real and nominal interest rates. The advantage of this approach is that it unifies a theory of short-run fluctuations in employment with a theory of long-term movements in the level of economic activity.

I have argued elsewhere that a contract theory based on asymmetric information and limited collateral has strong theoretical claims to be given serious consideration as a replacement to the Phelps-Friedman theory of the expectations-augmented Phillips curve.[2] I briefly review this argument in section 8.4 of this paper. The main contribution of this work is, however, empirical. In section 8.7 I present estimates of an AIL-based theory of supply from U.S. annual time-series data. The relationship not only fits well, it also remains structurally stable over the entire postwar sample period. A researcher who had estimated an AIL-based equation using only prewar data would not go far wrong if he or she applied the same parametric model to postwar data from 1946 up to the present day.

8.2 Related Literature

A number of authors have been concerned with the effects of collateral on macroeconomic theory and with the role of informational asymmetries in the theory of financial intermediation. I view the present work as complementary to this literature. One of the earliest theoretical pieces on the theory of financial intermediation is the work by Stiglitz and Weiss (1981) on credit rationing. Ben Bernanke and Mark Gertler (1987) have made a number of important contributions, and papers by Bruce Smith (1983), Steve Williamson (1986), Greenwald and Stiglitz (1986), and Fazzari, Hubbard, and Petersen (1987) have explored both theoretical and empirical implications of theories of imperfect financial intermediation. This literature is comprehensively surveyed in the paper by Mark Gertler (1988).

My difference is one of emphasis. Most of the work that I cite above is concerned with the implications of informational asymmetries for the theory of aggregate demand, and it is my impression that these authors have in mind a fairly standard transmission mechanism, from demand fluctuations to output, that operates through price inflexibility on the supply side. It is my contention, in this paper, that the same set of theories that offers a potential explanation of, for example, the Keynesian investment multiplier also suggests a very different mechanism for the transmission of policy shocks to aggregate supply. It is the theory of supply that I concentrate on below.

8.3   The Stylized Facts

In this section of the paper I summarize three stylized facts that concern the relationship between inflation, the rate of interest, and employment. I then offer an interpretation of these facts in terms of an AIL-based theory of aggregate supply.

Fact number 1. In the United Kingdom there was a marked and fairly stable inverse relationship between unemployment and the rate of wage inflation from 1861 well into the 1960s. Beyond this date the relationship appears to have broken down, and parts of the 1970s and 1980s have been characterized by the simultaneous occurrence of both high inflation and high unemployment.

Explanation. The traditional explanation for the Phillips curve relationship is as a wage-adjustment equation. According to this interpretation, high unemployment causes wages to fall as part of a disequilibrium adjustment process.

The AIL-based theory reverses the direction of causation. Under the AIL interpretation, a high rate of inflation is associated with a low realized rate of interest. When the real rate of interest is low, the equilibrium frequency of contract failures is low. These contract failures may manifest themselves as bankruptcies or as layoffs. In either case, contract terminations are rationally anticipated outcomes of negotiations between asymmetrically informed parties; that is, the form of the contract is *explained* not *assumed* as in more traditional ad hoc contract-based theories that have been advanced as possible justifications for sticky-price Keynesian theories of supply.[3]

The Phelps-Friedman explanation of the disappearing Phillips curve relies on the idea that original estimates of the relationship neglected to take account of the influence of expectations on the wage formation process. The AIL interpretation of the facts also relies on an omitted variable problem, but in AIL theory it is the influence of the rate of interest that has been omitted and not the effect of (unobservable) inflationary expectations. Until the mid 1960s the nominal rate of interest exhibited very little movement relative to its more recent fluctuations (see fig. 8.3 below, which demonstrates this assertion for U.S. data). Failure to take account of the interest rate as an explanatory variable in the aggregate supply equation caused the estimated Phillips curve to shift in the 1970s when a high and volatile rate of interest became part of the background of central bank monetary policy.

Fact number 2. In postwar U.S. time-series data there is a strong correlation between lagged values of the rate of interest and values of the unemployment rate. The mean lag is about nine months. If the influence of expected inflation is removed from the series, the role of the nominal interest rate is still significant; that is, the *nominal* interest rate exerts an influence on the level of aggregate economic activity that is independent of the expected real rate of return.[4]

Explanation. The role of the nominal interest rate fits naturally into AIL-based theories in which a lack of liquidity is an important factor that contributes to a high incidence of layoffs. The nominal rate of interest represents the opportunity cost of holding money, and an optimal contract balances this opportunity cost against the benefit of additional liquidity. In AIL theories this benefit arises from the fact that a high cushion of liquidity allows firms to offer a more stable wage. Ex post stability of the contracted wage, in the presence of fluctuations in the marginal productivity of labor, allows the firm to make more efficient employment decisions. If a firm had to raise the wage every time that it wished to expand output, then it would be less likely to expand in times of high productivity.

The simplest way to think of the chain by which the nominal rate of interest affects employment is to view money as a productive asset; money enters the production function and directly affects aggregate supply. If the opportunity cost of holding money rises, then firms will use less of it. Since money is a complement to labor, the net effect is that high interest rates are associated with less employment in equilibrium.

Fact number 3. The unemployment rate in the United States exhibits a significant degree of persistence. An ARIMA $(1,1,0)$ process fits reasonably well to twentieth-century annual data with an autoregressive coefficient of approximately 0.5.

Explanation. It has recently become common practice to explain the persistence of unemployment in terms of hysteresis effects.[5] Under this interpretation, unemployment has remained high in recent years because workers remain out of the labor force in the face of persistent spells of demand-induced unemployment. This effect causes an increase in the natural rate. Under AIL theories, on the other hand, unemployment is highly autocorrelated because the lagged value of the unemployment rate serves as a proxy for the effects of financial structure on the efficiency of labor contracts. I provide evidence in section 8.7 of this paper that the value of previous periods' profits is a more appropriate regressor, in an aggregate supply equation, than is the lagged value of the unemployment rate. The real value of last-period profits is an important explanatory variable, because when profits are high entrepreneurs do not need to borrow as much from external sources in order to finance their activities. High profits reduce the dependence of the entrepreneur on outside funding and, by so doing, reduce the production inefficiencies that are induced by contracts between asymmetrically informed parties.

8.4   A Review of AIL Theory

In this section I review the structure of AIL-based theories. The presentation is broken into three parts, each of which is designed to explain the role of three explanatory variables in the AIL theory of aggregate supply. These variables are the real rate of interest, the nominal rate of interest, and the profits that are earned by entrepreneurs.

Throughout this section, I maintain the simplifying assumption that future prices are perfectly foreseen. Although uncertainty is important in AIL theory, it is uncertainty about the productivity of individual enterprises that provides the motive for agents to write contracts. The basic theory does not differentiate between the anticipated real rate of interest and the realized real rate of interest, and it is eclectic on which of these variables should enter the aggregate supply function. This important issue is treated in section 8.5, in which I discuss the question of the indexation of nominal contracts to observed prices.

8.4.1   The Role of the Real Rate of Interest

The most direct way of explaining why the real rate of interest is a key variable in AIL theories of supply is by means of a parable. Think of a simple economy in which all output is produced by one-person firms. These firms are owned and operated by self-employed risk-neutral entrepreneurs, each of whom may combine a single unit of his own labor with a single unit of capital. Nothing of substance hinges on the assumption that the technology is of this rather simple form, although it is important that there should be at least two inputs. The second input introduces a role for a second individual and provides a motive for a contract. I refer to the second individual as a banker, and, to stress the fact that risk sharing does not play a role in AIL theories, I assume that this second individual is also risk neutral. The role of the banker is to provide sufficient funds to the entrepreneur to enable him to purchase a machine.

The process of production yields an uncertain future return, and the distribution of this return is known by both the entrepreneur and the banker. These two individuals must write a contract that specifies how the proceeds of the enterprise will be divided up between them. At this point AIL theories introduce a key assumption: *asymmetric information*—the entrepreneur has better information about the productivity of his own business than does the banker.

This assumption is an important ingredient of theories that rely on informational asymmetries and it is a feature that is missing in more familiar insurance-based approaches to contract theory. The role of the assumption is to limit the set of contracts that can be written to those that are indexed to common verifiable information. Its effect is to link together the employment rule and the loan repayment schedule in any contract that is acceptable to both parties. This linkage is achieved by the principle that a contract will be acceptable to the banker if it provides the entrepreneur with an incentive to truthfully reveal the productivity of the enterprise.[6] Any contract that has this property must take account of the fact that, ex post, the entrepreneur will make the employment decision that is in his own best interests. Since the entrepreneur will make this decision by comparing the marginal product of employment with the marginal amount that he must pay to the banker, it follows that the loan repayment schedule and the employment level cannot be separated from each other.

At this point AIL theories introduce a second key assumption: *limited collateral*—the collateral of the entrepreneur is limited by his own wealth.

This assumption limits the amount that the entrepreneur can pay to the banker in the worst possible state of nature.

In order to clearly explain the combined implications of these two assumptions I make the simplifying assumption that the technology permits only two possible employment decisions. The entrepreneur may decide either to work or to lay himself off. Further assume that the banker observes whether or not the entrepreneur decides to work but that he cannot observe either the productivity of the enterprise or ex post profits. These assumptions imply that the set of acceptable contracts consists of those that make one payment to the banker if production takes place and a different payment if it does not.

It is at this point that the real rate of interest enters the picture. The expected real rate of interest represents the value of the banker's opportunity cost of funds. The higher is this ex ante expected return, the higher must be the expected value of the bankers's share of the enterprise. Since the payment received by the banker in the event of bankruptcy is limited by the wealth of the entrepreneur, an increase in the rate of interest must be accompanied by an increase in the payment that is promised to the banker in the event that production takes place. But herein lies the essence of the AIL approach to aggregate supply. The entrepreneur's ex post employment decision is itself a function of the amount that must be paid to the banker. Once a contract has been written and the state of nature is revealed to the entrepreneur, he will decide whether or not to declare bankruptcy by comparing his ex post utility under two alternative employment decisions. In order to induce the entrepreneur to work, the marginal product of employment must exceed his disutility of effort: *in addition* it must be sufficiently high to cover the marginal increment in the loan-repayment schedule. If the ex ante real interest rate increases, then the increment in the loan-repayment schedule must also increase and, ex post, there will be fewer states of nature in which the entrepreneur finds it worthwhile to employ himself.

In an economy that consists of a large number of self-employed entrepreneurs, each of whom receives an idiosyncratic productivity shock, the aggregate quantity of output that is produced will be a decreasing function of the real rate of interest because a higher real interest rate induces a higher equilibrium frequency of contract failures. This is the basic mechanism that underlies AIL theories of aggregate supply.

8.4.2 The Role of the Nominal Rate of Interest

A slight modification to the above story will serve to illustrate the role that money may play in the productive process. Consider a scenario in which an entrepreneur must write a contract with a single worker. In order not to complicate this picture unnecessarily let us assume that the entrepreneur has no need of a banker since he has sufficient collateral to purchase his own capital equipment. As in the previous discussion, assume that there are only two possible employment states—the worker may work or he may be laid off. Unlike the previous story, however, it is now the worker, and not the entrepreneur, who supplies his labor time to the enterprise. The worker observes his own ex post labor supply, whereas the entrepreneur observes the random productivity of the enterprise.

The way that one may introduce money into this story is by requiring that the worker should be paid in cash. The entrepreneur may invest his wealth in the form of productive capital in the enterprise, but in so doing this capital is tied up and becomes unavailable for use in making wage payments to the workers. He must decide, ex ante, how much of his wealth to retain in the form of liquid assets and how much of it to sink into more productive, but less available, capital.[7]

The worker and the entrepreneur must negotiate a contract that offers the worker a sufficiently high ex ante expected return to induce him to forgo his next-best alternative. But, as in the situation that we discussed above, the set of acceptable contracts is limited to those that make one payment to the worker if he is employed and another payment if he is laid off. The payment that the worker receives if he is laid off is limited by the liquid assets of the entrepreneur. It follows that the lower the liquidity position that is taken by the entrepreneur the larger must be the wage that is paid to the worker if he is employed; that is, a low level of liquidity will be associated with a high degree of variability in the contracted-wage schedule. But the degree of variability of the contracted-wage schedule will itself affect the probability that the entrepreneur will decide to employ the worker. In making an ex post employment decision, the entrepreneur will compare the worker's marginal product to the marginal increment in his wage schedule. The larger the gap is between the layoff payment and the employment payment, the lower is the probability that the worker will be employed.

It is at this point that the role of the nominal interest rate enters the picture. The money rate of interest represents the opportunity cost of holding cash, and the entrepreneur must balance this opportunity cost against the benefit that is afforded by a less volatile employment schedule. If the interest rate rises then the entrepreneur will hold less cash. To compensate the worker for the fact that he will be paid less if he is laid off, the contracted-wage schedule must promise to pay more to the worker if he is employed. But this additional variability in the wage schedule will cause the entrepreneur to be less likely, ex post, to decide to employ the worker. Across the whole economy a higher rate of interest will be associated with a lower level of liquidity and with a higher frequency of layoffs. It is this basic mechanism that causes the nominal rate of interest to be an important explanatory variable in AIL theories of aggregate supply.

8.4.3 The Role of Profits

In AIL theory, contracts will be more efficient if entrepreneurs are able to finance a higher proportion of their activities with internally generated sources of funds. Take a simple example in which all output is produced by entrepreneurs who face a set of identical projects of the type that I discussed in section 8.4.1. If all projects are of given size, then the most efficient way of organizing production is for each entrepreneur to own a single plant that is purchased with his own funds. A social organization of this type will maximize the social product since it eliminates the efficiency distortions that are introduced by contracts between asymmetrically informed agents. Whether or not such an organization will arise in a competitive economy depends on the relationship between technology, which dictates efficient plant size, and the wealth distribution, which determines the extent to which production requires individuals to share the entrepreneurial role. Those individuals who are wealthier are more likely to become entrepreneurs because they will need to borrow less from other individuals in order to set up a firm. Wealth bestows a comparative advantage in the role of entrepreneurship because it permits the individual to make more efficient production decisions. As an economy evolves over time, the distribution of income between entrepreneurs and other members of society will itself affect the efficiency with which productive activity is organized. If entrepreneurs receive a large share of national income, then these individuals will need to borrow less in future periods from other members of society. A high current level of profit will be associated with a high future level of economic activity because it reduces the dependence of entrepreneurs on less efficient sources of outside funding. It is this basic mechanism that explains why profits are included as an explanatory variable in AIL theories of aggregate supply.

8.5   The Indexation of Contracts

One of the issues that has caused problems for neo-Keynesian contract theories concerns the indexation of contracts. According to these theories, firms offer contracts to workers in which wages are stable because workers are risk averse and, ceteris paribus, they would prefer a stable income stream to one that fluctuates. But this explanation is widely recognized to be flawed. The neo-Keynesian theory of aggregate supply relies on an assumption that agents write contracts in which money wages are predetermined. Stable money wages do not insure workers against fluctuations in the value of the monetary unit; indeed, quite the opposite is the case. Predetermined money wages expose workers to the risk of income fluctuations in the face of demand disturbances that presumably these individuals would prefer to avoid.

However, AIL theories do not face this problem. In the basic theory that I outlined in Section 8.4, I made the strong assumption that there was no aggregate uncertainty. This assumption is clearly counterfactual, and it must be modified if the theory is to be applied to the data. The most straightforward way in which to introduce aggregate uncertainty is to assume that the price level fluctuates randomly and that this fluctuation is independent of the idiosyncratic production uncertainty that is faced by any particular entrepreneur. This would be the case, for example, if all aggregate fluctuations arose as a result of random policy actions on the part of the central bank. In this situation it is meaningful to distinguish between the ex ante expected real rate of interest and the ex post realized real rate. Which of these two variables is the appropriate regressor in an AIL theory of aggregate supply? The answer to this question is that, if both parties are risk neutral, then they will be indifferent to a contract in which the money wage rate is indexed to the observable price level and one in which it is not. If one party is more risk averse than the other, the details of the employment contract and, in particular, the degree to which the contract is indexed to the price level, will depend on the relative curvature of the utility functions of the entrepreneur and of the worker. In AIL theory, unanticipated shocks do not play a central role in explaining employment fluctuations, and, consequently, the issue of contract indexation is secondary.

Although from a theoretical point of view one might be happy with this approach, it does lead to a number of difficulties in empirically testing the theory. It is clearly not a good description of the real world to assume that future prices are perfectly foreseen, and it is almost certainly true that one of the roles of liquid assets (a role that is not captured by the theory that I have discussed) is to provide a guarantee of payment against *aggregate* fluctuations in income. By neglecting to model the role of aggregate uncertainty it is likely—to the extent that aggregate uncertainty is important in the real economy—that the theories that I have described above will generate predictions that are at odds with the facts. One place in which this problem is likely to manifest itself is in the counterfactual implication, of the simple AIL theory, that the business cycle is symmetric. Upswings are predicted to last for just as long, and to be just as severe, as downswings,[8] although we know that this is not the case at least in the United States.

In applying the theory to U.S. data I have taken account of the fact that most contracts seem to contain only limited indexing provisions, and I shall therefore interpret the real interest rate variable as an ex post rate. This approach sidesteps the issue of aggregate fluctuations, and it does not offer a satisfactory solution. However, in the absence of a well-formulated theory of contracts in general equilibrium, one that takes account of the effects of aggregate disturbances, it is as close as I am able to come to providing a consistent theoretical implementation of the ideas that I have described above. The details of the empirical implementation of my approach are described in the next section.

8.6   From Theory to Evidence

In the next two sections of the paper I explore the statistical evidence for an AIL-based theory of supply. My data consists of annual time series on four basic explanatory variables for the period from 1929 to 1986. These variables are:

PRATE 1   =   the period $t-1$ interest rate on six month commercial loans;
DLPRICE   =   the logarithmic difference of the period t and period $t-1$ values of the gross national product (GNP) deflator;
UNEM   =   the period t unemployment rate;

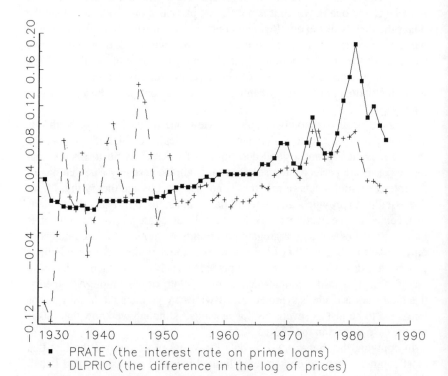

Fig. 8.1   The interest rate and the inflation rate

Source: Prewar data on interest rates is from *Banking and Monetary Statistics of the United States;* prewar data on the GNP deflator is from the *National Income and Product Accounts;* postwar data on both variables is taken from the *Economic Report of the President.*

LRPROF 1 = the logarithm of the period $t-1$ value of real national income, net of real compensation to employees.

These variables are graphed in figures 8.1 and 8.2. It is apparent that each of
these variables has experienced a marked upward trend over the sample period. The Durbin-Watson statistics for the residuals of a regression of each of
these series on a constant are presented below:

$$PRATE = .13 \quad DLPRICE = .78$$
$$UNEM = .18 \quad LRPROF = .04$$

J. D. Sargan and Alok Bhargava (1983) present a test for stationarity of a time
series that is based on the Durbin-Watson statistic. The critical value of this
test for a simple random walk with a sample size of 57 is approximately .49
and hence three of these series (the inflation series is the exception) do not
seem to be stationary. Since standard asymptotic theory does not apply to
nonstationary data, the regression results that I report below are based on first
differences.[9] The data in first-difference form is presented in figures 8.3 and
8.4 and the corresponding Durbin-Watson statistics are given by:

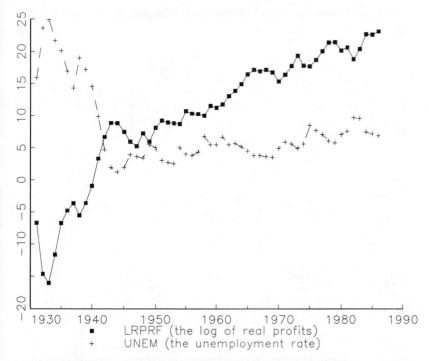

■ LRPRF (the log of real profits)
+ UNEM (the unemployment rate)

Fig. 8.2   The unemployment rate and the logarithm of real profits

Source: Profits is taken from the *National Income and Product Accounts*; Real Profits is national
income net of compensation to employees all deflated by the GNP deflator. Unemployment data
are from the Bureau of Labor Statistics.

DPRATE 1 =   1.57   DDLPRICE =   2.02
DUNEM   =   .93   DLRPROF   =   1.02

The profits variable that I have chosen to work with consists, essentially, of the sum of proprietor's incomes, rental income, corporate profits, and net interest as reported in the national income and product accounts of the United States. This is a very broad interpretation of entrepreneurial income but has the advantage of avoiding the problem that the category in which profits are reported depends in an arbitrary way on the tax laws.

In addition to the four basic variables I have also used annual data on the real values of consumption, GNP, and the stock of high-powered money as instruments in instrumental-variables estimation of aggregate supply. The consumption and GNP data are taken from the national income and products accounts: the series on high-powered money for earlier years is assembled from various Federal Reserve publications and for the postwar period it is taken from the Economic Report of the President.

8.7   The Evidence for a Stable Supply Relationship

The regression equation that I have estimated for these data series takes the form

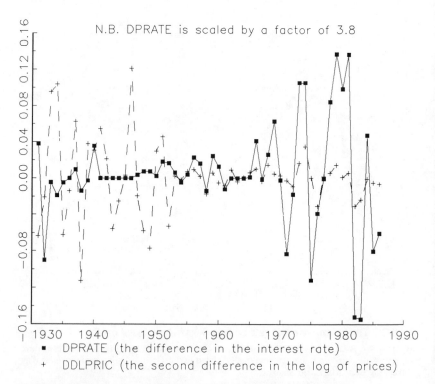

N.B. DPRATE is scaled by a factor of 3.8

•   DPRATE (the difference in the interest rate)
+   DDLPRIC (the second difference in the log of prices)

Fig. 8.3   The interest rate and the inflation rate in first differences

(1)   DUNEM = $-19.5 \times$ DDLPRICE $+ 42.7 \times$ DPRATE 1
      (5.5)   (11.4)
      $-10.7 \times$ DLPROF 1,
      (1.6)

where standard errors appear in parentheses. The equation was estimated for
the entire sample period and for various subperiods to check stability across
prewar and postwar samples. Equation (1) reports the results that I obtained
for the full sample using a recursive instrumental-variables estimator.[10] I used
instrumental variables because the current value of the price level appears as a
regressor on the right-hand side of the equation, and one would expect that
this variable would also enter an aggregate demand equation in a complete
system. I used a recursive estimator as a means of checking the stability of the
parameter estimates over the sample period.

The instruments were chosen by picking lagged values of variables that one
would expect to appear in the reduced form of a small econometric model.
The complete set of instruments that was used to estimate equation (1) is listed
below:

DDLPRICE 1   =   the lagged difference in the inflation rate;
DLPRICE 1   =   the lagged value of the logarithmic inflation rate;
DLHMON 1   =   the lagged value of the logrithmic money growth rate;

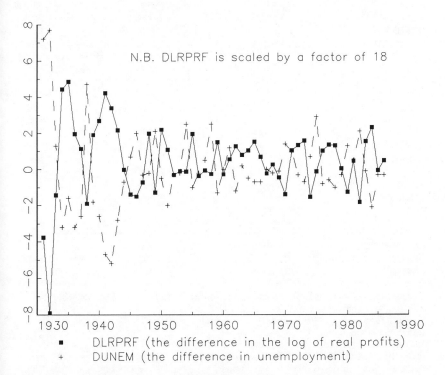

Fig. 8.4   **The unemployment rate and real profits in first differences**

DDLRGNP 1   =   the difference in the real logarithmic growth rate of
                    GNP, lagged once;
DDLRGNP 2   =   the difference in the real logarithmic growth rate of
                    GNP, lagged twice;
DDLHMON 2   =   the difference in the logarithmic money growth rate,
                    lagged twice;
DLRCONS 1   =   the lagged value in the logarithm of real consumption
                    expenditure.

The reduced form equations for DUNEM and for DDLPRICE are presented
in table 8.1, which also reports some additional statistics for the instrumental

Table 8.1   **Reduced Form and Two-Stage Least Squares (2SLS)**

Variable	Coefficient	Standard Error	t-value
	A. Reduced Form Estimate for DUNEM[a]		
DPRATE 1	30.86013	13.55965	2.2759
DLRPRF 1	− 8.62344	3.33673	− 2.5844
DDLPRIC1	− 6.02328	5.11099	2.2154
DLPRICE1	11.32267	5.11099	2.2154
DLRCONS1	3.03328	7.86273	.3858
DLHMON 1	− 9.44258	2.94940	− 3.2015
DDLRGNP1	− 5.58095	4.58824	− 1.2164
DDLHMON2	.62968	4.84670	.1299
DdLRGNP2	4.67657	4.32808	1.0805
	B. Reduced Form Estimates for DDLPRIC[b]		
DPRATE 1	.39698	.24265	1.6360
DLRPRF 1	− .22701	.05971	− 3.8019
DDLPRIC1	.28557	.09678	2.9507
DLPRICE1	− .57685	.09146	− 6.3070
DLRCONS1	.64766	.14070	4.6030
DLHMON 1	.17976	.05278	3.4059
DDLRGNP1	.16045	.08211	1.9542
DDLHMON2	.01495	.08673	.1724
DDLRGNP2	− .06147	.07745	− .7936
	C. 2SLS Estimates for DUNEM[c]		
DDLPRIC	− 19.50165	5.54802	− 3.5151
DPRATE1	42.73199	11.41742	3.7427
DLRPRF1	− 10.68548	1.64866	− 6.4813

[a]Reduced form σ = 1.3797980; residual sum of squares = 85.6729126; R^2 = .50888; $F(9,45)$
= 5.18089; Durbin-Watson statistic = 2.52.
[b]Reduced form σ = .0246917; residual sum of squares = .0274355; R^2 = .67899; $F(9,45)$ =
10.57576; Durbin-Watson statistic = 2.01.
[c]Instruments used: DDLPRIC1, DLPRICE1, DLRCONS1, DLHMON1, DDLRGNP1,
DDLHMON2, and DDLRGNP2. Residual sum of squares = 77.831906990; σ = 1.2353606;
Durbin-Watson statistic = 2.033; reduced form σ = 1.37979799; specification χ^2 (6)/6 = 1.89;
$\chi^2(3)/3$ testing β = 0: 16.95.

Table 8.2   **Comparisons of Two-Stage Least Squares Estimates for Different Sample Periods: One Endogenous and Two Exogenous Variables with Six Instruments**

Variable	Coefficient	Standard Error	t-value
	A. Period 1944–45[a]		
DDLPRIC	− 32.00162	8.68435	− 3.6850
DPRATE1	48.55340	116.41942	.4171
DLRPRF1	− 14.88498	2.56745	− 5.7976
	B. Period 1946–86[b]		
DDLPRIC	− 7.14713	9.70822	− .7362
DPRATE1	39.03005	9.22832	4.2294
DLRPRF1	− 6.29407	2.32061	− 2.7122
	Full Sample Period[c]		
DDLPRIC	− 21.59181	7.33891	− 2.9421
DPRATE1	42.19304	11.67587	3.6137
DLRPRF1	− 11.30842	1.85985	− 6.0803

[a]Instruments used: DDDLRGN2, DDLRCON1, DDLHMON2, and DDLPRIC1. Residual sum of squares = 16.157650115; σ = 1.3398860; Durbin-Watson statistic = 1.763; reduced form σ = 2.85964940; specification χ^2 (3)/3 = .89; χ^2 (3)/3 testing β = 0: 12.47.
[b]Instruments used: DDDLRGN2, DDLRCON1, DDLHMON2, and DDLPRICI; residual sum of squares = 35.137310873; σ = .9615956; Durbin-Watson statistic = 2.371; reduced form σ = .95093673; specification χ^2 (3)/3 = 1.70; χ^2(3)/3 testing β = 0: 7.95.
[c]Instruments used: DDLRCON1, DDLHMON2, and DDLPRICI. Residual sum of squares = 76.435856954; σ = 1.2364130; Durbin-Watson statistic = 2.054; reduced form σ = 1.48459869; specification χ^2(3)/3 = .24; χ^2(3)/3 testing β = 0: 15.98.

variable regression. The choice of instruments does not make a great deal of difference to the instrumental-variables estimates, and I experimented with a number of alternatives including lagged values of investment, of government expenditure, and various lags of the first and second differences of the logarithm of the price index and of the money stock.

Equation (1) is typical of the results that I obtained using a number of different sample periods and a number of different instrument sets.[11] I have not restricted the coefficient on DDLPRICE to be equal and of opposite sign to the coefficient on DPRATE 1, and it is clear from the precision with which these coefficients are estimated that a restriction of this nature would be rejected by the data with high probability. That is, one cannot accept the proposition that it is only the real rate of interest that belongs in the aggregate supply equation rather than real and nominal rates of interest separately. This statement does, however, deserve some qualification since the effects of the nominal interest rate and of the inflation rate are being picked out by the data over very different sample periods.[12]

Figure 8.3 graphs the difference in the inflation rate and the difference in the nominal interest rate over the period from 1931 to 1986. Notice that for the initial part of the sample period there is a great deal of variability in the inflation rate but not much movement at all in the rate of interest. In the latter part of the sample period this situation is reversed. One might suspect that the data will be unable to identify the coefficient on the interest rate in prewar data and that it will similarly be unable to identify the separate effect of the inflation rate in postwar data. This suspicion is born out in table 8.2 in which I present separate estimates for pre-1945 and postwar samples. Since there are only 12 observations in the pre-1945 sample I was forced to use a restricted instrument set that drops DDLRGNP 1, DLHMON 1, and DLPRICE 1 as a way of increasing the number of degrees of freedom. Table 8.2 also reports estimates for the pooled sample using the restricted instrument set.

The remarkable feature of all of the estimates that I obtained is that they remain stable over the entire postwar sample period. Figures 8.5, 8.6, and 8.7 present recursive estimates of the coefficients on the realized inflation rate, on the lagged interest rate, and on profits, for sequential sample periods beginning with the period 1933 to 1964 and ending with the sample period 1933 to 1986. The dashed lines are approximate 5% standard error bounds. As an indication of the stability of this relationship in post-war data, figure 8.8 presents a graph of fitted versus actual values of DUNEM for the period from 1933 to 1986. This equation is estimated using data from 1933 to 1958, but it

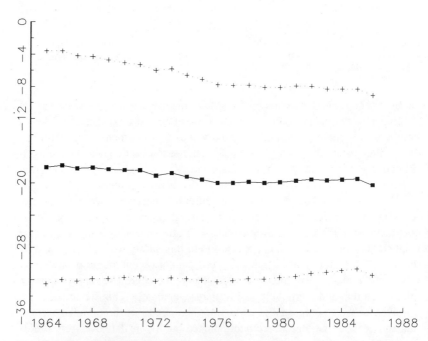

Fig. 8.5   The coefficient on inflation with two standard-error bounds using a recursive two-stage least squares estimator

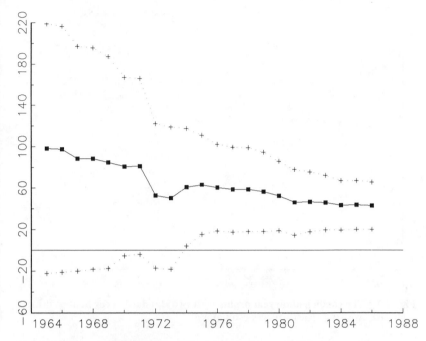

Fig. 8.6   The coefficient on the interest rate with two standard-error bounds using a recursive two-stage least squares estimator

is graphed for the entire sample period. Although there is some evidence of a break between prewar and postwar samples, a researcher who had estimated equation (1) using data from 1929 up until 1945 would not have gone far wrong in applying these estimates to the postwar period.[13]

In section 8.4 of this paper I discussed the issue of the persistence of unemployment. As a test of whether lagged profits is an appropriate explanatory variable in an aggregate supply equation, I ran a number of encompassing tests in which various additional explanatory variables were tested as alternatives to lagged profits. In all of the equations that I tested the functional form that includes only DLRPROF 1, DDLPRICE, and DPRATE 1 performed significantly better than the joint model, and the alternative model that did not include lagged profits was rejected. Table 8.3 reports the outcome of two of these tests. The top panel of the table tests an alternative model in which lagged profits are replaced by the lagged unemployment rate. Notice that this alternative model is overwhelmingly rejected against the joint model, which includes both DLRPROF 1 and DUNEM 1 as regressors—the F-statistic of 27.425 is well outside the 5% error bound, under the null, of 4.034. The model that drops lagged unemployment and includes only lagged profits, however, cannot be rejected with an F-statistic of .096. The second panel of table 8.3 presents similar results for a test of the model that replaces lagged

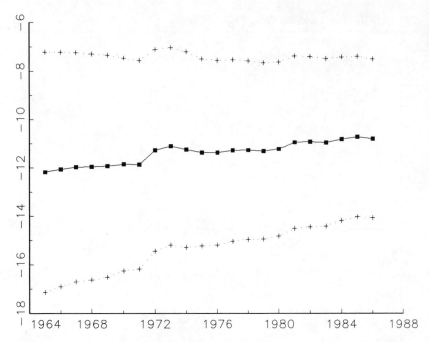

Fig. 8.7   The coefficient on real profits with two standard-error bounds using a recursive two-stage least squares estimator

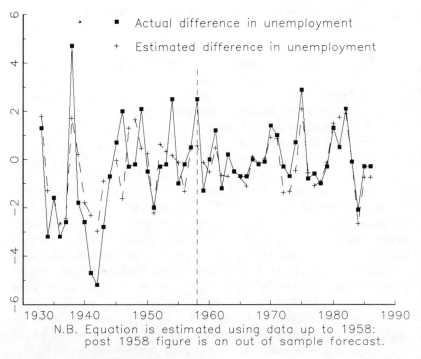

■   Actual difference in unemployment

+   Estimated difference in unemployment

N.B. Equation is estimated using data up to 1958:
post 1958 figure is an out of sample forecast.

Fig. 8.8   Out-of-sample forecasts

Table 8.3   Alternative Specifications

A. Test of DUNEM1 vs. DLPRPF1

Model 1 regresses DUNEM on DDLPRIC, DPRATE1, and DLRPRF1; model 2 regresses DUNEM on DDLPRIC, DPRATE1, and DUNEM1; both regressions use the instruments: DPRATE1, DLRPRF1, DDLPRIC1, DLPRICE1, DLRCONS1, DLHMON1, DDLRGNP1, DDLHMON2, DDLRGNP2, and DUNEM1.

Model 1 vs. Model 2	Form	Test	Form	Model 2 vs. Model 1
− .303	$N(0,1)$	Ericsson IV	$N(0,1)$	7.629
10.717	$\chi^2(7)$	Sargan	$\chi^2(7)$	22.669
.096	$F(1,50)$	Joint model	$F(1,50)$	27.425
4.034	$F[1,50]$	Critical values	$F[1,50]$	4.034

B. Test of DLRCMP1 vs. DLRPRF1

Model 1 regresses DUNEM on DDLPRIC, DPRATE1, and DLRPRF1; model 2 regresses DUNEM on DDLPRIC, DPRATE1, and DLRPRF1; both regressions use the instruments: DPRATE1, DLRPRF1, DDLPRIC1, DLPRICE1, DLRCONS1, DLHMON1, DDLRGNP1, DDLHMON2, DDLRGNP2, and DLRCMP1.

Model 1 vs. Model 2	Form	Test	Form	Model 2 vs. Model 1
.561	$N(0,1)$	Ericsson IV	$N(0,1)$	4.427
10.716	$\chi^2(7)$	Sargan	$\chi^2(7)$	19.439
.291	$F(1,50)$	Joint model	$F(1,50)$	14.526
4.034	$F[1,50]$	Critical values	$F[1,50]$	4.034

Note: Part A tests whether lagged unemployment is a better explanatory variable than lagged profits. Part B tests if lagged real compensation to employees is better. Both tests overwhelmingly pick lagged profits over the alternative.

profits with the lagged value of compensation to employees. This model is again overwhelmingly rejected in favor of the AIL specification.

8.8   Conclusion

I hope to have persuaded the reader that the statistical evidence that I have presented lends qualified support to AIL theories of aggregate supply and that these theories offer a more promising research agenda for macroeconomics than the Phelps-Friedman alternative. In concluding I should add that if this view is correct it follows that expectational surprises play, at best, a secondary role in the business cycle. One is left with a view of the transmission mechanism, from policy to output, that occurs through the effects of intertemporal relative prices. According to this view, fiscal and monetary policy can affect the level of economic activity in the long run if and only if these policies can influence real and nominal rates of interest. There is little doubt that the money rate of interest is free to be chosen in a fiat money economy and, in this sense, the nonsuperneutrality of money that I have described above is likely to prove uncontroversial. One may reasonably argue that these kinds of nonsuperneutralities are likely to be unimportant in practice, but this is a matter that is at least potentially capable of being decided by the evidence. The ability of policy to influence the real rate of interest is a different matter. There are skeptics who will point to both theoretical and empirical reasons for doubting that this theory will provide a successful explanation of the transmission mechanism. On the empirical side, the real rate of interest in the postwar United States seems to be quite well described by a first-order autoregressive process and it does not seem to be Granger caused by any other economic time series.[14] On the theoretical side, if one works within the representative agent paradigm, then one would not expect that fiscal policy could influence the real rate of return in the long run. But this is not the only possible interpretation of the facts and the representative agent paradigm is not the only framework that one might use to organize the data. The overlapping generations model is an equally useful framework and, within this structure, one would predict that fiscal policy can have permanent long run effects on the rate at which agents can make intertemporal trades. From the overlapping generations perspective, the finding that fiscal policy does not Granger cause the real rate of interest represents evidence of a highly elastic aggregate supply curve.[15]

In any event, these issues will not be decided by the evidence that I have presented in this paper: they require a more fully specified theoretical model and a more complete simultaneous equations approach to the data: there is still much work to be done. In 1958, A.W. Phillips closed his paper with the lines: "These conclusions are of course tentative. There is need for much more detailed research into the relations between unemployment, wage rates, prices and productivity." Thirty years of intensive theoretical and applied work does not seem to have brought us much closer to a resolution.

Notes

1. Some of the more recent approaches to contract theory combine asymmetric information with an insurance based approach. The *Quarterly Journal of Economics* supplement (98:1983) edited by Costas Azariadis and Joseph Stiglitz contains a number of such papers. This volume goes only part way to providing the kind of alternative theory of supply that I am referring to and, for the most part, it is oriented to the task of explaining the neo-Keynesian assumption of sticky prices. But AIL theories require the *additional* assumption of limited collateral.

2. Roger E. A. Farmer (1984); also (1988a) which discusses the effect of nominal interest rates on aggregate supply in a general equilibrium model.

3. It should be pointed out that the implications of AIL-based theories of aggregate supply are distinct from New-Classical intertemporal-substitution (ITS) theories, which also stress the role of real interest rates. In ITS theories, agents supply more labor today if the currently anticipated real rate of interest is high. In contrast, AIL theories predict that employment will be high today if the rate of return that is realized

today is low. Both the timing and the sign of the relationship differ between the two theories. Thus AIL theories are also eclectic on the distinction between the effects of the anticipated real rate of interest and the realized rate. Which of these variables is important depends on whether contracts are indexed to the observable rate of inflation. This in turn depends on agents' attitudes to risk sharing, which in AIL theories are seen as second-order effects. Section 8.5 discusses the indexation issue in more depth.

4. Sims (1980) documents this assertion for small vector autoregressions. Evidence for the effect of nominal interest rates after correcting for anticipated inflation is found in Litterman and Weiss (1985).

5. See, e.g., the paper by Blanchard and Summers (1986). A number of authors have recently begun to question the natural rate hypothesis in the light of recent European experience. Several papers on the issue are collected in the *American Economic Review* May 1988 papers and proceedings. Most writers on the topic, however, maintain the distinction between a theory of short-run fluctuations and a theory of movements in the natural rate. It is my contention that this distinction is artificial and anachronistic.

6. A contract that has this property is said to be incentive compatible and the principle is usually referred to as the revelation principle. See Myerson (1979).

7. One might argue that a theory that relies on an assumption that workers are paid in cash does not fit well with recent experience. However, the critical feature of the AIL explanation is that the opportunity cost of liquidity is an increasing function of the nominal rate of interest. In U.S. time-series data the gap between the loan rate of interest and the deposit rate is a stable linear function of the level of the three-month Treasury-bill rate. It follows that even if firms hold their liquid assets in the form of interest bearing deposits they will still face a cost of liquidity that increases systematically with the rate of interest. The papers by Farmer (1988a,b) discuss this issue in more depth and provide evidence of the relationship between loan rates and deposit rates for postwar U.S. time-series data.

8. I am grateful to Glenn Hubbard for drawing my attention to this issue. At the present time an approach that integrates theory and data with the same degree of precision as real business cycle theory is beyond our grasp. Economies with informational perfections of the kind that I describe in this paper cannot be described as solutions to a planner's problem and one cannot, therefore, exploit the second welfare theorem and reduce the equilibrium of such an economy to a representative agent problem.

9. See J. D. Sargan and Alok Bhargava (1983). The Sargan-Bhargava test is uniformly most powerful against the alternative of a first-order stationary Markov process and seems to be preferable to the alternative Dickey-Fuller (1981) test, which is not invariant to whether the alternative hypothesis is a pure random walk or a random walk with drift.

10. All regressions were run using David Hendry's program GIVE.

11. The residuals of the regression do not show evidence of autocorrelation, although I did find evidence of heteroscedasticity and they do not pass tests for normality. There is no evidence of ARCH effects. There is some evidence of misspecification of the functional form although I did not manage to find a parsimonious representation of the relationship that performed better than the equation that is reported. A functional form in which the logarithmic difference of the unemployment rate appears on the left-hand side does significantly worse.

12. Since there is some reason to believe that the methods of data collection differ between prewar and postwar samples (see Romer (1986), it is possible that the hypothesis that only the real rate of interest is important would not be rejected if one had access to a consistently collected sample in which there was substantial variation in both variables.

13. There is no evidence of a structural break in the data at any point beyond 1947. The pre-1946 and postwar samples do show some evidence of structural instability, but this result is highly sensitive to the single observation for 1946, which corresponds to the removal of wartime price controls. If 1946 is included in the postwar sample, it dramatically reduces (in absolute value) the magnitude of the postwar inflation coefficient. If 1946 is excluded from the postwar data, the effect of inflation in the postwar sample is much closer to the pre-1946 value, although it is still estimated very imprecisely.

14. See Litterman and Weiss (1985).

15. There are also open economy issues that I have not touched on. For example, it may well be that, in addition to real rates of return, policy may affect unemployment through effects on relative prices of domestic versus foreign goods. By changing fiscal policy, the government may induce a transition to a new equilibrium relative price. During the transition, the effective real rate of interest will fluctuate. This offers a possible channel by which fiscal policy may alter output in the short run even if the long-run rate of return is pegged by the world rate.

References

Azariadis, Costas and Joseph E. Stiglitz, eds. 1983. *Quarterly Journal of Economics,* suppl., vol. 98.

Blanchard, Olivier, and Lawrence H. Summers. 1986. Hysteresis and the European unemployment problem. In *NBER macroeconomics annual 1986,* ed. S. Fischer. Cambridge, Mass.: MIT Press.

Bernanke, Ben, and Mark Gertler. 1987. Banking and Macroeconomic equilibrium. In *New approaches to monetary economics,* ed. William A. Barnett and K. Singleton. New York: Cambridge University Press.

Dickey, J. A., and W. A. Fuller. 1981. Likelihood ratio statistics for autoregressive time series with a unit root. *Econometrica* 49:1057–72.

Farmer, Roger E. A. 1984. A new theory of aggregate supply. *American Economic Review* 74, no. 5 (December):920–30.

———. 1988a. Money and contracts. *Review of Economic Studies* 55:431–46.

———. 1988b. What is a liquidity crisis. *Journal of Economic Theory* 46(1): 1–15.

Fazzari, Stephen, Glenn Hubbard, and Bruce Petersen. 1987. Financing constraints and corporate investment. Mimeograph. Northwestern University.

Gertler, Mark. 1988. Financial structure and aggregate economic activity: An overview. *Journal of Money Credit and Banking,* vol. 20, pt. 2 (August): 559–88.

Greenwald, Bruce, and Joseph E. Stiglitz. 1986. Information, finance constraints, and business fluctuations. Mimeograph. Princeton University.

Greenwald, Bruce, Joseph E. Stiglitz, and Andrew Weiss. 1984. Informational imperfections in the capital market and macroeconomic fluctuations. *American Economic Review* 74:194–200.

Litterman, Robert B., and Laurence Weiss. 1985. Money real interest rates, and output: A reinterpretation of postwar U.S. data. *Econometrica* 52, no. 1 (January):129–56.

Myerson, Roger. 1979. Incentive compatibility and the bargaining problem. *Econometrica* 47:61–74.

Phillips, A. W. 1958. The relationship between unemployment and the rate of change of money wage rates in the United Kingdom, 1861–1957. *Economica,* n.s., 25 (November):283–99.

Romer, Christina. 1986. Spurious volatility in historical unemployment data. *Journal of Political Economy* 94, no. 1 (February):1–37.

Sargan, J. D., and Alok Bhargava. 1983. Testing residuals from least squares regression for being generated by the Gaussian random walk. *Econometrica* 51, no. 1 (January):153–74.

Sims, C. A. 1980. Comparison of interwar and postwar cycles: Montarism reconsidered. *American Economic Review* 70:250–57.

Smith, Bruce. 1983. Limited information, credit rationing, and government lending policy. *American Economic Review* 73:305–18.

Stiglitz, Joseph, and Andrew Weiss. 1981. Credit rationing in markets with imperfect information. *American Economic Review* 71:393–410.

Wiliamson, Stephen. 1986. Costly monitoring, financial intermediation, and equilibrium credit rationing. *Journal of Monetary Economics* 18:159–79.

9 Liquidity Constraints in Production-Based Asset-Pricing Models

William A. Brock and Blake LeBaron

9.1 Introduction

Economists have simulated Lucas's (1978) exchange economy asset-pricing model to show how mean reversion could appear. (See Cecchetti, Lam, and Mark 1988; Bossaerts and Green 1988; and Kandel and Stambaugh 1988.) In this paper we study the impact of liquidity constraints on market valuation of firms in general equilibrium rational expectations asset-pricing models. To do this we must introduce production.

Our approach uses the production-based asset-pricing models of Brock (1982) and Cochrane (1987) with liquidity constraints added on the firm side. Model parameters are chosen to line up with data in the style of the "real business cycle" school. Hence we will concentrate on explaining phenomena at business cycle frequencies. Robustness of the results to reasonable variations in parameter values is probed.

We show that a production-based asset-pricing model generates mean reversion that is strengthened for liquidity constrained firms. In other words, variance ratio plots drop more for liquidity constrained firms. This is consistent with Fama and French (1988), Poterba and Summers (1987), and with De Bondt and Thaler's (1985, 1987, 1989) "over reaction" effect. We will show that for this result to be visible credit constraints must be binding very tightly on small firms. The fact that it takes strongly binding credit constraints and

Both authors are at the University of Wisconsin-Madison. William Brock is the F. P. Ramsey Professor of Economics and Blake LeBaron is assistant professor of economics.

William A. Brock wishes to thank the National Science Foundation grant 144-AH01 for financial support. Both authors wish to thank the University of Wisconsin Graduate School for financial support. The authors wish to thank Mark Gertler, Glenn Hubbard, Nobu Kiyotaki, Bruce Lehmann, Ken West, and the participants of the NBER conference for helpful comments. None of the above are responsible for errors or shortcomings in this paper.

what amounts to 1,000 years of simulated data to show significant results agrees with some of the recent results putting the 3–5 year mean reversion phenomena on much weaker ground statistically.[1]

Large-firm returns strongly lead small-firm returns at the weekly frequency and weakly lead at monthly and quarterly frequencies. This kind of effect is suggested by Lo and MacKinlay (1988b) as a partial explanation for the striking results on short-term mean reversion found by Lehmann (1988). It is difficult to get this effect out of our model. We are not too unhappy with this aspect of the model, however. This is so because we believe that the lead-lag pattern across small- and large-firm returns found by Lo and MacKinlay is stronger at higher frequencies than at lower frequencies.

We found two other results that are consistent with the real data, but very weak. The model generates slightly higher unconditional variance for liquidity constrained firms, and nonlinearity tests performed on simulated constrained and unconstrained returns are consistent with results of nonlinearity tests performed on Center for Research in Security Prices (CRSP) decile-1 (small) firms and decile-10 (large) firms.

In equilibrium, returns $R_i(t, t + 1)$ on firm i over $[t, t+1]$ are constrained by

$$(E) \qquad\qquad 1 = E\{R_i(t, t + 1)b(t + 1)|I(t)\}$$

where $\{b(t)\}$ is the discounting process and $I(t)$ denotes information at time t. In Lucas (1978), $b(t) = bu'[c(t)]/u'[c(t - 1)]$, where u is the utility function of the representative consumer. For the economy as a whole the "market" portfolio return over $[t, t, + 1]$ is given by $R(t, t + 1) = [v(t + 1) + c(t + 1)]/v(t)$. Here $v(t)$ and $c(t)$ are value of the market portfolio and aggregate consumption, respectively, at date t. The constraint (E) makes interpretation subtle. Economic reasoning in rational expectations general equilibrium asset-pricing contexts is treacherous. "Perhaps it has been good judgment, not merely timidity, which has led aggregate theorists to steer clear of any attempt to 'understand the market'" (Lucas 1978, 1441). However, mean reversion in the market portfolio can be made reasonably intuitive.

Mean reversion at the market level is generated by noting that a relatively high consumption (good times) today ($c[t]$ is high) implies a relatively high $b(t + 1) = bu'[c(t + 1)]/u'[c(t)]$ because $u'' < 0$. Hence (E) implies that $R(t, t + 1)$ must be relatively low. Hence ergodicity (the tendency for relatively high consumption $c[t]$ to revert back to average consumption) will cause $R(t, t + 1)$ to revert back to its mean level. This explains mean reversion of returns on the market portfolio. We turn now to explaining why mean reversion is stronger for liquidity constrained firms versus unconstrained firms, ceteris paribus.

We ignore general equilibrium feedback from both unconstrained and constrained firms into the discounting process. In our model, constrained and unconstrained firms are exactly the same in every respect except that constrained firms cannot borrow to finance investment. Production functions for both types are hit by aggregate and idiosyncratic production shocks. Hence returns are contemporaneously correlated. Unconstrained firms are always forward-looking in choosing investment projects for the future. Therefore in maximizing market value today they choose investment projects that trade off systematic risk and expected return optimally. Constrained firms are constrained by past shocks. They are limited in borrowing by current income. Hence they will invest less than or equal to their desired level for future periods. Therefore they cannot achieve the optimal trade-off between systematic risk and expected return. This lack of optimality causes the market to push up their expected return.

Mean reversion is magnified by liquidity constraints. On the one hand, a low-valued constrained firm (relative to unconstrained) is relatively low valued because the constraint is binding relatively tightly. Since production shocks are independently and identically distributed (i.i.d.), the low-valued constrained firm has an even-money chance of being loosely constrained next period. Hence a good aggregate shock will bounce value back more than the value of an unconstrained firm under the same conditions. This is so because relaxation of the constraint allows the constrained firm to more closely mimic an unconstrained firm and thus achieve a higher market value. On the other hand, if the constrained firm is high valued this is so because the constraint is not binding (although it may bind in the future) so that it can mimic an unconstrained firm. But a negative shock in the future may cause the firm to be constrained for several periods and, hence, lose a lot of value.

The paper is organized as follows. Section 9.1 contains the introduction. Section 9.2 presents stylized facts and the simplest model that can illustrate the basic economic mechanism that we focus on. The basic economic mechanism is the role of liquidity constraints on the firm side in transforming production shocks of short memory into shocks of value and returns of longer memory. Section 9.3 expands upon the simple model. The fourth section presents results of computer simulation of the model. To our knowledge this is the first computer simulation study of production-based asset-pricing models. In addition we add liquidity constraints. The results show that the model is capable of generating mean reversion patterns as measured by Cochrane (1988) and Poterba and Summers (1987). Variance ratio plots across constrained and unconstrained firms compare fairly well with those generated by decile-1 (small) firm returns and decile-10 (large) firm returns. The model does this for parameter values appropriate to the time scale of the returns under comparison. Section 9.5 contains time-series plots illustrating the results. The paper ends with section 9.6, which is a summary with speculations and suggestions for future research.

9.2   The Simplest Model

In this section we present the simplest model that we can think of that generates returns consistent with the observed differences in return dynamics between the small firms and the large firms. The model will be an asset-pricing model of Lucas's (1978) type with financing constraints. It will show how financing constraints can turn nonpersistent production shocks into highly persistent ex post asset returns. This simple economic mechanism shows promise to rationalize a wide spectrum of stylized facts on differences in return behavior in smal and large firms.

Before presentation of the model we list the "stylized facts." Decile 1 (decile 10) denotes the smallest (largest) 10% of CRSP firms. A nice survey of the main stylized facts that we are interested in explaining is De Bondt and Thaler (1989). References are given for the facts that are not in De Bondt and Thaler.

9.2.1   Stylized Facts

1. Unconditional variance, skewness (positive), kurtosis, are larger for decile 1 than for decile 10 (see table 9.1).

2. Mean reversion is stronger for small firms. Mean reversion is essentially zero for largest firms after World War II. It is stronger during periods that include the Great Depression and is weaker during the postwar period. See Lo and MacKinlay (1988a), Fama and French (1988), Poterba and Summers (1987), as well as De Bondt and Thaler (1989). The top part of figure 9.1 displays the variance ratios for the largest and smallest CRSP deciles from monthly returns data, 1926–86.[2] In this panel we see that the variance ratios fall more for the smaller firms than the large firms. The lower panel presents the difference of the large- versus small-firm variance ratios along with simulations taken from resampled (with replacement) data taken from the respective returns series. One hundred simulations are performed on data sets of the same size as the monthly CRSP series. Variance ratios are constructed for both the scrambled large-firm series and small-firm series and the difference is

Table 9.1   Unconditional Moments: Smallest and Largest Deciles

	Mean	Standard Deviation	Skewness	Kurtosis	BDS(2)
Monthly (26–87)					
Largest	.009	.053	.28	7.45	4.95
Smallest	.017	.114	2.90	20.7	9.08
Monthly (47–87)					
Largest	.009	.03	.00	.88	− .17
Smallest	.014	.07	1.53	13.6	2.71
Annual (26–87)					
Largest	.086	.19	− .948	1.13	
Smallest	.139	.38	− .312	.54	

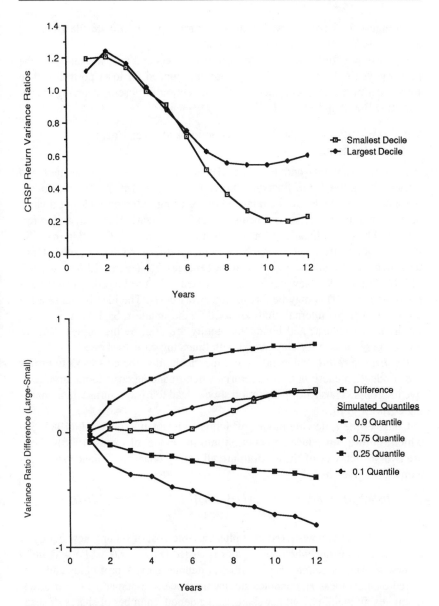

Fig. 9.1   Variance ratios: largest and smallest deciles

taken. This picture shows that in these small samples the variance ratios are not very different statistically. They just barely break through the 0.75 quantile at 10 years.

3. Rejection of i.i.d. returns by the nonparametric (BDS) test for independence (Brock et al. 1988) for monthly CRSP returns from 1926 to the present

is strongest for small firms. Decile-10 returns appear i.i.d. to the BDS test after World War II, but decile-1 returns do not.

4. Form portfolios of stocks that are past losers and past winners over the past few years. Price reversals are more pronounced for loser portfolios than for winner portfolios, with much of the correction for losers occurring in January (De Bondt and Thaler 1989).

9.2.2   Asset-Pricing Model with Production and Fixed Cost of Stock Issue

Fazzari, Hubbard, and Petersen (1988a, 1988b) have documented and stressed the influence of financing hierarchies across firm size. These financing hierarchies are due to the relative cost of using different modes of finance across different size classes of firms. Table 2 of Fazzari, Hubbard, and Petersen (1988b) shows financing for firms with assets under $10 million (over $1 billion) coming from short-term bank debt, long-term bank debt, other long-term debt, and retained earnings in percentages 5.1 ($-.6$), 12.8 (4.8), 6.2 (27.9), 75.9 (67.9). New equity issue seemed to be used as a last resort even for large firms. This may be due to higher tax costs. The idea is that relative costs are such that internal funds are used by the smallest, bank loans are used by the next smallest, and bonds and equity are used by the largest. We are going to use an asset-pricing model with financing costs to show:

Persistence result: Independent and identically distributed shocks to profits and production cause non i.i.d. returns when financing costs loom large relative to profits. Thus i.i.d. production shocks lead to i.i.d. returns when financing costs are zero.

Consider the following model, which is an adaptation of Brock (1982, 36) which, in turn, introduces production into the model of Lucas (1978). There are two size classes of firms. Both are all equity financed. Balance sheet dynamics are given by

$$(1) \quad p_i(t)[z_i(t) - z_i(t - 1)] - [F + c(t)]I(t) + f_i[x_i(t - 1), r(t)] = x_i(t) + d_i(t)z_i(t - 1),$$

where $F + c(t)$ denotes fixed cost plus variable cost of issuing new equity at date t, and $I(t)$ is one when new equity is issued $[z_i(t) - z_i(t - 1)] > 0$ and 0 otherwise. Here x denotes capital stock, f denotes current profit plus undepreciated capital stock, $r(t)$ denotes stochastic process (assumed i.i.d. for now), d denotes dividend payout per share, and z denotes number of shares of security outstanding. We can view z as a type of long-term bond if the "divident payout" is constant. This interpretation is more consistent with the Fazzari, Hubbard, and Petersen (1987, 1988) evidence because new-share issues are a small part of actual financing.

At first, suppose that small firms, denoted by $i = 1$, choose not to issue new securities because F is too high relative to f. So their balance sheet dynamics are given by

(2) $f_i[x_i(t - 1), r(t)] = x_i(t) + d_i(t)z_i(t - 1).$

At first we suppose that large firms can issue new securities for free. The idea is that $F + c(t)$ is so small relative to f that to a first approximation we can ignore the floatation costs. Large-firm balance sheet dynamics are given by

(3) $p_i(t)[z_i(t) - z_i(t - 1)] + f_i[x_i(t - 1), r(t)] = x_i(t) + d_i(t)z_i(t - 1),$

Turn now to the consumer side. As in Lucas (1978), the Euler equation of the consumer is given by

(4) $p_i(t - 1) = E\{b(t)[p_i(t) + d_i(t)]|I(t - 1)\},$

where $b(t)$ denotes a discounting process (the marginal rate of substitution between date $t - 1$ and date t consumption) and $I(t - 1)$ denotes information available to condition on at date $t - 1$. Let the process $b(t)$ be the constant b, $0 < b < 1$, for now. Let both firms be intial stock market value maximizers. Assume, for all values of r, that f is zero at $x = 0$, $f'(\cdot)$ is infinity at $x = 0$, $f'(\cdot)$ is zero at x equal to infinity, and that f is strictly concave and continuously differentiable.

It is easy to see that the large firms jump to a steady state $\bar{x}_2$ given by the unique solution to,

(5) $bEf'_2(x, r) = 1.$

Net cash flow is given by

(6) $n_2(t) = f_2[x_2, r(t)] - x_2.$

Now multiply both sides of the Euler equation by the number of equities outstanding and use the balance sheet to find

(7) $p_i(t - 1)z_i(t - 1) = v_i(t - 1) = E\{[v_i(t) + n_i(t)]|I(t - 1))\}.$

Ex post returns are given by

(8) $R_2(t) = \dfrac{[v_2(t) + n_2(t)]}{v_2(t - 1)} = \dfrac{[\bar{v}_2 + n_2(t)]}{\bar{v}_2},$

for the large firms, where $\bar{v}_2$ is the constant solution of (6) and (7) for the large firms. Hence we have proved:

PROPOSITION 1.   Ex post returns are i.i.d. when production shocks are i.i.d. provided that financing costs are zero so that there are no constraints on borrowing through the stock market.

Let us now examine the polar case of the small firms who cannot borrow at all and, hence must finance accumulation to the desired level of capital stock internally. Since the small firms choose not to issue new securities, and since they are not allowed to pay out negative "dividends," one can show that initial "stock market value" maximization implies that the optimal investment path takes the form

(9)
$$x_1(t) = \min\{\bar{x}_1, f_1[x_1(t - 1), r_1(t)]\},$$
$$\bar{x}_1 = \underset{x}{\operatorname{argmax}} \{bE[f_1(x, r_1)] - x\}.$$

It is instructive to graph the stochastic dynamics of (9) assuming that higher r generates higher f. Look at net cash flow and ex post returns:

(10)
$$n_1(t) = f[x_1(t - 1), r_1(t)] - x_1(t),$$

(11)
$$R_1(t - 1, t) = \frac{[v_1(t) + n_1(t)]}{v_1(t - 1)},$$

(12) $v_1(t) = E\{bn_1(t + 1) + \ldots\} = $ expected discounted sum
of future net cash flow.

The desired level of capital stock is $\bar{x}_1$. When a low shock occurs, the firm wants to accumulate at the maximal rate and pay no dividends. If it gets hit with a very low shock at t it is likely that several periods will pass before it has reached $\bar{x}_1$. Hence there will be spells where zero dividends are paid out. We sum this up into:

PROPOSITION 2.   The solution of (9)–(12) transforms i.i.d. production shocks into non-i.i.d. ex post returns.

Unfortunately, we can not hope to explain mean reversion or the phenomenon of large-firm returns leading small-firm returns with this model.

PROPOSITION 3.   Returns across size classes of firms are uncorrelated at all leads and lags.

Proof. This follows from the Euler equation:

(13) $1/b = E\{R_i(t, t + 1)\}, i = 1, 2.$

We must show that

$$E\{R_i(t, t + 1)R_j(t + L, t + L + 1)\} = (1/b)^2, \quad \text{for } L > 0, \forall i, j.$$

To do it use iterated expectations and (13). Q.E.D.

REMARK.   Any formulation where conditional expectations are independent will yield this result. Dependence induced by the discounting process is a useful way to remove this independence.

9.3   The Extended Model: The Case $b(t)$ Stochastic

In order to get mean reversion and large-firm returns leading small-firm returns we must have $b(t)$ stochastic since returns are uncorrelated when $b(t) = b$ for all t. In the case $b(t)$ stochastic the Euler equation for a value-maximizing firm can be written in terms of returns:

(14) $1 = E\{b(t + 1)R(t, t + 1)|I(t)\},$

where $I(t)$ denotes information available at date t.

It is relatively straightforward to work out some results for the case $u(c) = \ln(c), f(x, r) = rx^d$. Unfortunately, this form of the prodution function implies that capital lasts only one period. Nevertheless, working out the solution is instructive.

Let the economy as a whole choose nonanticipating functions $\{x\}, \{c\}$ (as in Brock [1982]) to solve

$$(15) \qquad \max E \Sigma b^{(t-1)} \ln[c(t)],$$

subject to

$$(16) \qquad c(t) + x(t) = r(t)[x(t-1)]^d, \quad x(0) \text{ given.}$$

Here the sum runs from $t = 1, 2, \ldots, \infty$.

It is well known that the solution is given by

$$(17) \qquad x(t) = ey(t), e = bd, y(t) = r(t)[x(t-1)]^d.$$

The value of the "market portfolio" is given by

$$(18) \qquad \begin{aligned} v(t) &= bE(\{u'[c(t+1)]/u'[c(t)]\}[v(t+1) + n(t+1)) \\ &= bE\{[y(t)/y(t+1)][v(t+1) + (1-e)y(t+1)]\}, \end{aligned}$$

where net cash flow $n(t+1) = c(t+1)$ equals aggregate consumption at date $t+1$. Conjecture a solution $v(t) = vy(t), v$ constant. We find

$$(19) \qquad v = b[v + (1-e)].$$

Returns are defined by

$$(20) \qquad \begin{aligned} R(t, t+1) &= [v(t+1) + n(t+1)]/v(t) \\ &= \{[v + (1-e)]/v\}[y(t+1)/y(t)] \\ &= k[y(t+1)/y(t)] = kr(t+1)[x(t)]^d/y(t) \\ &= ke^d[r(t+1)][(y(t)^{(d-1)})]. \end{aligned}$$

It is well known that (17) converges to a stationary distribution (see Brock [1982] for references). This is easy to see by noting that (17) is linear in logs. The ergodic property inherent in (17) leads to behavior much like "mean reversion" in returns (20). For example, both $E\{R(t, t+1)|t\}$, var$\{R(t, t+1)|t\}$ fall as $y(t)$ increases. Hence, since a high return last period is associated with a low y this period, and since y converges to a limit distribution, this will cause a tendency for high past returns to be followed by lower future returns. Turn now to the effect of introducing credit-constrained firms.

Look at the valuation equation for firm i,

$$(21) \qquad v_i(t) = bE\{u'[c(t+1)]/u'[c(t)][v_i(t+1) + n_i(t+1)]\},$$

where

$$(22) \qquad \begin{aligned} n_i(t+1) &= y_i(t+1) - x_i(t+1) \\ &= a_i(t+1)r(t+1)[x_i(t)]^d - x_i(t+1). \end{aligned}$$

Here $a_i(t),(t)$ are i.i.d. and independent of each other. We will assume that constrained firms at date t maximize market value subject to the constraint

(23) $x_i(s) \leq y_i(s)$ $\forall s$.

Unconstrained firms just maximize market value. Both types face the discounting process parametrically. It is easy to find the solutions if we ignore general equilibrium feedback from the firms i to the economy as a whole. We assume that the collectivity of firms to be valued is small relative to the economy as a whole.

9.3.1   Unconstrained Firms

For i in U (U = unconstrained), conjecture $x_i(t) = e_i y(t)$, $v_i(t) = v_i y(t)$ and insert this into the valuation equation (21). Use (17) and simplify to obtain

(24) $v_i = b[v_i + E\{a_i(t)\}[e_i/e]^d - e_i]$,

(25) $e_i = (bdE\{a_i(t)\})^{1/(1-d)}$,

(26) $R_i(t,t + 1) = [y(t + 1)/v_i y(t)][v_i + a(t + 1)(e_i^d) - e_i]$.

9.3.2   Constrained Firms

For i in C(C = Constrained), one can show the optimum x satisfies,

(27) $x_i(t + 1) = \min\{a_i(t + 1)r(t + 1)x_i(t)^d, e_i y(t + 1)\}$.

Conjecture a solution to the valuation equation of the form

(28) $v_i(t) = v[i, y_i(t), y(t)] = y(t) j[i, w_i(t)]$,
                         $w_i(t) = y_i(t)/y(t)$.

Use (17), (18), and (28) to obtain

(29) $j[i, w_i(t)] = bE\{j[i, w_i(t + 1)] + \max[0, w_i(t + 1) - e_i]\}$,

(30) $w_i(t + 1) = a_i(t + 1)\{(1/e)\min[w_i(t), e_i]\}^d$.

Apply standard techniques as in Lucas (1978), for example, to show that (29) has a unique solution. (It is a contraction map since $0 < b < 1$.) Note that $j[i,0] = 0$ and $j[i,w] \leq v_i$. This is so because the value of a constrained problem must be less than or equal to the value of an unconstrained problem, and j is nondecreasing in w. Note that if the dynamics (30) ever hits zero, it stays at zero forever. Let us now look at returns.

Returns, $R_i(t,t + 1)$ are given by

(31)
$$R_i(t,t + 1) = \frac{y(t + 1)\{j[i, w_i(t + 1)] + m_i(t + 1)\}}{y(t) j[i, w_i(t)]},$$

$$m_i(t + 1) = \max(0, a_i(t + 1)\{(1/e)\min[w_i(t), e_i]\}^d - e_i).$$

Although (31) is a complicated expression, it is not hopeless to compare constrained returns with unconstrained returns ceteris paribus. Let $w_i(t)$ tend to zero. Notice that unconstrained returns (26) do not depend upon $y(i,t)$. The only date t data they depend upon is $y(t)$. So let a firm take a very negative shock relative to the whole economy so that $w_i(t)$ is small. Then if the firm is constrained its returns will "tend" to be high from $[t, t+1]$ relative to the returns of a constrained firm. But at each point in time the pricing equation (21) must be satisfied. Hence for conditional expected returns of a constrained firm to be higher than that for the unconstrained firm, the constrained firm must put more of its payoff on states of the world where marginal utility is low. This effect is not easy to get out of the analytics, but it appears in the computer results reported in Section 9.4 below. We are still working on an analytic formulation of this effect.

9.4   Computer Results

Some of the models presented in the previous sections are simulated in this section. The models are designed to look like real business cycle models and generate reasonable numbers for aggregate fluctuations. From the simulations of aggregate fluctuations, policy and pricing functions are developed for the "small" firms (unconstrained and constrained). With these functions, complete returns series can then be simulated and compared.

The first part of the exercise is to solve for the optimal policy function for the economy as a whole. The economy is assumed to chose nonanticipating $\{x\},\{c\}$ to maximize

$$(32) \qquad E \sum_{t=1}^{\infty} b^{t-1} \frac{1}{\gamma} c(t)^{\gamma},$$

where

$$(33) \qquad y(t) = r(t)x(t-1)^d + (1-\delta)x(t-1),$$
$$c(t) = y(t) - x(t).$$

Here $\{r\}$ is i.i.d. with finite mean and variance, and is bounded away from zero and infinity. This can be easily solved numerically on a discrete grid, given the parameters and the stochastic process $r(t)$. The solution to problem (32) gives a policy function for $c(t) = g[y(t)]$, and therefore gives us the means to simulate the $c(t)$ and $y(t)$ processes.

With the aggregate $c(t)$ process our small firms taking the aggregate as exogenous can be priced as follows:

$$(34) \qquad y_i(t) = r(t)a_i(t)x_i(t-1)^d + (1-\delta)x_i(t-1)$$
$$x_i(t) = y_i(t) - \theta[y_i(t), y(t)].$$

Here $\theta(y_i, y)$ is the optimal policy for the firm given its output and the aggregate output levels. The price of the small firm is a function of both its output level and the aggregate consumption level.

(35) $p[y_i(t),y(t)] = \max E\{\Gamma[y(t),y(t + 1)]\theta[y_i(t + 1),y(t + 1)]$
$\qquad + p[y_i(t + 1),y(t + 1)]\},$

(36) $\Gamma[y(t),y(t + 1)] = \left[\dfrac{c(t + 1)}{c(t)}\right]^{\gamma - 1}.$

Here $\theta(y_i,y)$ is the optimal policy for the firm given its output and the aggregate output levels. In the unconstrained case θ may take on any value positive or negative. For the constrained firms we force the firms to pay out a minimum dividend, $\bar{c}$, in every period. If they cannot meet this payment they will pay out dividends of zero. More formally this puts the following constraint on θ.

$$\theta \geq \begin{cases} \bar{c}, & \text{if } y_i \geq \bar{c}; \\ 0, & \text{otherwise.} \end{cases}$$

These models will now be simulated for several different parameter values. For the first set of simulations we will use $(d = 0.4;\bar{c} = 0.4;b = 0.9;\delta = 0.2;\gamma = 0)$. This is the case of logarithmic utility. The two shock processes are simulated with discrete random variables. The aggregate shock, $r(t) = \{0.9,0.95,1,1.05,1.1\}$, each with probability 0.2. The small-firm shocks for both the unconstrained and constrained cases will be $a_i(t) = \{0,0.8,1,1.2,2\}$, each with probability 0.2, and $a_i(t)$ is independent of $r(t)$. The structure of the stochastic shocks for production will remain the same for all the examples in this paper. Some experiments have been done to see that minor changes in these distributions will have no effect on the results here. It remains to be seen what effect major changes to the shock processes will have.

Time series of percentage changes of consumption and returns are presented in figures 9.2 and 9.3, respectively. Figure 9.2 shows the consumption series to be a choppy series reflecting the discrete shocks that it is built from. The mean percentage change in consumption is 2%, which is comparable to that for the United States (see Mehra and Prescott 1985). One problem with comparing our numbers with others' estimated numbers is that the model simulated here is stationary. It is hoped that growth can be worked into this system without affecting the results, but this has not been tested yet.

The returns time series in figure 9.3 shows more blurring around the main bands. This is due to the additional shocks for small firms. Simulated time series of length 1,000 are replicated 100 times to produce the results in figures 9.4–9.10 and table 9.2 below. For these simulations, two sets of shocks are drawn, the $r(t)$ aggregate shocks and the $a_i(t)$ individual shocks. The results for the constrained and unconstrained firms are simulated for the same set of individual shocks, the only difference being the constraint.

Figure 9.4 presents the variance ratio tests used by Cochrane (1988) and Poterba and Summers (1988). Under the hypothesis that the generated returns are i.i.d., the expected value of the variance ratio should be one. (We follow the same bias adjustment of Cochrane 1988 and Poterba and Summers 1987.)

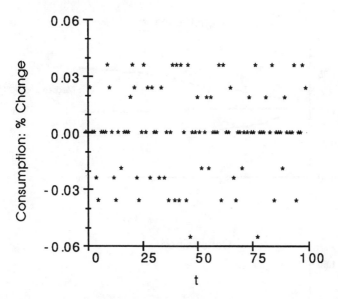

Fig. 9.2   Simulated consumption: percentage change

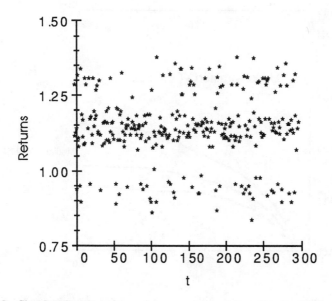

Fig. 9.3   Simulated returns

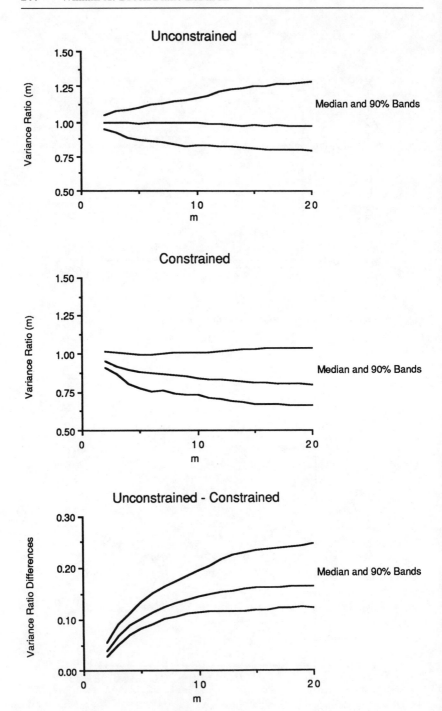

Fig. 9.4   Simulated variance ratios: $\gamma = 0, b = 0.9, d = 0.4, \delta = 0.2, \bar{c} = 0.4$

We do not have any reason to believe that the returns from either generated series are i.i.d. What we are interested in here is comparing the results for the two different types of firms. The top two panels of figure 9.4 show the median and 5% and 95% quantiles for the simulations performed on the unconstrained and constrained firms, respectively. We see that the constrained firms generate more evidence of variance ratios dropping off. This is made clearer in the lower panel where we look at the difference between the variance ratios for each type of firm for a given set of individual shocks. The differences here are significantly positive.

Table 9.2 presents some statistics on the simulated series. The first four columns present the mean, standard deviation, skewness, and kurtosis. For these simulations compare the first two rows. The numbers in parenthesis are the 5% and 95% quantiles. This table shows very little difference between the two series. The constrained series does have a "significantly" larger standard deviation, but it is no where near the order of magnitude difference in the actual data (about a factor of 2). The other moments show few patterns that line up with the data. The hope here was not to line up all moments, but to see that the simulated data generated roughly the same type of results as the data. The last column gives the BDS statistic (Brock et al. 1988, Hsieh and Le-Baron 1988). This is a nonparametric test for any kind of dependence in the data. Under the null hypothesis of i.i.d., the BDS statistic is distributed normal with mean zero and unit variance. In table 9.1, the BDS statistic is applied to the monthly series. It is not used for the annual series since this series has too few points. In table 9.2 we see that the BDS statistic generates slightly larger values for the constrained firms. This is consistent with the presence of more dependence of any form in the constrained samples.

To test robustness of these results they are first tested against other preferences. They are run for $\gamma = -0.5$ and $\gamma = -1.5$. Figures 9.5 and 9.6 present variance ratios and differences for these preferences. They repeat the results obtained with logarithmic preferences. In table 9.2 we see that the results for the logarithmic case are repeated for the other two preferences.

The next experiment is to check the importance of $\bar{c}$, the constrained payout amount. We will repeat the first three simulations for $\bar{c} = 0$. In figure 9.7 the variance ratios for logarithmic preferences are given. The differences here are much smaller. Very little difference can be seen in the first two figures. The differences show that the variance ratio are still smaller for the constrained firms, but the magnitude of the spread is now much smaller. Table 9.2 shows very little difference in the statistics from the unconstrained and constrained firms. These results are repeated for the other preference parameters $\gamma = -0.5$, and $\gamma = -1.5$ in figures 9.8 and 9.9 and in table 9.2.

From these results we see that the value of $\bar{c}$ is crucial for obtaining mean reversion for our parameter values. It is necessary to keep the constrained firm up against the constraint for a large enough fraction of time to generate different numbers. So far, our most efficient way to do this is to increase $\bar{c}$. At the

Table 9.2   **Simulated Moments and BDS results**

	γ	Mean	Std.	Skewness	Kurtosis	BDS(2)
Experiments 1–3:[a]						
Unconstrained	.0	.13	.11	−.15	−.51	.31
		(.12, .13)	(.10, .11)	(−.20, −.11)	(−.65, −.36)	(−1.15, 1.97)
Constrained	.0	.13	.12	−.30	−.35	1.78
		(.12, .13)	(.12, .12)	(−.36, −.24)	(−.49, −.18)	(.01, 3.95)
Unconstrained	−.5	.13	.11	−.12	−.47	.99
		(.13, .14)	(.11, .12)	(−.18, −.06)	(−.62, −.31)	(−.49, 2.74)
Constrained	−.5	.13	.13	−.25	−.34	1.76
		(.13, .14)	(.12, .13)	(−.32, −.18)	(−.50, −.15)	(.14, 3.46)
Unconstrained	−1.5	.13	.11	−.14	−.50	.58
		(.12, .13)	(.11, .11)	(−.19, −.08)	(−.64, −.33)	(−1.25, 2.23)
Constrained	−1.5	.13	.12	−.29	−.34	1.91
		(.12, .14)	(.12, .13)	(−.36, −.22)	(−.47, −.15)	(.29, 3.66)
Experiments 4–6:[b]						
Unconstrained	.0	.13	.11	−.15	−.52	.38
		(.12, .13)	(.10, .11)	(−.21, −.09)	(−.64, −.36)	(−1.08, 2.02)
Constrained	.0	.13	.11	−.12	−.50	.61
		(.12, .13)	(.10, .11)	(−.18, −.07)	(−.63, −.35)	(−.64, 2.01)
Unconstrained	−.5	.13	.11	−.12	−.48	.98
		(.12, .13)	(.11, .11)	(−.19, −.06)	(−.60, −.32)	(−.52, 2.50)
Constrained	−.5	.13	.11	−.09	−.47	1.38
		(.12, .13)	(.11, .11)	(−.16, −.02)	(−.57, −.31)	(−.31, 2.98)
Unconstrained	−1.5	.12	.11	−.05	−.53	.38
		(.12, .13)	(.10, .11)	(−.20, −.09)	(−.67, −.38)	(−1.13, 2.16)
Constrained	−1.5	.12	.11	−.12	−.52	.63
		(.12, .13)	(.10, .11)	(−.17, −.07)	(−.66, −.36)	(−.93, 2.29)
Experiment 7:[c]						
Unconstrained	.0	.07	.07	.06	−.42	.49
		(.07, .07)	(.06, .07)	(.01, .11)	(−.54, −.27)	(−1.05, 2.26)
Constrained	.0	.07	.07	−.03	−.36	1.05
		(.07, .07)	(.07, .07)	(−.08, .03)	(−.50, −.15)	(−.84, 3.41)

Note: Results for seven experiments performed on varying parameters. The parameter values ($\bar{c}$, b, d, δ, γ) are given in notes. Each experiment is run for one firm subject to the $\bar{c}$ constraint (constrained) and one firm not subject to the constraint (unconstrained). Numbers in parentheses are 5% and 95% quantiles from 100 replications of length 1,000.
[a]$\bar{c} = .4$; $b = .9$; $d = .4$; $\delta = .2$.
[b]$\bar{c} = 0$; $b = .9$; $d = .4$; $\delta = .2$.
[c]$\bar{c} = .6$; $b = .95$; $d = .4$; $\delta = .1$.

current values of $\bar{c}$ the constrained firm is at the constraint about one-third of the time.

The last simulation changes b and δ to more common real business cycle values. The first parameters were chosen to generate roughly the same levels of volatility and consumption and returns as in the data. These are chosen as being a little closer to those used in other simulations. (King, Plosser, and Rebelo 1988 and Cecchetti, Lam, and Mark 1988). Here we run $b = 0.95$, $d = 0.4, \delta = 0.1, \gamma = 0$. For these values we needed to increase $\bar{c}$ to a larger

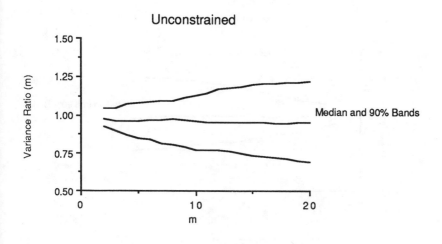

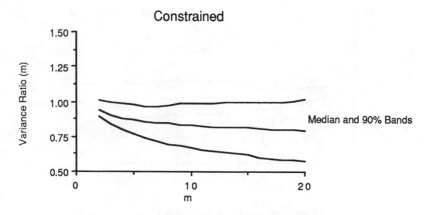

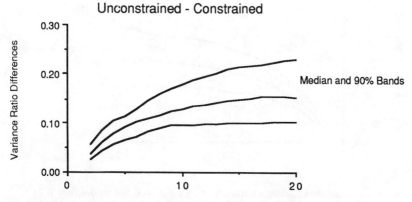

Fig. 9.5   Simulated variance ratios: $\gamma = -0.5, b = 0.9, d = 0.4, \delta = 0.2,$
$\bar{c} = 0.4$

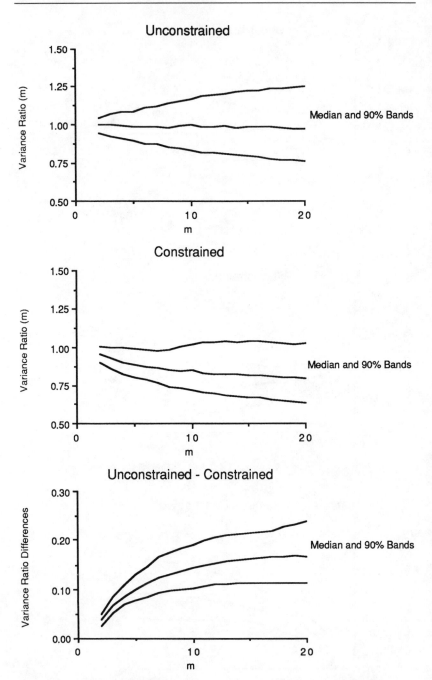

Fig. 9.6   **Simulated variance ratios:** $\gamma = -1.5, b = 0.9, d = 0.4, \delta = 0.2,$ $\bar{c} = 0.4$

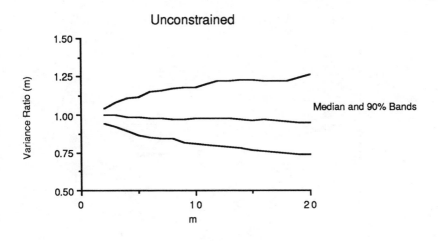

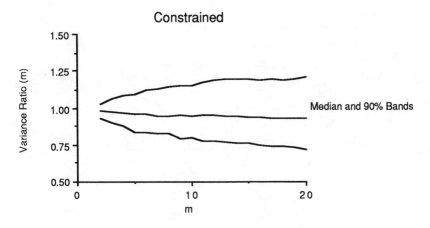

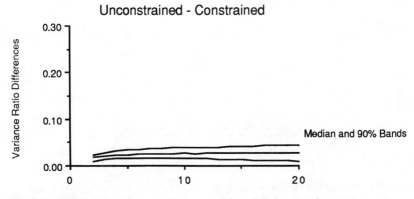

Fig. 9.7   **Simulated variance ratios: $\gamma = 0, b = 0.9, d = 0.4, \delta = 0.2, \bar{c} = 0$**

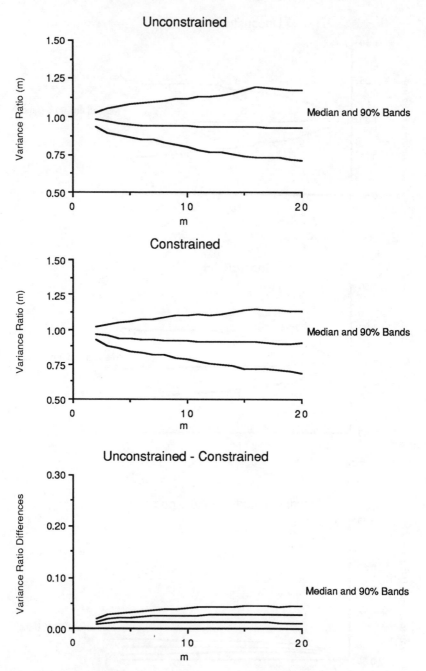

Fig. 9.8   Simulated variance ratios: $\gamma = -0.5, b = 0.9, d = 0.4, \delta = 0.2, \bar{c} = 0$

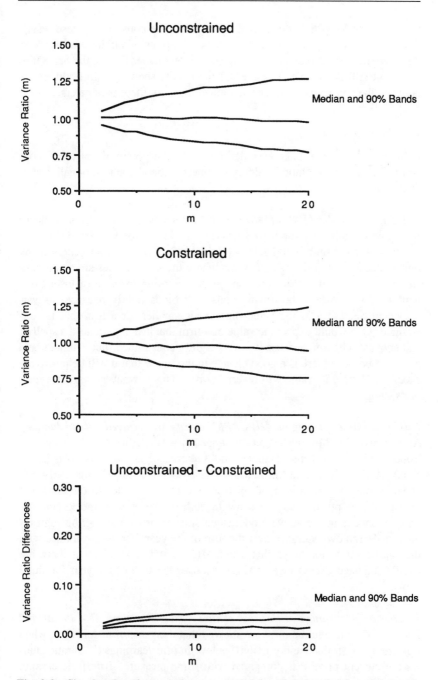

Fig. 9.9   Simulated variance ratios: $\gamma = -1.5, b = 0.9, d = 0.4, \delta = 0.2, \bar{c} = 0$

level, 0.6, to keep the constrained firm against the constraint. These results repeat those of the first three experiments. The plots of variance ratios are in figure 9.10. The differences here appear a little smaller than in the first set of runs, but still detectable. In table 9.2 the results show very little difference between the constrained and unconstrained firms for these parameters.

9.5 Speculations

In this section we make speculations about the possibility of credit constrained asset pricing models along the lines of the above to rationalize stylized facts.

1. De Bondt/Thaler (1985),(1987),(1989) loser/winner effect. Look at firm i whose production function is $a_i(t)r(t)x_i(t - 1)^d$ in Section 9.3 above. Imagine conducting De Bondt and Thaler's (1985,1987) study on data generated by our model for $i = 1,2, \ldots, F$ firms where the smaller ones are credit constrained because of scale economies in underwriting loans. Past loser firms would be ones whose borrowing constraint binds tightly because, as was shown in Section 9.3, the value function is smaller for a firm that is constrained. One would expect the value of a firm that had experienced a spell of bad shocks to be low because it is very tightly constrained, but it should be a good bet because there is a good chance in the future that it will be positively shocked. Hence, its value will revert upward. This is what our variance ratio plots suggest.

2. (Capital asset-pricing model) CAPM returns are received only in January. And excess CAPM-adjusted returns appear for small firms in January (De-Bondt and Thaler 1989, Haugen and Lakonishok 1988, Lakonishok and Smidt 1987). Barsky and Miron (1989) have documented a strong yearly seasonal in output with a sharp drop from the fourth quarter to the next first quarter. If we put a yearly seasonal in both the systematic shocks and the specific shocks in the above model, then smaller firms may exhibit high returns and high own variance over the turn of the year. Yet the covariance with the market may not move that much. Hence it is possible that there are CAPM-adjusted excess measured returns over the turn of the year for small firms.

3. Low price/earnings ratio firms exhibit "excess" returns (De Bondt and Thaler 1989). In Section three we showed that the value of firm i is low when it is credit constrained and y(i,t)/y(t) is low. In price/earnings (P/E) ratio studies the current price P is compared with some measure of intrinsic earning power. Since that measure is usually some kind of backward or estimated forward average, therefore, the measure of P/E will proxy current $y(i)/y$ in our model. We have shown by simulation that low enough current $y(i)/y$ predicts

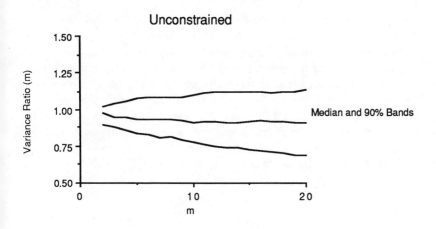

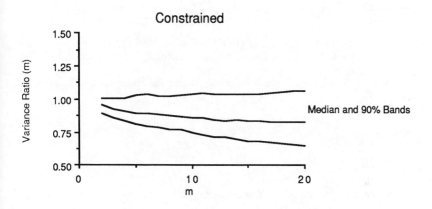

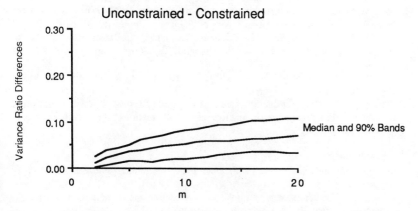

Fig. 9.10   Simulated variance ratios: $\gamma = 0, b = 0.95, d = 0.4, \delta = 0.1, \bar{c} = 0.6$

high returns next period. Hence it seems plausible that P/E ratio studies conducted on simulated data from a many firms version of our model may show "excess" returns to low P/E firms.

This paper set out to explain some stylized facts about small firms using a production-based asset-pricing model. We have been successful in some areas and unsuccessful in others. Simple credit-constraint restrictions, when the constraints are binding, much of the time can account for mean reversion types of effects in return series. There were several other issues that we had hoped to explain, but have been unable to do so with this model. Differences in unconditional moments do not show up in this model with these simple discrete shocks. Also, the lead-lag patterns discovered by Lo and MacKinlay (1988) were not seen here.

Notes

1. See Kim, Nelson, and Startz (1988) and Richardson (1988) for some of this evidence. Bruce Lehmann has chosen the term "factoids" for these stylized facts of questionable significance.
2. Variance ratios are calculated following Poterba and Summers (1987) and Cochrane (1988).

References

Barsky, R., and J. Miron. 1989. The seasonal cycle and the business cycle. *Journal of Political Economy* 97(3):503–34.
Bossaerts, P., and R. Green. 1988. A general equilibrium model of changing risk premia: Theory and tests. Typescript. Carnegie Mellon University.
Brock, W. A. 1982. Asset prices in a production economy. In *The economics of information and uncertainty,* ed. John J. McCall. Chicago: University of Chicago Press.
Brock, W. A., W. D. Dechert, J. A. Scheinkman, and B. LeBaron. 1988. A test for independence based on the correlation integral. Typescript. University of Wisconsin—Madison.
Cecchetti, S., P. Lam, and N. Mark. 1988. Mean reversion in equilibrium asset prices. Typescript. Ohio State University.
Cochrane, J. H. 1987. Production based asset pricing: Using producer's first order conditions to link asset prices to macroeconomic fluctuations. Typescript. University of Chicago.
———. 1988. How big is the random walk in GNP? *Journal of Political Economy* 96(5):893–920.
De Bondt, W., and R. Thaler. 1985. Does the stock market overreact? *Journal of Finance* 15(3):793–805.
———. 1987. Further evidence on investor overreaction and stock market seasonality. Typescript. University of Wisconsin—Madison.

————. 1989. Anomalies: A mean-reverting walk down Wall Street. *Journal of Economic Perspectives* 3(1):189–202.

Fama, E., and K. French. 1988. Permanent and temporary components of stock prices. *Journal of Political Economy* 96(2):246–73.

Fazzari, S., R. Hubbard, and B. Petersen. 1988a. Financing constraints and corporate investment. *Brookings Papers on Economic Activity,* no. 1, 141.

————. 1988b. Finance and investment reconsidered. Typescript. Northwestern University, Department of Economics.

Haugen, R., and J. Lakonishok. 1988. The incredible January effect. Homewood, Ill.: Dow Jones-Irwin.

Hsieh, D., and B. LeBaron. 1988. The small sample properties of BDS statistics. Typescript. University of Chicago, Graduate School of Business.

Kandel, S., and R. Stambaugh. 1988. A model of expected returns and volatilities for various forecast horizons. University of Chicago, Graduate School of Business.

Kim, M. J., C. R. Nelson, and R. Startz. 1988. Mean reversion in stock prices? A reappraisal of the empirical evidence. NBER Working Paper no. 2795.

King, R. G., C. I. Plosser, and S. T. Rebelo. 1988. Production, growth, and business cycles: 1. The basic neoclassical model. *Journal of Monetary Economics* 21:195–232.

Lakonishok, J., and S. Smidt. 1987. Are seasonal anomalies real? A ninety year perspective. Typescript. University of Illinois at Urbana-Champaign.

Lehmann, B. 1988. Fads, Martingales, and market efficiency. Stanford University, Hoover Institution.

Lo, A., and C. MacKinlay. 1988a. Stock market prices do not follow random walks: Evidence from a simple specification test. *Review of Financial Studies* 1:41–66.

————. 1988b. When are contrarian profits due to stock market overreaction? Typescript. University of Pennsylvania.

Lucas, R. E. 1978. Asset prices in an exchange economy. *Econometrica* 46:1429–45.

Mehra, R., and E. Prescott. 1985. The equity premium: A puzzle. *Journal of Monetary Economics* 15:145–61.

Poterba, J., and L. Summers. 1987. Mean reversion in stock prices: Evidence and implications. Typescript. MIT and Harvard University.

Richardson, M. 1988. Temporary components of stock prices: A skeptic's view. Typescript. Stanford University, Graduate School of Business.

10 Understanding Stock Price Behavior around the Time of Equity Issues

Robert A. Korajczyk, Deborah Lucas, and Robert L. McDonald

10.1 Introduction

The link between the real and financial decisions of firms has been studied for many years, yet it remains poorly understood. Neoclassical investment theories such as Tobin's q posit a direct, simple link between the market's valuation of the firm and investment decisions: firms invest when the market value of an investment exceeds the cost of the investment. For a variety of reasons—agency conflicts between management and security holders, conflicts among security holders, and asymmetric information between management and security holders—the relation between real and financial decisions may be quite complex.

In this paper we study seasoned equity issues as one piece of the corporate financing and investment puzzle. We expect equity issues to be particularly revealing about the role of asymmetric information in financing decisions. First, to the extent that there is asymmetric information between management and outside security holders, the asymmetry should be of greatest concern to potential buyers of common stock since stock is the residual claim on the firm. Second, it is well documented that stocks exhibit large abnormal returns during the period surrounding an equity issue. This suggests that equity issues do in fact reveal valuable information to the market. It is therefore natural to

Robert A. Korajczyk is visiting associate professor of finance, Graduate School of Business, University of Chicago and associate professor of finance, Kellogg Graduate School of Management, Northwestern University. Deborah Lucas is assistant professor of finance, Kellogg Graduate School of Management, Northwestern University. Robert L. McDonald is visiting associate professor of finance, Graduate School of Business, University of Chicago, associate professor of finance, Kellogg Graduate School of Management, Northwestern University, and Research Associate, NBER.

The authors wish to thank Glenn Hubbard, Jeremy Stein, and participants in the NBER conference, "Information, Capital Markets, and Investment."

consider whether the price behavior of an equity-issuing firm sheds light on the importance of asymmetric information in the investment process.

Section 10.2 summarizes the observed aggregate price behavior around equity issues and reviews alternative theories explaining these phenomena. In Section 10.3 we examine the empirical evidence in more detail with the goal of linking the evidence to the predictions of the various theories. We conclude that informational theories in which managers have superior information about the quality of the firm are capable of providing a parsimonious explanation for much of the observed price and timing behavior, although other factors also appear to be relevant.

Most tax- or information-based theories suggest that debt issues are less costly than equity issues. Consequently, one might expect the debt-equity ratio to rise before an equity issue, since firms with sufficient "debt capacity" will tend to finance with debt. In Section 10.4 we track the history of the debt-equity and debt-asset ratios prior to equity issues. It is surprising to find that the debt-equity ratio, however measured, falls or remains constant in the two years prior to an equity issue. Section 10.4 also examines the effect of issue size on price behavior and the relation between the abnormal price rise prior to issue and the price drop at issue. As in previous studies, we find that a larger issue results in a somewhat larger price drop, but the explanatory power is low. We find that the correlation between the rise prior to the issue and the drop at the announcement period depends on the time period considered, reconciling the contradictory results of earlier studies.

In Section 10.5 we discuss some of the welfare implications of the asymmetric information models that are supported by the data. Although equity issues induce a substantial price drop, we argue that these price effects may not provide a reliable guide to the welfare cost of asymmetric information. The social cost may be either larger or smaller than it would appear from examining stock price data alone. Section 10.6 concludes the paper.

10.2   The Stock Price Behavior around Equity Issues

Before discussing the theoretical reasons for the unusual behavior of stock prices around the time of equity issues, we present a brief overview of our evidence on stock price behavior. Figure 10.1 displays the cumulative excess return (the stock's return over and above the return on an equal-weighted index) in the 500 days preceding and 100 days following the issue announcement for primary issues and mixed primary and secondary issues. Figure 10.2 displays the same information for pure secondary issues (i.e., equity issues that add no capital to the firm.) We divide the sample between New York Stock Exchange/American Exchange (NYSE/AMEX) firms and over-the-counter (OTC) firms since previous authors only examine NYSE/AMEX data. Figure 10.3 shows the return on the market, in excess of the return on short-term Treasury bills, in the 500 days preceding and 100 days following the equity issues. The data and measurements are discussed in detail in the next section. Several facts are readily apparent:

1. In the 500 days prior to the issue announcement, there is a cumulative excess return for the NYSE/AMEX firms of 43.8% for primary and combined primary and secondary issues and 29.3% for pure secondary issues. For OTC firms, the corresponding numbers are 68.8% and 44.5%.

2. On the two days on and preceding the equity issue announcement, there is a total abnormal price drop of 3.0% for NYSE/AMEX and 2.9% for OTC primary and combined issues. For pure secondary issues, the drop is 2.8% for NYSE/AMEX firms and 1.7% for OTC firms.

3. The pattern of price behavior is generally similar for pure secondary and other issues, though primary issue announcements are preceded by a larger price run-up. The OTC and NYSE/AMEX firms also have qualitatively similar price patterns, with a larger rise for OTC firms.

4. Equity issues follow rises in the market as a whole (fig. 10.3).

These results are consistent with the findings of Asquith and Mullins (1986) and Masulis and Korwar (1986).[1] Barclay and Litzenberger (1988) provide complementary evidence on the intra-day behavior of stock prices for firms announcing equity issues.

Theoretical explanations for facts 1–4 above can be loosely divided between those based on asymmetric information, and those based on other factors. The following descriptions are organized along these lines.

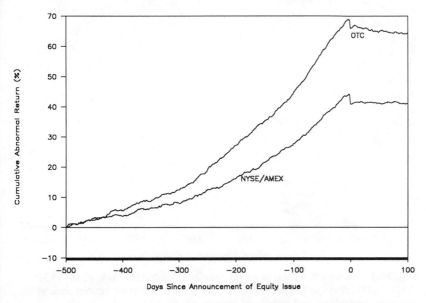

Fig. 10.1   Cumulative abnormal returns in the period surrounding an equity issue announcement for primary and combined primary/secondary issues

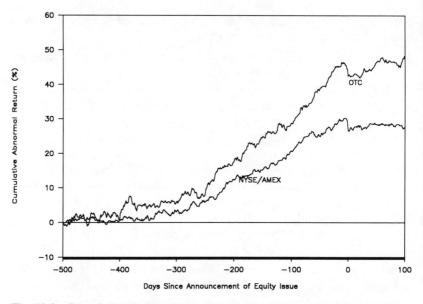

Fig. 10.2   Cumulative abnormal returns in the period surrounding an equity issue announcement for secondary issues

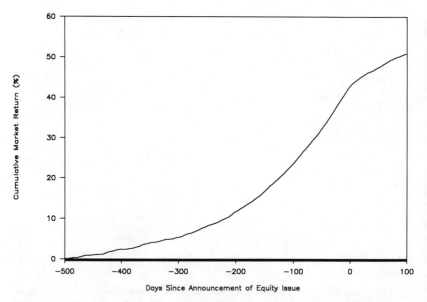

Fig. 10.3   Cumulative returns on an equally weighted portfolio of all NYSE/AMEX/OTC firms in the period surrounding an equity issue announcement for primary, secondary, and combined issues

10.2.1 Information-based Theories of Stock Price Behavior

Most information-based theories presume that managers (or, more generally, existing shareholders) know more about the value of the firm than do potential new investors. This asymmetric information creates an adverse selection problem (the "lemons" problem of Akerlof 1970), which can explain the existence of a price drop when an equity issue is announced. Myers and Majluf (1984) apply this idea to security issues and create a framework that is used in much of the subsequent literature. They assume that managers know more about the firm's true value than do outside investors and also that managers act in the interests of existing shareholders. Rational investors correctly value firms on average, but individual firms can be mispriced, conditional on managers' private information. Since managers act in the interests of existing shareholders, there is an incentive to sell new equity when it is overvalued. Thus, selling equity on average conveys negative information about the firm, and the stock price drops at the equity issue announcement.

Lucas and McDonald (1990) demonstrate that a similar story can simultaneously explain the extended price rise preceding the equity issue, the drop at issue, and the clustering of issues following a market rise. The key assumptions behind their model are (a) managers know more about the value of the firm than do outside investors, (b) delaying an equity issue is costly (it lowers the net present value of projects), and (c) the market assesses firm values correctly on average, but individual firms may be temporarily mispriced. As the market receives new information over time, the valuation of undervalued firms tends to increase while the valuation of overvalued firms tends to decrease.

Under these assumptions, consider two firms that for some reason plan to issue equity. Suppose the two firms are identical except that one is overvalued and one is undervalued. The undervalued firm expects the market to revise upward its estimate of the firm's value, hence there is an incentive to postpone the equity issue until the stock price is higher. The overvalued firm, on the other hand, expects that the market will learn its true value over time, and it bears the cost of waiting. This firm, therefore, issues equity as soon as the opportunity arises.

This issue policy for the two types of firms implies that equity issues will be preceded by positive abnormal returns on average. Undervalued firms wait for their price to rise before issuing so that their average price path prior to issue will be upward sloping. Overvalued firms, on the other hand, do not wait. If the arrival of profitable opportunities for issuing equity is uncorrelated with a firm's price history, then their price path prior to issue will, on average, be flat. Thus the average price path prior to issue for all firms that issue equity will be upward sloping. As in Myers and Majluf (1984), when firms do issue they tend to be overvalued, so the price drops at issue announcement.

Asquith and Mullins (1986) offer an informal explanation for the connection between the price rise preceding issue and the drop at issue. They find empirically that the smaller the price drop is at issue, the greater the excess return preceding the issue. They suggest that if there is a positive correlation between price increases and a reduction in asymmetric information, firms experiencing price increases will have a smaller price drop at issue and therefore are more likely to issue equity. A problem with this explanation is that Masulis and Korwar (1986) find the opposite result in their data: the greater the price rise preceding the issue the greater the price drop. We show in Section 10.4 below that the sign of the relationship between the price run-up and the price drop is not monotonic; it depends upon the length of time over which the price run-up is measured.

There are other information-based models of financing behavior. For example, Leland and Pyle (1977) and Ross (1977) suggest that a reduction in management's stake in the firm conveys negative information, since management should be willing to bear more of the risk of a more profitable firm. This is distinguished from the adverse selection explanation in that the owner-manager bears personal costs from selecting a suboptimal debt ratio. A test of this explanation presumably requires information about the manager's incentives. Miller and Rock (1985) also present a model in which signalling leads to suboptimal investment. All these theories share with Myers and Majluf (1984) the feature that equity issues convey bad news about the firm. We now turn to several competing and complementary explanations for the price behavior around equity issues.

10.2.2 Other Explanations for the Price Rise Prior to Issue

The price rise prior to the announcement of an equity issue has received less attention in the literature than the subsequent price drop, but there are several other possible explanations.

The Market Learns about a Positive Net Present Value (NPV) Project

One appealing alternative to the asymmetric information story for the price rise rests on the observation that if the market can observe the arrival of valuable investment projects, firms receiving these projects will experience a price rise. Certainly one reason to issue equity is to finance valuable new projects. Thus, observed prices will tend to rise prior to equity issues if the purpose of the issues is to finance observable new projects. This hypothesis is empirically distinguishable from the asymmetric information hypothesis, as is discussed in Section 10.3 below.

Naive Trading Rule

Suppose that managers and shareholders believe that the stock price is likely to fall after it has had a sustained positive abnormal return. Then issues will follow price rises, and the trading rule may do no harm, apart from possibly wasting the resources involved in a sale of equity.

10.2.3   Other Explanations of the Price Drop

Price Pressure

The issuance of new shares represents an increase in the supply of shares to the market. Therefore, the price will decline if the demand for an individual stock is not perfectly elastic, and the decline should be greater for a larger issue. Note that although the ultimate impact of price pressure occurs on the issue date, the price declines at the announcement in anticipation of the lower price at issue.

Issue Costs

This explanation holds that equity issues are costly to the firm (due to administrative expenses and underwriting fees) and that the price drops because the firm bears this cost.

10.2.4   Equity Issues in the Aggregate

So far we have discussed firm-level characteristics of equity issues. There are also two interesting characteristics of equity issues on a more aggregate level. First, as table 10.1 shows, there is substantial variation over time in the number of equity issues. In 1980, for example, there were approximately three times as many equity issues as in 1979 and almost twice as many in 1983 as in 1980.[2] Second, figure 10.3 shows that equity issues on average follow increases in the market.

There are at least two information-based explanations for variation over time in the quantity of equity issues. First, it is possible that the adverse selection problem is less important at some times than at others. Choe, Masulis, and Nanda (1989) argue that the adverse selection problem varies over the business cycle, and that this can explain "bunching" of equity issues.[3]

Second, it is possible for there to be bunching even if the adverse selection problem is constant over time. Lucas and McDonald (1990) show that if managers wait for good news to be revealed before issuing equity, and if good news is correlated across firms, then equity issues will be correlated with market price rises.

Both theories are consistent with the market price pattern illustrated in figure 10.3. Figure 10.3 was constructed by tracking the returns, in excess of the daily equivalent of the one-month Treasury-bill rate, on an equally weighted market portfolio of NYSE/AMEX/OTC firms around the time of each equity issue in our sample. Figure 10.3 is a plot of the cross-sectional average of the market excess returns around each issue.

10.3   Empirical Implications and Tests

10.3.1   Data Overview

Our sample comprises 1,480 seasoned equity issues by industrial firms over the period 1974–83. The sample includes issues that were solely primary issues (underwritten issues by the firm), solely secondary issues (underwritten sales by large stockholders), and combinations of these. Of the 1,480 equity issues, 789 are for NYSE/AMEX firms and 691 are for OTC firms. Table 10.1 provides information on the number of issues by type and by year. The data were obtained from Drexel Burnham Lambert's *Public Offerings of Corporate Securities* (various years). This source includes only issues in excess of $3 million.

Historical data on daily equity returns and prices were obtained from the Center for Research in Security Prices (CRSP) NYSE/AMEX and NASDAQ data files. Data on accounting-based variables and announcement dates of quarterly earnings were obtained from the quarterly Compustat (industrial and full coverage) files. A smaller sample remains after matching and screening for missing observations. Observations are omitted for any of the following reasons: inability to match company name with CRSP or Compustat, missing data, or apparent data errors.[4]

The balance sheet variables are constructed from Compustat data. Debt was measured net of liquid short-term assets.[5] Data definitions are as follows (names of Compustat variables are italicized):

Cash   =   *total current assets – total inventories;*
Debt   =   *total long-term debt + total current liabilities*
                             + preferred stock (Liquidating Value) – cash;
Equity (market value)   =   *end-of-quarter closing price × common shares*
                             outstanding;
Assets (market value)   =   equity (market value) + debt;

Table 10.1   Number of Issues by Type and by Year

Year	Primary	Secondary	Combined
1974	6	8	9
1975	27	22	20
1976	40	23	31
1977	12	13	22
1978	56	12	27
1979	48	9	23
1980	144	21	73
1981	135	13	62
1982	98	20	55
1983	253	54	144
Total	819	195	466

Table 10.2   **Mean Abnormal Returns around Announcements of Equity Issues**

Period	Mean Abnormal Return	t-statistic	Observations
All issues			
− 500 to − 251	13.20	11.21	939
− 250 to − 101	19.59	21.32	1,097
− 100 to − 2	18.84	25.54	1,175
− 1 to 0	− 2.89	− 20.70	1,197
1 to 100	− .00	− .20	1,223
Primary and combined issues:			
− 500 to − 251	14.35	11.15	813
− 250 to − 101	19.98	20.23	956
− 100 to − 2	20.02	25.06	1,027
− 1 to 0	− 2.94	− 19.39	1,048
1 to 100	− .01	− .67	1,070
Secondary issues:			
− 500 to − 251	5.78	2.10	126
− 250 to − 101	16.91	6.77	141
− 100 to − 2	10.63	6.07	148
− 1 to 0	− 2.49	− 7.33	149
1 to 100	.02	1.37	153

Assets (book value)   =   *total assets* − cash;

Equity (book value)   =   *total assets* − debt − cash.

We wish to study the abnormal price behavior of firms engaging in issues of seasoned equity. We define abnormal returns on asset i on day t, A_{it}, as the difference between the rate of return on asset i on day t, R_{it}, and the return on a control portfolio on that day, R_{ct}, $A_{it} = R_{it} − R_{ct}$. The control portfolio is defined as the equal-weighted portfolio of all NYSE/AMEX/OTC stocks. Abnormal returns computed in this manner are commonly referred to as "market adjusted returns" (see Brown and Warner 1985). We use this measure of abnormal returns to investigate the price behavior around announcement of the equity issue and announcement of accounting measures of earnings.

The cumulative abnormal returns around the announcement and issue dates are defined by

$$CAR_t = \sum_{\tau = \tau_0}^{t} \bar{A}_\tau, \quad t = \tau_0, \tau_0 + 1, \ldots, T,$$

where $\bar{A}_\tau$ is the cross-sectional average one-day abnormal return over the firms.

Table 10.2 documents the statistical significance of both the price rise and price drop in this sample. Note that the abnormal returns over the 100 days after the issue date are insignificantly different than zero. The t-statistics provided in table 10.2 are calculated for each period using a cross-sectional estimate of the variance of abnormal returns. Simulation results in Collins and

Dent (1984) indicate that this method of calculating t-statistics leads to appropriate inferences in experimental designs similar to ours.

Abnormal return calculations over long periods tend to be sensitive to the method used to determine the normal return. To ascertain how robust the results are to different specifications, we also calculated abnormal returns using a variety of alternative methods. These include (a) market-adjusted returns relative to the value-weighted NYSE/AMEX/OTC portfolio; (b) market-adjusted returns comparing NYSE/AMEX and OTC firms to their respective equal-weighted and value-weighted indices; (c) capital asset-pricing model adjusted returns where abnormal returns are defined as

$$A_{it} = \{R_{it} - [R_{Ft} + \beta_{im}(R_{mt} - R_{Ft})]\},$$

where R_{mt} is the return on a "market" portfolio as defined in the various permutations described above, $\beta_{im} = \text{cov}(R_i, R_m)/\text{var}(R_m)$, and $R_{Ft} =$ return on a riskless asset. For the risk-free rate we use the one-month Treasury-bill return from Ibbotson Associates (1985) and assume that the daily return is constant over the month. Assets' sensitivity to market movements, beta, are measured using the techniques of Scholes and Williams (1977) over periods prior to the announcement of the issue, after the announcement, and combined prior/post announcement periods. The final alternative method is (d), abnormal returns relative to a beta-sorted comparison portfolio as calculated in the CRSP excess-returns file (NYSE/AMEX firms only). Assets' betas are estimated over a year and allocated to one of 10 portfolios on the basis of the estimates of beta. Over the following year the abnormal return for asset i is its return less the return on the comparison portfolio, which is an equal-weighted average of the returns on the component securities.

We find that the basic pattern of abnormal returns around the announcement of equity issues is similar across all methods of calculating abnormal returns, although the magnitudes of abnormal returns cumulated over long periods differ substantially across methods. For instance, the abnormal price rise over the 500 days preceding the announcement for the NYSE/AMEX firms ranged between 20% and 65%. We calculate cross-sectional correlations across methods of measuring cumulative abnormal returns over 50-day windows over the period from 500 trading days before the announcement to 100 days after. The correlations are generally high (.85–.99) with the exception of abnormal returns from the CRSP excess-returns file. Thus, inferences drawn from cross-sectional relations (aside from intercepts) should be robust to the method of calculating abnormal returns.

10.3.2   Evidence on the Price Rise

We have discussed several plausible reasons for the price rise prior to an equity issue. One is that the market, on average, receives good news about the value of the firm's current assets since some issues are postponed in anticipation of good news (the information theory). Another is that the market learns of the arrival of a valuable new project that the firm has yet to undertake, and the expected value of the new project is immediately impounded into the firm's price (the good-project theory). Our first task empirically is to distinguish between these two explanations.

One test is to compare the price path prior to seasoned equity issues with the price path prior to large block sales by existing equity holders (secondary offerings). With a secondary offering, no new capital is added to the firm. Hence the purpose of the sale cannot be to finance a new project. Observing a significant price rise before secondary offerings would therefore support the information hypothesis over the good-project theory.

Figures 10.1 and 10.2 and table 10.2 compare the price behavior surrounding primary and secondary issues. The behavior in both cases appears to be similar both qualitatively and quantitatively, supporting the information theory. There is an apparent difference: the rise before primary issues is steeper than the rise before pure secondary issues. Of course, the price rise preceding pure secondary issues could occur for reasons unrelated to the price rise for primary issues. For instance, uninformed large shareholders may wish to diversify after a large price run-up to rebalance their portfolios. Nevertheless, the similarity between the patterns in figures 10.1 and 10.2 is striking.

A related test involves examining stock price behavior around the time of low-risk debt issues. Since some projects are presumably debt financed, the project-arrival theory also predicts a price rise preceding debt issues. On the other hand, if the price rise and subsequent drop upon announcement of the equity issue are due to adverse selection, this price pattern should not occur for firms issuing riskless debt. Mikkelson and Partch (1986) present evidence that is consistent with the information theory and inconsistent with the project arrival theory. For a sample of 135 NYSE/AMEX firms issuing straight debt between 1972 and 1982, they find a statistically significant abnormal *negative* return of -4.11% in the 60 days preceding the announcement of an issue and a change of only $-.39\%$ on the announcement date.

Since accounting earnings before the equity issue can only reflect returns from existing assets, observing positive earnings surprises in the months preceding the equity issue would support the information theory over the good-project theory. To implement this idea, we sum the excess returns on earnings announcement dates in the eight quarters preceding the announcement of an equity issue and compare this with the excess return over the 500 days preceding the announcement of an issue. The earnings announcement event is defined as the day preceding and the day of an earnings announcement in the *Wall Street Journal*. For NYSE/AMEX firms, the average daily abnormal return over the earnings announcements is 0.26%, while for OTC firms the average daily abnormal return over the earnings announcements is 0.28%. By comparison, the average daily abnormal returns over the entire period, from day -500 to day -2, were 0.08% for NYSE/AMEX firms and 0.13% for OTC firms. Thus, earnings announcements do appear to have an effect on excess returns for these firms.[6]

We do find some evidence in support of the good-project theory. On average, firms issuing equity experience a rise in Tobin's q prior to the issue and then a fall following the issue (see figure 10.4). Here Tobin's q is measured as the ratio of market value of assets to book value of assets. This pattern is consistent with the view that firms issue equity to finance a growth opportunity, and that once the project is undertaken the ratio of growth opportunities to assets in place falls.

The third potential explanation for the price rise was the "naive trading rule" under which managers issue after observing a rise in share price. If this is the case, we would expect to see few firms with a price decline prior to issue. Figure 10.5 illustrates the cross-sectional distribution of excess returns over the 500 days preceding an equity issue announcement for primary, secondary, and combined issues. Although rises predominate, 18% of firms experience a price drop relative to the market in the period preceding the issue announcement.[7] Although this distribution is inconsistent with the naive trading rule, it corresponds to the predicted distribution in Lucas and McDonald (1990).

10.4   Other Empirical Results

10.4.1   Does a Debt Capacity Constraint Induce Equity Issues?

Information-based models of capital structure generally imply that firms are better off issuing lower risk securities; debt dominates equity (see, e.g.,

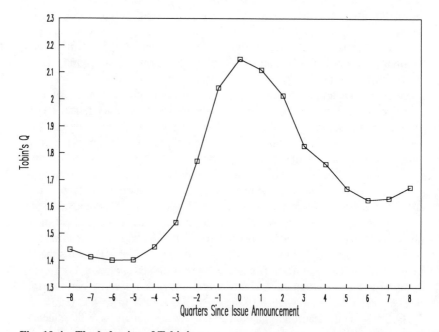

Fig. 10.4   The behavior of Tobin's q

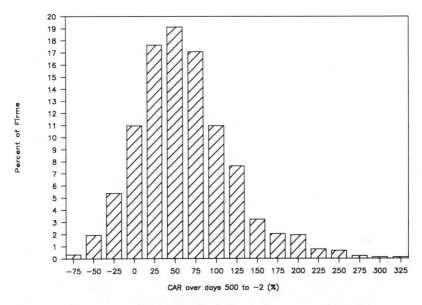

Fig. 10.5   The cross-sectional distribution of cumulative abnormal returns prior to an equity issue announcement.
Note: A histogram bar represents the percentage of firms with a CAR between the previous and current values on the horizontal axis.

Myers and Majluf 1984; and Narayanan 1988). However, situations may arise in which issuing more debt is no longer feasible or desirable. For example, a firm may have reached a point at which the costs of debt financing outweigh the benefits, and the firm issues equity to increase "debt capacity." We examine the capital structure of firms around the time of equity issues to see whether firms issuing equity appear to be short on debt capacity.

In figures 10.6 and 10.7 we plot the ratio of the book value of debt to market and book value of assets, respectively, over the four-year period surrounding the announcement of the issue. Debt ratios based on market values decline dramatically before the issue of equity, while ratios based on book value decline slightly. This seems to be inconsistent with a story in which the firm is issuing equity because its debt levels have become too high, since issues of debt in the period before the equity issue would tend to lead to increases in the book debt to asset ratios. Also, the cash to book asset ratio increases slightly before the equity issue, increases dramatically at issuance, and falls after the issue (see fig. 10.8). The fact that cash ratios fall while debt ratios rise after the issue is not consistent with a scenario in which the firm uses cash from the equity issue to retire debt. What factors cause these firms to choose equity over debt remains an interesting and open question.

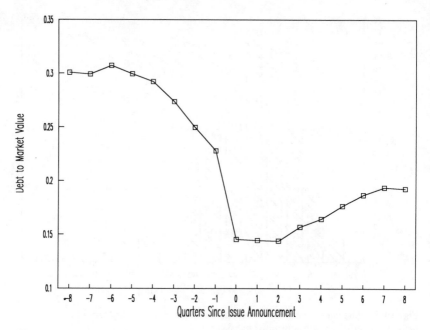

Fig. 10.6   The behavior of the ratio of debt to market value of assets

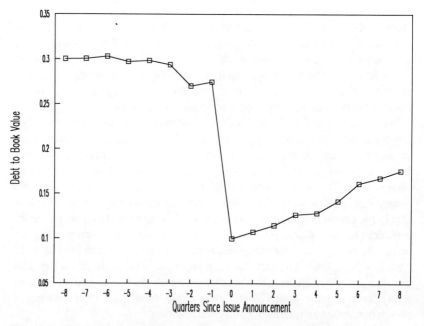

Fig. 10.7   The behavior of the ratio of debt to book value of assets

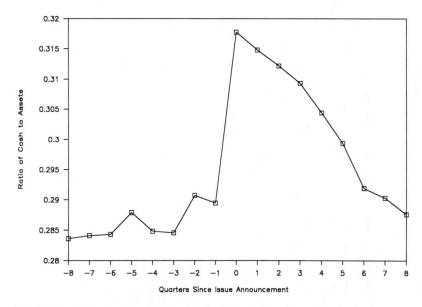

Fig. 10.8   The behavior of the ratio of cash to book value of assets

10.4.2   Explaining the Magnitude of the Price Drop

Table 10.3 shows the relation between the announcement day price drop, the size of primary and secondary issues (expressed as the number of new shares issued divided by the preissue number of shares outstanding), abnormal price movements prior to the announcement, and a measure of the direct cost of the issue (the underwriters' spread).

There is a negative relation between the announcement period abnormal return and the abnormal price change from day -100 to day -2. This negative relation is statistically significant at the 5% level in one case and is occasionally statistically significant at the 10% significance level. There is no relation between the announcement period return and the abnormal return over the period from day -250 to day -101. On the other hand, there is a positive (significant at the 10% level but not at the 5% level) relation between the announcement period returns and the returns from day -500 to -251.

The earlier empirical literature explored the relation between the slope of the price rise preceding issue and the drop at issue. Asquith and Mullins (1986) find a positive relation between the announcement period returns and prior period returns while Masulis and Korwar (1986) find a negative relation. The former study uses a longer prior period (11 months) while the latter uses a shorter prior period (three months). There appears to be no compelling theoretical reason that the relation should go in either direction. The regressions reported in table 10.3 partially reconcile these opposite findings.

The effect of issue size on the price drop is traditionally used as a test of the

Table 10.3 Regression of Announcement Period Abnormal Return on Size of Primary and Secondary Issues, Abnormal Price Movements prior to Announcements, and Measures of the Cost of Underwriting

Intercept	$100 \times$ CAR $(-100, -2)$	$100 \times$ CAR $(-250, -101)$	$100 \times$ CAR $(-500, -251)$	Size of Issue		Underwriter Discount	Discount $\times$ Size	N	R^2
				Primary Size	Secondary Size				
−2.49 (−12.30)				−2.30 (−2.21)	−1.46 (−.86)			1,195	.00
−1.39 (−1.77)				−2.61 (−.58)	−.78 (−.40)	−22.53 (−1.34)	19.24 (.26)	1,179	.01
−2.64 (−16.91)	−1.37 (−2.18)							1,174	.01
−2.29 (−11.16)	−1.17 (−1.83)			−2.33 (−2.20)	−1.13 (−.64)			1,172	.01
−1.52 (−1.91)	−1.14 (−1.79)			−2.04 (−.44)	−.56 (−.29)	−15.60 (−.95)	5.09 (.07)	1,156	.01
−2.90 (−18.13)		−.08 (−.17)						1,096	.00
−2.48 (−11.84)		.11 (.21)		−2.76 (−2.50)	−1.45 (−.82)			1,094	.01
−1.36 (−1.64)		.21 (.41)		−2.01 (−.44)	−.76 (−.38)	−24.04 (−1.39)	5.25 (.07)	1,079	.01

							N	R²
−2.95 (−19.20)	−1.23 (−1.75)	.91 (1.90)					938	.01
−2.66 (−12.28)	−1.08 (−1.51)	.88 (1.85)	−1.52 (−1.31)	−2.39 (−1.84)			937	.01
−1.91 (−2.30)	−1.08 (−1.48)	.91 (1.89)	−.20 (−.04)	−1.79 (−1.25)	−16.60 (−.96)	−7.99 (−.09)	922	.01
−2.83 (−15.77)	.48 (.78)	.91 (1.89)					938	.01
−2.61 (−11.88)	.63 (1.04)	.86 (1.79)	−1.29 (−1.09)	−2.43 (−1.87)			937	.01
−1.88 (−2.27)	.68 (1.11)	.88 (1.81)	−.23 (−.05)	−1.86 (−1.31)	−16.07 (−.92)	−4.99 (−.06)	922	.02

Note: The first three data columns show regression of CAR(−1,0) on abnormal returns prior to announcement; under Size of Issue, Primary Size = number of primary shares issued divided by the number of shares outstanding prior to issue, while Secondary Size = secondary shares issued divided by number of shares outstanding prior to issue. Underwriter Discount = offer-price proceeds to the company divided by the offer price. Discount × Size = the underwriter's discount multiplied by the size of the primary issue. Heteroscedastic robust t-statistics are in parentheses (see White 1980).

price pressure hypothesis. As in previous studies, the evidence seems to be mixed.[8] In table 10.3, the relation between the announcement period price change and the size of the primary and secondary components of the issue is consistently negative. The relation is occasionally significant (at the 5% level) for primary issues. Also, note that a negative relation between the announcement period price change and the size of the issue, while being consistent with a price-pressure story, is not necessarily inconsistent with an information-based explanation of the price behavior. Presumably the more overvalued the equity, the larger the incentive to issue more equity. Thus, the size of the issue may partially reveal the managers' private information.

In order to test the hypothesis that anticipated issue costs cause the price drop upon announcement, we include the underwriters' discount and the product of the discount and the size of the primary issue as explanatory variables.[9] While the underwriters' fees are not the only cost of the issue, they are generally the major component of the cost (see Smith 1977). Neither of the issue cost variables have significant explanatory power.

The issue cost variables' lack of explanatory power may be due to the fact that the actual costs are not known at the announcement date. However, if the issue cost hypothesis were true and investors had rational expectations of the costs, then we should find significantly negative coefficients. It should be noted that in all of the above cases the explanatory power of prior period abnormal returns, size of the issue, and issue costs are very low.

10.5   Welfare Implications

The preceding empirical results lend support to the hypothesis that asymmetric information has an important role in explaining stock price behavior around the time of seasoned equity issues. In this section we turn to the question of whether the magnitude of the price drop is likely to be informative about the extent of investment inefficiency. We argue that the magnitude of the price drop is not necessarily related to the extent of investment inefficiency.

Asymmetric information has implications for the real investment policies of firms in most of the information-based models we have discussed. Myers and Majluf (1984) show that asymmetric information can lead to underinvestment because some undervalued firms forgo valuable projects to avoid issuing equity at an unfavorable price. Miller and Rock (1985) develop a signaling model in which firms choose to pay dividends rather than to invest optimally. On the other hand, Narayanan (1988) shows that it is possible to obtain overinvestment in similar circumstances. For example, firms with no need for funds may attempt to benefit shareholders by mimicking high-quality firms and issuing equity. If equity issues are costly, this dissipates resources.

One way of interpreting the size of the price drop is to look at the "offering dilution." Asquith and Mullins (1986) compute the offering dilution as the ratio of the drop in valuation for the firm as a whole to the amount of equity issued. They show that the average offering dilution is 31% for primary and combined issues. Viewed in this way, one might conclude that firms take strong measures to avoid equity issues, and that the induced investment inefficiency will be large.

The offering dilution may be a gross overestimate of the issuing cost, however. Suppose that managers know the firm is overvalued and issue equity. As a result, the stock price drops and there is substantial offering dilution. Presumably the firm's true value would have become known eventually. The equity issue merely serves as a signal of the overvaluation and hastens the release of this information. Despite appearances, there is no social cost associated with the equity issue. The "offering dilution" statistic computed by Asquith and Mullins (1986) is, according to this explanation, irrelevant for measuring the cost of the equity issue.

On the other hand, price changes can underestimate the cost of asymmetric information. Suppose that some firms without valuable projects issue equity in order to pool with higher-valuation firms that do have projects. This has the dual effect of discouraging some high quality firms from issuing equity (as in Myers and Majluf 1984) and also wastes the resources used in issuing equity. Lucas and McDonald (1990) find that, in theory, the stock price could actually increase upon issue announcement even if some issuing firms dissipate resources. This can occur when the average project financed increases firm value by more than the announcement signals low asset quality.

Perhaps most important, estimating the welfare loss due to asymmetric information requires an understanding of the costs of substituting alternative sources of financing. A convincing estimate would require a more complete characterization of the costs of debt as well as equity.

10.6 Conclusions

This paper studies stock price behavior around the time of an equity issue and also examines the contemporaneous behavior of balance sheet variables. We have argued that information-based theories are consistent with much of the evidence about stock price behavior, in particular the rise preceding the issue, the fall at the announcement of the issue, and the tendency for issues to be clustered after market rises. Furthermore, the evidence weighs against several alternative theories. In the information theories the welfare costs of suboptimal investment cannot be estimated by solely studying asset price reactions to financing announcements. We conclude that a large price drop at issue announcement need not indicate large inefficiencies in the investment process.

There are still significant gaps in our understanding of equity issues. Most fundamentally, we still do not understand how firms choose the method of finance. Our evidence that the debt-to-value ratio does not rise preceding an equity issue deepens this puzzle.

Notes

1. For example, Asquith and Mullins (1986) obtain a two-day announcement return of -2.7% for all firms in their sample, with a cumulative excess return of about 36% for primary and combination issues and 20% for pure secondary issues in the 480 days preceding the issue.
2. Our source for equity issues may not have comprehensive coverage of equity issues, so table 10.1 must be viewed as only suggestive. Choe, Masulis, and Nanda (1989), however, also show substantial year-to-year variation in the quantity of equity issues.
3. Korajczyk, Lucas, and McDonald (1988) observe that periodic information releases by the firm will generate time-varying asymmetric information, and that firms will issue equity following such information releases. This does not explain aggregate low-frequency variations in the quantity of equity issues, however.
4. We lose 12 issues (10 firms) by not matching firms with the data from CRSP. An additional 202 issues are eliminated because we did not find announcement dates for the issues. The largest source of data loss was missing observations in the Compustat data.
5. Essentially identical results were obtained measuring debt gross of short-term assets.
6. The significance of the effect of earnings announcements must be qualified by the observation that a significant proportion of abnormal returns occur on earnings announcement dates for all firms (Chari, Jagannathan, and Ofer 1988). Healy and Palepu (1988) compare earning growth rates before and after equity issues and find no evidence of a significant change.
7. For 22% of NYSE/AMEX firms and 13% of OTC firms, a negative CAR preceded the equity issue announcement.
8. Scholes (1972) studied secondary issues and found the price drop at issue to be permanent and unrelated to the size of the issue. Asquith and Mullins (1986) find that the price drop at announcement appears to be weakly related to the size of the issue, while Masulis and Korwar (1986) and Barclay and Litzenberger (1988) find no relation for industrial firms.
9. We only include the product of the discount and size of the primary issue since the firm only bears the underwriting cost of the primary issue.

References

Akerlof, George A. 1970. The market for "lemons": Qualitative uncertainty and the market mechanism. *Quarterly Journal of Economics* 84(August):488–500.
Asquith, Paul, and David W. Mullins, Jr. 1986. Equity issues and offering dilution. *Journal of Financial Economics* 15 (January/February):61–89.
Barclay, Michael J., and Robert H. Litzenberger. 1988. Announcement effects of new equity issues and the use of intraday price data. *Journal of Financial Economics* 21(May):71–99.
Brown, Stephen J., and Jerold B. Warner. 1985. Using daily stock returns: The case of event studies. *Journal of Financial Economics* 14(March):3–31.
Chari, V. V., Ravi Jagannathan, and Aharon R. Ofer. 1988. Seasonalities in security returns: The case of earnings announcements. *Journal of Financial Economics* 21(May):101–21.

Choe, Hyuk, Ronald W. Masulis, and Vikram Nanda. 1989. On the timing of seasoned common stock issues: Theory and evidence. Working paper (June). Southern Methodist University.

Collins, D. W., and W. T. Dent. 1984. A comparison of alternative testing methodologies used in capital market research. *Journal of Accounting Research* 22(Spring):48–84.

Drexel Burnham Lambert. *Public offerings of corporate securities.* 1974–83.

Healey, Paul, and Krishna Palepu. 1988. Earnings and risk information from primary stock offerings. Working paper (September). MIT.

Ibbotson Associates. 1985. *Stocks, bonds, bills, and inflation.* Yearbook.

Korajczyk, Robert A., Deborah Lucas and Robert L. McDonald. 1988. The effect of information releases on the pricing and timing of equity issues: Theory and evidence. Working paper no. 2727. NBER.

Leland, H. E., and D. H. Pyle. 1977. Informational asymmetries, financial structure, and financial intermediation. *Journal of Finance* 32(May):371–87.

Lucas, Deborah, and Robert L. McDonald. 1990. Equity issues and stock price dynamics. *Journal of Finance,* forthcoming.

Masulis, Ronald W., and Ashok N. Korwar. 1986. Seasoned equity offerings: An empirical investigation. *Journal of Financial Economics* 15(January/February):91–118.

Mikkelson, Wayne H., and M. Megan Partch. 1986. Valuation effects of security offerings and the issuance process. *Journal of Financial Economics* 15(January/February):31–60.

Miller, Merton, and Kevin Rock. 1985. Dividend policy under asymmetric information. *Journal of Finance* 40(4):1031–1051.

Myers, Stewart C., and Nicholas S. Majluf. 1984. Corporate financing and investment decisions when firms have information that investors do not have. *Journal of Financial Economics* 13(June):187–221.

Narayanan, M. P. 1988. Debt versus equity under asymmetric information. *Journal of Financial and Quantitative Analysis* 23(March):39–51.

Ross, Stephen A. 1977. The determination of financial structure: The incentive-signalling approach. *Bell Journal of Economics* 8(Spring):23–40.

Scholes, Myron S. 1972. The market for securities: Substitution versus price pressure and the effects of information on share prices. *Journal of Business* 45(April):179–211.

Scholes, Myron S., and Joseph Williams. 1977. Estimating betas from nonsynchronous data. *Journal of Financial Economics* 5(December):309–27.

Smith, Clifford W., Jr. 1977. Alternative methods for raising capital: Rights versus underwritten offerings. *Journal of Financial Economics* 5(December):273–307.

White, Halbert. 1980. A Heteroskedasticity-consistent covariance matrix estimator and a direct test for heteroskedasticity. *Econometrica* 48(May):817–38.

11　Investment, Financial Factors, and Cash Flow: Evidence from U.K. Panel Data

Michael Devereux and Fabio Schiantarelli

11.1　Introduction

Most empirical models of company investment rely on the assumption of perfect capital markets. One implication of this assumption is that, in a world without taxes, firms are indifferent to funding their investment programs from internal or external funds. However, there is a rapidly growing body of literature examining the possible existence of imperfections in capital markets and their effects on firms' financial and real decisions. In this paper we provide some econometric evidence on the impact of financial factors like cash flow, debt, and stock measures of liquidity on the investment decisions of U.K. firms. These variables are introduced via an extension of the Q model of investment, which explicitly includes agency costs. We discuss whether the significance of cash flow is due to the fact that it proxies for output or because it is a better measure of market fundamentals than Q. Moreover, we investigate if the effect of financial factors varies across different types of firm. The cross-sectional variation of the impact on investment of flow and stock measures of liquidity has been analyzed also by Fazzari, Hubbard, and Petersen (1988) and by Gertler and Hubbard (1988) for U.S. firms and by Hoshi, Kashyap, and Scharfstein (1988) for Japanese firms. The former studies distinguish between firms according to their dividend payment behavior, while the latter

Michael Devereux is director of the Corporate Sector Research Programme at the Institute for Fiscal Studies, London. Fabio Schiantarelli is associate professor at Boston University and research associate at the Institute for Fiscal Studies.

This paper forms part of the research carried out at the Institute for Fiscal Studies on the impact and incidence of corporate tax, which is financially supported by the ESRC under grant B00222009. The authors are grateful to the following for helpful comments: R. W. Blundell, S. R. Bond, F. Hayashi, R. G. Hubbard, F. Huizinga, K. Lang, C. Meghir, J. Poterba, A. Weiss, and a discussant and participants at the NBER conference, "Information, Capital Markets and Investment." Errors remain their own.

classifies firms according to the strength of their institutional relationships with banks. Instead, we group observations according to firm size, age, and type of industry (growing and declining). The empirical importance of this breakdown is a natural subject of investigation and moreover allows us to minimize the problems of endogenous selection. In the theoretical section we outline a simple model that illustrates how cash flow can be introduced in Q models. We discuss the determinants of the size of the cash-flow effect and explain why caution must be exercised in attributing interfirm differences only to differences in the importance of agency or financial distress costs.

In Section 11.2 we briefly review recent contributions to the literature on credit market imperfections, and in Section 11.3 we show how features appearing in these models might be expected to influence investment decisions. Section 11.4 develops a simple extension of the investment model with adjustment costs that explicitly allows for agency costs of external finance. Section 11.5 describes the behavior and performance of a sample of 720 manufacturing firms in the United Kingdom, split by size and age, and Section 11.6 presents some econometric results, obtained using instrumental variables, which indicate that financial factors, principally in the form of lagged cash flow, do have an independent effect on investment. Section 11.7 is a brief conclusion.

11.2   The Cost of External Finance

During the last few years there has been a renewed interest in understanding the relationship between investment and financing decisions, at both the theoretical and empirical levels. The common theme underlying the various contributions is the lack of perfect substitutability between inside and outside financing. The existence of differential information and incentive problems makes external finance more costly than internal finance. In this setting the availability of internally generated funds, and/or of assets that can be used as collateral, may have an effect on investment decisions.

Let us briefly review the disadvantages and benefits of external finance. Starting with debt finance, there are different reasons why there may be a conflict between shareholders and debtholders, giving rise to agency costs of debt. Jensen and Meckling (1976) suggest that stockholders will have an incentive to engage in projects that are too risky and so increase the possibility of financial distress and bankruptcy. If successful, the payoff to the owners of the firm is large. If unsuccessful, the limited liability provision of debt contracts implies that the creditors bear most of the cost. Myers (1977) suggests that if the firm is partly debt financed, it may underinvest in the sense that it forgoes projects with a positive net present value. This problem is particularly severe when assets in place are a small proportion of the total value of the firm. Other areas of conflict between bondholders and shareholders are represented by the claim dilution resulting from the issue of additional debt and by the possibility that the firm may pay out excessive dividends financed by reduced investment.

Since potential creditors are assumed to understand the incentives facing stockholders and are aware of the risk of bankruptcy when loans are negotiated, the owner will ultimately bear the consequences of these agency problems in terms of a higher cost of debt. With asymmetric information about borrower quality, rationing may also occur (see Jaffee and Russell 1976; Stiglitz and Weiss 1981). As a way to control the conflict between bondholders and shareholders and to minimize the agency cost of debt, bond covenants are observed, limiting the discretionary action of the owners regarding dividends, future debt issues, and maintenance of working capital (Smith and Warner 1979). Debt covenants usually contain a maximum limit on the amount of dividends that can be paid out that depends positively upon accumulated earnings. Restrictions on the minimum value of the ratio between tangible assets and debt, working capital and debt and, finally, between interest payments and cash flow are also common. The greater is the amount of debt in the firm's capital structure, the more severe the incentive problems become, and the more likely it is that the firm will face financial distress and ultimately bankruptcy. Because of the less favorable terms on which debt can be obtained and because of the cost associated with tighter monitoring and bonding activities, agency costs are therefore likely to be increasing in the level of debt. On the other hand, it is likely that such costs are a decreasing function of the level of past and present earnings and of assets, particularly if liquid in nature, that can be used as collateral.

While agency costs make debt less attractive, the tax deductibility of interest payments makes it more attractive. In the absence of such costs, debt is preferred to retentions if $(1 - m)/(1 - z) > 1 - \tau$, where m is the marginal personal tax rate on interest income, z the tax rate on capital gains, and τ the corporate tax rate (King 1977). In the United Kingdom this inequality is satisfied for most investors.[1]

New share issues may be disadvantageous because of transaction costs, tax reasons, or asymmetric information. Informal evidence on transaction costs in the United Kingdom suggests that there are large fixed costs in issuing new equity.[2] The tax disadvantage of new share issues relative to retentions in a classical system of company taxation depends upon the relationship between personal tax rates on dividends, m, and capital gains, z. If m is greater than z, as is usually the case, new equity issues are relatively more expensive (see, e.g., King 1977). In an imputation system, like the one in existence in the United Kingdom since 1973, the situation is more complex. New share issues are a cheaper source of finance for a full tax paying firm if $(1 - m)/[(1 - z)(1 - c)] > 1$, where c is the rate of imputation. This condition will be satisfied for institutional investors for whom $m = z = 0$ and for other investors with a low marginal tax rate on dividends.[3]

Finally, new share issues may be more costly because of asymmetric information. Myers and Majluf (1984) suggest that, if managers have inside information, it may happen that that information is so favorable that management, acting in the interest of old shareholders, will not issue new shares, which are perceived as being underpriced. Investors will therefore interpret the decision to issue new shares as a bad signal. In this case, new equity finance can only be obtained at a premium because of the adverse selection problem.

Up to this point in the discussion we have implicitly assumed that management acts in the interest of shareholders. Allowing for the possible divergence of interest between managers and outside shareholders provides an additional rationale for the disadvantage of external finance. If managers have a less than 100% ownership stake in the company, they will be encouraged to use a greater than optimal amount of the firm's resources in the form of perquisites (Jensen and Meckling 1976). Such activities can be monitored by the outside shareholders, but such monitoring is costly, and the insiders will ultimately bear the cost in terms of a reduced price that prospective outside shareholders are willing to pay for a stake in the firm. This consideration suggests that the cost of outside financing is related to the stake of insiders and to the dispersion of outside ownership.

11.3   Financial Factors and Investment Decisions

What is the effect of credit availability, cash flow, and collateralizable assets on investment decisions? The literature on this issue has been conducted in the context of models with different structures concerning information and technology. One group of papers adds financial considerations to standard investment models based on the assumption of convex adjustment costs, usually estimated in their Q form. For example, credit rationing with an exogenously given ceiling can be easily added to Q models. If there are tax advantages to debt, firms will borrow up to capacity. Under the standard assumptions (perfect competition, constant returns to scale, a single quasi-fixed factor), marginal Q will continue to equal average Q, with the caveat that the present value of the interest payments net of new debt issued should be added to the market value of shares in defining average Q. The present value of these flows can be approximated by the current value of the stock of debt. One could also assume that the maximum amount of debt is a fixed proportion of the capital stock (Summers 1981) with basically the same result.

Alternatively one could include in the objective function an additional cost term, increasing in the level of debt, that summarizes the agency/financial distress cost of debt, as in Chirinko (1987).[4] In this case, an internal solution for debt can be obtained. If the agency cost of debt is linear homogeneous in its arguments, and the change (as opposed to the level) of debt does not enter the agency cost function, marginal Q again equals average Q. If the change in debt does appear in the agency cost function and the latter is not linear homogeneous, the difference between marginal and average Q depends upon the present and future values of the change and level of debt (Chirinko 1987).

When personal taxation is taken into account, and if capital gains are taxed less heavily than dividends, one can distinguish between three financing regimes.[5] In regime 1, investment can be financed at the margin by retentions, positive dividends are paid, and no new shares are issued. In regime 3, the firm issues new shares and pays no dividend. In the intermediate case, regime 2, both dividends and new share issues are zero and the marginal source of finance is debt. A relationship between investment and tax-adjusted average Q can be derived only in regimes 1 and 3. In regime 2 no such relationship exists, and investment equals cash flow plus new debt issued. In this context, an increase in cash flow makes the probability that investment is financed at the margin by retentions more likely, and this can be shown to increase investment (Hayashi 1985). However, conditional on Q, cash flow does not have an additional explanatory power in regimes 1 and 3. In regime 2, increases in cash flow (and debt) translate into a one-to-one increase in investment and Q does not matter.

Fazzari, Hubbard, and Petersen (1988) extend Q models by including a premium for issuing new shares, based on the adverse selection argument put forward by Myers and Majluf (1984). The existence of this premium increases the cost differential between internal finance and new equity, and it increases the likelihood that the firm will find itself at the point of discontinuity where all profits are retained, no dividends are paid, and the firm's future prospects are not good enough to induce it to issue new shares. For those firms Q does not matter, while cash flow does matter.

In another group of papers the role and consequences for investment of informational imperfections are more closely analyzed. In this context the amount of net assets that can be used as collateral is a determinant of the agency cost of external finance and has an effect on investment. The particular informational asymmetry and the details about technology differ across papers, but the common theme is that insiders have less incentive to cheat and more incentive to act in the interest of outside investors when their stake in the project is greater (see the contributions by Bernanke and Gertler 1989; Gertler 1988; and Gertler and Hubbard 1988). The link between the firm's value and the fraction of entrepreneur wealth invested in the project is also emphasised by Leland and Pyle (1977). Since the borrower's net worth is likely to be procyclical, incentive problems may be particularly severe in a recession. This may lead to an asymmetric effect of financial variables on investment during the business cycle.

The existence of informational asymmetries that restrict the firm's ability to raise external equity plays a crucial role also in the paper by Greenwald and Stiglitz (1988). They show that production and investment depend upon the equity position. Since there is only limited access to equity markets, the main way to change firms' equity is to accumulate cash flow, net of financial obligations. All these models imply that an increase in collateralizable net worth may stimulate investment. The more precise modeling of the informational asymmetries and of the possibility of bankruptcy is clearly a strength of these models. However, they do not yield an investment equation that explains how financial factors and expectations about firms' prospects jointly determine investment.

11.4   From Theory to Testing

The empirical importance of financial variables, in particular cash flow and stock measures of liquid assets, characterizes many econometric studies of investment based on firm-by-firm data (see Fazzari, Hubbard and Petersen 1988, and Gertler and Hubbard 1988 for the United States; Hayashi and Inoue 1988, and Hoshi, Kashyap, and Scharfstein 1988 for Japan; and Blundell et al. 1989 for the United Kingdom). Most of the testing has been conducted in the context of Q models in which average Q is used to control for the investment opportunities open to firms. Fazzari et al. and Gertler and Hubbard analyze the cross-sectional variation in the importance of financial factors by classifying firms according to their dividend payout behavior, while Hoshi et al. make a distinction between firms with and without strong links with a single bank.

We discuss the role of financial factors in the context of a simple variant of a Q model of investment. The model includes on the cost side a term, A, representing agency/financial distress costs which is a function of the stock of debt B, the capital stock K, the stock of liquid assets L, and cash flow X. Debt and liquid assets are chosen endogenously, together with investment and new share issues. On the basis of the arguments of the previous section, agency costs are an increasing function of debt and a decreasing function of cash flow and of liquid assets. The agency cost function is expected to vary for firms in different age and size classes and in different industries. The reasons why this may be the case are summarized in Section 11.5. Moreover there is a premium that must be paid for issuing new shares. This way of summarizing informational asymmetries and the risk of bankruptcy is obviously ad hoc. It is adopted here to provide some unifying principle to our discussion and to our empirical testing and to make clear the implicit assumptions underlying the type of equations that have been used so far to test for the importance of financial factors in equations containing average Q. In particular, we want to specify a model that is consistent with the fact that cash flow may matter (albeit differently) for all firms, and not only for those that have used up all retentions and are not issuing any new shares. Under the assumption of perfect competition and linear homogeneity of the production, adjustment, and agency cost functions, the marginal condition for investment, I, implies that when positive dividends are paid (see Appendix),

$$(1) \qquad \left(\frac{I}{K}\right)_t = \frac{1}{b(1 - A_X)}\left\{\frac{\lambda_t^K/\gamma}{(1 - \tau)p_t^y} - \frac{p_t}{(1 - \tau)p_t^y}\right\},$$

where A_X denotes the partial derivative of the agency cost function with respect to cash flow, λ_t^K is the marginal shadow value of capital, p_t^y the output price, p_t the investment price, all in period t, b is a parameter from the adjustment cost function (defined in the Appendix), τ the corporate tax rate, and γ the tax discrimination parameter between dividends and retentions equal to $(1 - m)/[(1 - z)(1 - c)]$. The linear homogeneity assumption, although not necessarily realistic, allows one to show that the following relationship holds between the marginal and average values of the capital stock:

$$(2) \qquad \lambda_t^K K_{t-1}(1 - \delta) + \lambda_t^B B_t + \lambda_t^L L_t = V_t\left(1 + \frac{R}{1 - z}\right),$$

where V_t is the market value of the firm's shares at the beginning of period t, R is the market return on equity, δ is the depreciation rate, and the λ's are the shadow values of the state variables. If the firm is on its optimal path, it is possible to show that $\lambda_t^B = -(\gamma + \mu_t^D)[1 + R/(1 - z)]$ where μ_t^D is the multiplier on the nonnegativity condition for dividends. Similarly, $\lambda_t^L = (\gamma + \mu_t^D)[1 + R/(1 - z)]$. If positive dividends are paid, as is almost always the case in our sample, the multiplier, μ_t^D, is zero. Using this result in (2) and taking a first-order approximation of (1) around sample averages or steady state values we can write:

$$(3) \qquad \left(\frac{I}{K}\right)_t = \beta_0 + \beta_1 Q_t + \beta_2\left(\frac{X}{pK}\right)_t + \beta_3\left(\frac{B}{pK}\right)_t + \beta_4\left(\frac{L}{pK}\right)_t,$$

where I/K denotes investment expenditures and

$$(4) \qquad Q_t = \frac{(V_t/\gamma + B_t - L_t)\left(1 + \dfrac{R}{1 - z}\right)}{(1 - \delta)K_{t-1}(1 - \tau)p_t^y} - \frac{p_t}{(1 - \tau)p_t^y}.$$

The coefficients, denoting sample averages or steady state values by bars, are:

$$(5) \qquad \beta_1 = \frac{1}{b(1 - \overline{A_X})}; \ \beta_2 = \frac{\overline{\left(\frac{I}{K}\right)}\overline{A}_{X,X/K}}{1 - \overline{A_X}}; \ \beta_3 = \frac{\overline{\left(\frac{I}{K}\right)}\overline{A}_{X,B/K}}{1 - \overline{A_X}}; \ \beta_4 = \frac{\overline{\left(\frac{I}{K}\right)}\overline{A}_{X,L/K}}{1 - \overline{A_X}}$$

where subscripts again denote partial derivatives.

This equation suggests that the coefficient in front of average Q reflects both the adjustment cost parameter b and the derivative of the agency cost function with respect to cash flow. The coefficient of cash flow is positive if $A_{X,X/K} > 0$, as is reasonable to assume (i.e., increasing cash flow reduces agency costs at a decreasing rate). The coefficient increases with the average investment rate. It also depends upon average cash flow/capital, debt/capital, liquid assets/capital. Similar comments apply to the coefficients of B/K and L/K, the signs of which depend on the cross partial derivatives of A. If the agency cost function is additively separable in the pairs (X,K), (B,K), and (L,K), the last two regressors can be omitted and the coefficient of X/K depends only upon the average cash flow to capital ratio (in addition to the investment rate). Unless more specific assumptions are made about the functional form of A, little can be said a priori on its effect on the size of the coefficient, and this is a source of ambiguity in forecasting the expected strength of the effect of cash flow, debt, and liquid assets on investment for different types of firms. Aside from this ambiguity, we allow the agency cost function to be displaced upward or downward by a multiplicative constant that is specific for each group of firms and therefore varies according to size, age, and sector. An increase in the constant unambiguously increases the coefficients of cash flow, debt, and liquid assets.

There are several reasons why the agency cost function may vary across firms. First, it might be expected that young and small firms may be at a disadvantage, ceteris paribus, when raising external finance. Younger firms are likely to be a riskier prospect since the shorter track record makes it more difficult to judge their quality. Moreover smaller firms often tend to be less diversified, to display greater earnings volatility, and to be more prone to bankruptcy (Titman and Wessels 1988). However, there are also reasons why it might be the case that incentive problems are more severe for firms in which insiders own a smaller proportion of the firm and outside ownership is more dispersed. Since size may proxy for ownership structure, there is some ambiguity in assessing the effect of size on agency cost. Finally, it is intuitively more probable that firms in declining sectors may face financial distress. The second-hand market for capital goods is likely to be less active, the liquidation value of assets to be smaller, and, therefore, the cost of financial trouble greater in this case.

We have assumed so far that positive dividends are being paid because this is what our data suggests happens most of the time. In this case the first-order condition on new share issues implies that $\gamma - 1 - \omega_t + \mu_t^N = 0$, where ω_t is the marginal adverse selection premium firms have to pay when issuing new shares, and μ_t^N is the nonnegativity constraint on new equity issues. If ω_t is independent of V_t^N as in Fazzari, Hubbard, and Petersen (1988), then we need to assume that γ is less than $1 + \omega_t$, otherwise it would pay to finance continuous new dividend distributions by issuing new shares. If the above condition holds, firms will not issue new shares and pay dividends at the same time. In order to provide a satisfactory rationale for an internal solution for dividends and new share issues, it would be necessary to provide an analysis of the signaling role of dividends and of the possibility of tax exhaustion, but this goes beyond the purpose of this paper. The specification of Q models when the various asymmetries of the tax schedule are explicitly modeled is contained in Devereux, Keen, and Schiantarelli (1989), where it is shown that an internal solution for dividends and new share issues can be obtained because the possibility of tax exhaustion reduces the effective value of γ. Alternatively, it must be assumed that personal tax rates vary across investors and that the condition $\gamma = 1 + \omega_t$ determines the marginal investor in the case of an internal solution.

11.5 Interfirm Differences in Financing, Investment and Profitability in the United Kingdom

In this section we discuss how financing, investment, profitability, and other characteristics vary across different types of firms according to size, age, and sector. The results presented here are based on a sample of 720 firms in the U.K. manufacturing sector over the period 1969–86, quoted on the London Stock Exchange. Because of births and deaths and an increase in the number of firms available in 1975, the number of records on each firm varies between 4 and 18; only 89 firms existed for the entire sample period. Data have been obtained from two sources. Accounting data on each firm has been provided by Datastream, and market valuations have been taken from the London Share Price Database (LSPD). These two sources have been merged for each firm in each year to provide the data used in this paper.[6] These firms account for approximately 65% of total investment in manufacturing between 1977 and 1985. The construction of the variables follows that in Blundell et al. (1989). Company investment includes direct purchase of new fixed assets and those acquired through acquisitions. The firm's market value is an average for the three months prior to each accounting year. Replacement cost estimates of the capital stock are estimated using the perpetual inventory method.[7]

The discussion above implied that there are several reasons why one might expect the location of the agency cost function to differ across firms. Given its location, the expectation of the relative effect of financial factors on investment would also depend on their relative investment rates and their cash flow, debt, and other liquid assets relative to their capital stock. In this section we present some evidence on the relative sizes of these ratios and more generally on firms' characteristics according to size, age, and whether they operate in a growing or declining sector.

It is also worth commenting briefly on the difference between these splits (by size, age, and sector) and that used by Fazzari, Hubbard, and Petersen (1988). Fazzari et al. split their sample of firms according to their dividend payout ratios. This was an attempt to identify those firms that were likely to pay no dividends and at the same time did not find it profitable to issue new shares. In the United States, this may be reasonable (Fazzari et al. show that, among their group of firms having a low payout rate, dividends are paid only 33% of the time). However, in the United Kingdom, the vast majority of firms pay dividends every year while some firms also raise external equity finance fairly frequently. Without explicitly modeling why firms pay dividends—for example, because of a possible signaling role (see, e.g., John and Williams

1985; Ambarish, John, and Williams 1987; and Edwards 1987 for a critical discussion)—it is not clear which firms are constrained by their earnings and which are not. For example, if cutting dividends is taken to be a negative signal, firms that have paid high dividends in the past will be forced to maintain a high dividend strategy. Alternatively, following Easterbrook (1984) and Rozeff (1982), it might be argued that firms with a more widespread ownership are required to pay a higher dividend because this implicitly forces them to submit to scrutiny from the market when they raise external funds.

In table 11.1 we present some summary statistics in which each observation on each firm is classified into one of three size categories according to the real value of the capital stock (1980 prices) at the beginning of the preceding period (pK_{t-2}). The observation is classified as small if pK_{t-2} is less than £6 million, medium if pK_{t-2} is between £6 million and £50 million, and large if pK_{t-2} is above £50 million. Note that, as a firm grows, it may move from one

Table 11.1   **Split by Size**

Case 1 $pK_{t-2} < £6m$
Case 2 $£6m < pK_{t-2} < £50m$
Case 3 $pK_{t-2} > £50m$

	Case 1 (%)	Case 2 (%)	Case 3 (%)
Number of observations	2,681	3,966	2,059
Investment/capital stock	13.4	11.1	10.2
Sales/capital stock	318.8	232.9	170.8
Cash flow/capital stock	17.8	13.6	11.4
Profit/capital stock	12.4	8.8	6.6
Dividends/cash flow	23.3	23.8	22.4
Dividends/profit	33.5	36.6	38.7
Investment/total funds[a]	66.4	70.0	78.3
Retentions/total funds	67.9	65.5	68.0
New equity/total funds	13.2	14.8	12.3
Change in long-term debt/total funds	5.7	7.8	13.3
Change in short-term debt/total funds	13.2	11.9	6.5
Change in bank debt/total funds	12.1	10.8	5.2
Long-term debt/market value[b]	7.6	12.5	23.3
Interest paid/(interest + cash flow)	16.6	18.1	20.3
Current assets[c]/capital stock	24.5	20.6	23.2
Average Q[d]	−.13	−.19	.11
Standard deviation of real sales growth	16.1	15.4	12.7
Frequency of dividend payments	89.2	94.5	97.5
Frequency of new equity issues	13.6	27.5	49.8

[a]Total funds are the sum of retentions, new equity, and the change in long-term and short-term debt.
[b]Market value is taken as the market value of equity plus the book value of debt.
[c]Current assets comprise inventories and work in progress, financial investments, the stock of cash, and trade debtors less trade creditors, and other short-term liabilities (excluding short-term debt).
[d]Q is defined in equation (4). V_t is measured at the beginning of the period.

group to another. As explained in the next section, we split the sample according to the size of pK_{t-2} in order to minimize problems of endogenous selection in estimation.[8] The table indicates that investment and cash flow, each as a percentage of the end-of-period capital stock, decrease with size. This is particularly true of cash flow, with small firms generating a return of 18% compared to only 11% for large firms. Ceteris paribus, the existence of higher cash flows for small firms makes it less likely that they will face financial constraints. The dividend payout ratio is higher for larger firms, although this appears to be mainly due to the fact that depreciation (the difference between cash flow and profit) represents a higher proportion of cash flow for large firms; the average dividend-to-cash-flow ratio is remarkably constant across the three size categories. The frequency with which dividends are paid increases with size, but even for small firms, however, the average dividend payout ratio is approximately 34% and dividends are paid 89% of the time.

Prima facie evidence that internal sources of finance are preferred to external sources is represented by the fact that investment is financed mainly through retentions, which constitute about 67% of the total sources of funds. Perhaps it is a surprise that the proportion of funds raised from retentions by large firms is almost identical to that raised by small firms. New equity varies between 12% and 15% of total new funds.[9] The frequency of new share issues increases with size. The lower frequency of new equity issues for small firms is consistent with the observation that flotation and underwriting costs are a decreasing function of the value of the issue.

Long-term debt represents a small percentage of investment finance, especially for smaller firms. This suggests that it is expensive for small firms to rely on market debt. Note, however, that the percentage of new finance derived from short-term debt (with maturity of less than one year) is greater for smaller firms. The vast majority of their short-term debt is provided by banks. This indicates that the difficulty of borrowing in the open market may be partly relieved by the ability to borrow from institutions that can more easily monitor the borrower through a continuing relationship. It is not clear, however, that the duration of bank debt matches the requirements imposed by investment projects that will provide a return over a long period of time.

A final piece of interesting evidence from table 11.1 is that the standard deviation of real sales growth falls with size, although this effect is not very large. The slightly higher figure for small firms may be reflected in the relatively high ratio of current assets to the capital stock, in that such firms may find it useful to maintain a sizeable reserve of liquid assets in order to buffer the volatility of sales revenues and to avoid being forced to borrow on unfavorable terms. Moreover, this ratio is one of the indices commonly used by lenders to judge the credit worthiness of potential borrowers. Another indicator of the ability to meet financial obligations is the ratio between interest payments and cash flow, which is smaller for smaller firms. By presenting a healthy liquid asset position firms may be able to reduce the cost of borrowing.

Table 11.2   **Evidence from CBI Industrial Trends Survey of U.K. Manufacturing Companies**

		Size by Number of Employees (%)			
Question Response	Whole Sample	0–199	200–499	500–4,999	More than 5,000
Inadequate net return on proposed investment	39.5	26.3	38.5	41.7	46.5
Shortage of internal finance	21.2	15.4	15.5	8.5	29.2
Inability to raise external finance	2.6	3.0	2.3	2.1	2.9
Cost of finance	8.5	10.6	8.5	8.0	8.4
Uncertainty about demand	46.3	56.7	52.8	48.2	36.9
Shortage of labor (including management & technical staff)	3.1	3.7	3.5	2.4	3.1
Other	2.3	2.0	2.8	2.4	2.4
N.A.	12.2	14.2	9.6	10.3	13.4

Note: This table reflects the average response to the question, "What factors are likely to limit (wholly or partly) your capital expenditure authorizations over the next 12 months?" The question was posed over the period 1981–86 in 24 quarterly surveys.

Table 11.2 presents some independent evidence on the degree to which financial factors are perceived to influence the investment decision of different sizes of firms. The figures are taken from the quarterly survey of U.K. manufacturing industry conducted by the Confederation of British Industry. It indicates that over the period 1981–86, virtually a third of the respondents cited some financial factor as constraining their investment (although it is hard to distinguish the three questions related to financial factors). The most striking feature of the table is, however, the proportion of the largest firms that cited "shortage of internal finance" as a significant constraint on their investment. While the sample of firms in this category is low,[10] this does suggest that very large firms may face financial constraints. The table suggests, however, that slightly less large firms (in the third category) face somewhat lower financial constraints.

Another dimension that has a potential bearing on investment and financing decisions, especially in the presence of asymmetric information, is the firm's age. Although we do not have exact information on each firm's age, we do know when firms went public. In table 11.3, we distinguish between observations on firms that have been quoted for at least 12 years and observations on firms younger than 12 years. In this table we examine only small and medium-size firms (i.e., pK_{t-2} less than £50 million). Since larger firms are almost exclusively more than 12 years since their first quotation, they would all fall into the "old" category. By concentrating on the remainder, we consider firms which, apart from age, are more nearly alike.

Within this size category, new firms have a higher investment rate and cash flow. The payout ratio is fairly stable across the two categories. New firms have a higher use of retentions and also derive a slightly larger fraction of new funds from new share issues. The higher profitability and investment of the new firms is reflected in a higher value of Q. There is little variation in the standard deviation of sales growth, thus suggesting that sales volatility does not depend to any great extent on firm age.

It was also suggested that the location of the agency cost function, and hence the degree to which companies face financial constraints, depends on the sector in which it is operating. We have therefore also considered the difference between companies in growing and declining sectors, this time conditioning on size by splitting the sample according to whether pK_{t-2} is greater or less than £10 million. (The state of manufacturing industry in the United Kingdom in the 1970s and early 1980s was such that a majority of our sample of firms belonged to sectors that declined over the period considered.) As might be expected, comparing firms of similar size, both investment and profitability are, on average, higher for firms in growing sectors. Again, however, the average dividend payout ratios are very similar across the different categories. Further, no clear pattern emerges concerning the use of different sources of finance, although small firms in growing industries make less use of retention finance (only 59% of total new funds).

Table 11.3 **Split by Size and Age**
Case 1 $pK_{t-2} <$ £50m; less than 12 years since first quotation
Case 2 $pK_{t-2} <$ £50m; more than 12 years since first quotation

	Case 1	Case 2
Number of observations	773	5,874
Investment/capital stock	14.4	11.0
Sales/capital stock	282.5	238.0
Cash flow/capital stock	18.0	13.6
Profit/capital stock	12.3	8.9
Dividends/cash flow	23.6	23.7
Dividends/profit	34.5	36.4
Investment/total funds	72.3	69.2
Retentions/total funds	69.0	65.5
New equity/total funds	15.3	14.5
Change in long-term debt/total funds	5.9	7.7
Change in short-term debt/total funds	9.8	12.3
Change in bank debt/total funds	9.3	11.1
Long-term debt/market value	10.1	12.2
Interest paid/(interest + cash flow)	17.4	18.0
Current assets/capital stock	13.2	21.8
Average Q	.81	−.30
Standard deviation of real sales growth	17.1	15.6
Frequency of dividend payments	95.5	92.0
Frequency of new equity issues	24.1	21.6

Notes: For information on variables, see table 11.1.

11.6   Empirical Results

What does the empirical evidence say about the role of financial factors in investment decisions for U.K. firms? We start our discussion from the results obtained from estimating equation (3) for the entire sample. We wish to allow for the possibility of time-specific (α_t) and firm-specific (α_i) effects. Introducing the subscript i to distinguish companies, we therefore wish to estimate

$$
(6) \qquad \left(\frac{I}{K}\right)_{it} = \beta_0 + \beta_1 Q_{it} + \beta_2 \left(\frac{X}{pK}\right)_{it} + \beta_3 \left(\frac{B}{pK}\right)_{it}
$$
$$
+ \beta_4 \left(\frac{L}{pK}\right)_{it} + \alpha_i + \alpha_t + \upsilon_{it}
$$

The stochastic term, υ_{it}, arises from disturbances to the adjustment cost function, as in the standard Q model. There is nothing in the theory that restricts this term to be an innovation error, and, indeed, related research estimating the Q model on similar data has suggested that υ_{it} follows an AR(1) process (Blundell et al. 1989). To allow for this possibility, lagged values of the dependent variable and of each regressor are included in the equation (although we estimate the model without imposing the common factor restriction). The lagged values may, of course, also reflect the ambiguities involved in choosing the timing of the various variables.

The model has been estimated in first differences to allow for firm-specific, time-invariant effects and an instrumental variable procedure is used to allow for the endogeneity of the regressors.[11] This endogeneity arises because current cash flow, debt, current assets, Q, and investment may all be simultaneously determined (although Q, unlike the other variables, is constructed by dating it at the beginning of the period). In addition, care must be taken to allow for the possibility of measurement error, particularly in Q. Not only are contemporaneous values of these variables invalid instruments, but first differencing introduces the correlation between, for example, Q_{t-1} and υ_{t-1} into the equation. In the absence of serial correlation in υ_{it}, however, further lags of each of the regressors are valid instruments. Thus, in the third period, variables dated $t = 1$ may be used as instruments in the differenced equation (as well as Q_{i2} if it is uncorrelated with υ_{i2}). Similarly, in the fourth period, variables dated $t = 1$ and $t = 2$ are valid instruments. Since this gives more instruments in later periods, and since υ_{it} may be heteroscedastic across companies, we use an application of Hansen's (1982) generalized method of moments estimator. However, computing restrictions force us to restrict the instrument set.[12] Below, we denote the instrument set used in the form $Q(n,m)$, where n indicates that the latest lag used is dated $t - n$, and m indicates the number of lags used.[13]

In column 1 of table 11.4 we present the estimated coefficients for the equation containing, in addition to Q and lagged investment, both flow and stock

Table 11.4   **The Full Sample**

Dependent Variable $\Delta(I/K)_t$	Period 1972–86 720 Companies, 6,546 observations		
	1	2	3
$\Delta(I/K)_{t-1}$	.1896	.1896	.1907
	(.0306)	(.0286)	(.0284)
ΔQ_t	.0180	.0166	.0158
	(.0051)	(.0079)	(.0074)
ΔQ_{t-1}	−.0044	−.0039	−.0036
	(.0019)	(.0025)	(.0023)
$\Delta(X/pK)_t$	.1168	−.0086	.0481
	(.0788)	(.1494)	(.1180)
$\Delta(X/pK)_{t-1}$	.1584	.2309	.2179
	(.0582)	(.0894)	(.0798)
$\Delta(B/pK)_t$	−.0772	—	—
	(.0300)		
$\Delta(B/pK)_{t-1}$	.0581	—	—
	(.0418)		
$\Delta(L/pK)_t$	−.0149	—	—
	(.0130)		
$\Delta(L/pK)_{t-1}$	.0153	—	—
	(.0138)		
$\Delta(Y/pK)_t$	M	—	−.0059
			(.0043)
$\Delta(Y/pK)_{t-1}$	—	—	.0023
			(.0033)
$m2$	−1.26	−1.17	−1.21
Sargan	59.0 (55)	97.7 (70)	95.5 (68)
W	52.1 (15)	49.5 (15)	51.1 (15)
Instruments	$Q(2,2),CF/pK(2,1)$ $B/pK(2,1),$ $I/K_{t-2},I/K_{t-3},$ $L/pK_{t-2},L/pK_{t-3}$	$I/K(2,1), Q(2,2)$ $CF/pK(2,1)$ $Y/pK(2,1)$	$I/K(2,1),Q(2,2)$ $CF/pK(2,1)$ $Y/pK(2,1)$

Note: Time dummies are included in all equations. Asymptotic standard errors are reported in parentheses. Standard errors and test statistics are asymptotically robust to heteroscedasticity across companies. The notation $m2$ is a test for second-order serial correlation in the residuals, asymptotically distributed as $N(0,1)$ under the null of no serial correlation (see Arellano and Bond 1988). The Sargan statistic is a test of the over-identifying restrictions, asymptotically distributed as $\chi^2(k)$. Here W is a Wald test of the joint significance of the time dummies, asymptotically distributed as $\chi^2(k)$, under the null of no significance. The instrument sets are explained in the text.

measures of liquidity and the stock of debt.[14] Time dummies are included as regressors and instruments in all equations. The results suggest that contemporaneous Q is a significant determinant of investment although, as in most other empirical studies, the size of its coefficient is small. Cash flow, especially dated $t − 1$, plays an important role with large coefficients. The coefficient on contemporaneous debt is negative and significant, as one would expect if an increase in cash flow decreases the marginal agency cost of debt, so that $A_{X,B/X} < 0$ (see [5]). The stock of liquid assets does not play a significant role in this equation. Dropping liquid assets from the model in column 1 has very little effect on the other terms in the equation.

These results are generally robust to variations in the instrument set. The equation does not exhibit second-order serial correlation (see the $m2$ statistic), which would invalidate the instrument set. Moreover, the Sargan test of over-identifying restrictions suggests that the instruments are not correlated with the error term. If Q_{t-1} is included in the instrument set, the coefficient on contemporaneous Q falls, which is consistent with the possibility that downward bias due to measurement error in Q outweighs any upward bias due to the possible endogeneity of Q.[15] This result is also found when the same comparison is made for the other equations presented below, and so we generally exclude Q_{t-1} from the instrument set.

The positive effect of the lagged investment rate and the negative coefficient on the lagged Q term are consistent with an AR(1) error term in the underlying equation. However, the positive coefficients on both the cash flow terms is inconsistent with this explanation of the dynamic structure. (Replacing $[X/pK]_t$ with $[X/pK]_{t-2}$ provides a result consistent with the AR[1] process, although this would imply that lagged cash flow, not current cash flow, should be in the specification in eq. [3].) This suggests that the timing of the impact of cash flow in investment is more complex than suggested by the model in Section 11.4. Intuitively, the significance of lagged cash flow may be explained if external investors may observe only cash flow in the previous period or, more generally, may judge the firm's credit worthiness using a weighted average of past cash flows.[16]

In column 2 of table 11.4 we explore what happens when debt and liquid assets are excluded from the model (debt is rarely significant in the subsamples of the data examined below, mainly due to the fact that less data is available). The positive effect of contemporaneous cash flow disappears in the absence of the negative effect of contemporaneous debt, while lagged cash flow becomes more important. The coefficient on current Q falls slightly.

In column 3, current and lagged output, Y, as a proportion of the replacement value of the capital stock are added to this specification (contemporaneous output is not significant). Their coefficients are neither individually nor jointly significant. However, note that the negative coefficient on current output is consistent with the presence of imperfect competition, which introduces an additional wedge between marginal and average Q, which depends on the present value of current and future output.[17] The wedge captures the loss of monopoly profits due to the decrease in price associated with the additional output produced by new investment. Adding output to the equation to some extent proxies for the wedge, and therefore we would expect a negative coefficient.[18] We explore this issue further below for different subsamples of the data.

The presence of output in the equation has little effect on the coefficient of lagged cash flow. Its remaining significance suggests that even if cash flow is to some extent proxying for demand, this is not the main reason for its importance. The principal model investigated below is a parsimonious version of column 2 of table 11.4, dropping lagged Q and current cash flow (which are individually and jointly insignificant). The size and significance of the other variables are virtually unchanged when these two terms are omitted.

One reason for the significance of cash flow is that it may be a better proxy for market fundamentals than the market value of the firm, and entrepreneurs may respond only to fundamentals (Blanchard, Rhee, and Summers 1988). In this case one would expect that during periods of potential speculative bubbles or fads in the stock market, the coefficient for Q and cash flow should be different, compared with other periods. In particular one may expect that Q matters less relative to cash flow in such periods. It is obviously difficult to identify unambiguously when bubbles or fads caused share prices to be a poor reflection of fundamentals. During the years covered by our estimation, the years between 1981 and 1986 are possible candidates; average price–earnings ratios have been consistently higher from 1981 onward than over the previous 10 years. While this may, of course, simply reflect more optimistic expectations, this may also reflect the existence of a bubble.

We have therefore reestimated the specification used below, for example in table 11.5, allowing all of the slope coefficients to differ between the two subperiods. However, there is no strong evidence of a structural break. The Wald test statistic for the joint significance of the three additional terms (each variable interacted with a dummy equal to 1 for the period 1981–86 and 0 otherwise) is 6.83 (compared with a critical value of 7.81 at the 5% significance level). In addition, the coefficient on lagged cash flow for the whole period was 0.2951 (with standard error of 0.0462), while that for the additional variable lagged cash flow from 1981 to 1986 only was -0.0982 (with standard error of 0.0607). If Q_{t-1} is included in the instrument set, the three additional terms become jointly significant (with a Wald statistic of 15.3). The same pattern arises for the cash-flow terms, and additionally in this case, the coefficient on Q from 1981 to 1986 only is positive and significant. Any support for a structural break that might be found in these results would therefore be in the opposite direction to what would be expected if cash flow were merely proxying for market fundamentals. Rather, it seems that in the relative boom years of the 1980s firms were simply less financially constrained and hence cash flow was less important. The asymmetric effect of cash flow on investment during booms and recessions is emphasised by Gertler and Hubbard (1988). Of course, it may be that cash flow proxies both for market fundamentals and financial constraints, but that the change in the latter dominates in the 1980s. This is an issue that deserves further investigation. However, these initial results suggest that fads and bubbles are not the key explanation as to why cash flow is significantly related to investment.

The arguments summarized in the previous section suggest that cash flow and other financial variables may have a differential impact across different types of firms. In table 11.5 we present the results on the effect of cash flow for firms of three different sizes (small, medium, and large). We also consider "very large" firms (which are a subset of the group of large firms). Note that observations are classified according to the size of the capital stock at the end of time $t - 2$, pK_{t-2}. Under the assumption that the error term in the levels equation is not serially correlated, pK_{t-2} is predetermined with respect to the error term in the differenced equation. Current assets were not significant when added to the various equations. In addition, current cash flow and further lags of cash flow and Q were generally insignificant when added to the equations presented.

Consider, first, cases 1, 2, and 3 in table 11.5. The coefficient on cash flow is significant for all classes of firms. Perhaps surprisingly, it is greater for large firms, although there is not a statistically significant difference between the coefficients for large and small firms at normal significance levels (the t-statistic for the significance of the difference between the two coefficients is 1.13).[19] The coefficient and the significance of current Q increase across the size categories; for small firms Q appears to have no impact on investment, while for large firms the coefficient on Q is much greater. Given the increasing coefficient on cash flow as size increases, we also consider whether the impact of cash flow for large firms is dominated by very large firms. The results shown in case 4 show that this may be the case; although the coefficient on cash flow for very large firms is less precisely determined (due to fewer obser-

Table 11.5   **Split by Size**

Case 1 $pK_{t-2} < £6m$
Case 2 $£6m < pK_{t-2} < £50m$
Case 3 $pK_{t-2} > £50m$
Case 4 $pK_{t-2} > £100m$

Dependent Variable $\Delta(I/K)_t$	Case 1	Case 2	Case 3	Case 4
Number of firms	311	403	164	112
Number of observations	1,709	3,111	1,726	1,140
$\Delta(I/K)_{t-1}$	.1723	.1550	.1056	.1032
	(.0485)	(.0355)	(.0493)	(.0480)
ΔQ_t	.0011	.0144	.0188	.0085
	(.0052)	(.0082)	(.0101)	(.0058)
$\Delta(X/pK)_{t-1}$	.2275	.2263	.3163	.4050
	(.0413)	(.0385)	(.0667)	(.1113)
$m2$	−2.14	−.52	−.18	.03
W	67.3 (15)	67.1 (15)	38.0 (15)	59.7 (15)
Sargan	82.1 (72)	89.4 (72)	85.0 (72)	73.8 (72)
Instruments	$I/K(2,1)$, $Q(2,2)$, $CF/pK(2,1)$, $Y/pK(2,1)$			

Note: See notes to table 11.4.

vations) the significance of the difference between it and that for small firms is slightly higher (with a t-statistic of 1.50).

These qualitative results are invariant to alternative instrument sets. However, the significance of both the Q and cash flow does vary with the instrument set. In particular, if Q_{t-1} is included in the instrument set, current Q is statistically significant for medium, large, and very large firms although the estimated coefficients are slightly lower. In addition, the differences between the cash-flow coefficients are more significant (with t-statistics of 1.68 for the difference between small and large firms and 1.88 for the difference between small and very large firms).

With one main exception, adding other regressors has little impact on the coefficients and standard errors presented in table 11.5. The exception occurs when current output is added to the model for large firms. The coefficient on current output for large firms is -0.0106 with a standard error of 0.0026. Its negative sign is again consistent with the possibility that output is reflecting the existence of imperfect competition since large firms are more likely to be in a position to exploit the benefits of monopolistic competition. The coefficient on current cash flow for large firms increases substantially when current output is included, although it is less precisely estimated. Current debt also has a negative sign but is not significant when added to the models in table 11.5. Adding debt tends to increase the difference in the coefficients on cash flow between case 1 and case 3 firms, although their standard errors also increase.

In the context of the model sketched in Section 11.4, the size of the coefficient on cash flow for large firms cannot be accounted for by a higher investment rate of large firms (see [5]), because it is, in fact, lower. It could be explained by the lower cash flow/capital ratio that characterizes larger firms, if the coefficient of cash flow decreases with this ratio. It is easy to find parameterizations of the agency cost function that yield this result.[20] This factor may be dominant since differences in the investment rate are not very large and neither is the difference in the riskiness as measured by the variance of sales. It is also possible that the differential according to size may capture industry effects. Finally, it is possible that, ceteris paribus, agency costs may be more severe when insiders effectively controlling the firm hold a lower fraction of the equity and/or outside equity holdings are more dispersed. Size may proxy for the effect of these factors on the severity of the incentive problems.

Two criticisms might be made with regard to splitting firms according to the replacement cost value of the capital stock two periods ago. One is that there may remain some endogeneity introduced by serial correlation in the error term (although we do not find such correlation). The second is that whatever effects size is proxying for, an alternative would be to split by the size of a firm relative to the size of other firms in the industry in which that firm operates. Thus a "small" firm overall may seem larger relative to other firms in its own industry. To meet these possible criticisms, we first split firms according to their initial size (that is, their size when they first entered the data base). Of course, this takes no account of the rate of growth of a firm since it entered the data base, and, possibly as a result, there is much less variation in the value of the cash-flow coefficient between different size classes of firms measured by initial size. However, in table 11.6, we present the results of splitting firms according to their initial size relative to that of other firms in their industry that are also in the data base. Thus, case 1 firms are among the smallest 75% of firms in their industry measured by initial size and case 2 firms are among the largest 25%. It is clear from the table that the results concerning cash flow are similar to those in table 11.5 (indeed the size and significance of the difference across the two categories is greater in table 11.6; the t-statistic on the difference between the two cash-flow coefficients is 1.84). By contrast, however, Q appears more important for the smaller firms. This latter result may be partly due to grouping together all "nonlarge" firms in the first column.

While we do not have any data on ownership patterns, we can control for industry. An interesting distinction, as suggested above, is between growing and declining sectors. Table 11.7 contains the results of the size/sector split (using only two categories for size). Due to the small number of observations in some of the categories, parameters are estimated with less precision than in other tables. The perhaps surprising result from table 11.7 is that the coefficient on cash flow is greater for firms operating in growing sectors. This is true even if the long-run impact of cash flow is considered. This table also mirrors the result that cash flow is more important for large firms, with the largest coefficient being for large firms in growing sectors. This result is not

Table 11.6   **Split by Initial Size Relative to Distribution of Industry Initial Size**
Case 1 pK_0 within smallest 75% of firms in the same industry
Case 2 pK_0 within largest 25% of firms in the same industry

Dependent Variable $\Delta(I/K)_t$	Case 1	Case 2
Number of firms	4,530	2,016
Number of observations	541	179
$\Delta(I/K)_{t-1}$	.1741	.1782
	(.0325)	(.0546)
ΔQ_t	.0130	.0060
	(.0082)	(.0032)
$\Delta(X/pK)_{t-1}$	.2303	.3613
	(.0293)	(.0648)
$m2$	−1.67	−.33
W	96.9 (15)	38.5 (15)
Sargan	102.0 (72)	85.1 (72)
Instruments	$I/K(2,1)$, $Q(2,2)$, $CF/pK(2,1)$, $Y/pK(2,1)$	

Note: See notes to table 11.4.

Table 11.7   **Split by Size and Sector**

Case 1 $pK_{t-2} < £10m$; growing sectors
Case 2 $pK_{t-2} < £10m$; declining sectors
Case 3 $pK_{t-2} > £10m$; growing sectors
Case 4 $pK_{t-2} > £10m$; declining sectors

Dependent Variable $\Delta(I/K)_t$	Case 1	Case 2	Case 3	Case 4
Number of firms	157	298	132	279
Number of observations	859	1,775	1,356	2,556
$\Delta(I/K)_{t-1}$	.2222	.1246	.0614	.1149
	(.0674)	(.0454)	(.0613)	(.0413)
ΔQ_t	.0086	.0142	.0299	.0061
	(.0080)	(.0056)	(.0145)	(.0030)
$\Delta(X/pK)_{t-1}$	.2719	.1786	.3234	.2055
	(.0648)	(.0400)	(.0683)	(.0433)
$m2$	−3.05	−1.24	−.66	.02
W	39.8 (15)	55.8 (15)	30.9 (15)	48.5 (15)
Sargan	67.1 (72)	85.8 (72)	82.2 (72)	89.3 (72)
Instruments	$I/K(2,1)$, $Q(2,2)$, $CF/pK(2,1)$, $Y/pK(2,1)$			

Note: See notes to table 11.4. Growing sectors are chemicals and man-made fibers; electrical and instrument engineering; and food, drink, and tobacco. Declining sectors are metals and metal goods; other minerals and mineral products; mechanical engineering; motor vehicles, parts, and other transport equipment; textiles, clothing, leather, and footwear; and other industries.

sensitive to the instrument set used. One explanation for this effect may be that the lower investment rate of firms in declining sectors dominates empirically their lower cash flow and their higher agency costs, which, ceteris paribus, would be expected to arise. The table indicates that the impact of Q is mixed: among small firms it is more important for firms in declining sectors but among large firms it is more important for firms in growing sectors.

The final issue we wish to explore is the effect of age on the relevance of cash flow. In table 11.8 we report the results obtained when, excluding large firms, we distinguish between firms that have been quoted for more or less than 12 years. Twelve years may seem a rather long time, but it is imposed by the necessity of having enough observations in the "new" firms category for the purposes of estimation. The results suggest that cash flow is somewhat more important for new firms, although the differences between the two categories are not large. Once again, it should be noted that the category of new firms is very small, and that the variables consequently tend to be less significant.

11.7   Conclusions

The results discussed in this paper suggest that, in all cases, cash flow is significantly associated with investment. Stock measures of liquidity do not play an important empirical role. The stock of debt does appear to have a

Table 11.8   **Split by Size and Age**
Case 1 $pK_{t-2} < £50m$; less than 12 years since first quotation
Case 2 $pK_{t-2} < £50m$; more than 12 years since first quotation

Dependent Variable $\Delta(I/K)_t$	Case 1	Case 2
Number of firms	99	574
Number of observations	450	4,370
$\Delta(I/K)_{t-1}$	.0935	.1939
	(.0610)	(.0342)
ΔQ_t	.0122	.0095
	(.0099)	(.0066)
$\Delta(X/pK)_{t-1}$	.2720	.2242
	(.0662)	(.0302)
m2	−1.57	−.97
W	36.7 (15)	88.4 (15)
Sargan	48.3 (44)	100.7 (72)
Instruments	$(I/K)_{t-2}, (I/K)_{t-3},$	$I/K(2,1), Q(2,2),$
	$Q(2,1), CF/pK(2,1),$	$CF/pK(2,1),$
	$Y/pK(2,1)$	$Y/pK(2,1)$

Note: See notes to table 11.4.

negative impact on investment, although the significance of this term depends on the size of the sample. The performance of Q is mixed. While it plays a significant role in the full sample, there are subsamples, typically of small firms, in which it does not appear to have an independent effect on investment. The results for the full sample over different time periods suggest that the significance of cash flow is not due solely to the fact that, in proxying for demand, it is a better measure of fundamentals than Q, nor simply that it contains new information not captured by beginning-of-period Q, although more research is needed on this issue.

Cash flow does appear to differ across firms in the magnitude of its impact on investment. In particular, it appears to play a more important role for large firms than for small firms. While this may be surprising at first sight, there are several reasons why this effect might be observed. For example, it may reflect the fact that large firms tend to have a lower relative cash flow. In addition, it may reflect the possibility that large firms have a more diverse ownership structure, which tends to increase agency costs. Given size, the effect of cash flow tends to be larger for firms in growing sectors, contrary to what one would expect since collateralizable net worth is likely to be larger in this case and the risk of bankruptcy lower. However, firms in growing sectors need to finance a higher rate of investment. Finally, when firms are classified according to age, it appears that cash flow matters somewhat more for newer firms, as would be expected since information asymmetries are likely to be larger for such firms and they need to finance a higher investment rate.

Our results suggest that capital market imperfections should be an important ingredient of any extension to or reformulation of the adjustment cost model of investment. However, the mixed performance of Q suggests that such extensions should be pursued in future work.[21]

Appendix

The firm maximizes the market value of the shares of existing shareholders, V_t:

(A1) $V_t = E_t \sum_{j=t}^{\infty} \left(\frac{1}{1 + R/(1 - z)} \right)^{j+1-t} \{\gamma D_j - V_j^N(1 + \omega_j)\},$

where D_j denotes dividends, V_j^N new shares issued, ω_j the sample selection premium, all in period j, and $\gamma = (1 - m)/(1 - z)(1 - c)$, with m denoting the tax rate on dividends, z the tax rate on capital gains, and c the rate of imputation. Here R is the market rate of return on equity, assumed to be constant for simplicity.

The maximization is subject to the definition of sources and uses

(A2) $(1 - \tau)p_t^y \Pi(K_t, I_t) - A(X_t, B_t, L_t, p_t K_t) + V_t^N + B_{t+1}$
$+ L_t[1 + (1 - \tau)i^L] = D_t + p_t I_t + [1 + i(1 - \tau)]B_t + L_{t+1},$

where τ is the corporate tax rate, p_t^y the price of output, p_t the price of investment goods, $p_t^y \Pi(t)$ real revenues net of variable costs, K_t capital stock, $A(t)$ agency costs of debt, B_t debt, L_t liquid assets, all in period t, i the rate of interest on debt, and i^L the rate of interest on liquid assets. For ease of notation, we omit depreciation allowances; these are included, however, in the empirical work. Cash flow, denoted X_t, is defined as

$X_t = (1 - \tau)\Pi(t) - [1 + i(1 - \tau)]B_t + [1 + i^L(1 - \tau)]L_t.$

The capital accumulation equation is

(A3) $K_t = (1 - \delta)K_{t-1} + I_t$

and the nonnegativity conditions are $V_t^N \geq 0$ and $D_t \geq 0$.

The first-order conditions are:

(A4) $(\gamma + \mu_t^D)[(1 - A_X[t])(1 - \tau)p_t^y \Pi_I(t) - p_t] + \lambda_t^K = 0,$

(A5) $(\gamma + \mu_t^D)[(1 - A_X[t])(1 - \tau)p_t^y \Pi_K(t) - p_t A_K(t)]$

$- \lambda_t^K + \frac{1 - \delta}{1 + R/(1 - z)}\lambda_{t+1}^K = 0,$

(A6) $\gamma + \mu_t^D - 1 - \omega_t + \mu_t^N = 0,$

(A7) $\quad (\gamma + \mu_t^D) + \dfrac{(\gamma + \mu_{t+1}^D)}{1 + R/(1 - z)}[-(1 - A_X[t+1])$

$\quad (1 + [1 - \tau]i) - A_B(t+1)] = 0,$

(A8) $\quad (\gamma + \mu_t^D) + \dfrac{(\gamma + \mu_{t+1}^D)}{1 + R/(1 - z)}[(1 - A_X[t + 1])$

$\quad (1 + [1 - \tau]i^L) + A_L(t+1)] = 0.$

Also:

(A9) $\lambda_t^B + (\gamma + \mu_t^D)[(1 - A_X[t])(1 + [1 - \tau]i) + A_B(t)] = 0$

(A10) $\lambda_t^L + (\gamma + \mu_t^D)[(1 - A_X[t])(1 + [1 - \tau]i^L) + A_L(t)] = 0.$

λ's denote the multipliers associated with the state variables and μ_t^D and μ_t^N the multipliers associated with the nonnegativity condition for D_t and V_t^N. Equations (A4) to (A10), together with the complementary slackness conditions, summarize the conditions for an optimum.

If we assume that the adjustment cost function is separable and has the form

$$\frac{b}{2}\left[\left(\frac{I}{K}\right)_t - c\right]^2 K_t,$$

equation (A4) yields (1) in the main text when $D_t > 0$ so that $\mu_t^D = 0$.

In order to obtain the relationship between the marginal and average value of the capital stock, equation (2) in the main text, multiply (A4) by I_t, (A5) by K_t, (A6) by V_t^N, (A7) by B_{t+1}, (A8) by L_{t+1}, (A9) by B_t, (A10) by L_t, and add them together. Solve the resulting difference equation forward and note that (A7) and (A9) imply that

$$\lambda_{t+1}^B = -(\gamma + \mu_t^D)[1 + R/(1 - z)],$$

and that (A8) and (A10) imply that

$$\lambda_{t+1}^L = (\gamma + \mu_t^D)[1 + R/(1 - z)].$$

This yields equation (2) in the main text.

Notes

1. However, the possibility of negative profit, combined with corporate tax asymmetries, reduces the effective corporate tax rate because there may not exist taxable profits against which to offset an interest payment. This reduces the tax advantage of debt (see DeAngelo and Masulis 1980; Auerbach 1986; and Mayer 1986).

2. For example, typical transaction costs in raising £5 million would be around £250,000, compared with only £500,000 for raising £50 million.

3. The existence of a high allowance for capital gains results in a zero marginal tax

rate for investors earning less than about £6,000 per year in the form of capital gains. One should, in addition, consider the possibility that firms may not be able to offset their advance corporation tax against the mainstream corporation tax. This implies that the effective rate of imputation is smaller than the statutory rate, making new share issues less attractive (Keen and Schiantarelli 1988).

4. See also Steigum (1983) and Bernstein and Nadiri (1986) in which the cost of borrowing is made an increasing function of the debt/equity ratio.

5. Edwards and Keen (1985) discuss what happens when dividends are tax favored and a maximum limit is imposed on their distribution, as is the case in the United Kingdom.

6. The LSPD data is needed to calculate Tobin's Q.

7. Further details are available from the authors on request.

8. Splitting by payout behavior is more open to criticism from this point of view.

In order to allow for any distortion to these results arising from measurement error in K, a similar split was performed using the real value of sales two periods earlier as a measure of size. The results were very similar.

9. Mayer (1987, 1988) claims that the proportion of funds raised from new share issues is somewhat lower, although our figures are in line with official statistics (DTI Business Monitor, MA3).

10. Between 25 and 60 out of a sample of around 1,250.

11. Related research (Blundell et al. 1989) has indicated that the presence of firm-specific effects can lead to biased estimated coefficients when the model is estimated in its levels form. In addition, the presence of the lagged dependent variable in the more general equation makes the within-groups estimator inconsistent for dynamic models with small T (Nickell 1981).

12. We have used GAUSS 1986, version 1.49B, in which the instrument set must be restricted to 90 instruments. Thanks are due to Manuel Arellano and Stephen Bond for allowing the use of their GAUSS programs in this work.

13. For $m = 1$, the GMM instrument set differs from simply using Q_{t-n} essentially by allowing the reduced-form coefficient to vary over time.

14. We have experimented with alternative empirical measures for γ. The results are very similar whatever measure is used. The results are also not sensitive to the inclusion of the discount factor, R, in the definition of Q_t. In the tables we report the results obtained when γ and the discount factor are set equal to one.

15. In principle, including Q_{t-2} in the instrument set may also introduce measurement error since it also appears as a regressor in the differenced equation, although in later tables the first-differenced Q_{t-1} is omitted since it is not significant for subsamples of the data. This issue has been explored in detail by Blundell et al. (1989) on the same data set, and our choice of instrument set is consistent with their results.

16. This would require the inclusion of X_{t-1} and further lags in the agency cost function described in Section 11.4.

17. More precisely, omitting debt, liquid assets, and taxes, it can be shown that

$$\lambda_t^K = \frac{\left(1 + \frac{R}{1-z}\right)\left\{V_t - \sum_{i=1}^{\infty}\frac{1}{\epsilon_{t+i}}\left(1 + \frac{R}{1-z}\right)^{-i}p_{t+i}^y Y_{t+i}\right\}}{(1 - \delta)K_{t-1}},$$

where ϵ_{t+i} is the elasticity of demand.

18. However, if the equation is estimated in a quasi-differenced form, as suggested by Schiantarelli and Georgoutsos (1990) and Galeotti and Schiantarelli (1988), the contemporaneous investment rate, given "scaled" past investment, should be positively

related to $(Y/K)_{t-1}$. When this variable is added to our specification alone, it is rarely significant. This issue deserves additional investigation.

19. We need to test the hypothesis that the difference between the cash-flow coefficients equals zero. On the assumption that the error terms are independent across the two categories, the appropriate standard error is simply the square root of the sum of the squares of the two standard errors on the two coefficients. This allows a simple t-test to be performed on the difference between the coefficients.

20. This would be the case, for example, if, ignoring liquid assets

$$A = \{-a(X/K)^\alpha + b \, (B/K)^\beta\}K,$$

where $0 < \alpha < 1$, or if

$$A = (X/K)^\alpha(B/K)^\beta K,$$

where $\alpha < 0$.

21. For example, see Chirinko (1984) and Hayashi and Inoue (1988) for Q models with multiple capital inputs, Galeotti and Schiantarelli (1988) for a Q model with imperfect competition and labor as a quasi-fixed factor, and Bond and Meghir (1989) for an adjustment cost model that avoids the use of stock market values and parameterization of the gross production function.

References

Ambarish, R., K. John, and J. Williams. 1987. Efficient signalling with dividends and investments. *Journal of Finance* 43(2):321–43.

Arellano, M., and S. Bond. 1988. Dynamic panel data estimation using DPD: A guide for users. Working Paper no. 88/15. Institute for Fiscal Studies.

Auerbach, A. J. 1986. The dynamic effects of tax law asymmetries. *Review of Economic Studies* 53:205–25.

Bernanke, B., and M. Gertler. 1989. Agency costs, net worth and business fluctuations. *American Economic Review* 79(1):31–41.

Bernstein, J. I., and M. I. Nadiri. 1986. Financing and investment in plant and equipment and research and development. In *Prices, competition and equilibrium*, ed. M. H. Preston and R. E. Quandt. Oxford: Philip & Allen.

Blanchard, O. J., C. Rhee, and L. H. Summers. 1988. The stock market, profit and investment. Mimeograph.

Blundell, R., S. R. Bond, M. P. Devereux, and F. Schiantarelli. 1989. Does Q matter for investment? Some evidence from a panel of U.K. companies. Working Paper no. 87/12a. Revised. Institute for Fiscal Studies.

Bond, S. R., and C. Meghir. 1989. Dynamic investment models and the firm's financial policy. Mimeograph. Institute for Fiscal Studies.

Chirinko, R. S. 1984. Investment, Tobin's Q and multiple capital inputs. Working Paper no. 328. Cornell University.

———. 1987. Tobin's Q and financial policy. *Journal of Monetary Economics* 19:69–87.

DeAngelo, H., and R. W. Masulis. 1980. Optimal capital structure under corporate and personal taxation. *Journal of Financial Economics* 8:3–30.

Devereux, M. P., M. J. Keen, and F. Schiantarelli. 1989. Tax asymmetries, investment and financial decisions in a model with adjustment costs. Mimeograph. Institute for Fiscal Studies.

Easterbrook, F. H. 1984. Two agency-cost explanations of dividends. *American Economic Review* 74(4):650–59.

Edwards, J. S. S. 1987. Recent developments in the theory of corporate finance. *Oxford Review of Economic Policy* 3(4):1–12.

Edwards, J. S. S, and M. J. Keen. 1985. Taxes investment and Q. *Review of Economic Studies* 52:665–79.

Fazzari, F. M., R. G. Hubbard, and B. C. Petersen. 1988. Financing constraints and corporate investment. *Brookings Papers on Economic Activity,* no. 1, pp. 141–95.

Galeotti, M., and F. Schiantarelli. 1988. Generalised Q models for investment and employment. Working Paper no. 88/13. Institute for Fiscal Studies.

Gertler, M. 1988. Financial capacity, reliquification and production in an economy with long-term financial arrangements. Mimeograph.

Gertler, M., and R. G. Hubbard. 1988. Financial factors in business fluctuations. Prepared for the Federal Reserve Bank of Kansas City's Symposium on Financial Market Volatility, August, Jackson Hole, Wyoming.

Greenwald, B. C., and J. E. Stiglitz. 1988. Financial market imperfections and business cycles. Working Paper no. 2494. NBER.

Hansen, L. P. 1982. Large sample properties of the generalized method of moments estimator. *Econometrica* 50:1029–54.

Hayashi, F. 1985. Corporate finance side of the Q theory of investment. *Journal of Public Economics* 27:261–88.

Hayashi, F., and T. Inoue. 1988. Implementing the Q theory of investment on micro data: Japanese manufacturing 1977–1985. Mimeograph.

Hoshi, T., A. Kashyap, and D. Scharfstein. 1988. Corporate structure and investment: Evidence from Japanese panel data. Working Paper no. 2071-88. A. P. Sloan School of Management.

Jaffee, D. M., and T. Russell. 1976. Imperfect information, uncertainty and credit rationing. *Quarterly Journal of Economics* 90:651–66.

Jensen, M. C., and W. H. Meckling. 1976. Theory of the firm: Managerial behaviour, agency costs, and ownership structure. *Journal of Financial Economics* 3:305–60.

John, K., and J. Williams. 1985. Dividends, dilution and taxes: A signalling equilibrium. *Journal of Finance* 40:1053–70.

Keen, M. J., and F. Schiantarelli. 1988. Corporation tax asymmetries and optimal financial policy. Working Paper no. 88/2. Institute for Fiscal Studies.

King, M. A. 1977. *Public policy and the corporation.* London: Chapman & Hall.

Leland, H. and D. Pyle. 1977. Information asymmetries, financial structure and financial intermediaries. *Journal of Finance* 32:371–87.

Mayer, C. 1986. Corporation tax, finance and the cost of capital. *Review of Economic Studies* 53:93–112.

———. 1987. The assessment: Financial systems and corporate investment. *Oxford Review of Economic Policy* 3(4):i–xvi.

———. 1988. New issues in corporate finance. *European Economic Review* 32:1167–86.

Myers, S. C. 1977. Determinants of corporate borrowing. *Journal of Financial Economics* 5:147–76.

Myers, S. C., and N. S. Majluf. 1984. Corporate financing and investment decisions when firms have information that investors do not have. *Journal of Financial Economics* 13(June):187–221.

Nickell, S. J. 1981. Biases in dynamic models with fixed effects. *Econometrica* 49:1417–26.

Rozeff, M. S. 1982. Growth, beta and agency costs as determinants of dividend payout ratios. *Journal of Financial Research* 5(3):249–59.

Schiantarelli, F., and D. Georgoutsos. 1990. Monopolistic competition and the Q theory of investment. *European Economic Review.* Forthcoming.

Smith, C. W., Jr., and J. B. Warner. 1979. On financial contracting: An analysis of bond covenants. *Journal of Financial Economics* 7:117–61.

Steigum, E., Jr. 1983. A financial theory of investment behaviour. *Econometrica* 51:637–45.

Stiglitz, J. E., and A. Weiss. 1981. Credit rationing in markets with imperfect information. *American Economic Review* 71(June):393–410.

Summers, L. H. 1981. Taxation and corporate investment: A Q theory approach. *Brookings Papers on Economic Activity,* no. 1, pp. 67–140.

Titman, S., and R. Wessels. 1988. The determinant of capital structure choice. *Journal of Finance* 43(1):1–18.

12 Financial Systems, Corporate Finance, and Economic Development

Colin Mayer

12.1 Introduction

Over the past decade there has been increasing interest in the role of institutions in the financial and real activities of the corporate sector. That interest is most clearly reflected in the plethora of models on imperfect information that have recently appeared in the finance literature. Several attempts have been or are currently being made to establish the empirical significance of these models for the financial behavior of firms. This volume reports the results of a number of such studies. However, a majority of this work is confined to one country, namely the United States, and examines only a small segment of a country's total financial system at any one time. It is therefore difficult to judge the broader significance of these models for the overall functioning of a financial system and to determine the extent to which they are relevant to different countries.

It is well known that there are significant variations in the structure of different countries' financial systems. Since Marshall there has been much discussion about the role of banks in the German financial system. Schumpeter, Gerschenkron, and Cameron all pointed to banks as an engine of growth of the German economy. More recently, similar consideration has been given to the role of banks in the Japanese economy and contrasts have been drawn

Colin Mayer is professor of corporate finance at City University Business School in London and codirector of the Centre for Economic Policy Research's program in applied microeconomics.

This paper is part of the Centre for Economic Policy Research's "International Study of the Financing of Industry." The CEPR study is being financed by the Anglo-German Foundation, the Bank of England, the Commission of the European Communities, the Economic and Social Research Council, the Esmee-Fairbairn Charitable Trust, the Japan Foundation, and the Nuffield Foundation. This paper was presented at the NBER Conference, "Information, Capital Markets and Investment Conference," Boston, May 1989. The author is grateful to conference participants for their comments, and especially to Roger Farmer and Glenn Hubbard. Ian Alexander provided excellent research assistance.

between the importance of banks and securities markets in Japanese and Anglo-Saxon financial systems, respectively.[1]

Prima facie, banking systems would be expected to avoid some of the information deficiencies associated with securities markets. A primary rationale for the existence of banks is that they perform screening and monitoring functions that individual investors can only undertake at high cost. Resource allocation, credit availability, and terms of loans may all, therefore, be superior under a bank-based than a market financial system. On the other hand, transaction costs may be lower in the absence of intermediation, and taxation may militate in favor of market-based sources of capital.

There are then several factors that finance theory suggests should influence the financing patterns of different countries' corporate sectors. The purpose of this paper is to compare the industry financing of eight developed countries and to evaluate these patterns in the context of alternative theories of corporate finance. International comparison of the financing of industry is a familiar subject. However, it is probably fair to say that, to date, it has only shed limited light on the functioning of different financial systems. In large part this is due to the unreliability of the underlying data. There are, for example, well-known problems associated with international comparisons of corporate sector gearing: the valuation of assets, the treatment of reserves and goodwill, and the double counting of intrasector flows all present serious difficulties. The extent to which such inconsistencies can be overcome by ad hoc corrections is questionable.

One justification for a reexamination of this subject at this time is that more reliable methods of comparison have been developed that overcome many of the problems that have afflicted previous studies. Problems remain but the degree of comparability reported in this paper is almost certainly greater than that of previous studies and probably about as great as existing data allow the researcher to achieve at an aggregate level.

The results suggest 10 stylized facts about corporate finance. These concern forms of finance in different countries and the relation between different forms of finance over time. The stylized observations are reported in Section 12.2 of the paper. In Section 12.3, alternative theories of corporate finance are discussed, and their relevance to explaining the observed financing patterns is considered. This is not supposed to be a test of alternative theories, merely an examination of the extent to which they are consistent with aggregate financing patterns in different countries.

Theory and observation bear directly on many of the issues that have been central to policy debates about financial systems. In particular, there is currently much discussion about the relative merits of banks and markets for promoting economic growth. As noted above, banks have traditionally been regarded as central to the promotion of economic growth. More recently, disillusionment with the role of banks in developing countries has intensified in the face of widespread corruption and bank failures. The World Bank (1989) has, as a consequence, advocated the use of both securities markets and banks in promoting economic growth.

Likewise, as the emergence of a unified market in 1992 promises to create a high degree of homogeneity across the financial systems of member states, the strengths and weaknesses of different financial systems have been brought to the fore of policy discussions. Section 12.4 considers the implications of both empirical observations and theoretical models for the relative merits of securities markets and banks in promoting economic growth.

12.2   The Financing of Industry in Eight Countries

There are two sources of information available for studies of aggregate corporate financing patterns in different countries. The first is national flow-of-funds statements. These are records of flows between different sectors of an economy and between domestic and overseas residents. The relevant statement for this exercise is flows to and from nonfinancial enterprises. The second source is company accounts. These are constructed on an individual firm basis but are often aggregated or extrapolated to industry or economy levels.

Both sources have their merits and deficiencies. In theory, flow-of-funds statistics provide a comprehensive coverage of transactions between sectors. Company accounts are only available for a sample, often quite small, of a country's total corporate sector. However, the data that are employed in company accounts are usually more reliable than flow-of-funds. As Appendix A describes, flow-of-funds are constructed from a variety of different sources that are rarely consistent. As a consequence, statistical adjustments are required to reconcile entries.

As described in Mayer (1987, 1988) and Appendix B to this paper, the methodology employed in the Centre for Economic Policy Research Study of the Financing of Industry differs in several respects from that used by previous researchers. Greater emphasis is placed on flows of finance instead of stocks. Figures are recorded on a net (of accumulation of equivalent financial assets) as well as a gross funding basis. Financing proportions are aggregated over different time periods using a weighted as well as a simple average of individual years' proportions. Appendix B argues that these procedures achieve a greater degree of international comparability than has been available hitherto.

Tables 12.1, 12.2, and 12.3 report weighted and unweighted average financing proportions for the five countries of the international study (France, Germany, Japan, the United Kingdom, and the United States) and for Canada, Finland, and Italy using flow-of-funds statistics. Table 12.1 reports unweighted averages of net financing as a proportion of capital expenditures and stock building. Table 12.2 shows weighted averages of net financing using straight line depreciation over 16 years from 1970 to 1985. Table 12.3 records unweighted averages of gross financing as a proportion of total sources of finance.[2] The weighted and unweighted averages are similar.

Table 12.1   **Unweighted Average Net Financing of Nonfinancial Enterprises, 1970–85[a]**

	Canada[b]	Finland[c]	France	Germany[d]	Italy[e]	Japan[f]	United Kingdom[g]	United States[h]
Retentions	76.4	64.4	61.4	70.9	51.9	57.9	102.4	85.9
Capital transfers	.0	.2	2.0	8.6	7.7	.0	4.1	.0
Short-term securities	−.8	3.7	−.1	−.1	−1.3	N.A.	1.7	.4
Loans	15.2	28.1	37.3	12.1	27.7	50.4	7.6	24.4
Trade credit	−4.4	−1.4	−.6	−2.1	.0	−11.2	−1.1	−1.4
Bonds	8.5	2.8	1.6	−1.0	1.6	2.1	−1.1	11.6
Shares	2.5	−.1	6.3	.6	8.2	4.6	−3.3	1.1
Other	1.3	7.4	−1.4	10.9	1.0	−3.8	3.2	−16.9
Statistical adjustment	1.2	−5.0	−6.4	.0	3.2	N.A.	−13.4	−5.1
Total	99.9	100.1	100.1	99.9	100.0	100.0	100.1	100.0

Source: OECD Financial Statistics.

Note: Numbers are percentages.

[a] Net financing is shown as a proportion of capital expenditures and stock building. Gross financing is a proportion of total sources.

[b] For Canada, mortgages are included in loans, foreign investments are included in other, and capital transfers are included in retentions.

[c] Data on Finland refer to the period 1969–84. Errors in the OECD statistics have required that the statistical adjustment be altered as follows: 1971, DM 2 billion and 1973, +DM 89 billion.

[d] There is no statistical adjustment in German accounts. Funds placed with insurance companies and building and loans associations are included in loans.

[e] The Italian statistical adjustment was reduced by Lit2,070 billion in 1974 to make accounts balance. Trade credit is not recorded as a separate item in Italian flow-of-funds.

[f] Japanese flow-of-funds do not report retentions. The ratio of external to internal financing of Japanese enterprises has been obtained by applying proportions recorded in aggregate company accounts for the period 1972–84, as shown in tables 12.4 and 12.5. The Japanese figures therefore have to be treated with particular caution. Short-term securities are included in bonds.

[g] United Kingdom statistics refer to private enterprises only; were public enterprise to be included then entries would read as follows: retentions, 91.9; capital transfers, 5.7; short-term securities, 1.3; loans, 11.7; trade credit, −.7; bonds, −.9, shares, −2.5; other, 2.1; statistical adjustment, −8.5.

[h] The following modifications were made to the U.S. statistical adjustment to make accounts balance (in millions of dollars): 1970, −1; 1971, −3; 1973, +3; 1975, +1; 1976, −2; 1979, +2; 1981, −1; 1982, +1; 1983, −2; 1984, −1. Capital transfers are included under retentions in U.S. accounts. Acquisitions of central government short-term securities are not shown separately from bonds and have been subtracted from issues of bonds in table 12.2 below.

Observation 1.   Retentions are the dominant source of finance in all countries.

The United Kingdom has the highest proportion of retentions (107% excluding public enterprises, 97% including public enterprises on a weighted net financing basis). Italy has the lowest, but, even here, over half of investment in physical assets and stocks is funded from retentions. This is not just a consequence of the procedure of netting uses of finance from sources. Even on a gross basis U.K. corporations obtain just over 70% of their total sources from retentions and U.S. corporations just under 70%.

Table 12.2   Weighted Average Net Financing of Nonfinancial Enterprises 1970–85

	Canada	Finland	France	Germany	Italy	Japan	United Kingdom[a]	United States
Retentions	78.1	64.2	N.A.	72.6	N.A.	N.A.	107.2	89.2
Capital transfers	.0	.2	N.A.	9.4	N.A.	N.A.	2.7	.0
Short-term securities	-1.2	4.1	N.A.	-.1	N.A.	N.A.	2.8	1.0
Loans	15.9	27.8	N.A.	12.0	N.A.	N.A.	2.2	25.4
Trade credit	-3.7	-1.8	N.A.	-2.5	N.A.	N.A.	-1.7	-1.4
Bonds	7.2	3.2	N.A.	-1.9	N.A.	N.A.	-2.3	11.7
Shares	2.2	-1.4	N.A.	.6	N.A.	N.A.	-3.6	-2.8
Other	1.0	6.5	N.A.	9.9	N.A.	N.A.	3.5	-17.2
Statistical adjustment	.5	-3.0	N.A.	.0	N.A.	N.A.	-10.8	-5.9
Total	100.0	99.8	N.A.	100.0	N.A.	N.A.	100.0	100.1

Weights Used Above (The Product of Revaluation and Depreciation Factors)

	1970	1971	1972	1973	1974	1975	1976	1977	1978	1979	1980	1981	1982	1983	1984	1985
Canada	.20	.39	.55	.69	.74	.78	.84	.88	.91	.89	.89	.89	.89	.93	.97	1.00
Finland	.29	.52	.70	.85	.90	.86	.87	.91	.91	.98	1.01	.94	.97	.97	.99	1.00
Germany	.11	.22	.32	.40	.46	.53	.59	.76	.71	.75	.78	.81	.87	.92	.96	1.00
United Kingdom	.32	.58	.79	.89	.90	.91	.93	.95	.95	.90	.87	.89	.93	.97	.99	1.00
United States	.17	.33	.47	.59	.62	.67	.73	.77	.78	.80	.79	.78	.81	.89	.94	1.00

Source: OECD Financial Statistics.

Note: Numbers are percentages.

[a]United Kingdom statistics refer to private enterprise. If public enterprise were to be included, then Retentions, 97.5, capital transfers, 4.2; short-term securities, 2.1; loans, 5.9; trade credit, -1.1; bonds, -1.7; shares, -2.6; other, 2.4; statistical adjustment, -6.5.

Table 12.3   Unweighted Average Gross Financing of Nonfinancial Enterprises, 1970–85

	Canada	Finland	France	Germany	Italy	Japan	United Kingdom[a]	United States
Retentions	54.2	42.1	44.1	55.2	38.5	33.7	72.0	66.9
Capital transfers	.0	.1	1.4	6.7	5.7	.0	2.9	.0
Short-term securities	1.4	2.5	.0	.0	.1	N.A.	2.3	1.4
Loans	12.8	27.2	41.5	21.1	38.6	40.7	21.4	23.1
Trade credit	8.6	17.2	4.7	2.2	.0	18.3	2.8	8.4
Bonds	6.1	1.8	2.3	.7	2.4	3.1	.8	9.7
Shares	11.9	5.6	10.6	2.1	10.8	3.5	4.9	.8
Other	4.1	6.9	.0	11.9	1.6	.7	2.2	-6.1
Statistical adjustment	.8	-3.5	-4.7	.0	2.3	N.A.	-9.4	-4.1
Total	99.9	99.9	99.9	99.9	99.9	100.0	99.9	100.1

Source: OECD Financial Statistics.

Note: Numbers are percentages.

[a]With the inclusion of public enterprise, U.K. statistics would be: retentions, 67.9; capital transfers, 4.2; short-term securities, 1.9; loans, 22.4; trade credit, 3.6; bonds, .6; shares, 3.9; other, 1.9; statistical adjustment, −6.4.

Observation 2.   There are some marked variations in self-financing ratios across countries. In the United Kingdom and the United States, more than three-quarters of investment is funded from retentions. In Finland, France, Japan, and Italy, appreciably more is raised externally. Canada and Germany lie somewhere between the two groups.

Observation 3.   In no country do companies raise a substantial amount of finance from securities markets.

Summing together short-term securities, bonds, and shares reveals that the largest amount raised in securities markets is 19% in Canada on a gross basis (i.e., as a proportion of total sources) and 13% on a net basis in the United States. In Germany and the United Kingdom, net amounts raised from these three sources were negative and gross amounts were only 3% in Germany and 8% in the United Kingdom. Only in Canada and the United States do bond markets raise a significant proportion of external finance for industry.

Observation 4.   Banks are the dominant source of external finance in all countries.

Observation 5.   Bank finance is particularly pronounced in France, Italy, and Japan. It represents a surprisingly small proportion of German corporate financing.

Bank finance accounts for approximately 40% of gross sources in France, Italy, and Japan. In Germany, the United Kingdom, and the United States, it only contributes around 20% of total sources. Netting off deposits, this falls to 8% in the United Kingdom. Rather strikingly, then, there is no support from these figures for the commonly held view that German banks contribute a substantial amount to the financing of their industry (see Carrington and Edwards 1979).

Comparing the gross and net financing tables demonstrates some of the problems associated with interpreting gross funding figures. In some countries, trade credit appears to be an important source of finance, in particular in Finland (see table 12.3). But much of this is intracorporate sector and does not contribute to total net financing. Table 12.1 correctly records that, overall, nonfinancial enterprises are *suppliers* of credit to other sectors, in particular to consumers.

Comparing tables 12.1 and 12.3 reveals that U.K. enterprises have been particularly heavy purchasers of financial assets. This has been primarily in the form of deposits, but purchases of shares have also been large. Acquisitions of financial assets in the United States mainly take the form of intrasector flows of trade credit and purchases of domestic shares and overseas assets.

The quality of some flow-of-funds data is questionable. Statistical adjustments reveal inconsistencies between series, and the coverage of some items, in particular trade credit, is known to be inadequate. U.K. data are particularly deficient in this respect. Table 12.1 recorded the fact that the statistical adjustment averaged 13% of gross investment over the period 1970–85—approximately twice that of any other country.

Table 12.4   **Unweighted Average Net Financing of Non-financial Corporations**

	Finland	France	Japan	United States
Period	1975–84	1976–84	1972–84	1970–85
Retentions	66.4	66.9	57.9	87.9
Capital transfers	1.8	1.2	N.A.	.0
Short-term securities	3.1	} 36.1	N.A.	.0
Loans	34.7		46.2	10.8
Trade credit	−7.2	2.5	−8.6	−2.5
Bonds	1.1	} −6.7	} .2	15.8
Shares	−2.4			−1.3
Other	4.8	.0	2.4	−3.9
Statistical adjustment	−2.4	.0	1.9	−6.9
Total	99.9	100.0	100.0	100.0

Source: Company accounts as reported in OECD Financial Statistics.
Note: Numbers are percentages.

Table 12.5   **Unweighted Average Gross Financing of Nonfinancial Corporations**

	Finland	France	Japan	United States
Period	1975–84	1976–84	1972–84	1970–85
Retentions	41.3	36.1	33.7	64.6
Capital transfers	1.0	.6	N.A.	.0
Short-term securities	2.2	} 31.3	N.A.	1.5
Loans	34.5		36.4	12.5
Trade credit	13.0	25.4	15.0	10.4
Bonds	.6	} 6.6	2.1	12.5
Shares	4.3		4.9	4.0
Other	4.6	.0	7.8	−.2
Statistical adjustment	−1.6	.0	.0	−5.2
Total	99.1	100.1	99.9	99.8

Tables 12.4 and 12.5 repeat the financing proportion exercise using company accounting data where they are available. There is a strong similarity in the financing patterns that emerge from the two sources of data. However, there are a few differences. Bank loans are more significant in Finland but much less significant in the United States than suggested by the flow-of-funds data. Bonds are even more significant in the United States as a source of finance for industry than flow-of-funds data indicate.

Average financing ratios, therefore, look similar for the two sources of data. However, nothing has been said to date about the extent to which these proportions have changed over time or the correlation between different forms of finance. Flow-of-funds data are too short (16 observations per country for the series standardized by the OECD) to provide accurate guidance on either of these questions. In contrast, company accounting information has been collected for nearly 40 years in the United Kingdom.

The graphs in figure 12.1 and 12.2 are based on aggregate company accounting information. In interpreting the graphs it should be borne in mind that there was a significant change in sampling procedures in 1977.[3] The graphs suggest the following observations:

Observation 6.   U.K. investment has been consistently financed from retentions (91% on average). Bank finance has contributed close to zero (3% on average) on a net basis.[4]

Observation 7.   There is a strong inverse relation between the proportion of expenditure financed from retentions and bank credit.

Confirmation for observation 7 comes from an examination of correlations between different forms of finance. Table 12.6 records the correlation between retentions and other sources of finance. Retentions are strongly inversely correlated with trade credit and bank credit on both a gross and net basis. The fact that this is true of gross as well as net bank credit indicates that short-term financing requirements are satisfied by raising bank loans as well as reducing cash balances.

Despite only having a short time series available for other countries, table 12.7 reveals a remarkable consistency in this pattern of correlations. Loans and trade credit are inversely related to retentions in all countries. On a net

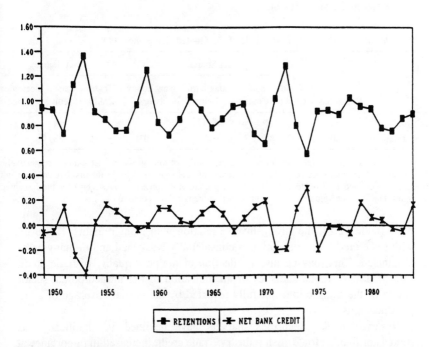

Fig. 12.1:   Retentions and net bank credit in the United Kingdom (proportions of physical investment)
Source: Goudie and Meeks (1986).

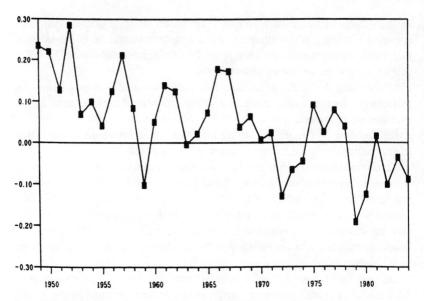

Fig. 12.2: Net issue of securities in the United Kingdom (proportion of physical investment)
Source: Goudie and Meeks (1986).

Table 12.6   Correlation Matrix for U.K. Quoted Companies, 1949–77

		Gross Source				Net Source		
	Retentions	Trade Credit	Bank Credit	Long-term Debt	New Equity Issues	Trade Credit	Bank Credit	Securities Issued
Investment	.23	− .17	.13	− .11	− .08	.66	.15	− .41
Retentions	1.00	− .73	− .73	− .07	.03	− .51	− .83	− .23

Note: (I) Gross and net sources are defined as a percentage of total gross and net sources, respectively. Investment and retentions are defined as a percentage of total gross sources for the first five columns and retentions is defined as a percentage of total net sources (i.e., physical investment) for the last three columns. The absolute value of investment is used in the last three columns.

basis (table 12.8), the strong inverse relation with loans remains. However, with trade credit the correlation is considerably weakened and in many cases eliminated. This may be just a reflection of the poor quality of trade credit data in flow-of-funds statistics or an indication of the intracorporate sector nature of the transaction, not fully revealed by the partial coverage of company accounts.

Observation 8. Securities markets have declined in significance as sources of finance for British industry. Trade credit increased in importance at the end of the 1960s and early 1970s.[5]

There is no evidence of financial innovation and deregulation being associated with a growth in the contribution of market sources of finance.[6] Cross-sectional evidence suggests that high retention proportions in the United Kingdom are not merely a consequence of low industrial growth. Two relatively high growth industrial sectors (chemicals and allied firms, and electrical engineering) recorded financing proportions that were equal to or in excess of those in other industries (table 12.9).

However, there are marked differences in financing proportions of different size of firms within industries. Since 1977, the U.K. Department of Trade and Industry has categorized firms by two size groups: (1) large and (2) medium and small companies.[7] Table 12.10 below records the following:[8]

Observation 9. Small- and medium-sized firms are considerably more reliant on external finance than large firms. A smaller proportion of small- than large-company finance comes from securities markets.

Confirmation for the greater role of banks in small company financing comes from an examination of stock as well as flow proportions in table 12.11. However, it should be borne in mind that pre- and post-1977 data are not directly comparable.

Observation 10. Bank (and short-term) finance account for approximately two-thirds of U.K. companies' total debt but more than five-sixth of small companies' total debt.

These ten observations, or stylized facts, warrant explanation.

Table 12.7   Correlations between Proportions of Retentions and Proportions of Other Forms of Gross Finance

Proportion of	Canada	Finland	France	Germany	Italy	Japan	United Kingdom	United States
Short-term securities	.05	− .58	.00	.02	.34	N.A.	− .11	− .31
Loans	− .78	− .43	− .37	− .59	− .74	N.A.	− .73	− .45
Trade credit	− .40	− .33	− .37	− .36	N.A.	N.A.	− .69	− .84
Bonds	.16	− .14	.43	− .55	− .32	N.A.	− .34	.42
Shares	− .01	.26	− .25	.05	− .12	N.A.	.45	− .20

Table 12.8   Correlations between Proportions of Retentions and Proportions of Other Forms of Finance

Proportion of	Canada	Finland	France	Germany	Italy	Japan	United Kingdom	United States
Short-term securities	− .54	− .67	− .40	− .01	− .52	N.A.	− .25	− .40
Loans	− .78	− .47	− .45	− .57	− .88	N.A.	− .70	− .67
Trade credit	.03	− .40	− .41	− .07	N.A.	N.A.	.02	.01
Bonds	− .30	.12	.13	− .76	− .03	N.A.	− .36	.02
Shares	.72	− .17	− .47	.32	.05	N.A.	− .10	− .09

Table 12.9   Financing Proportions in Two Industries in the United Kingdom

	Gross Proportions			Net Proportions		
	Total Sample	Chemicals and Allied Industries	Electrical Engineering	Total Sample	Chemicals and Allied Industries	Electrical Engineering
Retentions	59.1	62.7	59.2	91.0	89.7	117.3
Trade credit	17.5	12.7	17.1	1.5	−2.2	−11.9
Bank credit	5.6	3.2	1.6	2.7	−2.2	−20.4
Long-term liabilities	6.8	13.3	6.7	4.8	14.7	15.0
Issues of Shares	10.9	8.0	15.4			
Total	99.9	99.9	100.0	100.0	100.0	100.0

Source: Goudie and Meeks (1986); Business Monitors (M3).
Note: All averages are unweighted. The total sample refers to the period 1949–84; chemicals and allied and electrical engineering industries relate to the period 1949–82.

Table 12.10   Financing Proportions of Large, and Medium- and Small-Sized Companies in the United Kingdom: Average, 1977–1982

	Retentions	Banks, Short-term Loans and Trade Creditors	Issues of Shares and Long-term Debt	Other Sources
All companies:				
Large	70.9	23.2	5.7	.2
Medium and small	52.6	45.7	1.3	.3
Chemical companies:				
Large	70.5	20.2	7.6	1.6
Medium and small	50.3	50.5	3.8	−4.7
Electrical companies:				
Large	79.4	19.4	3.1	−1.9
Medium and small	60.4	37.4	2.4	.1

Source: Business Monitors (M3).

12.3   Alternative Theories of Corporate Finance

There are five classes of theory to which one might turn for an explanation of the above financing patterns: an irrelevance proposition, transaction costs, taxation, information and control theories. These will be considered in turn.

12.3.1   Irrelevance

The most widely cited theory of corporate finance is the Modigliani and Miller proposition. This states that in the presence of perfect and complete capital markets and in the absence of taxation, corporate valuations, and costs of capital are independent of firms' capital structures.

At face value, this proposition suggests no underlying determinant of corporate capital structure: the financing of industry is a matter of indifference—

an accident of history and a product of random influences. However, the stability of financing patterns over time and countries that has been noted above argues strongly against the thesis of indifference. The 10 stylized observations warrant explanation. The indifference proposition does not provide it and cannot, on its own, be treated as a serious basis for explaining international patterns of corporate finance.

12.3.2   Transaction Costs

Combined with transaction costs or taxation, the theory is much more powerful. The most immediate implication of introducing transaction costs is to establish a preference for retention over external finance. This is quite consistent with observation 1.

However, the United Kingdom and the United States are generally regarded as possessing the most highly developed and efficient financial systems of any country in the world. This proposition rests uneasily alongside the observation that they have the lowest external financing proportions of any of the countries in the study (observation 2).

Of course, this may merely reflect a low demand for external finance. But even the composition of external finance does not correspond with the predictions of a transaction cost theory. The most striking case of international variations in transaction costs comes from observations on equity markets. In some countries, stock markets are very small. For example, in France and Germany, less than 500 companies are quoted. This compares with 1,700 in Japan and 2,000 in the United Kingdom. French and German market capitalizations were 20% of gross domestic product (GDP) at the end of 1986 as against nearly 90% in Japan and the United Kingdom and 50% in the United States. But, over the period of this study, the United Kingdom and the United States raised, at best, approximately the same amount of (and probably in practice rather less) new equity finance for their industries as France and Japan. It is not merely a matter of transaction costs being a few percentage

Table 12.11   **Ratio of Stock of Bank and Short-term Loans to Total Short- and Long-term Debt: Average 1977–82 (in percentages)**

All companies:	66
Large companies	63
Medium and small companies	87
Chemical companies:	47
Large chemical companies	46
Medium and small chemical companies	93
Electrical companies:	73
Large electrical companies	66
Medium and small electrical companies	94

Source: Business Monitors (M3).
Note: Bank loans relate to both short- and long-term loans. The table is not therefore informative about maturity of debts.

points higher in some countries than others but a difference between companies having very general access to securities markets in some countries and
very limited access elsewhere.

Turning to bond finance, the surprising feature is how little is raised in a
low-cost, unregulated Eurobond market by European corporations in relation
to domestic issues by North American firms. Over the period of this study
British firms were net purchasers (or repurchasers of bonds) and Canadian
firms significant net issuers. In contrast, according to one report (OECD
1989), direct costs of issuing bonds were relatively high in Canada (1.7% for
large issues) in 1982/83 and low in the United Kingdom (1.1% for large issues).

Finally the notion that ratios of external to internal finance merely reflect
investment demands is undermined by comparisons of low- and high-growth
sectors. Two of the highest-growth sectors (electronics and pharmaceuticals)
had the highest retention proportions.[9] In any event, transaction costs are
probably in general swamped by tax considerations.

12.3.3   Taxation

The first point to note about taxation is that in virtually every country of
this study (with the possible exception of Finland) debt finance has been favored over equity. This stands in marked contrast to the universal preference
for equity finance (including retentions) over debt finance (observation 1).

More generally, table 12.12 records a poor relation between tax incentives
to employ different forms of finance in the eight countries of the study and
actual financing proportions. On the left-hand side, table 12.12 ranks the tax
incentive to use debt in preference to retentions, new equity issues in preference to retentions and new equity in preference to debt. Countries at the top
have the highest incentive to use the first form of finance in each case. On the
right-hand side, it reports actual financing proportions from table 12.1 of this
paper.

The most striking country in the first part of table 12.12 is Germany, which
has the highest incentive to use debt in relation to retentions and the second
lowest use of debt relative to retentions. The United Kingdom has the lowest
debt-to-retentions ratio and the third highest tax incentive. The picture is not
very much better for the ratio of new equity to retentions where Germany now
has the third lowest new equity proportion and the highest incentive and the
United Kingdom still has the lowest proportion and the fourth highest incentive.

It might be objected that comparisons of internal and external financing
proportions and incentives are distorted by transaction costs and investment
requirements. The third part of the table may therefore be regarded as more
instructive. There the most striking case is Finland, which has the highest
incentive to use new equity in preference to debt and the second lowest proportion. The United Kingdom also has a remarkably low new equity propor-

Table 12.12   **Comparison of Ranking of Eight Countries' Tax Incentives to Employ Different Forms of Finance with Average Financing Ratios over the Period 1970–85**

Tax Incentive[a]	Financing Ratio[b]
Debt/retentions:	
Germany	Japan
Japan	France
United Kingdom	Italy
Canada	Finland
Italy	United States
France	Canada
United States	Germany
Finland	United Kingdom
New equity/retentions:	
Germany	Italy
Italy	France
Canada	Japan
United Kingdom	Canada
France	United States
Finland	Germany
Japan	Finland
United States	United Kingdom
New equity/debt:	
Finland	Italy
Italy	France
Canada	Canada
France	Japan
United Kingdom	Germany
Germany	United States
United States	Finland
Japan	United Kingdom

Source: OECD (1986) and table 12.1 of this paper.

[a]Tax incentives are based on the approach described in King and Fullerton (1984). The OECD calculations are based on the "fixed-p" case and the results reported above relate to "actual inflation." Tax incentives are computed as the ratio: $\dfrac{(1 - t_i)}{(1 - t_j)}$, where t_i is the effective tax rate on source of finance i. Tax incentives relate to tax exempt institutional investors and investment in equipment.

[b]Financing proportions are based on table 12.1 in this paper, that is, unweighted average net financing from flow-of-funds sources. Debt is defined as the sum of short-term securities, loans, trade credit, and bonds.

tion in the face of a high incentive resulting from its imputation system of taxation.

There are several objections that can be raised against this type of comparison. There are well-known problems in comparing tax incentives across countries. The figures on which table 12.12 are based come from an OECD extension of the King-Fullerton (1984) study. These derive tax incentives created by both corporate and personal taxation on the basis of a Modigliani and Miller (as against a Miller) equilibrium model of the economy. They do not take account of cross-border tax incentives to locate, finance, and invest in different countries, and they have been found to be very sensitive to respecifications of the model. In addition, the tax incentives in the OECD study relate to investment in equipment, not structures, and tax-exempt institutions, not households. In fact, the ranking of incentives is virtually identical for structures and equipment but is sensitive to the assumed tax rate of investors.[10] Finally, the tax incentives refer to one year, 1983, while the financing proportions are averages over the period of the study, 1970–85. Averaging over the period 1982–84 revealed that the ranking of external to internal financing proportions is similar around the date of measurement of tax incentives. Despite all these possible sources of inaccuracy, there would have to be a remarkable level of mismeasurement for taxation to provide a credible explanation for observed financing proportions.

12.3.4   Information Theories

At first sight, information theories appear to be quite consistent with many of the results reported in this paper. For example, Myers's (1984) pecking-order hypothesis suggests that riskless securities (debt) are used in preference to risky (new equity) and retentions are used in preference to external sources of finance (observations 1 and 3).

However, the thesis on which the aversion to new equity finance is based (Myers and Majluf 1984) is an insider-outsider model in which owners are raising finance from outside investors. It says nothing about the preference of owners between subscribing themselves in the form of new equity issues and increasing retentions by cutting dividends. Since rights issues are frequently employed in Europe (almost all new equity issues are rights issues in France and the United Kingdom), the sale of equity to external investors does not arise in many of the countries of this study.

Furthermore there is little support for Myers's prediction that equity finance is employed at high levels of gearing when debt becomes risky. Even in Japan and Italy, where gearing levels have been high, there is little new equity finance (observation 5).

Some aspects of international patterns of corporate finance appear consistent with information models. Observation 3, that bond finance is significant in Canada and the United States, is consistent with the unusually large number of bond-rated companies in these countries. In contrast, there are just 30 bond-rated nonfinancial corporations in the United Kingdom, 14 in France, and 4 in Germany.

However, if anything, this relation between bond finance and ratings raises something of a puzzle. If it is possible to establish institutions that perform a pure information-gathering exercise, then what is the role of banks? Information theory cannot explain why there is a clear preference for bank finance in most countries (observation 4) and why bank finance remains important in the United States.

On a similar score, an analysis of credit evaluation procedures of banks in different countries reveals that the information content of banks is similar in different countries. There may be two exceptions to this: Germany and Japan. Both countries have close relations between banks and industry. In Germany, banks frequently have representatives on the boards of large firms (Edwards and Fischer 1990). In Japan there is regular interchange of personnel between banks and firms (see Corbett 1987). But in Germany an unusually small proportion of corporate sector finance comes from banks, while Japan has an unusually large proportion (observation 5).

Information deficiencies do not provide a convincing explanation for observed international patterns of corporate finance on their own. There is an aspect of the relation between institutions and firms that information theories fail to capture. The next subsection suggests that this has to do with control rather than monitoring of firms.

12.3.5   Control theories

The previous subsection has noted that agent-principal problems can arise where information asymmetries exist. Imperfect information is one but not the only explanation for why agent-principal problems may arise. Problems of verifiability and enforceability of contracts as well as observability may undermine the writing and implementation of complete contracts. Alternatively, writing complete contracts may simply be too expensive.

In the absence of complete contracts, the allocation of control over the deployment of assets matters. Those who control the employment of assets should be residual claimants. The amount of finance that those who are not in control are willing to provide will be dependent on the amount that they can realize if they do take control (see Mayer 1989a).

Control theory is most closely associated with Philippe Aghion and Patrick Bolton.[11] They argue that the amount of debt finance that a firm will choose is dependent on the point at which it is optimal for control to be transferred from entrepreneur to creditor. Thus external financing is dependent on the relative productivity of creditors and entrepreneurs in particular states of nature.

More generally, control theory suggests that external financing is dependent on (see Mayer 1989b): (i) the managerial ability of creditors; (ii) the nature of assets (the higher their realizable value, the higher is the creditor's reservation valuation and the greater is the amount of external finance that is available); (iii) the costs of coordinating creditors and the costs of bankruptcy and liquidation; and (iv) other nonfinancial controls that investors can exert on firms. More specifically, control theories lead to the following predictions.

PREDICTION 1.   Gearing levels will be high where the value of assets under creditor management is high.

PREDICTION 2.   Assets that are not specific to their current employment will attract more external finance.

PREDICTION 3.   Where the costs of organizing external control are high, there will be little external finance.

PREDICTION 4. The relation between control and finance is weakened where interests of investor and manager do not diverge.

The observations of the previous section can be assessed in relation to these predictions. The first five observations on the dominant role of retentions, low contributions from securities markets, and the importance of banks in some countries are consistent with predictions 1 and 3. If external intervention is costly because creditors are either poor managers or difficult to organize, then own finance will dominate (observation 1) and be particularly large in countries in which management and finance are separated (observation 2). Creditors that are dispersed and difficult to organize will play an especially small role (observation 3). Instead, finance will come from intermediaries (observation 4) that are closely integrated into their corporate sectors (observation 5).

The relation between finance and control is particularly evident in the provision of working capital. The main providers of working capital (banks and trade creditors—observation 7) also have the most direct claim on assets in the event of default (fixed and floating charges). The ability to trigger these claims automatically with little direct managerial input means that institutions can smooth cash flows even where their longer term involvement is small (comparison of observations 2 and 7).

Predictions 2 and 3 help to account for observations 9 and 10. Small and newly formed companies have a low intangible (goodwill) to tangible valuation ratio. Therefore a smaller proportion of their assets are specific to their current employment, and investors can realize a larger proportion of their ongoing value in the event of default. As a consequence, the external financing ratio of small companies is higher than average (observation 9) and finance is provided by investors who can take control at low cost (observation 10). By way of a corollary, it is worth noting that capital market deficiencies will be particularly pronounced in firms with a high proportion of intangible assets (i.e. companies involved in substantial research and development (R&D) programs) and few own resources. This is consistent with the Schumpetarian hypothesis that product market dominance is required to provide finance for R&D.

As for the other two observations, the apparent constancy of financing patterns (observation 6) supports the emphasis that is placed on structural factors (quality of management, nature of assets, and costs of creditor coordination) by control models. The decline in the proportion of certain classes of external finance (observation 8) probably then reflects a shift in the balance of corporate and investor control as the complexity of corporate organizational arrangements increases in the United Kingdom.

Observations on international patterns of corporate finance are therefore suggestive of the relevance of control theories of finance. However, there is one observation that at least at first sight appears inconsistent with control theories. Despite having a banking system that is closely integrated with its corporate sector, German industry raises a comparatively modest proportion of its finance in the form of loans (observation 5).[12] Prediction 4 was that the relation between finance and control would break down where investor and management interests do not diverge. This description, it is suggested, is applicable to German bank-investor relations.

Schonfield (1965), in his classic account of the German financial system, saw banks as the prefects of German industry. Their power derived from their equity investments, their proxy votes, and their representation on supervisory boards (the *Aufsichtsrat*). Knight (1988) views the relation as more advisory than dictatorial and echoes the sentiments of German bankers when he concludes, "The evidence then points to the banks as sometimes providing companies with independent, well-informed and well-connected nonexecutive chairmen able to make a powerful contribution to the board's performance" (15). Consensus or command, the need for financial control is lessened by the other instruments that German banks have at their disposal.

12.4 Conclusions and Policy Implications

A quite striking observation to emerge from the empirical analysis is that in no country do securities markets contribute a large proportion of corporate sector financing. In some countries, the average net contribution was close to or less than zero. Equity markets are particularly deficient in this respect. That is not to say that equity markets do not perform an important function. They may promote allocative efficiency by providing prices that guide the allocation of resources or productive efficiency through reallocating existing resources via, for example, the takeover process. But in terms of aggregate corporate sector funding, their function appears limited. Instead, a majority of external finance comes from banks. Why?

Neither transaction costs nor taxation were found to provide adequate descriptions of corporate financing patterns in different countries. One interpretation for the preponderance of bank finance is that financial intermediaries perform a central function in diminishing one of the most serious deficiencies of financial markets: asymmetries in information. According to this view, banks play an important role in collecting and processing information that markets are unable to do or can do only at high cost.

There is almost certainly a large element of truth in this story. But the analysis of the section 12.3 suggested that imperfect information is not an adequate description on its own. Information gathering can be quite effectively performed by institutions other than banks. Furthermore, the distinguishing feature of banks in different countries does not appear to be the nature of or the way in which they collect information.

Instead, it is the extent to which and the form in which institutions influence the activities of firms that appear to show marked variations across institutions and countries. Is control direct in the form of representation on the boards of firms or indirect in the form of takeovers? Do financial institutions or individual shareholders initiate changes in control? How easy is it to form coalitions of shareholders or bond holders and how serious are free-rider problems of control?

The analysis in the previous section suggested that control theories provide a good basis for understanding the 10 stylized observations of this paper. They emphasize the managerial functions of financial institutions and suggest that the central role of banks comes from their ability to intervene and take control at comparatively low cost.

If this is right, then the implication of both the empirical observation of a preponderance of external finance coming from banks and control models of corporate finance is that banks may be superior to markets in promoting economic development and growth. This may be particularly true in the early stages of development of both economies and firms before reputations have been established and adequate incentives exist to bring borrowers' and lenders' interests into line. In the longer term intermediaries may be less central to the development of firms.[13] But in the early stages of the growth of firms and economies an efficient banking system may be an essential requirement for expansion. During these periods, securities markets are unlikely to be effective substitutes.

Appendix A
Alternative Sources of Data

There are two sources of information on corporate financing: flow-of-funds statistics and company accounts. Company accounts are available on an individual firm basis; flow-of-funds are aggregated across sectors. For this purpose, the relevant flow-of-funds sector is nonfinancial enterprises.

The primary advantage of flow-of-funds data is that their coverage is comprehensive. In contrast, company accounts are only available for a limited number of firms and samples are frequently a small proportion (by number) of all enterprises. On the other hand, definitions of enterprise sectors differ across countries. In theory, Standard National Accounting (SNA) conventions stipulate that private and public corporations should be included in the nonfinancial enterprise sector. Unincorporated businesses should be included in the household, not the nonfinancial enterprise sector. In practice, as table 12A.1 records, only Canada abides by the SNA definition.

The major problem with flow-of-funds data is that they are collected from a variety of different sources. For example, in the United Kingdom, profits are largely based on tax returns to the Inland Revenue and loans and securities

Table 12A.1   Definitions of Nonfinancial Enterprise Sectors

Country	Definition
Canada	As for SNA
Finland	Includes unincorporated enterprises
France	Excludes large public corporations
Germany	Includes unincorporated enterprises
Italy	Excludes some public corporations
Japan	Excludes large public corporations
United Kingdom	Excludes public corporations
United States	Includes unincorporated enterprises, excludes public corporations

issued on returns by financial institutions to the Bank of England. As a consequence, sources and uses do not, in general, balance and a statistical adjustment is required to reconcile entries.[14]

A fundamental distinction between flow-of-funds statistics and company accounts is that the former only relate to domestic activities while the latter are constructed on a worldwide basis including foreign subsidiaries. Thus issues of bond and equity securities are restricted to those made on domestic markets in flow-of-funds accounts but include issues on all markets in company accounts. Company accounts are therefore more suitable for analyzing how different countries' corporate sectors fund themselves, but flow-of-funds allow the contribution of a domestic sector's financial system to be identified.

Overall there is a presumption that company accounts are more accurate than flow-of-funds. However, company accounting analyses are lengthy exercises, frequently involving the manipulation of very large data banks. As yet comprehensive information is only available on the United Kingdom. Even here, there are serious discontinuities in aggregate series. For example, in 1977 the sample of U.K. company accounts was extended from firms quoted on the stock exchange to a representative sample of all companies.

For other countries, aggregate company accounts constructed by the OECD have had to be used. These suffer from similar discrepancies in the definitions of sectors to flow-of-funds. Eventually, comprehensive accounting information on the five countries of the study will be available which will provide a greater degree of comparability than has been available to date. In the meantime, more emphasis is placed in this article on flow-of-funds sources. The relative merits of company accounts and flow-of-funds are summarized in Table 12A.2.

Table 12A.2   A Comparison of Flow-of-Funds and Company Accounts as
Descriptions of the Funding of Industry

	Flow-of-Funds	Company Accounts
Consistency in definitions of corporate sectors	Can be poor	Own aggregation is possible
Coverage of companies	Comprehensive	Limited, sometimes very limited
Coverage of items	Domestic	Global
Internal consistency	Poor	Good
Quality of data	Can be very poor	Good

Appendix B
Derivation of Financial Statistics

This study differs from previous international comparisons in both the data it uses and the way in which those data are presented.

The Data

Most existing international comparisons use stock data from company balance sheets to derive gearing levels. Two serious objections have been raised against this approach. First, in the absence of inflation corrections, capital stock and equity valuations can be substantially underrecorded. In Japan revaluations of company accounts are uncommon and in Germany they are forbidden by law. As Aoki (1984) has noted, the failure of Japanese accounts to revalue assets, in particular land, has resulted in Japanese gearing levels being considerably overstated. Second, book values of assets and reserves are sensitive to depreciation schedules.[15] Accounting conventions on depreciation vary appreciably across countries, partly in response to differences in corporate tax regimes.

Problems with accounting valuations have led several authors to advocate the use of market valuations. However, consideration of the use of market valuations suggests a more fundamental objection to stock measures. Market valuations respond not only to inflows and outflows of new financial resources but also to changes in valuations of existing resources. Valuations serve many useful purposes but do not assist in measuring financial flows.

To see this, consider a company that purchases land on the uncertain prospect of striking oil. Suppose that the land costs £1 million and the company funds this entirely from a bank loan. Assuming no other resources, its initial gearing is 100%. If the company subsequently strikes oil and the valuation of the land rises to £100 million, its gearing level will drop to 1%. If it does not, then values of both land and debt fall to £100,000 and the company is insolvent. The outcome of explorations appropriately affects valuations of debt and equity but does not alter the way in which the original investment was financed.

For this reason flows are used in preference to stocks. One implication of using flows rather than stocks is that retentions are defined on a gross of depreciation rather than a net basis. The reason for this is that by subtracting depreciation, financing is being distorted by accountants' estimates of valuation changes. These should not be part of a sources of funds account and are in any event inconsistently measured across countries.

Data Presentation

All financing proportions are recorded on a net basis: acquisition of financial assets are subtracted from increases in corresponding liabilities. The rationale behind using net financing proportions is that aggregate corporate financing figures attempt to answer the question, in what form did the nonfinancial corporate sector as a whole fund its physical investment? Intracorporate sector flows should net out, and offsetting flows should be eliminated. Thus, for example, from the perspective of the company sector as a whole, new equity issues by one company are offset by repurchases of equity of equal magnitude by another company. Any other approach leads to nonsensical results.

Consider, for example, a company that is required to make a compensating deposit of £30 for £100 of finance raised. Compensating deposits are common in Japan and the United States. The company has raised £100 gross but only £70 net. But suppose the company voluntarily holds £40 in deposits; should it be treated as having raised £70 or £60? Clearly net financing raised from the bank in this period has been £60. It may choose at a later date to increase this to £70 but the additional £10 has to be attributed to that period in which financial assets are reduced.

Economic theory does not currently allow reductions in stocks of financial assets to be distinguished from increases in financial assets. When a robust theoretical distinction is available then separate classification will be appropriate. Control theory offers just such a distinction by distinguishing finance by degrees of intervention. Ironically then, the theory that this paper emphasizes will in time invalidate the netting approach that has been advocated here. However, at the current time the appropriate null hypotheses that should guide the construction of financing data are Modigliani and Miller irrelevance propositions and corporate taxation models.

In moving from single projects to company finance, flows in different time periods have to be aggregated. The most straightforward approach is simply to average financing proportions. However, that does not take account of amounts of finance raised and so puts undue emphasis on periods of low investment. Instead, averages could be created by revaluing flows of different classes of finance to constant prices and then aggregating them. If a capital goods price index is used for revaluations, this is equivalent to weighting financing proportions by gross levels of investment at constant prices. An appealing alternative is to weight by *depreciated* values of investment at constant prices. This answers the question, what would the capital structure of a company be if it replicated its existing capital stock using the same sources of finance as it employed in the past? The average is calculated as follows:

$$\frac{\sum_{t=1}^{T}(I_t^j \times a_{t,T}) \times (P_T^k/P_t^k)}{\sum_{t=1}^{T}\left(\sum_{j=1}^{j}I_t^j \times a_{t,T}\right) \times (P_T^k/P_t^k)},$$

where I_t^j = amount of type j finance raised in period t ($j = 1, \ldots J$, t = 1, $\ldots$ T); $a_{t,T}$ = depreciated value in period T of a unit investment in period $t;$ P_t^k = capital goods price index in t.

Notes

1. See, e.g., Carrington and Edwards (1979) and Rybczynski (1988).
2. There is a strong similarity between the financing proportions recorded for the United States in table 12.3 and those reported in Goldsmith (1965) for earlier periods. Goldsmith reports the following for the period 1946 to 1958: retentions, 58.2; loans, 25.7; bonds, 9.6; equities, 6.4.
3. See App. A for details.
4. It is only slightly in excess of this on a gross basis—6% on average.
5. Comparisons of financing proportions in n. 2 above with table 12.3 suggests that a similar decline has occurred in the United States over the second World War period. Taggart (1985) demonstrates that the decline has been a long-run one. He reports the following financing proportions for the U.S. nonfinancial corporations since the turn of the century:

Period	Retentions (%)	Short-term Liabilities (%)	Bonds & Mortgages (%)	Equities (%)
1901–12	55	8	23	14
1923–29	55	4	22	19
1949–53	64	16	14	6
1979–83	64	26	9	2

6. That observation is not dependent on netting uses from sources. Issues of long-term liabilities and shares averaged as follows:

	1950–59	1960–69	1970–79	1980–84
Long-term liabilities	7.5	10.8	5.6	−.7
Shares	11.1	14.9	8.5	8.0

However, it should be borne in mind that pre- and post-1977 data are not directly comparable.

7. For the period shown in table 12.10 large firms are defined as those with capital employed of more than £4.16 million.

8. Goldsmith (1958) records a similar distinction between small and large firms in the United States in an earlier period. Gross financing proportions for the period 1946–52 were:

	Retentions (%)	Bank Loans & Trade Credit (%)	Bonds & Mortgages (%)	Equities (%)	Other (%)
300 large corporations	59.1	7.2	14.1	8.1	11.3
All other corporations	53.0	22.7	12.6	5.0	6.8

9. Research on individual company data in several countries, not reported here, confirms that electronic and pharmaceutical firms generally use little external finance.

10. The orderings of France and Italy in the debt: retentions comparison and of Japan and the United States in the new equity: debt comparison are reversed when investment in structures is considered instead of investment in equipment. Otherwise the orderings are unaffected.

11. See Aghion and Bolton (1988). See also Hart and Moore (1989) and Williamson (1988).

12. There are, of course, numerous other services that German universal banks provide for their customers, for example, bond and equity issuing facilities, and portfolio management services for investors. In addition, banks were probably a more important source of finance in earlier periods.

13. See Diamond (1989) for a theory of choice between bank and bond finance that is consistent with this.

14. There is no statistical adjustment in Germany. Instead, adjustments are made to recorded items to eliminate any discrepancy.

15. For a convincing demonstration of this point see Fisher and McGowan (1983). See also Harcourt (1965).

References

Aghion, P., and P. Bolton. 1988. An incomplete contract approach to bankruptcy and the financial structure of the firm. Mimeograph.

Aoki, M. 1984. *The economics of the Japanese firm.* Amsterdam: North Holland.

Carrington, J. C., and G. T. Edwards. 1979. *Financing industrial investment.* London: Macmillan.

Corbett, J. 1987. Interntional perspectives on financing: Evidence from Japan. *Oxford Review of Economic Policy* 3:30–55.

Diamond, D. W. 1989. Monitoring and reputation: The choice between bank loans and directly placed debt. Mimeograph.

Edwards, J., and K. Fischer. 1990. *The German financial system.* Forthcoming.

Fisher, F., and J. McGowan. 1983. On the misuse of accounting rates of return to infer monopoly profits. *American Economic Review* 73:82–97.

Goldsmith, R. W. 1958. *Financial intermediaries in the American economy since 1900.* Princeton, N.J.: Princeton University Press.

Goldsmith, R. W. 1965. *The flow of capital funds in the postwar economy.* New York: National Bureau of Economic Research.

Goudie, A. W., and G. Meeks. 1986. *Company finance and performance.* Cambridge: University of Cambridge.

Harcourt, G. C. 1965. The accountant in a golden age. *Oxford Economic Papers* 12:66–80.

Hart, O., and J. Moore. 1989. Default and renegotiation: A dynamic model of debt. Mimeograph.

King, M., and D. Fullerton. 1984. *The taxation of income from capital.* Chicago: University of Chicago Press.

Knight, A. 1988. The Deutsche Bank and industry post 1945: Interpreting the evidence. Mimeograph.

Mayer, C. P. 1987. Financial systems and corporate investment. *Oxford Review of Economic Policy* 3:i–xvi.

———. 1988. New issues in corporate finance. *European Economic Review* 32:1167–89.

———. 1989a. Finance and investment. Mimeograph.

———. 1989b. Myths of the West: Lessons from developed countries for development finance. World Bank discussion paper and background paper for the 1989 World Bank Development Report.

Myers, S. C. 1984. The capital structure puzzle. *Journal of Finance* 39:575–97.

Myers, S. C., and N. S. Majluf. 1984. Corporate financing and investment decisions when firms have information that investors do not have. *Journal of Financial Economics* 13:187–222.

OECD. 1986. Marginal tax rates on the use of labour and capital in OECD countries. *OECD Economic Studies* 7:45–99.

———. 1989. *Economies in transition: Structural adjustment in OECD countries.* Paris: OECD.

Rybczynski, T. M. 1988. Financial systems and industrial restructuring. *National Westminster Bank Quarterly Review,* 3–13.

Schonfield, A. 1965. *Modern capitalism: The changing behaviour of public and private power.* Oxford: Oxford University Press.

Taggart, R. A. 1985. Secular patterns in the financing of U.S. corporations. In *Corporate capital structures in the United States,* ed. B. M. Friedman. Chicago: University of Chicago Press.

Williamson, O. 1988. Corporate financing and corporate governance. *Journal of Finance* 43:567–91.

World Bank. 1989. *World development report 1989: Financial systems and development.* New York: Oxford.

Contributors

William A. Brock
Department of Economics
University of Wisconsin
1180 Observatory Drive
Madison, WI 53706

Michael Devereux
Institute for Fiscal Studies
180/182 Tottenham Court Road
London W1P 9LE, United Kingdom

Roger E. A. Farmer
Department of Economics
University of California
Los Angeles, CA 90024

William G. Gale
Department of Economics
University of California
Los Angeles, CA 90024

Bruce C. Greenwald
Bell Communications Research
435 South Street
Morristown, NJ 07901

Takeo Hoshi
Graduate School of International Relations and Pacific Studies
University of California, San Diego
La Jolla, CA 92093-0001

R. Glenn Hubbard
Graduate School of Business
Columbia University
New York, NY 10027

Anil Kashyap
Division of Research and Statistics
Federal Reserve Board
Washington, DC 20551

Robert A. Korajczyk
Department of Finance
Kellogg Graduate School of Management
Northwestern University
Evanston, IL 60208

Blake LeBaron
Department of Economics
University of Wisconsin
1180 Observatory Drive
Madison, WI 53706

Deborah Lucas
Department of Finance
Kellogg Graduate School of Management
Northwestern University
Evanston, IL 60208

Jeffrey K. MacKie-Mason
Department of Economics
University of Michigan
Ann Arbor, MI 48109

Colin Mayer
City University
Business School
Frobisher Crescent, Barbican Centre
London EC2Y 8HB, United Kingdom

Robert L. McDonald
Department of Finance
Kellogg Graduate School of Management
Northwestern University
Evanston, IL 60208

John R. Meyer
John F. Kennedy School of Government
Harvard University
Cambridge, MA 02138

John Pound
John F. Kennedy School of Government
Harvard University
Cambridge, MA 02138

Peter C. Reiss
Graduate School of Business
Stanford University
Stanford, CA 94305

David Scharfstein
Sloan School of Management
Massachusetts Institute of Technology

Fabio Schiantarelli
Department of Economics
Boston University
Boston, MA 02215

Joseph E. Stiglitz
Department of Economics
Stanford University
Stanford, CA 94305

John S. Strong
School of Business Administration
College of William and Mary
Williamsburg, VA 23185

Richard J. Zeckhauser
John F. Kennedy School of Government
Harvard University
Cambridge, MA 02138

Discussants and Other Participants

Carliss Y. Baldwin
Harvard Business School
Boston, MA 02163

Ben S. Bernanke
Woodrow Wilson School
Princeton University
Princeton, NJ 08544

David Bizer
Department of Economics
The Johns Hopkins University
Baltimore, MD 21218

Charles W. Calomiris
Department of Economics
Northwestern University
Evanston, IL 60208

Geoffrey Carliner
National Bureau of Economic Research
1050 Massachusetts Avenue
Cambridge, MA 02138

Steven M. Fazzari
Department of Economics
Washington University
St. Louis, MO 63130

Martin Feldstein
National Bureau of Economic Research
1050 Massachusetts Avenue
Cambridge, MA 02138

Benjamin M. Friedman
Department of Economics
Harvard University
Cambridge, MA 02138

Mark L. Gertler
Department of Economics
University of Wisconsin
Madison, WI 53706

Gary Gorton
The Wharton School
University of Pennsylvania
Philadelphia, PA 19104

James Kahn
Department of Economics
University of Rochester
Rochester, NY 14627

Bruce N. Lehmann
Graduate School of Business
Columbia University
New York, NY 10027

Andrew Lo
Sloan School of Management
Massachusetts Institute of Technology
Cambridge, MA 02139

Frederic S. Mishkin
Graduate School of Business
Columbia University
New York, NY 10027

335

Frank Packer
Graduate School of Business
Columbia University
New York, NY 10027

Bruce C. Petersen
Federal Reserve Bank of Chicago
230 South LaSalle Street
Chicago, IL 60690

James M. Poterba
Department of Economics
Massachusetts Institute of Technology
Cambridge, MA 02139

Jeremy Stein
Harvard Business School
Boston, MA 02163

Andrew Weiss
Department of Economics
Boston University
Boston, MA 02215

Mark Wolfson
Graduate School of Business
Stanford University
Stanford, CA 94305

Stephen P. Zeldes
The Wharton School
University of Pennsylvania
Philadelphia, PA 19104

Author Index

Subject Index